At 11:30 A.M. on December 7, 1941, a few hours after the attack on Pearl Harbor, Governor Joseph B. Poindexter of Hawaii issued a proclamation placing the Territory under martial law. The privilege of the writ of habeas corpus was suspended; the Commanding General was authorized to exercise the powers of governor during the emergency and also those normally pertaining to the judicial officers and employees. For the first time in American history a military government was established on loyal American territory and civil courts were completely superseded by military tribunals.

In *Hawaii Under Army Rule*, J. Garner Anthony, who served as attorney general of Hawaii from October 1942 to December 1943, gives a complete and accurate account of the institution, administration, and termination of martial law in Hawaii— a period during which, according to the author, thousands of persons were convicted in provost courts, some with trials and some without, and sentences were imposed without regard for the limitations of law in the offenses involved and for offenses unrelated to military security. Persons were held without bail and were obliged to purchase war bonds and donate blood in lieu of prison sentences. "Even the military governments imposed on the South during the Civil War did not cover the sweep of power that was exercised in Hawaii by the military arm from December 7, 1941, to March 10, 1943."

HAWAII UNDER ARMY RULE

I have often asked myself what would happen if, amid the laxity of democratic customs, and as a consequence of the restless spirit of the army, a military government were ever to be established among any of the nations of our times. . . . The result would be a regular, clear, exact, and absolute system of government; the people would become the reflection of the army, and the community be regimented like a garrison.

DE TOCQUEVILLE, *Democracy in America*

HAWAII
UNDER ARMY RULE

By

J. Garner Anthony

STANFORD UNIVERSITY PRESS
STANFORD, CALIFORNIA

AUTHOR'S NOTE

Material in Chapter Four, "The Military Government in the Courts," has been drawn, with extensive revision, from articles by the author published in the *California Law Review* ("Martial Law in Hawaii," Volume 30, 1942, and "Martial Law, Military Government and the Writ of Habeas Corpus in Hawaii," Volume 31, 1943) and the *Yale Law Journal* ("Hawaiian Martial Law in the Supreme Court," Volume 57, 1947).

STANFORD BOOKS IN WORLD POLITICS

A complete list of titles in the series will be found at the back of this book.

STANFORD UNIVERSITY PRESS, STANFORD, CALIFORNIA

Published in Great Britain, India, and Pakistan by Geoffrey Cumberlege, Oxford University Press, London, Bombay, and Karachi

The Baker and Taylor Company, Hillside, New Jersey
Henry M. Snyder & Company, Inc., 440 Fourth Avenue, New York 16
W. S. Hall & Company, 457 Madison Avenue, New York 22

Copyright 1955 by the Board of Trustees of the Leland Stanford Junior University
Printed and Bound in the United States of America by Stanford University Press

Library of Congress Catalog Card Number: 54-10677

To the memory of

PROFESSOR ROBERT C. BROOKS

Swarthmore College

CONTENTS

CHRONOLOGY

The chronology which follows lists the principal events relating to military control of civil affairs in Hawaii covering the period December 7, 1941, to February 25, 1946.

December 7, 1941: Hawaii Defense Act invoked by Governor Poindexter.
Martial law declared by governor.
General Short proclaims himself "Military Governor of Hawaii."
Governor Poindexter wires President Roosevelt for his action under Section 67, Hawaiian Organic Act.
Provost courts for the trial of civilians established.

December 8, 1941: Civil courts closed by military order.

December 9, 1941: President approves martial law and suspension of habeas corpus.

December 17, 1941: General Short replaced by General Emmons, who proclaims himself military governor.

December 22, 1941: Roberts Commission arrives in Hawaii (Sen. Doc. 159, 77th Cong., 2d Sess.).

February 19, 1942: *Ex parte Zimmerman,* 132 F.2d 442 (1942). Petitioner denied habeas corpus.

March 21, 1942: Congress authorizes creation of military areas and regulation by military commanders (56 Stat. 173).

June 2–6, 1942: Japanese defeated at Midway and threat of invasion of Hawaii lifted.

July 23, 1942: President appoints I. M. Stainback governor of Hawaii.

October 16, 1942: Hawaii designated as a military area pursuant to Executive Order No. 9066 and 56 Stat. 173.

December 1942: Washington conferences on termination of martial law.

February 8, 1943: Governor Stainback issues proclamation restoring civil authority in Hawaii; General Emmons issues similar proclamation.

March 10, 1943: Civil authority restored. General Emmons revokes Military Orders 1 to 181 inclusive and issues new orders.

June 1, 1943: General Emmons replaced by General Richardson, who assumes military governor role.

July 30, 1943:	*Ex parte Seifert,* U.S.D.C. (Haw.) No. 292; *Ex parte Glockner,* U.S.D.C. (Haw.) No. 295, petitions for writs of habeas corpus.
August 25, 1943:	General Richardson found in contempt of District Court and fined $5,000.
	General Richardson issues G.O. No. 31, providing fine and imprisonment for filing or entertaining petitions for writs of habeas corpus.
October 21, 1943:	Glockner and Seifert removed to San Francisco and freed.
November 23, 1943:	Gilbert Islands captured by our forces.
March 14, 1944:	*Duncan v. Kahanamoku,* petition for writ of habeas corpus filed.
April 13, 1944:	District Court holds martial law illegal.
May 4, 1944:	Curfew relaxed to 10 P.M. (G.O. 57).
June 30, 1944:	Title of military governor relinquished by General Richardson (G.O. 61).
July 21–29, 1944:	President Roosevelt arrives in Honolulu for military conference; "Office of Military Governor" changed to "Office of Internal Security" (G.O. 63).
October 24, 1944:	President Roosevelt terminates martial law and restores writ of habeas corpus by Proclamation No. 2627 (9 F.R. 12831).
November 1, 1944:	*Ex parte Duncan* reversed by Court of Appeals *en banc,* 146 F.2d 576 (CCA 9th 1944).
May 8, 1945:	V-E Day.
July 11, 1945:	Curfew and blackout lifted by Security Order No. 10.
August 14, 1945:	Japan surrenders.
February 25, 1946:	Supreme Court holds military trials of civilians invalid, *Duncan v. Kahanamoku,* 327 U.S. 304.

MARTIAL LAW DECLARED

$\mathcal{I}$T would have been odd if the people of Hawaii had witnessed the feverish activity that took place in the Islands for more than a year prior to Pearl Harbor without being aware of the imminence of war. Hawaii's intimate knowledge of the Army and Navy has never been approached by the civilian population of any state. For over a century the Navy and for almost half that period the Army have had a deep significance to the people of Hawaii. Hawaii needed no Captain Mahan to teach it the importance of sea power any more than that other island—England—needed him. The lesson was ingrained in the life and history of the people.

In 1939 the city of Honolulu, in co-operation with the Army, organized a complete blackout. The following year the board of supervisors took up a comprehensive Emergency Disaster Plan. By April 1941 unmistakable danger signals prompted the supervisors of Honolulu to enact an ordinance creating a Major Disaster Council.[1] This was simply a legislative recognition of the ferment that had been working in the community for over a year.

The Major Disaster Council[2] was charged with the duty of administering and co-ordinating certain essential civilian activities in the event of war. This comprehensive program included the M-Day plans of the Medical Society;[3] plantation provisional police in the rural districts;[4] on the island of Oahu, the Honolulu Police Department,[5] all

---

[1] Revised Ordinances, Hon. (1942), Sec. 746.
[2] Civilian Preparedness Activities and Establishment of Major Disaster Council, Pearl Harbor Attack, Hearings 79th Cong., 2d Sess. Part 18, p. 3401 *et seq.*
[3] *Id.* at 3421.   [4] *Id.* at 3360.   [5] *Id.* at 3387.

of which was done with the co-operation of the Hawaiian Department then under the command of Lieutenant General Walter C. Short and his immediate subordinates, Lieutenant Colonel Casey Hayes, Colonel H. K. B. Lyman, as well as the naval representative, Captain C. C. Baughman, Fourteenth Naval District, Pearl Harbor.

The medical profession under the leadership of Dr. Harry L. Arnold, chairman of the Preparedness Committee of the Honolulu Medical Association, had begun in earnest to get ready for M-Day. It devised a plan giving specific duties to all physicians in the Islands. A blood bank was formed and put in operation. Emergency beds in civilian hospitals were designated. Local doctors were grouped and assigned to hospitals or first-aid stations. Twenty such stations were established in schools and other public places throughout the city of Honolulu. A training program was organized by Dr. Robert Faus. The doctors gave training courses to more than 3,000 individuals of all races in first aid, nursing, ambulance training and related activities.[6] The profession publicized its work in the press and meetings of organizations. This was financed by the American Red Cross, which filled the gap left by the local legislature when it adjourned on April 30, 1941, without appropriating funds for the purpose. Dr. Robert B. Faus of the Preparedness Committee and Mr. Alfred L. Castle, vice-chairman of the American Red Cross in Hawaii, issued a joint statement on April 25, 1941, which was prophetic:

While the United States is not actually at war, and there is no occasion for war hysteria, the international situation is so critical that the civilian population of Honolulu must realize that the time has come *now*—not tomorrow—for intelligent, adequate, civilian defense preparedness. No sane person can think otherwise. The Army and Navy are not here to protect the population of Honolulu; their duty is to defend Hawaii as one of the most vital parts of the American Defense system. In case of emergency the civilian population must be prepared to care for itself.[7]

A reserve volunteer police force was recruited from the civilians of Honolulu. It was organized by Major Douglas G. King, an ex-officer in the British Army, the purpose of which was to have a trained body of men to augment the Honolulu police force in an emergency. One hundred forty-four were enrolled in the first training group and attended lectures on police work such as the apprehension of criminals, searches and seizures, criminal investigation, traffic, identification, drilling, and the use of firearms. Businessmen would appear in their offices the day of their shift in the neat uniform of the reserves pre-

6 Pearl Harbor Attack, Hearings 79th Cong., 2d Sess. Part 18, pp. 3421–27.
7 *Id.* at 3416.

pared to report for the night shift following their regular employment. The reserve police were jokingly known as the "society cops" but the people came to respect the organization which later was to do yeoman service throughout the war.

With the sharp rise in the population of the island of Oahu by the influx of military and civilian personnel (from some 200,000 in 1940 to approximately 500,000 at the height of the war) it can be readily seen that Honolulu was confronted with a police problem of the first order. Civilian defense workers were imported with no effective screening as to their health, character, or fitness, all of which added to the police problems of the city. The other islands of the group were similarly affected. Almost overnight sleepy country villages became beehives of activity seething with defense workers and military personnel.

The Navy's construction program in the islands of the Pacific was probably the most stupendous building program ever undertaken in history. It was done by a group of contracting companies working under an agreement with the Navy on a cost-plus-a-fixed-fee basis. The combination was called the Pacific Naval Air Base contractors or PNAB. Several of the constituent organizations were giants in their own right. The original Navy contract, NOy-4173 began with an estimated expenditure of $31,000,000, but it expanded rapidly to $200,000,000.[8]

Hawaii, Midway, Wake, Johnston, Palmyra, and many other obscure islands of the Pacific were transformed with lightning speed to military establishments by a nation grimly girding itself for war— Pearl Harbor was the focal point of all this activity.

The Hawaiian Sugar Planters Association (world-renowned in scientific agriculture) reported to Governor Joseph B. Poindexter its plans for the production of diversified crops to meet the Territory's needs. The report stated:

It is quite probable that if an emergency develops, the Territory will experience a gradual curtailment of transportation facilities but we should be prepared to promptly meet the worst possible situation.[9]

In February 1941 the legislature[10] met in its regular session, de-

---

[8] Woodbury, Builders for Battle (1946), 227.
[9] *Id.* at 3394 (Report, Dr. Harold L. Lyon, June 19, 1941).
[10] Congress by the Hawaiian Organic Act (31 Stat. (1900) 141; 48 U.S.C. Sec. 491 (1940)) created a territorial government which, in the traditional American pattern, embodies the doctrine of the separation of powers into the legislative, executive, and judicial. The legislature consists of an elective senate and house of representatives. The governor, the secretary and the judges of all courts of record are appointed by the President by and with the advice and consent of the senate.

bated the enactment of an M-Day law, but adjourned without its adoption. The objection to the bill was that it deposited too much power in the governor. Opponents wanted some check by a council.

On September 15, 1941, the legislature was called into special session by Governor Poindexter for the purpose of enacting legislation which would grant extraordinary powers to the governor for use in the event of war. Governor Poindexter (a cautious, elderly ex-federal judge) addressed the legislature prophetically:

That we will be drawn into actual hostilities is an apprehension which all of us share, but which we must face with courage and determination. That our cities may be bombed . . . are possibilities which may be deplored, but which must be vigorously prepared for. . . .

I recommend the enactment of a measure which will make suitable and adequate provision for the immediate and comprehensive designation and delegation of powers which under normal times would be unnecessary in a democratic form of government.[11]

On September 17, 1941, Lieutenant General Walter C. Short, commanding general of the Hawaiian Department, appeared before the senate of Hawaii, urging its enactment, and testified:

Many of these things can be done better by the civil authorities than by the military authorities, even after we possess the necessary powers to execute them. Many of them even after the declaration of martial law the military authorities would call on the civil authorities to perform. The proper action at this time might do much to delay or even render unnecessary a declaration of martial law. . . .

The essential legislation to provide this protection is entirely a function of the government and the legislature. The military authorities have no place in such action. If we tried to prescribe action we would be invading the public affairs of the civil authorities.[12]

The legislature went to work with a will. Thus the Hawaii Defense Act[13] which Governor Poindexter and General Short advocated speedily passed both houses and was approved on October 3, 1941. It vested in the executive sweeping powers over the inhabitants of Hawaii and their property, powers adequate to meet any emergency limited only by minimum safeguards for the rights of the individual. No state in the history of the nation had previously enacted so complete a delegation of power to the executive. Thus the machinery was at hand to be used in the anticipated crisis, but when the bombs dropped on Pearl Harbor it was rejected for a more dubious course.

With these activities going on before his eyes, the average citizen

11 Hawaii Sen. Jour. (1941) Spec. Sess. 14, 15.
12 Hawaii Archives, Minutes, Sen. Com. of the Whole (Sept. 17, 1941).
13 S.L. Hawaii, Spec. Sess. (1941), Act 24, p. 1.

of Hawaii realized that war in the Pacific was inevitable. In his Sunday morning paper for November 30, 1941, he read the banner headline of the *Honolulu Advertiser*:

JAPANESE MAY STRIKE OVER WEEKEND
KURUSU BLUNTLY WARNED NATION READY
FOR BATTLE[14]

At 11:30 A.M., on December 7, 1941, a few hours after the attack on Pearl Harbor, Governor Joseph B. Poindexter issued a proclamation invoking the powers conferred on him by the legislature under the Hawaii Defense Act. At 3:30 P.M. the same day he issued a proclamation placing the Territory under martial law and suspended the privilege of the writ of habeas corpus pursuant to Section 67 of the Hawaiian Organic Act which provides:

The governor shall be responsible for the faithful execution of the laws of the United States and of the Territory of Hawaii . . . and he may in case of rebellion or invasion or imminent danger thereof when the public safety requires it, suspend the privilege of the writ of habeas corpus or place the territory or any part thereof under martial law until communication can be had with the president and his decision thereon made known.[15]

The governor in his proclamation[16] not only suspended the privilege of the writ of habeas corpus and proclaimed martial law, but went beyond the provision of Section 67 by proclaiming:

. . . and I do hereby authorize and request the Commanding General, Hawaiian Department, during the present emergency and until the danger of invasion is removed, to exercise all of the powers normally exercised by me as governor; and I do further authorize and request the said Commanding General . . . during the present emergency and until the danger of invasion is removed to exercise the powers normally exercised by judicial officers and employees of this territory. . . .

Simultaneously with the issuance of the governor's proclamation, Lieutenant General Walter C. Short issued a proclamation in which he declared:

I announce to the people of Hawaii, that, in compliance with the above request of the governor of Hawaii, I have this day assumed the position of military governor of Hawaii, and have taken charge of the government of the Territory, . . .

[14] Pearl Harbor Attack Hearings, 79th Cong., 1st Sess., Part 29, p. 1647.
[15] 31 Stat. (1900) 153; 48 U.S.C. Sec. 532.
[16] For the text of the governor's proclamation and the proclamation of General Short taking over the government of Hawaii, see Ex parte White, 66 F. Supp. 982, 989, 990 (U.S.D.C. Hawaii 1944); the proclamations of the governor, the commanding general, and some of the more important general orders issued by the military governor are set forth in the Appendix.

. . . I shall therefore shortly publish ordinances governing the conduct of the people of the Territory with respect to the showing of lights, circulation, meetings, censorship, possession of arms, ammunition, and explosives, and the sale of intoxicating liquors and other subjects.

In order to assist in repelling the threatened invasion of our island home, good citizens will cheerfully obey this proclamation and the ordinances to be published; others will be required to do so. Offenders will be severely punished by military tribunals or will be held in custody until such time as the civil courts are able to function.[17]

The text[18] of the governor's proclamation was not communicated to President Roosevelt, but the governor on December 7, 1941, sent the following cable to the President:

I have today declared martial law throughout the Territory of Hawaii and suspended the privilege of the writ of habeas corpus. Your attention is called to Section 67 of the Hawaiian Organic Act for your decision on my action.[19]

President Roosevelt on December 9 gave the governor his decision as follows:

Your telegram of December 7 received and your action suspending the writ of habeas corpus and placing the Territory of Hawaii under martial law in accordance with U.S.C. Title 48, Section 532, has my approval.[20]

Neither the governor's proclamation in which he purported to turn over the powers of his office and the powers of judicial officers of the Territory to the commanding general nor the commanding general's proclamation in which the general assumed the role of military governor of Hawaii was ever submitted to the President.

General Short's proclamation contained internal evidence that it was his intention to administer martial law along orthodox lines, i.e., that the "ordinances" which he forecast would have some relevance to military necessity to resist the "threatened invasion."

The reference in General Short's proclamation to holding offenders in custody "until the civil courts are able to function" evidently contemplated a situation of civil disorder (which never in fact occurred), during which period, of necessity, the courts could not function. It is clear that martial law was initiated by the Army and that both Governor Poindexter and General Short thought that it would be of short duration unless the raid proved to be a prelude to a land invasion. The following facts came to light in 1946.

[17] Appendix A, p. 127.
[18] Duncan v. Kahanamoku, 327 U.S. 304, 308, note 2. (See Addendum, p. 33.)
[19] Ex parte White, 66 F. Supp. 989.
[20] *Ibid.*

On March 15, 1946, Lieutenant General Robert C. Richardson, Jr., addressed the Honolulu Chamber of Commerce on the subject of the Army rule in Hawaii and referred to certain recent broadcasts by a radio commentator as being "full of inaccuracies." The general said that he listened to them for a while and then "I turned it off." He continued:

There are misapprehensions about the declaring of martial law in Hawaii. The Army did not initiate martial law. The governor of the territory turned over his powers to the military commander and the President approved the action taken.

It was the governor, a civilian, who turned over the powers of the territory to the military.[21]

General Richardson was not in Hawaii on December 7; he had no firsthand knowledge of the facts, and the error of his statement "the Army did not initiate martial law" is readily demonstrated.

The Secretary of War, Robert P. Patterson, defended the Army rule in Hawaii in a letter dated March 25, 1946, addressed to Representative Walter G. Andrews which was inserted in the *Congressional Record*.

Secretary Patterson: The fact is that martial law was proclaimed for Hawaii on the afternoon of Pearl Harbor Day by the civilian Governor who requested the Army to take over and exercise the powers of government. . . . The Army did not in any sense oust or overthrow the civil government of the Territory. The civil authorities of the Territory continued for the most part to function as before, their authority supported and assured by martial law.[22]

Secretary Patterson (like General Richardson) had no knowledge of the facts and undoubtedly was relying (quite properly) upon information supplied to him by his subordinates.

The inference of Secretary Patterson's letter was that Governor Poindexter was responsible for the institution of martial law and that the Army was simply doing his bidding. The facts do not bear out this conclusion.

Governor Poindexter was emphatic in his denial when he described the scene which took place between himself and General Short on December 7, 1941. Governor Poindexter said:

Owing to the statements made recently by high officers in the War Department as reported by the press that martial law in the Territory of Hawaii was instituted by the civil authorities and that the governor had requested the military authorities to assume control which have led many

21 Honolulu Star-Bulletin, March 15, 1946.
22 Cong. Record, March 25, 1946, Appendix A1699.

people, so I am informed, to believe that the idea of martial law for the
territory had originated with me, the governor of Hawaii, on Pearl Harbor
Day, and there being in fact no basis for such a belief, it seems fitting that
I should at this time set out the facts and circumstances that led to the
declaration of martial law and the suspension of the writ of habeas corpus. . . .

Shortly after noon on December 7, 1941, Lt. Gen. Walter C. Short,
commanding general of the Hawaiian Department, called at the governor's
office. During the conference that followed, Hon. Charles M. Hite, secretary of the territory, was present also.

General Short stated that his call was for the purpose of requesting that
I declare martial law and suspend the writ of habeas corpus in the territory. . . . During the conference I put this question to Gen. Short: "As
commanding general, charged with the defense of these islands, do you
consider it absolutely essential to the defense of these islands that martial
law be declared and the privilege of the writ of habeas corpus be suspended?"

He answered emphatically: "I do."

I then told him that I was reluctant to do as he requested, that I was a
civilian unversed in military matters but he was a soldier charged with the
duty of safeguarding Hawaii from the enemy, and that I must yield to his
judgment as to what measures should be taken in discharging this duty.

I asked him how long martial law would continue. He replied that he
was unable to say but if it developed that this was a raid only and not the
prelude to a landing, martial law could be lifted within a reasonably short
time. . . .

I thereupon directed that the Attorney General's office prepare the necessary proclamation and when this was presented to me, about 4:30 P.M.,
I signed and promulgated the same.[23]

Although it was the fact that the proclamation was typed in the
office of the attorney general of Hawaii, Ernest K. Kai, acting attorney general at the time, made it clear that the attorney general's
department had nothing to do with the drafting of the proclamation.
Mr. Kai stated:

A previously prepared proclamation of martial law reached my desk
on December 7 with instructions to have it copied. This was done and sent
to the governor. I do not know where it was prepared, but I do know it
was not prepared in the Attorney General's office. It was typed there.[24]

The myth that Governor Poindexter was the moving spirit behind
the declaration of martial law and the assumption by the military
authorities of the civil government of Hawaii was carefully nurtured
by the War Department. President Roosevelt dispatched the Roberts
Commission to Hawaii to investigate and report on the Pearl Harbor
attack. It was evident that at the outset of the inquiry, the chairman,

[23] Honolulu Star-Bulletin, April 27, 1946.
[24] Honolulu Star-Bulletin, May 4, 1946.

Mr. Justice Roberts of the Supreme Court, had been briefed to the effect that martial law was proclaimed at the instigation of Governor Poindexter rather than upon the insistence of the Army, but he was quickly disabused of this, as shown by the transcript of the hearing.

The Chairman: As I understand it, was it at your initiation that martial law was declared in the emergency? At your request?
Governor Poindexter: No. It was at the request of the Army.
Chairman: Do you think it was a good thing to do that in the emergency?
Governor Poindexter: Well, this was the way it was represented. Of course being a civilian I was not very keen about having martial law, you will understand. But a disturbance that we had here and the large Japanese population we have in Hawaii was the reason that was advanced why that could be better handled through martial law than by civil authorities.[25]

After these disclosures, the *Honolulu Star-Bulletin* commented editorially:

Slowly but surely the "inside story" of the establishment of martial law in Hawaii on December 7, 1941, is coming to light.
The Army started the revelations—obviously without intending to do so—when its representatives began entering gratuitous disclaimers.
. . . It is important to know—officially—whether this surrender of his powers by the governor of Hawaii was continued month after month with his consent; and whether having once established itself by a proclamation, the terms of which were dictated by itself, the military government was ever challenged by the then Chief Executive.
The Army's studied effort now to show that the civil government initiated martial law should not pass unquestioned.[26]

So much for who planned and instituted martial law in Hawaii. The record is clear that it was planned by the Army months before Pearl Harbor. It was instituted at the instance of General Short and a proclamation was signed by a reluctant governor acting under the belief that it would be lifted "within a reasonable time." We turn to what happened after December 7, 1941.

Promptly after the declaration of martial law Lieutenant Colonel Thomas H. Green[27] (executive officer under General Short, the "military governor") set up a new system for the administration of criminal law throughout Hawaii. Civilians thenceforth were tried in provost

[25] Pearl Harbor Report, Part 23, p. 820.
[26] Honolulu Star-Bulletin, May 7, 1946.

[27] Lieutenant Colonel Green's advance in rank as executive to the military governor of Hawaii was rapid. In 1941, lieutenant colonel; January 1942, colonel; May 1942, brigadier general. He was transferred to Washington and appointed Assistant Judge Advocate General on April 14, 1943; appointed Judge Advocate General on December 1, 1945, with the rank of major general.

courts presided over by Army officers who meted out penalties without regard to the provisions of the statutes of Hawaii or of the United States.

On the Monday following the attack the civil courts were suppressed by oral order of General Short transmitted to Samuel B. Kemp, the chief justice of the Supreme Court of the Territory of Hawaii, who signed the following notice which was posted at the entrance to the Judiciary Building in Honolulu:

Under the direction of the commanding general, Hawaiian Department, all courts of the Territory of Hawaii will be closed until further notice. Without prejudice to the generality of the foregoing, all time for performing any act under the process of the territory will be enlarged until after the courts are authorized to resume their normal functions.

Army personnel moved in, took over the courtrooms, clerks' offices, clerks, and facilities of inferior courts throughout the Territory.

THE GENERAL ORDERS OF THE MILITARY GOVERNOR[28]

The commands of the military governor were made through the issuance of general orders which were published in the daily press. They were promulgated by the military governor through a subordinate "executive" who directed the daily press to publish the military orders at its own expense. Certain small newspapers in rural islands were paid by the Army for the space taken up with military orders.

The orders of the military governor were separated chronologically into two parts: the first covering the period December 7, 1941, to January 30, 1943, numbered consecutively 1 to 181. The second series included military orders issued after the partial restoration of civil government on February 8, 1943. These were numbered consecutively from 1 to 68, inclusive.

Under General Orders No. 1, an advisory committee to the military governor was appointed. The members were Governor J. B. Poindexter, Secretary of the Territory Charles M. Hite, Mayor Lester Petrie of Honolulu, Charles R. Hemenway, Frank H. Locey, Acting Attorney General Ernest K. Kai.

Mr. Charles R. Hemenway was the president of a leading trust

[28] The more important general orders of the military governor are set forth in full in the Appendix. General Orders Nos. 1 to 181 cover the period December 7, 1941, to January 30, 1943; on February 8, 1943, proclamations were issued by the governor of Hawaii and the military governor effective March 10, 1943, at which time General Orders 1 to 181 inclusive were revoked and a new set of general orders was issued covering the period March 10, 1943, to October 24, 1945.

company and a well-known civic leader, arid Frank H. Locey was the head of the Board of Agriculture and Forestry. It was assumed by the community that this committee of highly placed civilians would in fact advise. The committee, however, held no meetings and the military governor, according to the members, never requested the committee's opinion. It died a natural death.

General Orders No. 2 wisely commanded that all saloons be closed and it prohibited dealers from disposing of liquor stocks. However, prohibition by military order was short-lived, for by February 4, 1942, the bars were reopened and an elaborate permit system for the sale and distribution of liquor was established by General Orders No. 68. The fact that the bars were opened as early as February 4, 1942, when the military orders prohibited the impaneling of juries for the trial of cases, was later referred to by Chief Justice Stone in his concurring opinion in *Duncan v. Kahanamoku*. The Chief Justice observed:

After closing places of amusement, and after closing the civil courts on December 8, 1941, the military authorities, on December 24, 1941, ordered places of amusement to be opened.

On January 27, 1942, they permitted the courts to exercise their normal functions except as to jury trials and the issuance of writs of habeas corpus. On February 4, 1942, they authorized the sale of liquor at bars.

The full record in this case shows the conditions prevailing in Hawaii throughout 1942 and 1943. It demonstrates that from February 1942 on, the civil courts were capable of functioning, and that trials of petitioners in the civil courts no more endangered the public safety than the gathering of the populace in saloons and places of amusement, which was authorized by military order.[29]

The first military commission created by General Orders No. 3, on December 7, 1941, consisted of three civilians: James L. Coke, a former chief justice of the Supreme Court of Hawaii, Alva E. Steadman, the president of a local trust company and former circuit judge, and Angus Taylor, the acting United States District Attorney, along with four Army officers. This commission held its one and only meeting in the office of the attorney general in Iolani Palace[30] on December 10, but it tried no cases and never functioned. In fact, its existence on paper lasted only a week when General Orders No. 25 of December 14, 1941, was issued revoking the appointment. The members of the original military commission first learned of their removal upon reading it in the newspapers.

[29] Duncan v. Kahanamoku, 327 U.S. 304, 336 (1946). This case is discussed at length in Chapter Five.

[30] Colonel Green by this time had moved in and taken possession of the attorney general's office.

The events of the one meeting of the military commission created
by General Orders No. 3 were rather significant. The meeting was
called by Colonel Thomas H. Green. The purpose was to organize
the newly erected military tribunal. The author was invited to the
meeting by one of the civilian members, Mr. Steadman, who sensed
that troublesome legal problems would arise immediately.

Two of the civilian members (Steadman and Coke) at once inquired as to the kind of commission that would issue to them as military judges; who was to sign it? what oath would they take? where did
General Short get his authority to appoint judges to try civilians?
The inquiries were in no sense hostile, but were simply an attempt on
the part of two former judges to get at the foundation of whatever
judicial power they were supposed to exercise.

The author volunteered to draft a radiogram to the Attorney
General, Francis Biddle, which would set forth the facts and ask his
opinion. Messrs. Steadman and Coke thought this would be a good
idea, but it found no favor with Colonel Green or his subordinates;
a major present at the conference said with finality, "We have the
order of General Short, that's enough." "But what if General Short
is wrong?" asked Mr. Steadman. The major replied, "A commanding
general is never wrong." The conference ended on this note; the
proposed radiogram to the Attorney General was drafted and delivered to Colonel Green but never sent to Mr. Biddle.

One of the first official acts of the military government was to
move into Iolani Palace and take over the office of the attorney general. This was made easy by reason of the fact that Attorney General
Joseph V. Hodgson was temporarily on the mainland.

On December 7, Lieutenant Colonel Thomas H. Green took up
his headquarters together with his staff in the attorney general's
offices. As one member of the staff of the military governor accurately described the situation:

LIEUTENANT GENERAL DELOS C. EMMONS
RULES ALL HAWAII UNDER MARTIAL LAW

Authority over business deals, labor disputes, police, transportation,
daily movement of citizens, even their very lives, centers in the General's
office here in the old royal Iolani Palace.[31]

The orders of the military governor proceeded upon the theory
that after the declaration of martial law and the assumption by the

[31] Frederick Simpich, Jr., Life on the Hawaii Front, 82 National Geographic
Magazine 544 (1942).

commanding general of the office of military governor of Hawaii all power, legislative, executive, and judicial, vested in him; that he was not bound by the laws of the United States, the Territory of Hawaii, or the Constitution itself. As the matter was later described by the Supreme Court:

Thus the military authorities took over the government of Hawaii. They could and did, by simply promulgating orders, govern the day to day activities of civilians who lived, worked, or were simply passing through there. . . .

And finally, there was no specialized effort by the military, here, to enforce orders which related only to military functions, such as, for illustration, curfew rules or blackout.[32]

The orders themselves covered the entire sweep of government (except for taxation), such subjects as forbidding the civil courts to exercise criminal jurisdiction or to impanel juries, the erection of military tribunals for the trial of civilians, the decreeing of extensive offenses punishable in the provost courts, regulation of traffic, firearms, gasoline, liquor, foodstuffs, radios, the regulation and censorship of the press, wireless, cable and wireless telephone, the freezing of wages and employment, the regulation of hours of work, the possession of currency, the collection of garbage, blackout and curfew, rent control, regulation of restaurants, places of amusement, bars, establishment of one-way streets, the removal of keys from parked cars, interisland travel, speed limits, regulation of nationals of foreign countries, registration of females over sixteen, chlorination of water, regulation of bowling alleys, penalties for false statements to military authorities, registration of solicitors including union representatives.

In short, the military orders covered the whole range of government affairs. Whenever any new civilian problem arose, the quick answer was another military order. Every violation of an order called for punishment by fine or imprisonment or both. By and large the orders were ineptly drawn by persons who, judging from the finished product, served their apprenticeship in the art of draftsmanship in the office of the military governor. Deficiencies in the text of orders presented no difficulty to the provost court judges since the outcome of the military trials rarely resulted in anything but a finding of guilty.

The orders themselves were not without occasional bits of humor, both in the text and the association of subjects. For example, Section 1 of General Orders No. 57 dealt with the importation of flour,

[32] 327 U.S. 309, 314.

potatoes, onions, sardines, and canned tomato juice. Section 2 of the same order dealt with the jurisdiction of the Hawaiian courts ordained by Congress. It permitted them to open to a limited degree as "agents of the military governor" to perform certain functions "normally exercised by them during the existence of civil government" but prohibiting, however, the trial of criminal cases, the summoning of a grand jury, trial by jury, compulsory attendance of witnesses, the maintenance of any action against any member of the armed forces or other persons employed under the direction of the military governor or engaged in defense work for any act done in the course and scope of their employment.

The limitations thus imposed by the military governor upon the civil courts for all practical purposes rendered them powerless except in cases where no jury was demanded or in equity and probate cases where the compulsory attendance of witnesses was not required. Any party wishing to avoid a trial in a law case could do so by the simple expedient of demanding a jury. The reference in the order as to what judges formerly did "during the existence of civil government" left no doubt so far as the Army was concerned that the civil government of Hawaii was a thing of the past and that the supersession by the military was complete.

It is difficult to see how a judge holding a commission from the President of the United States, who had taken an oath to faithfully and impartially discharge the duties of his office and to support and defend the Constitution and laws of the United States, could act as the "agent for the military governor." The agency concept probably was designed to preserve a logical consistency with the theory that upon the declaration of martial law, the appointment of a military governor, and the closing of the courts by order of the commanding general, no residue of judicial power was left in the courts and that the source of all power (executive, legislative, and judicial) resided in the military governor. Hence, for the courts to act at all they could do so only as agents of the military governor. It is perhaps only a natural desire of man to clothe his act (no matter how wide a departure from the norm) with an aura of legality.

General Orders No. 54, issued by the military governor on January 20, 1942, was divided into five sections which covered the following subjects:

SECTION I	ISSUANCE OF GAS MASKS TO CIVILIANS
SECTION II	TRAFFIC DURING AIR RAID ALARMS
SECTION III	TRIAL JUDGE ADVOCATE, MILITARY COMMISSION
SECTION IV	DOGS
SECTION V	CLOSING HOURS OF BUSINESS ESTABLISHMENTS ON WEEKDAYS

Section IV, relating to dogs,[33] provided:

1. All dogs will be confined during the hours of blackout.
2. All dogs will wear at all times, except when actually confined, license tags issued by the proper authorities.

One characteristic of the military orders was that mandatory provisions were invariably expressed in the language of simple futurity but deficiencies in the text of orders afforded defendants little chance to escape a fine or imprisonment in the provost courts.

Although one could hardly expect a rational, workable, legal order to have been created by a military government which itself had no constitutional, statutory, or even executive order basis, there appears little excuse for the carelessly drafted orders that issued from the office of the military governor.[34]

General Orders No. 4 erected military tribunals for the trial of civilians. It was under this order that most of the civilians were tried in the provost courts. The full text of this order follows:

TERRITORY OF HAWAII
OFFICE OF THE MILITARY GOVERNOR
FORT SHAFTER, T.H.

7 December 1941

GENERAL ORDERS }
No. 4   }

By virtue of the power vested in me as Military Governor, the following policy governing the trial of civilians by Military Commission and Provost Courts is announced for the information and guidance of all concerned:

1. Military commissions and provost courts shall have power to try and determine any case involving an offense committed against the laws of the United States, the laws of the Territory of Hawaii, or the rules, regulations, orders or policies of the military authorities. The jurisdiction thus given does not include the right to try commissioned and enlisted personnel of the United States Army and Navy. Such persons shall be turned over to their respective services for disposition.
2. Military commissions and provost courts will adjudge sentences commensurate with the offense committed. Ordinarily, the sentence will not exceed the limit of punishment prescribed for similar offenses by the laws of the United States or the Territory of Hawaii. However, the courts may adjudge an appropriate sentence.
3. The record of trial in cases before military commissions will be substantially similar to that required in a special court-martial. The record of trial in cases before provost courts will be substantially similar to that in the case of a Summary Court-Martial.
4. The procedure in trials before military commissions and provost courts

---

[33] On the question of whether animals may be subject to legal duties, see Gray, The Nature and Sources of the Law, 44 (2d ed. 1924).

[34] Cf. Randall, Lincoln, The Liberal Statesman, 124 (1947).

will follow, so far as it is applicable, the procedure required for Special and Summary Courts-Martial respectively.

5. The records of trial in all cases will be forwarded to the Department Judge Advocate. The sentences adjudged by provost courts shall become effective immediately. The sentence adjudged by a military commission shall not become effective until it shall have been approved by the Military Governor.
6. All charges against civilian prisoners shall be preferred by the Department Provost Marshall or one of his assistants.
7. The Provost Marshall is responsible for the prompt trial of all civilian prisoners and for carrying out the sentence adjudged by the court.
8. Charges involving all major offenses shall be referred to a military commission for trial. Other cases of lessor degree shall be referred to provost courts. The maximum punishment which a provost court may adjudge is confinement for a period of five years, and a fine of not to exceed $5,000. *Military commissions may adjudge punishment commensurate with the offense committed and may adjudge the death penalty in appropriate cases.*
9. In adjudging sentences, provost courts and military commissions will be guided by, but not limited to the penalties authorized by the courts-martial manual, the laws of the United States, the Territory of Hawaii, the District of Columbia, and the customs of laws in like cases.

By order of the Military Governor:

(Signed) THOMAS H. GREEN
Lt. Col. J.A.G.D.
Executive Officer

A TRUE COPY:
(s)   JAMES F. HANLEY,
Major, J.A.G.D.

It should be noted that General Orders No. 4 created military tribunals for the trial of all civilians for offenses against "the laws of the United States, the laws of the Territory of Hawaii, or the rules, regulations, orders or policies of the military authorities." These tribunals were to "be guided by, but not limited to the penalties authorized by the courts-martial manual, the laws of the United States, the Territory of Hawaii, the District of Columbia, and the customs of laws in like cases." Thus the laws of Hawaii and the United States were abrogated by military fiat.

One writer, commenting on General Orders No. 4, in the *Harvard Law Review* for June 1942, said: "It is about what one acquainted with such situations would expect."[35]

In the same article the author gave his blessing not only to the

[35] Fairman, The Law of Martial Rule and the National Emergency, 55 Harv. L. Rev. 1253, 1296 (1942).

regime in Hawaii, but also to the Army evacuation program of the West Coast. On the subject of the detention of the peaceful residents of California of Japanese ancestry, he stated: "The detention of Japanese could, of course, be rendered legally impregnable for the duration of the emergency by an act of Congress suspending the writ of habeas corpus."[36]

It would seem clear that such a statute would have been contrary to the express command of Article I, Sect. 9, cl. 2, of the Constitution, which declares: "The Privilege of the Writ of Habeas Corpus shall not be suspended, unless when in Cases of Rebellion or Invasion the public Safety may require it."

The trials of minor offenses were conducted before the provost courts which imposed sentences up to five years' imprisonment or $5,000 fine or both. The vast majority of the cases tried in Hawaii by the military authorities were before the provost courts. Major offenses were tried before military commissions, which by the order were authorized to adjudge the death penalty. The order creating the military tribunals provided that the record and procedure in the provost courts should follow substantially that of a summary court-martial[37] and the procedure before a military commission was to follow that of a special court-martial.

There was no appeal from the sentences of the provost courts but sentences of military commissions required the approval of the military governor before execution. The accused in the provost courts was not even afforded the rights and privileges of an accused in a court-martial and, as has been noted, these are not entirely illusory.[38]

It will be observed that General Orders No. 4, coupled with Nos. 29 and 57, prohibiting the Territorial courts from exercising their statutory criminal jurisdiction, placed the entire administration of criminal law in the hands of military tribunals. The substantive crimes for which persons were tried before these tribunals were offenses against federal and Territorial statutes and violations of "the rules, regulations, orders or policies of the military authorities." From this it was clear that every violation of a general order issued by the military government carried with it criminal sanctions. Moreover since the Acts of Congress and the laws of Hawaii were merely

[36] *Id.* at 1302.

[37] The maximum punishment that could be adjudged by a summary court-martial was confinement for one month, restriction to limits three months, and forfeiture of two-thirds of one month's pay. Articles of War 14, 41 Stat. 789 (1920); 10 U.S.C. Sec. 1485 (1940).

[38] Gullion, How the Court-Martial Works Today, 27 A.B.A.J. 765 (1941).

"guides" for the imposition of sentence, the provost judge was not bound by the penalty prescribed in any written law.

Because of the absence of records, it is difficult, if not impossible, to recount accurately the activities of the provost courts. They exacted over $1,000,000 in fines, imposed prison sentences against hundreds of civilians along with such unusual punishments as compulsory blood donations and purchase of war bonds.

The provost courts not only passed upon offenses occurring after the declaration of martial law but disposed of criminal cases involving offenses prior to martial law. One example of this is found in *Ex parte Fred Spurlock*.[39] The petitioner, a Negro, came to Hawaii as a civilian defense worker. In November of 1941 he was ejected from a bar in Honolulu and, hurrying away from the scene, collided with two military policemen who turned him over to the civilian police. He was brought before the magistrate's court in Honolulu, charged with assaulting a police officer, and released on bond. His case was not called up for disposition until after the outbreak of war. In January 1942 he was summoned by a provost court on the charge previously made against him in the magistrate's court. In the interim the military courts had ousted the magistrate's court of jurisdiction. Spurlock entered the plea of not guilty and he was promptly found guilty and sentenced to five years' imprisonment. He begged the provost judge, Lieutenant Colonel John R. Herman, for mercy and was placed on probation. Several months later Spurlock was involved in a fight with another civilian and was taken into custody by the military police, held four days without bond, and then brought before the provost court. Spurlock was imprisoned in Oahu Prison from March 28, 1942, until he was released by Judge J. Frank McLaughlin of the United States District Court for Hawaii on a petition for a writ of habeas corpus on June 27, 1944.

Spurlock later testified in the United States District Court that when his case was called before Colonel Herman, the provost judge, the colonel said to him, "Oh, I see you are back—you are on probation, aren't you?"

To which he replied, "Yes, Sir."

Thereafter the charge was read by a police officer and the colonel promptly said, "Five years at hard labor—that's all."[40]

Spurlock asked to be sent into combat rather than prison, but Colonel Herman said, "Take him away."

[39] 66 F. Supp. 997 (D. Haw. 1944).
[40] Steere v. Spurlock, 146 F. 2d 652, CCA 9, 1944, cert. denied "on the ground that the cause is moot." 324 U.S. 868 (1945).

At most Spurlock was guilty of a trivial offense which might have drawn a $25 fine in a civil court. It is interesting to note that the Court of Appeals for the Ninth Circuit reversed the District Court *per curiam.* However, when Spurlock petitioned the Supreme Court of the United States for a writ of certiorari, the Solicitor General promptly filed a suggestion that the prisoner was released by the Army and the cause had become moot.[41]

The entire administration of criminal law in Hawaii was by military order placed in the hands of military personnel who tried civilians for felonies carrying the death penalty down to the most trivial misdemeanors without regard to whether they bore any relation to the public safety. As the Supreme Court later observed, "Thus the military authorities took over the government of Hawaii."[42]

The population of Hawaii remained under military rule from December 7, 1941, to October 24, 1944, when it was terminated by the proclamation of President Roosevelt.[43]

There never was anything resembling disloyalty, civil disorder, or misconduct on the part of the civil population which justified the proclamation of martial law on December 7, 1941, or its continuance in the days that followed the attack. The military establishment, to be sure, had received a staggering blow and was all but prostrate, but this was not the fault of the people of Hawaii or the civilian government nor could it justify taking military personnel away from military tasks to run the government of the Territory.

The duty of the military commander on such an occasion is to secure the defense of his command. He is not obliged to make a nice judgment on the facts to determine whether or not he should act in a given manner. He must take no chances, for the life of the state is in his hands. For example, the initial arrest and internment of persons of questionable loyalty after the suspension of the privilege of the writ would appear to be fully justified. A different question, however, is raised by the acts of military officers subsequently removing the internees from Hawaii and interning them on the mainland of the United States and thereafter again returning them to Hawaii for internment behind barbed wire on Sand Island[44] to avoid a challenge to their detention in places where the privilege of the writ was not suspended. In such a case internment of a citizen cannot be justified upon grounds of security.

---

[41] *Id.*
[42] Duncan v. Kahanamoku, 327 U.S. 304, 309.
[43] Proclamation No. 2627 (9 Fed. Reg. 12831).
[44] A small sandspit off Honolulu Harbor.

No valid case can be made either against the action of General Short in demanding the proclamation of martial law or against the action of Governor Poindexter in acceding to the general's demand. However, the continuance of the state of martial law for months and even years beyond the time when it was justifiable under any rational view of the facts was quite a different matter. It was clear that after the Battle of Midway, June 4–5, 1942, Hawaii was never threatened with or in danger of invasion.[45]

In April 1942 a military commission in Hawaii tried two civilians and sentenced them to be hanged. The first was a part-Hawaiian, Saffery Brown, who had been indicted by the grand jury prior to the outbreak of war, charged with killing his wife as a result of a domestic quarrel. After the declaration of martial law he was tried before a military commission. The other case involved a German, Otto Kuehm, who was tried in secret for espionage committed prior to the outbreak of war. Representations were made to Washington which resulted in a stay of sentences. As early as June 8, 1942, Secretary Ickes was advised by Nathan R. Margold, Solicitor of the Department, that there was no justification for the closing of the civil courts and the trials of Kuehm and Brown were invalid. He recommended, in the event the Attorney General took a different view, the matter be presented to the courts for judicial determination. Solicitor Margold said:

Commonly, the validity of action taken pursuant to a declaration of martial law reaches the courts after the emergency has passed. Where property rights have been concerned, and the court has ruled the acts invalid, Congress has usually indemnified the losers. Indemnity at some future time would, however, hardly benefit Kuehm and Brown who presently face death. Moreover, if the action of the Military Governor is determined to be invalid, such determination after men's lives have been taken, would be an unfortunate reflection on the administration.[46]

Shortly after the receipt of the Solicitor's opinion, E. K. Burlew, First Assistant Secretary of the Interior Department, upon instructions of his chief, Secretary Ickes, proposed a modification of the military rule in Hawaii to the War Department. Assistant Secretary of War John J. McCloy passed the request on to General Delos C. Emmons in Hawaii. Following a reply from the general, a conference was held in the Department of Justice at which Norman M. Littell,

[45] Biennial Report, Chief of Staff, U.S. Army (1943), House Document No. 288, 78th Cong., 1st Sess. 14, 30.
[46] Memorandum Opinion No. 31828, June 8, 1942, Department of the Interior.

Assistant Attorney General, E. K. Burlew, First Assistant Secretary, Department of the Interior, B. W. Thoron, Director of the Division of Territories, Samuel O. Clark, Jr., Assistant Attorney General Hugo Carusi, Executive Assistant to the Attorney General, John J. McCloy, Assistant Secretary of War, and Colonel J. L. McKee were present. Messrs. Thoron, Littell, Clark, and McKee had recently returned from Hawaii and had some firsthand information as to the state of affairs in the community.

The Interior Department's suggestion that the title of military governor was unlawful and should be eliminated was objected to by General Emmons on the ground it would detract from his authority; with regard to the suggestion that the civil courts be reopened for the exercise of their criminal jurisdiction, General Emmons objected upon the ground that it would be difficult to obtain impartial juries; it would take people away from defense work and the civil courts were too slow.[47] In this discussion it was pointed out by Assistant Secretary Burlew that Governor Poindexter signed the original proclamation, prepared by the Army, with great misgivings and only at the insistence of General Walter C. Short. Governor Poindexter had also advised Mr. Burlew:

. . . it was his definite understanding with General Short that the complete control of affairs by the military authorities would last only a few days or weeks until the immediate emergency was passed; but that this understanding had been ignored by General Emmons and the military rule had been perpetuated and extended.[48]

At the end of the conference Assistant Secretary McCloy stated he was inclined to agree that the ordinary courts should be allowed to function in criminal cases and juries should be impaneled; however, he indicated his agreement with the position of General Emmons that the military should have complete control of the administration of the government of Hawaii.

Governor Poindexter's term of office expired on March 9, 1942, and he was up for reappointment. Secretary of the Interior Harold Ickes had been informed of the complete supersession of the Territorial government by military authorities. Since Hawaii as a Territory was under the Department of the Interior, Secretary Ickes was hardly pleased with the War Department's invasion and conquest of his

[47] Two years later, Lieutenant General Robert C. Richardson, Jr., at the trial of the Duncan case, gave as one excuse for the existence of provost courts the "delays" of civil courts.

[48] Memorandum, July 10, 1942, Department of Justice files.

jurisdiction. He had the opinion[48] of Solicitor Nathan R. Margold of June 8, 1942, holding the military trials of civilians illegal and casting doubt upon the validity of the entire regime. A memorandum of Felix S. Cohen, Acting Solicitor of the Department of the Interior, dated June 9, 1942, had advised the Secretary that the delegation of power contained in Governor Poindexter's proclamation of December 7, 1941, was illegal. He stated: "Thus it was illegal for the governor to determine on December 7, that until the threat of invasion passes all civil functions should be performed by the military."

However, the Acting Solicitor did not know whether the proclamation itself had been submitted to the President or whether the President had approved it. Accordingly, he expressed the view that if the President had approved the proclamation, then it would be "improper" for the governor to modify it without the President's consent. As already noted, the proclamation was not approved by the President and it is doubtful whether or not he ever knew of its existence. The Department of the Interior for some unknown reason never furnished Governor Poindexter with either the memorandum or a copy of the Solicitor's opinion.

Secretary Ickes sent for Ingram M. Stainback, judge of the United States District Court for the Territory of Hawaii. After the declaration of martial law, Judge Stainback practically closed up his division of the United States District Court and was appointed legal advisor to the military governor under General Orders No. 17. He was assigned a cubicle directly adjoining General Green's office, but he rendered little advice to the military governor.

After talking with Judge Stainback, Secretary Ickes decided to appoint him as successor to Governor Poindexter. His name was sent to the Senate on July 23, 1942, he was confirmed four days later and took the oath of office on August 24, 1942. Before leaving Washington, however, the newly appointed governor reached an understanding with the Interior Department that there would be a substantial modification of martial law. It was agreed between the War Department and the Interior Department that the governor should promulgate a proclamation effecting the agreement. This was done on September 2, 1942, the proclamation reciting that the commanding general had determined it was "no longer impossible for the judicial officers and employees of this territory . . . to function with limits set forth in various orders."[49]

By General Orders No. 133, which was effective September 2,

[49] Ante note 46.

1942, the military governor authorized the civil courts to resume normal functions with certain stated exceptions among which were petitions for writs of habeas corpus, criminal proceedings against members of the armed forces or against any person engaged in defense activities under the direction of the military governor. For all practical purposes this would have been a complete restoration of criminal jurisdiction in the civil courts. General Orders No. 133 had been agreed upon in Washington in conferences between the two departments involved. However, on September 4, 1942, without taking the matter up with the Department of the Interior or Territorial officials, General Green promulgated General Orders No. 135, which was a substantial reversal of the agreement and the restoration effected by General Orders No. 133. General Orders No. 135 prohibited the Territorial and federal courts in Hawaii from trying criminal cases involving a number of offenses against federal and Territorial law. Moreover, jurisdiction over traffic violations which occurred after blackout was retained by the military authorities, as was jurisdiction over cases involving prostitution.

It is a curious thing how insistent the military authorities in Hawaii were upon maintaining jurisdiction over crimes involving prostitution and over the control of the vice itself. Unrelated, to be sure, to military security, it loomed large in the eyes of those in command in Hawaii. This was the subject of extended discussions between the lawyers of the War Department and the Department of the Interior. On November 4, 1942, Warner W. Gardner, the able Solicitor of the Department of the Interior, wrote a memorandum for Secretary Ickes on the subject of General Orders No. 135. He had been in consultation with General Cramer, Judge Advocate General, Colonel King, Major Fairman,[50] and Assistant Attorney General Tom C. Clark. Mr. Gardner reported:

The attached draft of a proposed order was agreed upon by General Cramer, Colonel King, Major Fairman, Assistant Attorney General Clark and myself on November 3. The 3-hour conference was devoted entirely to the minutiae of the particular crimes; the major retreats from General Order No. 135 received immediate and possibly uncomprehending approval. . . .

In a horse-trading deal at the end of the morning, we purchased approval of our distribution of crimes by giving the military jurisdiction over traffic offenses during blackout hours. Jurisdiction over prostitution offenses assumed major importance because McCloy had once mentioned this as a fit subject for military trial, so we held that in abeyance until advice from Hawaii. . . .

[50] The apologist for martial law in Hawaii. See Fairman, The Law of Martial Rule, 55 Harv. L. Rev. 1253 (1942).

I recommend the following program :

You should phone McCloy and tell him that the lawyers have reached an agreement on every issue save prostitution, and that in their painstaking way they undertook to get factual reports from Hawaii before solving that problem. You should then state that this matter has now dragged out for over two months and that anyone in their right mind knows that only contradictory information will come from Hawaii. Accordingly, you should be prepared to yield on prostitution if only the revised order will be sent at once to Hawaii, with directions to promulgate it at once. . . .

If McCloy will send the order out at once, I should withhold the letter to the President. If he insists on consultation with Hawaii, I should either send the letter along or should give him until Monday to receive cabled advice and to make up his mind.

In either case I think Stainback, who is reported as restive and indignant, should get some account of our activity, to dispel his natural impression that we are slumbering in peaceful indifference to his problems.

I may add that Cramer thinks we are entirely right on Green's appropriation of fines and forfeitures and states that he has a letter on McCloy's desk to halt that particular enterprise.[51]

Governor Stainback found himself the holder of a title to an office shorn of power. The military had taken over the executive, legislative, and judicial branches of the Territorial government, and in the words of the general's proclamation the general had "assumed the position of military governor." The press and the people generally referred to the governor as "the civil governor" in order to distinguish him from the real chief executive, "the military governor."

Governor Stainback soon learned that despite the agreement reached in Washington for a restoration of the civil government, the local military command did not propose to surrender the reins of power without a struggle.

The task of reviving and putting together the fragments of the civil government of Hawaii involved legal problems of considerable magnitude. To accomplish this Governor Stainback invited the dean of the bar, former Chief Justice A. G. M. Robertson, to become his attorney general. Judge Robertson, however, declined because of his advanced years. The governor then turned to the author, who accepted the office and was appointed attorney general on October 4, 1942.

On the day of his appointment the new attorney general called on General Green, who had continued to occupy the attorney general's suite of offices in Iolani Palace in Honolulu. He broached the sub-

[51] Memorandum of November 4, 1942, from Solicitor Gardner to Under Secretary Fortas, Department of Interior files.

ject of a return of the attorney general's offices for the use of the Territory's legal department. General Green stated he and General Emmons required offices commensurate with their rank, i.e., as military governor and executive to the military governor. He then added, "Moreover, if we were to move out of here, we would lose face." He closed the interview with the statement that the offices would not be returned. Although it took three months to accomplish it, General Green and his staff did evacuate Iolani Palace and took up quarters on the palace grounds. It later became known as the "Little White House" and was the site of the manhandling of deputy United States Marshal Bruns when he tried to serve General Richardson with a petition for a writ of habeas corpus.

The new attorney general proceeded to survey the Territorial government, or what was left of it, after the issuance of military orders. On December 1, 1942, he handed the governor a report on the status of the government which contained the following recommendations:

This report, already too long, is by no means exhaustive of the problems that exist under the present military rule. The solution of our present difficulties cannot be reached here but can only be settled in Washington.

I understand that in no single instance has any general order been submitted to you before it is promulgated. This is consistent with the view that the governorship is a mere figurehead and that the real governor of Hawaii is the "military governor." The situation can be clarified by reaching an agreement on the following points:

(1) The restoration of the courts to their normal functions, reserving to the military tribunals only those cases directly affecting the prosecution of war, such as sabotage, espionage, violation of the Articles of War, or crimes in and about military establishments, the jurisdiction to be determined by the United States District Court for Hawaii.

(2) A restoration to the territorial government of all civilian functions. This would involve the relinquishment by the military of all the civil functions presently usurped under military rule, such as food, price and liquor controls.

(3) The abolition of the assumption of military governorship by the Commanding General.

(4) A rescission of all general orders heretofore issued which are not based upon military necessity and an agreement that in the future the military orders dealing with the civilian population and civil government be predicated upon the ground of military necessity and, except in case of a real emergency which will not admit of delay, that such orders be submitted to you for approval before issuance.

In the event such a program cannot be agreed upon, the only alternative would seem to be the issuance of a proclamation terminating martial law. This, of course, should not be done without first having obtained the approval of the President. It could be done without restoring the privilege of the writ of habeas corpus. This would have the effect of placing us in approximately the same situation as exists in the West Coast where there is, in fact, a form of martial law, except that the writ of habeas corpus has not been suspended there. This would afford the military all necessary power, restore to civil authorities all civilian functions, and preserve to the citizen the substance of the Bill of Rights.[52]

Shortly after the receipt of this report, the governor and attorney general flew to Washington to put their case before the Secretary of the Interior. As a consequence the whole subject matter was open for conferences in Washington among the Departments of War, Interior, and Justice, together with representatives of the Territory. These continued for weeks until an agreement was finally reached between the three departments of government and the governor of Hawaii on the plan of modification of martial law.

In a memorandum dated December 10, 1942, to Secretary Ickes, Warner Gardner, Solicitor of the Interior Department, wrote:[53]

The military governor now exercises control over almost all civilian activities and his government includes almost every governmental power except taxation. Some of the principal civil functions exercised by the military are: (*a*) civil and criminal courts; (*b*) municipal affairs including taxicabs, rent control, garbage disposal, house numbering, traffic regulations, and direction of the police; (*c*) labor; (*d*) licensing of the press; (*e*) the local O.C.D. office; (*f*) public health, hospitals and waterworks; (*g*) prisons and insane asylums; (*h*) price control; (*i*) liquor control; (*j*) food control and production; (*k*) transportation; (*l*) gasoline rationing; (*m*) materials and supplies, including all W.P.B. functions.

And as to the provost courts, he said:

The administration of justice is among the worst features of the military conquest of the civilian government. Almost every offense is tried before the provost courts or the military commissions. The drum-head justice of the provost courts has the following characteristics: (*a*) The judge is often without legal training. (*b*) Copies of the charges are not given the accused, although he may read the prosecutor's copy at the outset of the trial. (*c*) The accused and the witnesses gather around the bench in a crowded courtroom, in which the officers are fully armed, and the evidence is taken through a general discussion; the aid of counsel and cross-examination are discouraged. It is uncommon that a trial exceeds thirty minutes in length. (*d*) It is ordinarily understood that a plea of "not guilty" draws a heavier sentence, and acquittals are rare. (*e*) Civil controversies are frequently ordered settled in the provost courts. (*f*) Defendants have been convicted of violating "the spirit of martial law" or "the spirit" of general orders when the text has been found inadequate.

---

[52] Report of Attorney General Anthony to Governor Stainback dated December 1, 1942, files of the attorney general of Hawaii.
[53] Department of Interior files.

(*g*) The penalties for conviction are severe and stand in sharp contrast to the nominal or much lighter penalties administered for the same offenses by way of military discipline to officers and enlisted men. These courts, subject to no obligatory review whatever, can impose penalties up to 5 years and $5,000.

While the civil courts are open for civil actions, the 50,000 defense workers and the civil employees of the military establishments and of the public utilities have a general immunity from civil suit and, no matter what their offense, are tried only in provost courts.

On the general administration of the military government, he concluded:

Such an administration of government would not be justified even if there were a corresponding gain in governmental efficiency. There has not been such a gain. Prostitution has flourished, ill-considered and poorly drafted orders are hastily issued, and a large uniformed bureaucracy has been set up.

Upon reading the report from Hawaii, Secretary Ickes promptly called a "full dress" meeting of the departments of government interested. It was convened in the impressive conference room of the Department of the Interior with Honest Harold in the chair. Around him at the table were Francis Biddle, Attorney General; James Rowe, the Assistant to the Attorney General; Samuel Clark, Assistant Attorney General; Ingram M. Stainback, Governor of Hawaii; J. Garner Anthony, Attorney General of Hawaii; J. J. McCloy, Assistant Secretary, War Department; Lieutenant General Delos C. Emmons, Commanding General, Hawaiian Department; Abe Fortas, Under Secretary, Interior Department; Warner W. Gardner, Solicitor, Interior Department; and B. W. Thoron, Director, Division of Territories and Island Possessions.

Secretary Ickes opened the conference by saying, "Gentlemen, the business before us is the emancipation of Hawaii." He outlined the events subsequent to December 7, the establishment of complete military rule in Hawaii, stating that in no place under the American flag from the beginning of the nation had such a rule been established except in rebellious or conquered territory, and that it was his purpose to see civil government restored in Hawaii. He recited the agreement reached between the War and Interior departments in August 1942 and charged the Army with bad faith in emasculating the agreement by subsequent orders. He paid his respects to General Green (as only Mr. Ickes could do) and then announced that "some other post should be found for that gentleman as soon as possible." Turning to the Army's use of funds allocated by the President for expenditure under the direction of the Department of the Interior he said, "I have just learned this morning that the Army has been spending my money"; and "that particular enterprise," continued the Secretary, "must stop at once." Moreover, he declared, "There must be an end to the trial of civilians in drum-head courts" and the Army would have to account for all fines and liquor permit fees collected by the military government. The field of civil government taken over by the Army, from provost court trials of civilians for all manner of crimes and misdemeanors to the military control of labor enforced by jail sentences in the military courts, was reviewed and the views of Secretary McCloy and General Emmons were solicited as to their justification of the Army's position.

At the end of the conference Attorney General Biddle read a draft of proclamation prepared in Solicitor Gardner's office. The meeting finally concluded with a general agreement on the document subject to minor modifications.

The newly elected delegate to Congress, Joseph R. Farrington, on December 21, 1942, made a public announcement, giving his unqualified support to the Territorial governor and attorney general in their efforts

to restore constitutional government under a reign of law in the Territory of Hawaii and to reestablish civil authority and responsibility consistent with the defense of the Islands. . . . Continuance of military rule and complete domination over civilians and civilian affairs not only is contrary to every tradition of America since the earliest days of this nation but is in fact a positive detriment to the total war effort.

The military rule is without precedent in history except in conquered or rebellious territory and is without constitutional or legal foundation.[54]

While the governor, his attorney general, and the delegate to Congress were in Washington pressing for a return of constitutional government, the military authorities in Hawaii were prompting the local business community to resist these efforts, and their activities met with some success. On December 27, 1942, the Honolulu Chamber of Commerce sent a wire to President Roosevelt, Attorney General Biddle, Delegate Farrington, Eric Johnston, Secretary Ickes, Secretary Knox, Governor Stainback, and Secretary Stimson, designed to frustrate the efforts of the Territorial officials. The wire read:

BECAUSE OF THE FACT THAT THE ISSUE HAS BEEN PUBLICLY RAISED CONCERNING THE OPERATION AND EXTENT OF MARTIAL LAW IN HAWAII THE CHAMBER OF COMMERCE OF HONOLULU WITH A MEMBERSHIP OF 950

[54] *Honolulu Star-Bulletin*, December 21, 1942.

INCLUDING ALL CLASSES OF BUSINESS AND PROFESSIONS WISHES TO
STATE THAT WE FEEL THERE NEED BE NO ESSENTIAL CONFLICT BETWEEN
LOCAL MILITARY AND CIVIL AUTHORITY BELIEVING FULLEST COOPERA-
TION AND UNITED EFFORT BETWEEN ALL PARTIES ABSOLUTELY ESSEN-
TIAL TO WIN THIS WAR PERIOD CIVIL MILITARY AND NAVAL AUTHORI-
TIES HAVE COOPERATED WITH OUTSTANDING RESULTS THIS PAST YEAR
WITH DUE RESPECT TO THE RIGHTS OF EACH PERIOD WE RECOGNIZE THAT
FULL RESPONSIBILITY FOR THE SAFETY AND WELFARE OF THIS TERRI-
TORY AND OUR COUNTRY RESTS ON THE COMMANDERS OF OUR ARMY AND
NAVY AND THAT WE CANNOT AFFORD TO HAMPER THEIR EFFORTS IN ANY
WAY PERIOD WHILE DESIROUS OF HAVING MORE FUNCTIONS OF CIVIL
GOVERNMENT GRADUALLY VESTED IN LOCAL AUTHORITIES AS OUTLINED
BY GENERAL EMMONS IN HIS PUBLIC STATEMENT OF DECEMBER 22, 1942,
WE RECOGNIZE THE DANGERS STILL CONFRONTING US AND DO NOT BE-
LIEVE THAT MARTIAL LAW SHOULD BE SUSPENDED AT THIS TIME PERIOD
WE RECOGNIZE THAT TIME AND EXTENT OF RESTORATION OF CIVIL
RIGHTS MUST BE FULLY COMPATIBLE WITH MILITARY NECESSITY PERIOD
WE FEEL THAT GENERAL EMMONS OUR MILITARY GOVERNOR HAS BEEN
EMINENTLY FAIR AND CONSIDERATE OF OUR CIVIL RIGHTS THIS PAST
YEAR AND WE HAVE EVERY CONFIDENCE THAT HE WILL CONTINUE TO
EXERCISE THIS CONSIDERATION
                    LESLIE A. HICKS, PRESIDENT CHAMBER COMMERCE
                    LAWSON H. RILEY, PRESIDENT RETAIL BOARD[55]

In fairness to the Chamber of Commerce it should be noted that
although the representation in the wire carried the implication that
950 businessmen of "all classes of business and professions" supported these views, as a matter of fact the issue was never submitted
to the membership. The radiogram simply stated the views of the
executive committee of the Chamber. The Chamber of Commerce,
of course, received no reply from the President, but it did receive
one from the Secretary of the Interior. In the Old Curmudgeon's
best style, he said:

January 9, 1943

MY DEAR MR. HICKS:

The President has referred to the Department of the Interior your
telegram of December 27, in regard to the operation and extent of martial
law in Hawaii. I am in full agreement that there need be no conflict between local military and civil authority. I believe, however, that the primary responsibility of the military authorities is for the security of the
islands and that the judicial and executive functions affecting civilian
affairs can best be carried on by the regularly constituted civil authorities
acting in full cooperation with the Commanding General.

Civil government has been successfully maintained and its responsibilities carried out by civilian authorities in other parts of the English-

[55] University of Hawaii War Records Depository (War Records Reel 27—Chamber of Commerce file).

speaking world under conditions of much more severe strain than exist in Hawaii. The idea that restoring the responsibility of civil government and the jurisdiction of the courts would hamper the defense of the territory by the Army and Navy is repugnant of every concept of American democracy and reflects upon the capacity of the people of Hawaii for self-government and self-discipline. The restoration of authority to the civil governor and to the civil courts is not a criticism of the manner in which the Commanding General has temporarily executed civil, executive and judicial functions but is a recognition of the fact that the people of the Hawaiian Islands are fully capable of administering their affairs in a manner consistent with American democratic principles.

Sincerely yours,
HAROLD L. ICKES
Secretary of the Interior[56]

The Chamber of Commerce also heard from Ben W. Thoron, Director, Division of Territorial and Island Possessions, who on January 21, 1943, wrote:

I was somewhat disturbed by the telegram from the Chamber of Commerce to the President which gave the impression that a large and responsible group of American businessmen had so far departed from normal American thinking as to prefer military control of all activities of civilian life and to be accorded access to the courts as an act of grace rather than a right instead of the normal process of American government. Mr. Hicks' circular of January 9 does little to clarify the attitude of the Chamber of Commerce. The whole thing seems to be based on a misapprehension of what has been going on here and the failure on the part of the group which prepared the telegram to take the trouble to inform itself of the facts.[57]

Mr. Thoron then quoted from a letter received from a high official of the British Colonial Office in response to an inquiry made by him about the war-torn island of Malta. He learned that it, too, had a military government, but maintained civil courts for ordinary offenses. Mr. Thoron concluded:

If the British are able to maintain civil government under circumstances as difficult as those in Malta and Ceylon, surely the people of Hawaii should not shirk the responsibility.[58]

The views of the Chamber of Commerce had little effect in Washington other than to bolster up the position of the War Department, which was demonstrably untenable and inconsistent with rudimentary concepts of American government. The backfire from the home front, no doubt, protracted the Washington negotiations.

At the conclusion of the conferences a compromise agreement

---

[56] University of Hawaii War Records Depository (War Records Reel 27—Chamber of Commerce file).   [57] *Id.*   [58] *Id.*

was reached between the military and civil authorities in Hawaii. The compromise resulted in a continuation of a modified form of martial law and the suspension of the privilege of the writ of habeas corpus. The compromise was embodied in two proclamations, one to be issued by the governor and the other to be issued by the commanding general. The device of issuing two identical proclamations (one by the governor and one by the general) was a satisfactory face-saving means of avoiding a public admission that the military were retreating from their illegal control of civil government. The two proclamations, together with a form of letter of instructions, were submitted to the White House for the approval of the President.

The solution was a compromise arrived at to avoid taking the issue to the President, who was then engaged with plans for the North African campaign. The compromise was presented by the Secretary of War, the Attorney General, and the Secretary of the Interior in a letter to the President which stated:

We are pleased to report that after lengthy discussions, the Departments of War, Justice and Interior have reached an operating agreement upon the distribution of governmental functions between the civil and military authorities in the Territory of Hawaii. . . . Copies of the proclamation are enclosed for your information. We also enclose a draft of a letter which we suggest you might appropriately send to the Secretary of War.[59]

The letter referred to, prepared for the President's signature, acknowledged receipt of the proclamations to be issued by the commanding general and the governor of Hawaii and then stated:

I wish to congratulate all departments concerned in their cooperative and successful effort to reach an amicable solution of the knotty problems involved. . . . I can readily appreciate the difficulty in defining exactly the boundaries between civil and military functions. I think the formula which this proclamation applies meets the present needs.[60]

It would seem obvious that the matter of defining the limits of military and civil jurisdiction could hardly be the subject of negotiation and compromise even though concurred in by the highest executive officer of the nation. The legislative branch of our government alone is the source of such powers and the executive is charged with carrying out the mandate of the Congress. The executive is not charged with rearranging the statutory scheme of government which Congress had enacted for Hawaii.

[59] Letter dated January 18, 1943, to President Roosevelt, see Duncan v. Kahanamoku (R. 74).
[60] Letter dated January 18, 1943, from President Roosevelt to Secretary Stimson (Duncan v. Kahanamoku, R. 74).

On February 8, 1943, proclamations which took effect March 10, 1943, were issued concurrently by the governor[61] and the commanding general,[62] substantially restoring civil authority; Territorial and federal functions which theretofore had been under complete military control were restored to the appropriate civil agencies, who were directed to resume "their respective jurisdictions, functions and powers according to law." Trial by jury and indictment by grand jury in the civil courts replaced the provost courts and military commissions for violations of Territorial and federal law. The OPA, which previously was an "advisor to the Military Governor" exercised its statutory powers in its own right as did other Territorial and federal agencies.

Among the matters enumerated in the proclamation were three main exceptions to a complete restoration of civil authority: (a) immunity[63] of members of the armed forces from criminal and civil proceedings under certain conditions; (b) criminal prosecution for violation of military orders; and (c) the control over labor working for the services or working on Army and Navy projects, stevedores, dock workers, and employees of public utilities.

The restoration of civil authority required the disposal of 181 general orders[64] covering all manner of civilian affairs which were issued in Honolulu since December 7, 1941. These were revoked and the subject matters regulated by them were turned over to the appropriate civil agencies. Regulations were promulgated by the governor under the Hawaii Defense Act, which replaced the rescinded military orders.

Some of the Defense Act regulations such as restrictions on interisland travel, freezing of certain essential workers, control over importation and distribution of food were strict, but it should not be overlooked that they replaced the control that theretofore existed under military orders enforceable in the provost courts. The Defense Act regulations were designed to afford due process of law to affected persons and to establish reasonable standards for the administrators. They became effective immediately upon publication (in the press or,

[61] Appendix A, p. 129.

[62] Appendix A, p. 131.

[63] Not to be confused with the Soldiers and Sailors Civil Relief Act of 1940 (52 Stat. 1178, 50 U.S.C. 501). This clause purports to grant a general immunity to members of the armed forces; it would seem that this is a judicial question, the answer to which would depend upon the facts in the specific case presented; it is doubtful whether the result can be accomplished by executive fiat.

[64] In addition there were a large number of orders issued by the commanding officers on the islands of Hawaii, Maui, and Kauai.

in time of emergency, by radio broadcast or posting).[65] Violations
of the regulations were made misdemeanors punishable by imprisonment not to exceed one year or a fine not to exceed $5,000, or both.[66]
The regulations could be challenged in the courts.

The Territorial legislature, which convened February 17, 1943,
in regular session, promptly amended[67] this act granting additional
powers to the governor to cope with any emergency and to make certain that no dearth of power would afford an excuse for the resumption
of military control. New military orders[68] were issued on March 10,
1943, designed to cover the few subjects left to military control under
the proclamation. The title and office of the "Military Governor"
were retained.

[65] Act 24, Sp. S.L. Hawaii 1941, Sec. 18.
[66] *Ibid.*, Sec. 22.
[67] Act 5, S.L. 1943, approved March 8, 1943.
[68] Honolulu Advertiser, March 10, 1943.

Addendum: Footnote 18 should read:

Duncan v. Kahanamoku, 327 U.S. 304, 308, note 2:
"The district court heard much evidence and from it found as follows on this
subject: 'By radio the Governor of Hawaii on December 7, 1941, notified the President
of the United States simply that he had placed the Territory under martial law and
suspended the writ. The President's approval was requested and it was granted by
radio on December 8, 1941. Not until 1943 was the text of the Governor's December 7
proclamation furnished Washington officials, and it is still doubtful if it has yet been
seen by the President.'"

Chapter Two

ORGANIZATION OF THE MILITARY GOVERNMENT

O<small>N</small> the Monday following the attack on Pearl Harbor the government of Hawaii had changed overnight. Few persons realized the import of what had taken place and those who did held their peace, thinking, of course, that it was a temporary expedient invoked by the military arm to assure swift and decisive action in defense of the Islands.

Lieutenant Colonel Thomas H. Green on December 8 had moved into Iolani Palace and established himself together with his subordinates in the office of the attorney general.

The general orders issued by the military governor of Hawaii were probably the most comprehensive orders of punitive martial law ever promulgated on American soil. Even the military governments imposed on the South during the Civil War[1] did not cover the sweep of power that was exercised in Hawaii by the military arm from December 7, 1941, to March 10, 1943. It has already been noted that every general order involved criminal sanctions. In other words, the military concept of law does not include law without punishment. While this may be the customary procedure among the military, it is novel from the point of view of the political scientist or the lawyer. The great body of commercial law, for example, deals exclusively with the rights of parties in civil controversies. Criminal law plays a relatively small part in the affairs of most men. Most people never enter a criminal court except in response to a traffic summons. The military system, however, is predicated upon a penal sanction attaching to every order even of the most trivial character.

---

[1] Cf. Robinson, Justice in Grey (1941). Chapter XVII contains an interesting discussion of martial law under the Confederacy.

THE OFFICE OF THE MILITARY GOVERNOR

There was, of course, no basis in federal or Territorial law for the use of the term "military governor" in the Territory of Hawaii. This phrase, applied to a loyal American community, is unknown to our law even in times of the direst emergency. It is a term properly applied only to conquered nations or areas of domestic territory in rebellion against the government. However, it was an accurate description of the military rule which existed in Hawaii.

The office of the "military governor" was organized under General Orders No. 56, which created first an executive, Lieutenant Colonel Thomas H. Green, whose function was to carry out "all policies and operations of martial law." Under the executive there was constituted an advisory committee of civilians which, as has been noted, never held a meeting.

The military governor's office also had an alien property controller, public relations department, personnel, finance, and morale sections. There were also created divisions handling priorities, civilian defense, food control, labor control, materials and supplies control, cargo and passenger control, land transportation control, cold storage control, and cloth control. The executive to the military governor appointed civilians as advisers of the several sections of the military government. However, they exercised no powers of government. All determinations were made by the military governor. Over each civilian head of a section was an Army officer who reported directly to the executive to the military governor. The complete displacement of the civil government is illustrated by the functional chart prepared by Colonel Green.

The organization chart discloses that there were no functions to be performed by the governor of Hawaii, who was designated as "civil governor," nor were there functions to be performed by the Territorial and county governments, all affairs of government having been placed under the direction of the executive to the military governor. This applied to federal as well as Territorial agencies. For example, the Office of Price Administration is designated on the chart under the executive to the military governor, and in fact price regulations which originated and were prepared by the OPA ultimately were issued as military orders, the OPA representative, Carl Borders, having been appointed director of price control of the office of military governor under General Orders 159.

On the staff of the military governor were a large number of civilian employees engaged in purely civilian governmental activities

FUNCTIONAL CHART

GOVERNMENT OF TERRITORY OF HAWAII UNDER MARTIAL LAW
REVISED MARCH 1, 1940
DATE OF GENERAL ORDER 56, SECTION 3, JANUARY 26, 1942
(SETTING FORTH THE ORGANIZATIONAL PLAN)

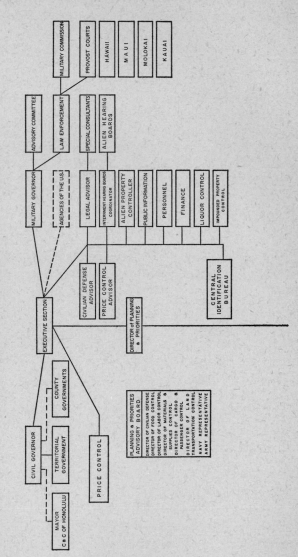

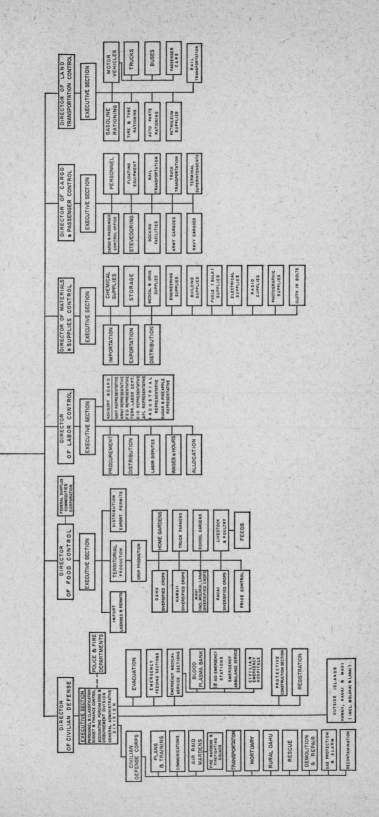

such as food control and labor control, and employees from other departments of the military government. The budget for the services of newly employed civilian personnel attached to the office of the military governor was approximately $50,000 per month. The positions filled by the new personnel were newly created by the military governor and had no basis in any legislative authority.

One of the projects of the military government was food production and distribution and included a plan to stimulate locally grown products. Vast sums were expended in this project, which ended in failure. This was conducted under the direction of Colonel William R. White who later became a general. It failed principally because the military authorities did not understand the agricultural problems of Hawaii. Military farms were operated at great expense and produced practically no food. Finally General Emmons decided to place this program in charge of a civilian. On November 6, 1942, under General Orders No. 153, he appointed Walter F. Dillingham director of food production.

The military governor maintained a public relations section consisting of a staff of four civilians whose duty it was to give out press releases which were designed to place the military government in a favorable light and to suppress news reflecting dissatisfaction with the regime. In addition to this, Lorrin P. Thurston, president and general manager of the *Honolulu Advertiser*, on November 9, 1942, was appointed "public relations advisor to the military governor" under General Orders No. 155. It was unfortunate that this newspaper thus foreclosed itself from being of any public service in criticizing the existing regime.

THE PROVOST COURTS

As has been seen, on December 7, 1941, all courts of Hawaii (civil and criminal) were ordered closed by the commanding general. On December 16, 1942, there was a slight relaxation of the original order by General Orders No. 29, which permitted the courts of Hawaii to try certain *ex parte* civil cases and there was a further relaxation on January 27, 1942, by General Orders No. 57, which allowed the courts to handle probate and divorce cases and certain civil actions which did not require the compulsory attendance of witnesses or the impaneling of juries.

In his report of December 1, 1942, to the governor of Hawaii, the attorney general of Hawaii stated:

In place of the criminal courts of this Territory there have been erected on all the islands provost courts and military commissions for the trial of all manner of offenses from the smallest misdemeanor to crimes carrying the death penalty. Trials have been conducted without regard to whether or not the subject matter is in any manner related to the prosecution of the war. These military tribunals are manned largely by Army officers without legal training. Those who may have had any training in the law seem to have forgotten all they ever knew about the subject.

Lawyers who appear before these tribunals are frequently treated with contempt and suspicion. Many citizens appear without counsel; they know, generally speaking, that no matter what evidence is produced the "trial" will result in a conviction. An acquittal before these tribunals is a rare animal. Accordingly, in most cases a plea of guilty is entered in order to avoid the imposition of a more severe penalty. Those who have the temerity to enter a plea of not guilty are dealt with more severely for having chosen that course.

Heavy fines and long prison sentences are meted out in many cases for comparatively trivial violations of military orders. The former practice of making people donate blood or buy bonds in expiation of their sins has been abandoned. In some instances persons have been found guilty of violating "the spirit of martial law" or "the spirit" of general orders, notwithstanding the act for which they are charged is not prohibited either by statute or military order.

The accused is not furnished with a copy of the charge against him but is permitted to examine the prosecutor's copy. Trials take place in crowded courtrooms in which the officers in charge are fully armed. The witnesses are brought before the provost judges en masse and stand in a circle about the bench together with the accused. The assemblage tells the judge their views of the matter. Cross-examination of witnesses is tolerated with none too much patience by the court.

There have been instances in which arrests have been made and the accused kept in jail three or four days awaiting trial, even in the case of comparatively minor offenses. With the writ of habeas corpus suspended, the unfortunate accused in such cases is without remedy.[2]

CENSORSHIP OF THE PRESS

In the year 1942 there existed no free press in Hawaii. The press operated under a military censorship—not the self-imposed censorship about which the mainland press complained, i.e., insufficient information about the conduct of the war, but censorship which prohibited publication of news items of general interest not related to the conduct of the war but related to the regime of military government. The military governor controlled the press through a licensing system which permitted it to publish "under such conditions and regulations as shall be prescribed from time to time by the military governor" (General Orders No. 14).

On one occasion Riley H. Allen, the editor of the *Honolulu Star-*

[2] See Appendix E.

Bulletin, wrote an editorial mildly criticizing the administration of the government. He was promptly given to understand by the executive to the military governor that such conduct would not be tolerated. Murders and rapes occurred in Honolulu, but the press was forbidden to publish the incidents and, of course, was denied access to police files since the police operated directly under the control of the military governor.

An illustration of the operation of the censorship of the press is afforded by the handling of the prostitution problem by the Army in 1942. For years the evil of prostitution was handled (*sub rosa*) by the local police who segregated the unfortunates in certain areas of the city. After the outbreak of war a substantial number of prostitutes were brought to Honolulu from the mainland under military priorities. The Army decided that it was inhuman to confine prostitutes to a red-light district and hence lifted the ban. As a result they were scattered throughout the residential districts of the city and in some instances homes in residential districts were converted to houses of prostitution. This met with vigorous objections on the part of neighbors who resented being awakened at all hours of the night by visitors to the approved Army brothels. This subject assumed such proportions that the Army decided to return the "jurisdiction" over this "function" to the local police commission. The police proceeded to return to their former segregation regulations. At this point the city of Honolulu was treated to the spectacle of a three weeks' strike by prostitutes who picketed the police station and the office of the military governor with placards announcing their grievances. Nothing appeared in the press in regard to the incident.

When civil government was partially restored by the proclamation of February 8, 1943, General Emmons endeavored to persuade the governor of Hawaii to take over the "function" of regulating prostitution but the governor declined. As a result, the police were ordered to close the houses of prostitution, and substantial numbers returned to the mainland.

The censorship of the press was easily imposed by the military control of shipping allocations and newsprint. Newspaper circulation by reason of the influx of troops and civilian workers soared. Any recalcitrant editor would have soon found his allocation of newsprint cut; the press was fully aware of its position and took pains to comply with the wishes of the military governor.

Some inkling of the extent to which vice flourished can be obtained from the records of the circuit court in Honolulu in a case tried in 1947, in which a safety deposit box of one police officer was opened by revenue agents who found $165,000 in cash which represented the officer's receipts from vice rackets that flourished in Honolulu during the reign of martial law.

MILITARY CONTROL OF LABOR

To understand the situation of labor it might be well to note the situation prior to December 7, 1941. Hawaii is an agricultural community economically dependent upon the two principal crops, sugar and pineapple, and of course overseas transportation. Labor in the principal industries is performed by persons of Asiatic ancestry, originally the Chinese, later the Japanese, and still later the Filipinos. Prior to the war there was no organized labor in the major industries. Dr. James H. Shoemaker, in his report to the Bureau of Labor Statistics in 1939, said:

Although many of the large enterprises maintained effective employee welfare policies, their attitude may best be described as benevolently paternal rather than liberal. The history of management in Hawaii broadly speaking is one of antagonism to labor organization.

The high degree of inter-corporate control makes it possible to monopolize the resources of all large enterprises to restrict the growth of labor unions and to combat strikes in whatever fields of industry they may occur. . . . Thus although management has done much for labor in Hawaii, it has also used every influence at its command to restrict labor organization. . . .

The position of the individual plantation worker is especially vulnerable. The house in which he lives, the store from which he buys, the fields in which he finds his recreation, the hospital in which he is treated are all owned by plantation management which in turn has its policies controlled from the offices of the factors in Honolulu.[3]

Prior to the outbreak of war Congress had appropriated vast sums for the defenses of Pacific bases. A joint venture of associated contractors known as "Contractors, Pacific Naval Air Bases (PNAB)" embarked upon the program of fortifying Hawaii and the islands of the Pacific under United States control. The Army, too, had been granted large appropriations by the Congress for the defenses of Hawaii and undertook construction programs of the first magnitude. These activities brought large numbers of skilled and unskilled workers to Hawaii from the mainland, workers who were accustomed to the rights of collective bargaining and union activity.

The military control of labor not only excluded Hawaii from the

[3] Shoemaker, Labor in the Territory of Hawaii, H.R. Doc. 848, 76th Cong., 3d Sess. 198 (1940).

National Wage Stabilization program, but also superseded the Fair Labor Standards Act of 1938.[4] On December 20, 1941, the military governor issued General Orders No. 38, which froze all wage rates as of December 7, 1941; it froze all employees of the federal, Territorial, and county governments, of contractors and public utilities "to their respective employers," and established an eight-hour day with time and a half for hours in excess of eight; it also suspended all labor contracts between contractors and their employees.

On March 31, 1942, General Orders No. 91 was promulgated. It was a comprehensive regulation of wage rates, overtime, and utilization of labor. It erected the system of releases from employment either with or without prejudice. An employee who failed to get a release without prejudice could not change his job. Any violation of this order, including failure to report to work, carried a jail sentence or a fine in the provost courts.

The order contained the sentence, "Nothing herein shall be construed as superseding or in conflict with the provisions of the Fair Labor Standards Act of 1938." However, it was explicit in providing for payment of one and one-half the regular rate for overtime in excess of 44 hours. Obviously there was no room for construction since the order was clear on its face and in direct conflict with the act of Congress requiring the payment of overtime compensation for hours worked after 40 hours a week. The "nothing herein" clause was window dressing, pure and simple. No employer or employee in Hawaii subject to the order could obey the command of Congress without risking punishment in the provost courts. Moreover, since the military governor's office of labor control had taken over complete jurisdiction of all labor employed by contractors engaged in work for the Army and Navy and all labor working for public utilities and stevedoring companies, any employer who did not obey the military order would be denied his supply of labor. As observed by Judge McLaughlin in a suit brought after the termination of martial law for unpaid overtime during the existence of the military control of labor, an employer had no alternative but to comply.

But certainly no one can question the fact that under the military government condition which confronted defendant it did act as a reasonable prudent man, having no army, would have acted. It was futile to mention what the law was, for the Military Governor was the law. The choice was clear: obey or be punished, irrespective of the law, whose force and effect had been supplanted by the force of military control.[5]

[4] 52 Stat. 1060, 29 U.S.C. Sec. 201.
[5] Kam Koon Wan v. E. E. Black, 75 F. Supp. 553, 561 (1948).

One of the greatest inroads on the liberty of the individual under the military regime in Hawaii was the control of labor under General Orders No. 91, which superseded General Orders No. 38. This order had the effect of freezing labor to a particular employer. It prohibited the Army, Navy, Contractors, the Territorial and county governments, hospitals, public utilities, and stevedoring companies from employing any individual formerly in the employ of any such agency or service unless the employee produced a "bona fide release without prejudice" from his previous employer. Workers who refused to report to the job after ordered to do so by their employers were subject to a $200 fine or imprisonment for two months. It was, of course, essential that labor should be prevented from constantly changing jobs during the war.

This objective was obtained throughout the rest of the country by the orders of the War Manpower Commission without putting anyone in jail for violations. However, General Orders No. 91 both in its substantive provisions and its sanctions differed widely from the orders of the War Manpower Commission. Under the General Orders No. 91, employees of utilities were frozen to their jobs and prohibited from leaving them. This resulted in great dissatisfaction, particularly in view of the higher wages received by others doing similar work. On occasions, drivers of the Honolulu Rapid Transit Company, Limited, would intentionally have "accidents," hoping that under the company's rules they would thus obtain a discharge for negligence and be free to seek other employment. Whatever might be said for industrial mobilization carried out by the government under a general law, there is little to be said for the freezing of men to their jobs for the benefit of private employers who stood to profit as the result of a job freeze.

One of the curious aspects of the military control of labor was the opposition of management to the imposition of wage controls which had been instituted throughout the nation. In continental United States the War Labor Board and Treasury regulations were effective to prevent the spiraling of wages. In Hawaii the programs effective in the rest of the nation were not applied, and in lieu of them was the military control of labor. The military orders made little or no attempt to halt the rapid increase in wages; upgrading and misgrading of employees and the pirating of labor were the order of the day. It would appear to have been to the interest of the Army and Navy and private industry to maintain the same pattern of wage controls as existed on the mainland. However, that program was resisted by all employers until June 6, 1944, when Chairman William

H. Davis of the National War Labor Board visited Hawaii for the purpose of inquiring into the labor situation and as a result revoked the exemption that had theretofore existed in Hawaii of federal wage controls.[6]

Another striking aspect of the military control of labor was the supine acquiescence of labor leaders. Not until after several years of the administration of military labor control did any labor leader protest the system. This may be attributed to ignorance on the part of those affected and possibly fear of the provost courts. In any event the first articulate protest was set forth in "Memorandum on Military Control of Hawaiian Labor," March 22, 1944, by a local of the AFL Teamsters' Union. The memorandum challenged the military governor's jurisdiction over labor. It asserted that the jurisdiction had no foundation in existing law; that the policies of the labor control office were antilabor; that the office approved the intimidation of organized labor even to the extent of having a bargaining agent arrested and held in jail for six months without charges or trial; that the military authorities on Kauai prohibited union officers from collecting dues or engaging in union activities; and that the policies adopted by the office of labor control were injurious to the war effort in Hawaii. The memorandum finally concluded with the statement:

We are convinced that the Office of the Military Governor is biased against unions and negligent of labor, that it has never worked out and will never work out a true labor policy, and that whatever partial policy it may adopt under the pressure of circumstances will be opportunistic and employer-biased. Above all, the legally precarious position of the "Military Governor's" authority will force him to avoid any decision or policy that may lead to his authority's being challenged in the courts. We consider the military incompetent to administer labor in Hawaii.

There exists no plausible reason for a continuance of this illegal military control over patriotic civilians. Any fancied need for this arbitrary subjugation of a free people that might once have existed when the military situation was critical has long since moved far over the western horizon with our powerful Pacific offensive.

Labor in the Territory of Hawaii, freed of its military shackles and controlled by constitutional civilian authority will make even greater contributions to our national war effort.

The workers of Hawaii are especially alert to their responsibilities. The record shows that. They have long been patient. They have kept their tongues in their cheeks and accepted the dictates of the "Military Governor" and his asserted subordinates so long as there appeared to be the remotest possibility that submission was necessary in furthering our offensive.

[6] National War Labor Board, General Orders No. 4, U.S.C. Cong. Service 1944, p. 1786.

Patience has ceased to be a virtue. Competent and constitutional civilian controls over labor must be established in Hawaii.

American free men are entitled to no less![7]

It is of interest that the Communist-dominated waterfront union, the ILWU, did not join in the protest of military control.

The enforcement of labor orders in the provost courts—the effect of the stringent military control of labor—naturally created resentment on the part of labor which was quickly expressed after the military controls were released and martial law was lifted. Prior to the war the basic industries of Hawaii, sugar and pineapples, were practically unorganized but within a short time after the lifting of military controls these industries became completely organized. As Doctor Shoemaker pointed out in his report:

Labor leaders contended that while Hawaiian enterprises both large and small were making unusual profits, while the Government was paying well for properties, materials, and services, and while prices were rising, labor was "frozen" and was carrying the weight of the civilian part of the local war effort without receiving its fair share of the payment for such effort.

It was further felt that after the summer of 1942 there was no justification for regulations controlling labor to be more restrictive in Hawaii than those on the mainland. Bitterness was especially expressed concerning the excessive power of management and the stringent regulations against absenteeism which made it possible for military courts to fine or imprison workers for being absent from their jobs under procedures which were considered arbitrary and were later judged by the Supreme Court to be illegal.

This resentment gradually grew to explosive proportions between 1942 and 1944 and was a primary reason for the sudden unionization of all important island industries as soon as restrictions were lifted.[8]

The backbone of the economy of Hawaii for the past century has been agriculture, the principal crops being sugar cane and pineapples. Generally speaking, agricultural labor on the mainland is not unionized. Today in Hawaii the organization of agricultural workers is almost complete. The wartime military control of labor contributed to this change. Once the military controls were lifted, organization followed.

[7] University of Hawaii War Records Depository.
[8] Shoemaker, The Economy of Hawaii in 1947, U.S. Department of Labor Bulletin 926, p. 26.

Chapter Three

OPERATIONS OF THE MILITARY GOVERNMENT

$\mathcal{J}$ooking back on the military regime in Hawaii, one is apt to wonder how a government of such magnitude could have sprung into being on American soil since Congress had not authorized a military government nor had it provided funds for the *de facto* military government. The appropriation acts themselves allotted no funds for these activities nor did any executive order of the President. How then was it financed?

Governor Poindexter had talked with the President by radio telephone on December 7. The President assured him that planes had already been dispatched and that orders were given for the immediate reinforcement of Hawaii with troops, ships, and supplies.

On January 12, 1942, the President, realizing the havoc brought by the attack, acting under the authority of the Independent Offices Appropriation Act 1942,[1] allocated $15,000,000 to the Secretary of the Interior,

to be expended by said Secretary, or such other person or persons as may be designated for the purpose for any and all emergencies due to the existing war conditions for the protection, care and relief of the civilian population in the Territory of Hawaii.[2]

and on the same day, the President addressed Secretary Ickes, advising him:

While this allocation is being made to you, I assume that the money will be transferred as and when needed to the governor of Hawaii for expenditure in connection with the emergency situations which may arise.[3]

---

[1] 55 Stat. 94.
[2] Letter of the President to the Secretary of the Treasury dated January 12, 1942.
[3] Letter of the President dated January 12, 1942, to the Secretary of the Interior.

Pursuant to this authorization, the Secretary of the Interior commissioned Benjamin W. Thoron of the Interior Department to work in co-operation with the governor of Hawaii in the disbursement of the $15,000,000 allocated by the President for the relief of the civil population of Hawaii.

When Mr. Thoron arrived in Hawaii he found that the civil government of Hawaii had been superseded and was no more than an appendix to the military government established by Colonel Green. The military orders, which issued in swift succession, established a military government of Hawaii vesting all powers—legislative, executive, and judicial—in the commanding general, who assumed the role and title of military governor. This was clear from the orders themselves, prohibiting the functioning of all processes of civil government except as "agents of the Military Governor" and was graphically emphasized by the functional chart drafted by Colonel Green, which accurately described the relationship of all government in Hawaii—federal and Territorial—as being under the supervision and control of the "executive section." The executive section was Colonel Thomas H. Green himself, who took on the title "Executive to the Military Governor." The functional chart disclosed, for example, the atrophy of the civil government of Hawaii, since on the left of the chart with no functions indicated whatsoever were placed the blocks containing the names "Civil Governor," "Mayor, City and County of Honolulu," "Territorial Government," and "County governments." These in the concept of the military governor had no functions to perform since all government was vested in him.

Not only was the Territorial government shorn of its authority, but this applied with equal force to the federal agencies operating in Hawaii, as, for example, the Office of Price Control, the Alien Property Controller, and all other agencies of the United States; all law enforcement was concentrated in military commissions and the provost courts. The two houses of the legislature of Hawaii as well as the judges of all courts, Territorial and federal, do not even appear on the chart as a part of the existing government. The reason for this was that under the regime erected there was no room for legislation other than the decrees of the military. The military governor did not recognize the legislature as a source of legislative power, and similarly, since all law enforcement was concentrated in the military commissions and provost courts, no place in the scheme of government was found for the courts ordained by law.

Hence, when Mr. Thoron arrived armed with the power of disbursing $15,000,000 allocated by the President "for the relief of the

civil population of Hawaii," he was immediately confronted with the
stubborn fact that the military governor asserted and exercised the
right to allocate the funds. Why Mr. Thoron did not make an issue
of this is not clear; possibly because of the absence of any complaint
from Governor Poindexter; possibly because he was unwilling to clash
with the military. At all events it was in this manner that the military
government of Hawaii was financed. A generous Congress had empowered to the President appropriate funds for such an emergency.
The President had acted for the relief of the civil population of
Hawaii, but by the time his instructions were translated into action
it turned out that what was earmarked "for the relief of the civil
population of Hawaii" was in fact used by the military governor to
keep the people under the subjection of a military rule which neither
the Congress nor the President had authorized.

An inkling of the extent of the jerry-built government may be
gathered from the fact that the expenditures for the maintenance of
the organization were of the order of $55,000 per month. These
sums went to pay the civilian employees who were placed on the payroll
of the military government. This budget of $55,000 per month did
not include the pay to officers and men of the United States Army who,
of course, were paid out of legitimate Army appropriations.

THE COLLECTION OF FINES

As might be expected, the rough justice meted out in the provost
courts was a source of large revenues. During the period December 7,
1941, to August 31, 1942, there was collected the sum of $789,417.08
from the operations of the provost courts and the issuance of individual liquor permits. Of this $562,674.67 constituted fines and for-
feitures exacted from civilians in the provost courts, and $226,742.41
represented fees paid by civilians to obtain permits for the purchase
of liquor. The funds themselves were deposited in the name of an
Army finance officer in the Bishop National Bank of Hawaii at Honolulu. The fact that the city government was deprived of its usual
revenues, which were intercepted by the military authorities, became
the subject of extended discussions between Colonel Green and officials of the city of Honolulu.

On March 5, 1942, Gerald R. Corbett, controller of the City and
County of Honolulu, wrote to General Emmons on the disposition
of provost court fines. Controller Corbett said:

Pursuant to your oral request made at our conference of Monday,
February 23, 1942, at which were present the writer, Chief Justice S. B.

Kemp, your legal advisor Judge Stainback and yourself, I present herewith a statement of the current facts pertinent to the problem confronting the Government of the City and County of Honolulu in connection with the non-receipt of our normal revenues from District Court fines and bail forfeitures. . . .[4]

Mr. Corbett pointed out that under military orders the criminal jurisdiction of the courts had been taken over by the provost courts; that he was advised by the Chief of Police "that the moneys are being held in the bank 'subject to the disposition of the military governor' at the orders of Colonel Neal Franklin, provost judge."

The controller then pointed out that from the beginning of county government, revenues from the courts in the form of fines and forfeitures had been included in annual budgets of the city. He then stated:

All of the facilities of the District Courts of Honolulu and the Rural Districts have been placed at the disposal of the Provost Judges to facilitate the discharge by them of their duties under your orders. These facilities include the housing of the courts in the courtrooms of the district magistrates, services of the courts' personnel, including clerks, reporters, stenographers, interpreters, bailiffs, assistant prosecutors and the Magistrates themselves, as well as stationery and office supplies and equipment. These expenses are being met out of the same fund into which the fines and bail forfeitures would normally be deposited.

It is my duty as Chief Financial Officer . . . to be concerned . . . since . . . we have been deprived of this . . . source of revenue . . . that you arrange for the restoration to the City and County Government of these normally expected revenues.[5]

The controller received a reply from Colonel Green on April 11, 1942:

As the matter now stands these are Federal funds. I have forwarded to the War Department a letter requesting instructions as to releasing a portion of such funds to the City and County. I have not yet received a reply from this request, and will advise you when the decision has been reached.

Having received no action, the controller on May 4 again wrote to Colonel Green in regard to these revenues:

I hesitate to reiterate my previous request to you for consideration in connection with the restoration to the City and County of our normal revenues from traffic waivers and court fines, since I know that your efforts in this connection have been continuous since the time the question was first raised. However, our need at the present time has become extremely urgent. . . .

[4] Files of controller, City and County of Honolulu.
[5] *Id.*

Finally on September 24, 1942, General Green wrote to the mayor of Honolulu:

It is proposed to reimburse the City and County of Honolulu for services rendered in connection with the enforcement of proclamations, regulations and orders issued by the Military Governor, the operation of the Provost Courts on the Island of Oahu and the keep of prisoners incarcerated in the County Jail upon order of the Provost Courts. A careful consideration of the many factors involved has led to the conclusion that the sum of $225,000.00 would compensate the City and County for such services.

Your advice is requested as to whether the settlement proposed above is acceptable. It is, of course, understood that the acceptance of this settlement is in full reimbursement for all claims against the United States or the Military Governor or any person connected with either growing out or in any way connected with the enforcement of proclamations, regulations and orders issued by the Military Governor, the operation of the Provost Courts on the Island of Oahu and the keep of prisoners incarcerated in the County Jail upon order of the Provost Court, for the period 7 December 1941 to 31 August 1942.

If the proposed settlement is not acceptable, it is requested that you submit for consideration with the least possible delay any modification you deem appropriate.

It should be noted that General Green's proposal included a full release and settlement "for all claims against the United States or the Military Governor . . . in any way connected with the operation of the Provost Courts. . . ."

General Green's proposal was referred by the city fathers to the attorney general, who vetoed it and brought the matter to the attention of Governor Stainback, who in turn wrote the Interior Department. Secretary Ickes, replying to the governor's letter, referred to a memorandum of Assistant Secretary of War John J. McCloy, dated July 13, 1942, which stated:[6]

The return of all fines, court costs and bail forfeitures to the Territory, after deducting such expenses as may have been incurred to date by the military authorities in the administration of justice, is looked on with favor by the War Department. Studies are now being reinstituted by the Judge Advocate General in order to bring this condition about. In this connection it will no doubt be necessary to establish an audit of the funds.

Secretary Ickes in his letter to the governor said:

I consider that General Green's proposal is completely at variance with the understanding between the War and Interior Departments. In the circumstances it is suggested that you inform General Green that his

6 Letter, Secretary of the Interior to Governor Stainback, October 16, 1942.

proposal is unacceptable and not in accord with the views expressed by the War Department and that you again request the return of the funds. I am bringing this matter and the question of the return of the liquor permit fees to the attention of the Secretary of War and will inform you of any decisions reached here.[7]

The matter was again brought to the attention of General Green by the governor, who had no more success than had the controller and the mayor. Upon learning this, Secretary Ickes on November 19, 1942, wrote the Secretary of War, Henry L. Stimson:

I have your letter of November 4 with regard to the return to the local civil authorities of the fines, court costs and bail forfeitures collected by the military authorities in the Territory of Hawaii.

This Department does not question the propriety of charging against the amounts collected the expenses incurred by the military authorities in the administration of justice in the Territory. Yet it is my understanding that these expenses are relatively small and are substantially less than the sum which General Green proposes to retain. I believe that neither of our departments wishes to withhold from the civil authorities the amounts which are not in dispute.

I hope, therefore, that the Commanding General, Hawaiian Department, will be instructed to return to the civil authorities all sums collected over and above an appropriate reserve for expenses incurred. The return of the balance found due would under this arrangement await an audit of the funds and an agreement as to the expenses properly deductible. If you should adopt this course, I assume, of course, that you will also instruct the Military Governor not to exact a general release of all claims in any way connected with the military government, as was proposed in the letter of September 24 of General Green, as a price for the return of these funds.[8]

The funds were finally turned over on December 15, 1943, at which time a finance officer drew a check on the Bishop National Bank in the sum of $732,116.42, which was made payable:

To The Order of Governor Territory of Hawaii, as Governor Territory of Hawaii and as Agent of the City & County of Honolulu, T.H., County of Maui, T.H., County of Hawaii, T.H., and County of Kauai, T.H., Honolulu, T.H.

The amount of the check represented the balance of the funds after deducting certain amounts claimed by the military authorities as expenses. No audit of the funds was ever submitted. Of the sum of $732,116.42 collected by the Territory, Honolulu alone received $619,804.80. The supervisors had done well not to accept General Green's initial offer of settlement of $225,000. Even more important

[7] *Id.*
[8] Files of the Department of the Interior.

was the fact that payment was not accompanied by any release of liability, which General Green had insisted on.

THE PROVOST COURT PRISONERS

The provost courts not only imposed heavy fines but they also handed out a generous number of stiff jail sentences even for minor offenses. It will be recalled that the provost courts operated without regard to the applicable provisions of the federal or Territorial criminal statutes, which served only as rough "guides" for the imposition of punishment. This left a wide discretion in the Army officers who sat as provost judges, many of whom were untrained in the law and those who were, for the most part, had little or no experience to fit them for the task of administering justice. As has already been noted, the Army rule of Hawaii would never have worked at all without the use of the existing facilities and services of the Territorial and county governments. The provost courts could never have functioned but for the assistance of the clerks, court attachés, and civilian personnel who staffed the civil courts and whose services were commandeered by the Army to perform the necessary clerical work in connection with the administration of the provost courts.

The newly erected military government, having been cut out of whole cloth and without regard to even an approximate co-ordination with the existing government, naturally made no provision for the execution of the sentences imposed by the provost courts. Here again it became necessary for the provost courts to compel the Territorial prison authorities to execute the sentences of the provost courts. As might be imagined, this posed a troublesome problem to the Territorial and county governments. The existing penal institutions consisting of Territorial prisons and county jails were geared to a judicial system which did not contemplate the wholesale imprisonment of persons for relatively minor offenses. The provost judges, however, being inexperienced in the art of administering criminal law, frequently imposed long prison terms for acts which under any normal system of law were misdemeanors and under any ordinary administration of criminal law would call for the imposition of a fine or short jail sentence.

Some idea as to the volume of business done in the provost courts can be gathered from the statistics applicable to one provost court in Honolulu during the year 1942. Records compiled by the Bureau of Crime Statistics and Identification revealed that there were 22,480 persons arrested; all but 359 were found guilty. Fines totaling

$532,539.50 were levied; 943 persons were sent to the county jail; 719 to the Oahu penitentiary. In the month of March 1942, 183 persons were fined and paid a total of $92,901, or an average fine of $500 per person. When it is considered that the provost court did not handle serious cases but concerned itself with what would be the equivalent jurisdiction of a police court it will be seen that the fines imposed were substantial.

Shortly after the inauguration of martial law the census of the jails and prisons experienced a sharp rise. No provision was made by the Army for the care, support, and custody of the provost court prisoners, but they were delivered to the warden or jailer with instructions to keep them incarcerated for the designated period. This, of course, constituted a heavy drain on the Territorial government.

There is no federal prison in the Territory of Hawaii. However, by a long standing arrangement between the Department of Justice and the Territory, persons convicted of crime in the federal courts are imprisoned in Territorial prisons, the federal government compensating the Territorial government for the custody and support of federal prisoners. This agreement naturally did not include payment for the keep of persons convicted and imprisoned by provost courts, which were unknown to our system of law.

When Oscar Goddard, the director of institutions of the Territory, who had charge of prisons, forwarded his bill in 1943 to the Attorney General of the United States, requesting reimbursement for the housing, custody, and support of the provost court prisoners, a novel problem was posed to the Department of Justice. Whose prisoners were these? They were not convicted in a federal court and hence did not fall within the existing contractual arrangement between the federal government and the Territory. They were not Territorial prisoners since they were not sentenced in a Territorial court. The Attorney General passed the problem on to the controller, who refused to pay the bill of the Territory upon the ground that the provost court prisoners were not federal prisoners, and the Territorial government was informed that these were "Army prisoners." The Territory was never reimbursed. Thus the Territorial government was obliged to support and maintain those persons who were sentenced by the provost courts and to foot their bill for room and board notwithstanding the fact that they were not imprisoned by any judgment of a judicial officer of the Territory, an anomalous situation.

The warden of Oahu prison, as might be expected, had special problems of his own arising out of the newly erected military government. He had been accustomed to receive prisoners in an orderly fashion, each prisoner being delivered to the institution along with a copy of the judgment and order of the court. These documents gave the warden specific instructions in regard to the custody of his prisoner, and the particular cases were dealt with in the manner as provided for by law by the Board of Paroles and Pardons, which would make the periodic statutory reviews, recommendations, and allowances for good behavior and other details of prison administration.

When the Army took over criminal law, all this went by the board. For several months the first prisoners who were incarcerated were delivered without any commitment papers whatsoever and the warden was supposed to keep track of the sentences imposed by either oral instructions or informal memoranda concerning them. In many cases he would not have any information as to the crime of which the prisoner was convicted.

By the early part of 1942 this situation assumed sizable proportions and the warden became concerned about his responsibilities. The matter did not trouble the military governor particularly but he finally agreed that it would be a good plan to have on file commitment papers. This, of course, posed a paper-work task of considerable size. The printed forms used by the Territorial courts did not fit the needs of the provost courts. Hence, it became necessary to devise new forms. The military governor having no funds for this purpose (none were authorized for him to erect provost courts or administer provost court prisons), again the task fell upon the director of institutions and the warden of Oahu prison. It was finally solved by the prisoners themselves. A form of commitment was drafted by Deputy Attorney General Sylva for the use of the provost courts, and the task of printing the forms was turned over to the inmates of the prison. The forms having been printed, the prisoners were then given the job of preparing the commitment papers which incarcerated them and their fellow inmates.

COMMUTATION FOR GOOD BEHAVIOR—BLOOD DONATIONS

The director of institutions on March 20, 1942, brought to the attention of the military governor the system that had obtained in Oahu prison whereby prisoners were given commutation for good behavior and requested that some action be taken in regard to the provost court prisoners. General Green, recognizing merit in the director's suggestion, authorized him

to allow the prisoners hereafter committed to Oahu Prison by the provost courts or military commission, commutation for good conduct at the same rate as the Federal government allows Federal prisoners committed to federal, state or territorial prisons.[9]

In June 1942 the census of Oahu prison reached a rather high point. General Green had previously authorized the provost courts to impose sentences in minor cases whereby the accused could donate a pint of blood to the blood bank in lieu of the payment of a fine. Evidently pleased with the results of this edict, he decided to extend the benefits of this system to the persons actually incarcerated in prison. On June 18, 1942, he issued a memorandum to the provost courts in regard to credit for donating blood:

1. Any prisoner sentenced by a Provost Court to a County Jail or Oahu Prison, who voluntarily donates his blood to a blood bank, shall be credited on his sentence as follows: For each pint of his blood so donated, fifteen days in case of a sentence of confinement, or thirty dollars ($30.00) in case of a fine. Two dollars of a fine shall be deemed the equivalent of confinement for one day for the purpose of this memorandum.
2. This credit, when earned, shall be applied automatically toward the satisfaction of such sentence by the person in whose official custody the prisoner may be and no action need be taken by the Provost Court sentencing such prisoner before such credit shall be given.
3. These credits shall apply to prisoners heretofore sentenced and now serving their sentences as well as to those hereafter sentenced.[10]

General Green's direction to the provost courts gives a clue to his idea of the relationship between a fine and imprisonment. According to his scale, a fine of $2.00 was the equivalent of one day in jail. Almost every defendant in a criminal case would prefer the imposition of a fine rather than a jail sentence. On General Green's formula, a year and a half in prison was the approximate equivalent of a $1,000 fine.

The allowance of credit to provost court prisoners for donating blood had its repercussions. In fact the inmates of the prison protested in *Paahao Press*, the prison organ. The nonmartial-law prisoners claimed discrimination by the edict of the military governor. This was brought to the attention of General Green by the warden. The Blood Bank, a civilian organization, had been planned prior to the war with a view to the coming emergency. It operated a substantial plant on the Queen's Hospital grounds. Those in charge skillfully enlisted the support of the community in the donation of blood, the giving of which appealed to the patriotic motives of the inhabitants. In the imposition by the provost courts of sentences to donate blood,

[9] Files of the director of institutions, Territory of Hawaii.
[10] *Id.*

the local high command responsible for the policy displayed a lack of judgment. Whatever may be said in defense of the general ineptness of the Army in the administration of civil affairs in Hawaii, it would tax the ingenuity of the most partisan to defend this practice.

The Blood Bank was a civilian project with a stirring public appeal, a patriotic act by which civilians could give tangible evidence of doing their bit. To make the act of donating blood a punishment for a trivial misdemeanor was destructive of the very idealism that sparked the program. Not infrequently the Sunday night drunks would be rounded up by the military police, held in jail overnight, and brought before the provost court the following Monday morning. When the calendar was called they were frequently sentenced to donate a pint of blood to the Blood Bank. The prisoners were taken from the provost court to the Blood Bank to have their blood drawn. The scientific screening (insisted on by the physicians) to eliminate tubercular and otherwise unfit donors was set at naught. Finally, on September 3, 1942, donating blood in satisfaction of provost court sentences was abolished with the following order:

No provost court shall as a sentence or a part thereof order a person sentenced by said court to give or donate his blood nor condition the suspension, execution or satisfaction of a sentence or a part thereof upon a blood donation by such person.[11]

While it was true that no military order commanded the donation of blood as punishment for an offense, it was hardly extracted on a voluntary basis. This form of punishment, as well as other unusual forms of punishment, was invented either by the executive to the military governor or the particular provost judge issuing sentence. To call these donations voluntary would be inaccurate. If, for instance, an individual convicted in the provost courts did not have the ready cash to meet his fine and was faced with the alternative of a jail sentence or donating a pint of blood, the act of donation was simply the choice of the lesser of two evils and could hardly be called voluntary. The terms of the order rescinding the practice shed light on this point: "No provost court shall . . . order a person sentenced by said court to give or donate his blood. . . ."[12]

The practice is reminiscent of archaic penalties that were discredited centuries ago and were expressly prohibited by the constitutional provision against "cruel and unusual punishments."

[11] Files of the director of institutions, Territory of Hawaii.
[12] *Id.*

COMPULSORY PURCHASE OF WAR BONDS

Akin to the punishment of extraction of blood was that of sentencing defendants to buy war bonds. The record of the civil population of Hawaii in the purchase of bonds was an enviable one. It probably led the nation. A number of factors contributed to this result: wages were high (after the initial freeze wages were freely increased without regard to federal wage controls), business flourished, with great numbers of Army and Navy personnel spending freely, but more important than all that was the fact that Hawaii regarded itself as the symbol of World War II. Bank deposits rose from $152,000,000 in 1941 to $493,000,000 in 1945.[18] In short, every factor was present to make for a favorable record in the purchase of bonds. The key to the program was the sense of community pride. Here was the spot of American soil which experienced and withstood the first shock of war. Ordering a citizen to purchase bonds as a penalty for the violation of a military order degraded what was otherwise a patriotic privilege and duty.

The unfamiliarity of the legal staff of the military governor with elementary principles of law was apparent every day. However, since they not only made the decrees but enforced and interpreted them in military courts, the anomalies were rarely exposed publicly. There was no separation of powers. All power had coalesced into a single hand—the military governor whose word was law. One unique example was the assertion by the military governor of the power to alter the terms of the United States War Bonds. These, of course, were obligations of the United States (drafted with care), bearing the facsimile signatures of the Secretary of the Treasury and the Treasurer of the United States. They were transferable or redeemable at the will of the holder. The provost judges, in pursuance of a "policy" formulated in the office of the military governor, adopted the practice of sentencing violators of martial law orders to purchase war bonds in lieu of fines or jail sentences. This required altering the tenor of the instrument by endorsing on the bonds a statement "not redeemable until victory" or "not redeemable until six months after V-J Day" or "Bonds not transferable and to be held for the duration of war." The particular provost judge who altered the bond would then sign his name under the endorsement.

To citizens the act of purchasing war bonds under military compulsion was distasteful. It is one thing to give freely to the nation but

[18] Hearings, Sub. Com. House Representatives, H. Res. 236, 79th Cong., 1st Sess. 678 (1946).

quite a different matter to buy bonds under pain of fine or imprisonment. The orders of the provost courts directing defendants to buy bonds probably had the opposite result from that intended.

This practice posed a problem with the local banks. The Bank of Hawaii, a leading banking institution of Honolulu, was concerned about the authority of a provost court to alter the tenor of a United States bond. The bank wrote the Secretary of the Treasury for his views on whether the solemn promise of the United States to pay or the order of the provost court was to be followed. The Secretary of the Treasury, after some delay, replied that the bank should abide by the tenor of the bond, regardless of the order of the provost court.

THE BLACKOUT AND CURFEW

The blackout which began on the night of December 7, 1941, continued for more than two years. It prohibited the showing of lights between the hours of sundown and sunrise. Civilians were not permitted on the streets after blackout hours. The blackout and curfew regulations were the subject of strict military orders under which violators were dealt with swiftly and severely in the provost courts. The restrictions imposed upon Hawaii were in sharp contrast with the mild blackout imposed upon the residents of besieged Britain. For civilians in Hawaii the blackout was total—not so much as a crack of light from an ill-fitting curtain escaped punishment. The liability imposed was absolute against the owner of the premises without regard to the individual who violated the order. Sentences were imposed without regard to the facts of the violation and even the most extenuating circumstances did not temper the judgment. For example, a light that went on by reason of a defective switch brought the owner the same punishment as though he had negligently failed to comply with the order.

The blackout and curfew restrictions were presumably regulations that related to the public safety. To question the necessity for these restrictions was to question the judgment of the military commander on an issue of security. Obviously, if regulations related to the public safety were rescinded, then all military orders relating to civil affairs generally would fall. If such restrictions had been lifted (after the need for them had disappeared), say, after the Battle of Midway in June 1942 or even as late as December 1942, this would have been a practical demonstration which would not have escaped the notice of the average citizen that the need for martial law and provost courts no longer existed. It was plainly the desire of the high command in

Hawaii to maintain the military government of Hawaii for as long a period as it could be maintained. This had the direct result of keeping the inhabitants under strict military control by the blackout and curfew for years after it could reasonably be said to be necessary. Troops would return to Hawaii from the Gilbert Islands and the Marshall Islands thousands of miles west of Hawaii and would be amazed to find a blacked-out city.

One thing particularly irritating to the civilian population was that the blackout and curfew were not applied to Army and Navy posts or to the waterfront in Honolulu. Civilians could look down from their homes in the heights above Honolulu and see the city below in total darkness except for the waterfront, which was ablaze, conducting the busy work of loading and unloading freighters. To the west of the city lay the Army airfield, Hickam Field, and farther on lay Pearl Harbor itself, both illuminated like Christmas trees. The same was true of Schofield Barracks, Bellows Field, and the Kaneohe Naval Air Station. Whenever a civilian had the temerity to ask why Honolulu should be subjected to a total blackout when the military objectives on the island were ablaze with lights, the stock answer was that the Army and Navy, in the event of an air raid alarm, could put out lights instantaneously—inferentially the civilian could not do so.

Chapter Four

THE MILITARY GOVERNMENT
IN THE COURTS

*T*HE history of the military government of Hawaii in the courts is a history of people reluctant to take their problems to the courts for the reason that it might be said they were "interfering" with the war effort. The tactics of the government, i.e., the War Department and the Attorney General, follow the pattern which was followed during the Civil War, namely, the resort to delays and devious devices to postpone a judicial determination by the highest court of the land on the validity of the exertion of military power over civilians.

It will be recalled that during the Civil War and reconstruction that followed, devices of questionable propriety were resorted to to prevent a determination by the Supreme Court of the grave issues involving the suspension of the privilege of the writ and the validity of military trials.[1] There were several important differences between the two situations. During the Civil War the nation itself was divided; persons in rebellion against the government were actually found within the Union ranks. It was the first occasion in which the national government was confronted with the necessity of suspending the privilege of the writ of habeas corpus. President Lincoln, it will be recalled, acted under the constitutional power of commander in chief without the sanction of Congress. As a matter of fact, Congress did not get around to sanctioning the presidential suspensions of the writ until 1863.

The situation in Hawaii, however, did not present a legal "no man's land." High officials in the government must have been aware of the limits of military power and particularly the illegality of the trial of civilians by military tribunals for ordinary crimes. Apart

[1] 2 Warren, The Supreme Court in U.S. History, p. 491 *et seq.*

60

from this, Congress promptly after the outbreak of war enacted a statute which clothed the military arm of government with every needed power to preserve the internal security of the nation but of course left enforcement of the orders to the federal courts.[2]

Congress had deposited in the executive an enormous delegation of power authorizing him, the Secretary of War, or any military commander, to prescribe rules of conduct for civilians within a military area. Under this statute 170,000 persons of Japanese ancestry including 70,000 American citizens were removed from the West Coast and placed in relocation centers in the interior of the United States, a program which was not only a frontal attack on basic principles of American democracy but also from a practical point of view was unwise and a useless waste of our energies at a time when they were most needed. No one with a knowledge of our past can look back on the handling of this problem without the conviction that we repudiated the ideals for which America had always stood and in defense of which we were waging the war. The social damage that was inflicted upon us as a result of the uprooting of these peaceful and law-abiding people may have its effects for years to come.[3]

The question which presents no ready solution is why, having ample statutory powers (sufficient to move 170,000 people en masse from their homes and confine them under military guard in relocation centers), was not this vast power employed to meet any real or fancied emergency that existed in Hawaii after the initial attack of December 7? It cannot be attributed to ignorance since the War Department had sponsored the legislation.[4] The statutory powers were never used by the Army in Hawaii until litigation in the courts finally brought the military government to an end.

ZIMMERMAN V. WALKER

The first challenge in the courts to the asserted military power in Hawaii involved a detention case.[5] The petition in this case alleged

---

[2] "Whoever shall enter, remain in, leave or commit any act in any military area or military zone prescribed, under the authority of the executive order of the President, by the Secretary of War, or by any military commander designated by the Secretary of War, contrary to the restrictions applicable to any such area . . . shall be guilty of a misdemeanor. . . ." Act of March 21, 1942, 56 Stat. (1942) 173; 18 U.S.C. 97(a).

[3] Hirabayashi v. United States, 320 U.S. 81 (1943); see Dembitz, Racial Discrimination and the Military Judgment, XLV Col. L. Rev. 175.

[4] This was the case of the author who in early 1942 suggested the establishment by Congress of combat areas to give the military authorities any needed powers; Anthony, Martial Law in Hawaii, 30 Calif. L. Rev. (1942) 371, 391. At the time this article was written the suggested legislation was an accomplished fact but the act of March 21, 1942, was not available in Hawaii.

[5] Zimmerman v. Walker, 132 F. 2d 442 (1942), cert. denied 319 U.S. 744.

that Zimmerman was a citizen of the United States, was unlawfully imprisoned by color of authority of the United States; that the "cause or pretext" of his detention was an order made by a board of officers and civilians appointed by the authority of the United States for the purpose of inquiring into the activities of residents to ascertain whether such activities were subversive of the best interests of the United States and to recommend detention or parole; that the Army was about to remove the prisoner beyond the jurisdiction of the court; that the order was predicated upon hearsay statements of persons unknown to the prisoner who neither saw nor heard his accusers; that he was not permitted to examine witnesses against him; was denied access to the statements submitted to the board concerning him and was denied access to its proceedings and was advised by respondent that the advice of counsel was neither necessary nor desirable.

The petition further charged that the detention was in violation of the federal Constitution and concluded with the prayer that a writ of habeas corpus issue directing respondent to produce the body of the prisoner before the court and certify the reasons for his detention and the order of removal.

The petition was served upon the United States Attorney who appeared, stating that he did not oppose any action by the court but was of the view that the existing military orders prohibited the issuance of the writ.

The Act of Congress provided:

The court, or justice, or judge, to whom such application is made, shall forthwith award a writ of habeas corpus unless it appears from the petition itself that the party is not entitled thereto.[6]

The petition, needless to say, having been prepared by counsel employed to secure the prisoner's release, did not disclose on its face any reason why the writ should not issue. In these circumstances the clear duty of the court was to issue the writ or an order to show cause.[7] Whether the prisoner was entitled to his discharge was a different matter.

Federal Judge Delbert E. Metzger,[8] before whom the application was made, entertained no doubt of the duty of the court under the Judicial Code but denied the writ on the ground that General

---

[6] R.S. 755, 28 U.S.C. Sec. 455.

[7] Walker v. Johnson, 312 U.S. 275, 282 (1941).

[8] The atmosphere of this hearing may be reconstructed from Judge Metzger's memorandum; see McColloch, Judge Metzger and the Military, 35 A.B.A.J. 365 (1949).

Orders 57[9] forbade its issuance, adding: "I feel that the court is under duress by reason of the order and not free to carry on the function of the court in a manner in which the court conceives to be its duty."

The compulsion which the District Court thought it was under certainly did not extend to the Circuit Court of Appeals sitting in San Francisco. The minimum requirements of due process and orderly judicial procedure would seem to have required a return setting forth the suspension of the privilege of the writ, the reasons for the prisoner's detention, and the allegation that the public safety required such action. Whether the petition and such a return would have raised issues for judicial determination could only be known after the writ (or an order to show cause) issued and the return was filed. The issuance of the writ, or an order to show cause, would not have concluded the question of the prisoner's right to be discharged.

The Circuit Court of Appeals, without any pleading other than the petition or evidence, concluded that the privilege of the writ was validly suspended on December 7, 1941, that the "petition and facts of which the court was required to take judicial cognizance were together to be considered as constituting the application"[10] and that since the petition disclosed that the detention was "after an inquiry related in some way to the public safety"[11] in an area where the privilege of habeas corpus had been lawfully suspended, concluded "the futility of further inquiry was apparent on the face of the petition."[12]

One of the facts of which the Court of Appeals took judicial notice as constituting (together with the petition) the application was that the "Hawaiian Islands, owing to their position and the inclusion in their population of so large an element presumptively alien in sympathy, are peculiarly exposed to fifth column activities."[13]

A vigorous dissent was filed by Judge Haney who, after reviewing the history of the writ, concluded that the petition was sufficient on its face to challenge the validity of the appointment of the board and that the court should have issued the writ or an order to show cause and passed upon the issue whether military necessity required

[9] This military order forbade, under heavy penalty, trial by jury and the issuance of the writ of habeas corpus.

[10] *Supra*, note 5 at 445.

[11] *Id*. at 446.

[12] *Id*. at 446.

[13] *Id*. at 446. How the court allowed unfounded rumor to creep into its opinion is puzzling in view of official statements to the contrary by the Attorney General and the highest military and naval authorities months before in the final Tolan Committee report (R.H. No. 2124, 77th Cong., 2d Sess.). The court was entitled to take judicial notice of such a report. Tempel v. United States, 248 U.S. 121 (1918).

the prisoner's detention. The dissent, unfortunately, confused martial law with military government.[14]

A petition for certiorari was filed in the Supreme Court. The Solicitor General filed a memorandum with the Supreme Court suggesting that the case had become moot by reason of action of the War Department removing Zimmerman from Hawaii and releasing him unconditionally the day before certiorari was applied for. Upon this showing the Supreme Court denied the petition, noting in the memorandum decision "that Hans Zimmerman, on whose behalf the petition is filed, has been released from the respondent's custody."[15]

There can be no doubt but that on December 7, 1941, the facts warranted the original declaration of martial law and the suspension of the privilege of the writ of habeas corpus. It may also be conceded that for a short period following the outbreak of war, martial law was lawfully in effect, and the privilege of the writ of habeas corpus was lawfully suspended. The Circuit Court of Appeals, however, proceeded upon the view that once it found the original declaration valid the duty of the court to look further was discharged. This might be termed the "blanket view" of martial law. In other words, a declaration once made is a permanent seal over cases that later arise, thus preventing judicial inquiry concerning them.

This view does not square with any accepted principle of martial law. The lawful existence of a state of martial law is a matter of fact, not a matter of proclamation; the validity of any act done in the name of martial law rests not upon the presence or absence of a proclamation but the existence of a military necessity justifying the act in question.

THE GLOCKNER AND SEIFERT CASES

The high prerogative writ remained unused in Hawaii until July 30, 1943, when two naturalized Germans filed petitions for writs. Their cases[16] later made the headlines from Maine to California. The petitioners alleged they were citizens of the United States held in custody by military authority (one since December 1941, the other since December 1942); that no charges had been made against them; that they violated no law of the United States, the Territory,

---

[14] *Supra*, note 5 at 449, 450.
[15] *Ibid.* Zimmerman v. Walker, *supra*, note 5, 319 U.S. 744. For Zimmerman's story of his internment on Sand Island, Hawaii, on December 8, 1941, his removal to Camp McCoy, Wisconsin, his return to Sand Island, the second removal from Hawaii and his final release, see Chicago Daily Tribune, August 20, 1943.
[16] Ex parte Seifert, U.S.D.C. (Hawaii) No. 296; Ex parte Glockner, U.S.D.C. (Hawaii) No. 295.

or any executive or military order but were confined in a military internment camp on the island of Oahu and were restrained of their liberty by Lieutenant General Robert C. Richardson Jr., commanding general, Hawaiian Department. The petitions concluded with the prayer that a writ or order to show cause issue. The government moved to dismiss the petitions.

The court overruled the motions upon two grounds: (1) that under the governor's proclamation of February 8, 1943, the privilege of the writ of habeas corpus was restored; and (2) that although a state of war existed, there was no showing that the Territory was in "imminent danger" of invasion and concluded that the petitions were prima facie sufficient and ordered the writ to issue. The writ in the usual form was handed to the marshal for service upon the general whose office was across the street from the federal court. A deputy marshal called at the office and upon being told that the general was in conference, waited outside. The deputy endeavored to serve the papers as the general left his office, but was manhandled by military police who prevented service.[17]

The court, upon being advised of this, instructed the marshal to continue his efforts to serve the general. On August 18 the marshal returned the writ as unserved for the reason that the general "evaded service." Time for service was extended until August 21, on which date the cause came on for hearing. The marshal's return disclosed that the general had been served with the writ on August 20. The United States Attorney requested ten days to file returns to the writs upon the ground that the petitioners were detained more than twenty miles' distance from the courthouse.[18] The court asked for evidence of the distance of the internment camp from the courthouse. Upon investigation the United States Attorney reported the distance to be 19½ miles. The court then fixed the time for the return of the writ and the production of the bodies.

On the return day, August 24, the United States Attorney advised the court that the bodies of the petitioners would not be produced[19]

---

[17] See Transcript of August 16, 1943, in Glockner and Seifert cases, *supra*, note 16.

[18] The Judicial Code provides: Any person to whom such writ is directed shall make due return thereof within three days thereafter, unless the party be detained beyond the distance of twenty miles; and if beyond that distance and not beyond a distance of a hundred miles, within ten days; and if beyond the distance of a hundred miles, within twenty days (R.S. 756, 28 U.S.C. Sec. 456). The time of return and distances were no doubt taken from the Habeas Corpus Act of 1670, 31 Charles II, c. 2; the writ is discussed at some length by Chancellor Kent; 2 Commentaries on American Law (14th ed.), 26 *et seq.*

[19] The Judicial Code provides: The person making the return shall at the same time bring the body of the party before the judge granting the writ. 28 U.S.C. Sec. 458.

and offered to read a statement from the general. The court declined to entertain the statement and instructed the United States Attorney to prepare a citation for contempt. A citation was prepared and served on August 24. On the following day the contempt proceedings[20] were heard, the court reviewed the habeas corpus cases, found the general in "open and notorious defiance of the mandate of the court" and sentenced him to pay a fine of $5,000. On the same day Lieutenant General Robert C. Richardson, Jr., issued the famous General Orders No. 31.[21]

The story can best be told by a reference to the transcript of the proceedings had in the United States District Court on August 16, 1943. Court was opened, Judge Metzger presiding, and the two habeas corpus cases, *Ex parte Seifert*, and *Ex parte Glockner*, were called by the clerk.

The Court: The United States marshal reported to me that he had difficulty and was defeated in an attempt to make service of the writ on General Richardson, and I wanted the marshal and the deputy marshal to make a statement before the Court as to their efforts and success. Mr. Marshal Heine, will you come forward.

The Clerk: Mr. Heine, will you raise your right hand, please?

(Otto F. Heine, being first duly sworn, testified as follows:)

Q. (*by the Court*): Mr. Marshal Heine, have you served the writs issued this morning in the cases now before the Court?

A.: I have not, your Honor.

Q.: Have you made an attempt to serve them?

A.: I did.

Q.: Will you state to the Court what experience you had in that connection?

A.: I received the writs from the clerk of the Court, Mr. Thompson, this morning at about 11 o'clock. Upon receipt of them I went over to the office of General Richardson in the Capitol grounds.[22] I entered and was greeted by a man named Mr. Slattery, I believe. I asked Mr. Slattery——

Q.: An officer, Captain Slattery?

A.: I don't know his title, Judge. I understand he is military aide to the military governor.

[20] United States v. Richardson, U.S.D.C. (Hawaii) Misc. No. 139.

[21] Honolulu Advertiser, August 26, 1943.

[22] The Capitol grounds referred to in the testimony are in the heart of the city directly opposite to the Federal Building which houses the federal court. General Richardson occupied a temporary structure built upon the Capitol grounds after the military governor had vacated the attorney general's office in Iolani Palace.

Q.: Mr. Slattery was in court here this morning, was he not, at the time the ruling was read?

A.: I don't know.

Clerk (*Mr. Thompson*): He was, your Honor.

Q.: Oh, yes. Proceed.

A.: Then Mr. Slattery told me to step into the next room, there was a young lady at the desk, to ask her for the General. I approached the young lady and I said to her, "Can I see General Richardson?" She said, "Your name, please?" I said, "Mr. Heine, United States marshal." Whereupon she left. I would say in about a minute she returned and told me the military governor would be unable to see me this morning as he was in conference. Then I asked her, "When would I be able to see General Richardson?" She said, "This afternoon he will be at Fort Shafter."

So upon receipt of that information I came to the office and told my deputy, United States Marshal George Bruns, to go to the Capitol Building and park himself up there by the General's car and wait there until the General returned to his car. So George Bruns went up and I believe you should get the story from George Bruns about what happened. . . .

(*The deputy, George Bruns, was then sworn as a witness and was questioned by the Court.*)

Q.: Now, Mr. Bruns, did you attempt to serve the writs of habeas corpus issued citing General Richardson this morning?

A.: I did.

Q.: What success or what experience did you have?

A.: I think it was about a quarter past 11, Marshal Heine came back and reported to me that General Richardson was going to be in conference all morning, and asked me to go over there and see if I could serve him. . . . .

I went over in the car and parked the car, came back down the roadway towards King Street to see if the General's car was still there. It was parked outside, on the *mauka*[23] of the door going into the building. I proceeded up the steps and went to the information desk. There were some M.P.'s in there and one of the M.P.'s standing outside the counter came up to me and asked me if there was anything he could do for me.

I said, "Yes." I showed him my badge and told him I was a United States deputy marshal and proceeded to take out my pocket commission. Before I was able to open it up and show it to him, he said, "Have you an appointment with the General?" I said, "No, I haven't an appointment with him, but I have some papers I would like to serve on him." He said, "I am sorry. The General is going to be in conference all morning."

[23] *Mauka* is a Hawaiian expression indicating the direction toward the mountains; the opposite direction being *makai*, or toward the sea.

I said, "All right. Thank you. I will wait for him."

So I walked outside and stood on the veranda, leaning against the post, the *mauka* post, which is near the steps going down and looking outside. I had only been there a few seconds when an M.P. came out and grabbed me by the shoulders and said to me, "You have to get up there," pointing to *mauka* on the veranda, where there was no outlet or anything, just a railing all the way down.

I said, "See here! You cannot handle me like that. I am a United States deputy marshal. If I can't wait on the veranda I will get out in the yard."

He said, "I have orders to tell you to get up there, so get up there."

So while he was holding onto me I happened to turn around and look and General Richardson and two other officers ran down the steps. I thought, "Well, I'll go over this bannister and break this fellow's hold." So I leaped over the bannister and he let go of his hand, putting it in between my collar and held on to me by my right arm, dragging me up against the railing.

General Richardson and the two officers got in the car and drove off through the Palace gate *ewa* on King Street. So then I went inside and this fellow Captain Slattery or Major Slattery was standing at the counter, and I said to him, "Do you allow a Federal officer to be treated this way? We give you more courtesy than I got over here this morning, and furthermore you are an officer of the court."

He didn't say a word. He walked inside. Then I came down the steps, got in my car, came down and reported it to the marshal.

(*The Court continued*:)

Q.: And you reported to the marshal your experience?

A.: Oh, yes. And in the meantime these papers were starting to blow all over the yard. I had to go pick them up.

Q.: That is, the papers you were attempting to serve?

A.: Yes.

Q.: That was the result of the manhandling you got there, was it, that you lost your hold on the papers or what?

A.: I was still being manhandled when I went over the railing. He was still holding onto me and kept holding onto me. That is when I lost the papers. That is when the papers got away from me.

The Court: Mr. Marshal, these writs were delivered to you to be served. You will continue to make every reasonable effort to serve them on General Richardson.

The spectacle of a commanding general of the United States Army evading the process of a middle-aged deputy United States marshal as though he were a fugitive from justice did not add to the prestige of the Army.

About the time of this incident Under Secretary of War Robert Patterson was in Honolulu en route to an inspection of the South

Pacific and had with him a number of high-ranking Army officers. A luncheon in his honor was arranged at the Pacific Club with General Richardson acting as host. Among the invited guests were the governor, the secretary, and the attorney general of the Territory. Preparatory to the luncheon, the office of the military governor felt obliged to take security measures to protect General Richardson from the United States marshal and so military police were stationed about the Pacific Club grounds and even in the reception lobby of the club itself.

The visit of Under Secretary of War Robert Patterson and his military aides to Hawaii was featured in the daily press, but no mention was made of the protection afforded General Richardson against the United States marshal. Referring to the luncheon in Secretary Patterson's honor, the press simply made mention that the general "entertained the group and territorial and civil officials at luncheon at the Pacific Club Tuesday."[24]

The *Honolulu Advertiser* wrote an editorial in praise of General Orders No. 31, which threatened Judge Metzger and all others with fine and imprisonment or worse in the provost courts if anyone participated in the habeas corpus proceedings.

The amazing situation in Hawaii in which it has been necessary in his judgment for the general commanding the department to issue a special order under martial law to prevent the extension of the privilege of the writ of habeas corpus to a military prisoner who he deems unsafe to be at large calls for an expression from Washington. This is due if for no reason than the salutary effect it will have upon the public morale here and throughout the country.[25]

The same issue of the *Honolulu Advertiser* carried a news story to the effect that General Richardson would appeal his sentence of contempt to the Circuit Court of Appeals.

Back in Washington, Assistant Secretary of War John McCloy issued the following statement as to the position of the War Department.

Memorandum to the press: The refusal of Lt. General Robert C. Richardson, Jr., to submit broad questions of Hawaiian defense to the decision of a federal court in test cases brought to put an end to martial law has the War Department's approval.[26]

The Assistant Secretary, himself an able lawyer, did not state that

<hr>

[24] Honolulu Star-Bulletin, August 18, 1943.
[25] Honolulu Advertiser, August 27, 1943; for the full text of General Orders No. 31, see Appendix C.
[26] Honolulu Advertiser, August 27, 1943.

the habeas corpus cases simply involved the right of the general to hold indefinitely without trial American citizens who were not charged with the commission of any crime. These were the "broad questions of Hawaiian defense" to which the Under Secretary referred. The immediate issue was settled in the *Glockner* and *Seifert* cases by the general accepting service of process and releasing his prisoners in San Francisco, thus rendering the case moot. The *Honolulu Advertiser* in an editorial said:

The question of the return of certain civil rights to the people here was not initiated by the civil community as a whole. The opinion of the civil population was neither asked nor expressed when "restoration demands were made." Hawaii naturally wanted such of its legal rights as would not interfere with the war but there was no popular voice raised against martial law as it has been administered since December 7, 1941.[27]

In a marked contrast the editor of the *Washington Post* wrote an editorial on the subject in which he first referred to President Roosevelt's speech at Ottawa on the Atlantic Charter and the Four Freedoms and then brought the matter down to earth on the immediate question of the writ of habeas corpus in Hawaii and pointed out that the Habeas Corpus Act, unlike the Atlantic Charter, was specific and not general and said:

It is by no means clear whence General Richardson derives the right he claims to have of suspending the writ. It would be difficult to show that the President himself has any such power which he could delegate to the general. . . .
To permit a military officer to assume such a power without restraint from the courts or authority from Congress would, it seems to us, set a highly dangerous precedent . . . It is, of course, true that Judge Metzger is without any physical power to enforce his writs or to collect the fine of $5,000 for contempt he has against General Richardson whereas General Richardson can enforce his decrees by a good many thousand bayonets. But it seems important to have the matter clear that General Richardson's authority to suspend the traditional liberties of American citizens within his military district rests not upon any legality but purely upon *force majeure*.[28]

The *Honolulu Advertiser* carried a lengthy editorial appearing on page 1 of the issue of September 12, 1943, which discussed the issues posed by the *Glockner* and *Seifert* cases and also the notorious General Orders No. 31. It endorsed the order in these words:

General Richardson's order closing the courts to habeas corpus proceedings has apparently found general community favor if for no other

[27] Honolulu Advertiser, September 1, 1943.
[28] Washington Post, September 2, 1943.

reason than it stopped the spectacle of a federal judge commanding and fining a commanding general . . . A declaration of martial law carries with it the suspension of habeas corpus and it is from this fact that it derives its potency as an effective measure in wartime . . . If there was any misunderstanding of that intent the local self-styled champions of "civil rights" might explain their delay of six months in bringing it to the attention of that same public they are now so busily engaged in "protecting."

The impression of those who have closely followed the case is that since the proclamation was issued with its attendant "restoration," legal lines have been drawn and strategy mapped to get rid of martial law. Perhaps it was to have been a legal blitz with a decision handed down quickly to catch the military napping. Never has a case of such import been "decided" so quickly in any branch of the local judiciary. Whatever the plan was, it promptly backfired with the issuance of General Richardson's General Orders No. 31.

The end sought by General Orders No. 31 was the prohibition of all pending and future habeas corpus proceedings in Hawaii and to provide penalties for its infraction—a simple task of draftsmanship.

The order is divided into six sections of sixteen paragraphs. The declared purpose (1.01) was to prevent "interference with military operations"; officers of the District Court were prohibited (2.01) from filing petitions or issuing process in habeas corpus; the judges (2.02) were similarly enjoined; the injunction was reiterated in the next two paragraphs (2.03, 2.04); the public generally and attorneys in particular were similarly enjoined (2.05), as was the United States marshal (2.06); judges of the District Court were directed to discontinue pending habeas corpus proceedings (2.07); Judge Metzger was ordered (2.08) to refrain from proceeding in *Ex parte Glockner*, and a companion order (2.09) was inserted in regard to *Ex parte Seifert*; officers of the federal court were ordered to refrain (3.01) from opposing any orders of the general or the military governor "regardless of whether or not such order or orders are published in the newspapers"; the order in its entirety was made applicable (4.01) to pending and future cases in the United States courts or any other[29] court of the Territory of Hawaii; lest the foregoing paragraphs be thought to leave any loophole, 4.01 added a rule of construction that the order "shall be liberally construed."

The penal provisions of the order made the punishment fit the crime. Any person who violated the order or aided and abetted its violation upon conviction in a provost court was subject to five years' imprisonment or $5,000 fine or both, or if convicted by a military

[29] The draftsman was either unaware of or not satisfied with the holding in Tarble's Case, 13 Wall. 397 (1871), giving the federal courts exclusive jurisdiction in such cases.

commission[30] was subject to such punishment as the military commission imposed; the order concluded with the recital that its issuance was by the general in his capacity as military governor and military commander and in the exercise of his martial law powers. A copy of the order was served in person by the provost marshal under arms upon the two federal judges.

When Judge Metzger was served with General Orders No. 31, commanding him to desist from further proceedings in the *Glockner* and *Seifert* cases he recorded his compliance with General Richardson's command by the following minute order:

At 11 A.M. the Court, by its senior judge, this 25th day of August 1943, in compliance with General Orders No. 31, dated August 25, 1943, received at this office at 10:40 A.M. this day from Lt. General Robert C. Richardson, commanding general, United States Army Forces, Central Pacific Area, also styling himself Military Governor of the Territory of Hawaii, directed the clerk to discontinue all activities in proceedings relating to habeas corpus and all matters related thereto or growing therefrom and that are now pending in this court.[31]

And then the district judge (probably with a twinkle in his eye) added for the record:

This direction shall be construed as a full and complete compliance with all lawful terms and provisions in every particular with said General Orders No. 31 and that everything therein lawfully commanded to be performed by any of the officers of this court is now fully done.

On August 18, 1943, the governor of Hawaii dispatched a letter to the Secretary of the Interior in which he said:

I am greatly disturbed at witnessing the spectacle of a commanding general in the United States Army defying an order of the Federal Court, refusing to accept the court's process and permitting a United States marshal to be abused in an effort to perform his sworn duty . . . Accordingly I request that you take this matter up directly with the Attorney General and, if necessary, the President to ascertain whether the process of a Federal Court . . . should be obeyed by the commanding general . . . and its legality tested in a proper manner or whether it should be defied and the United States marshal obstructed and mistreated for endeavoring to carry out the duties of his office.[32]

A similar letter was addressed by the governor to Francis Biddle, Attorney General.

[30] General Orders No. 2 (3.01) authorized the imposition of any sentence including the death penalty by military commissions; Honolulu Advertiser, March 10, 1943.
[31] U.S.D.C. (Hawaii) Ex parte Glockner, H.C. 295, Ex parte Seifert, H.C. 296, Ex parte Richardson, Misc. 139.
[32] Letter, Governor Stainback to Secretary of the Interior Ickes, August 18, 1943.

During the trial of the *Glockner* and *Seifert* cases, Judge Metzger was subjected to annoyance and threats by telephone which finally led him to address a letter to General Richardson which read in part:

I request that while you have your hand in at general orders you enunciate an order forbidding your officers to further annoying me by threats and abuses.

For the past several days my family and I have been repeatedly disturbed by telephone calls during dinner time and until late into the night by persons representing that they are Army officers or friends of General Richardson desiring to tell me the kind of a disloyal citizen and skunk they have concluded I am. Their vilifications and occasional threats are not particularly distressing to me personally but to shield members of my family I have made it a recent practice to answer the telephone myself . . . I dislike to be called from dinner, studies and slumber by intoxicated zealots who either refuse to give their names or indistinctly describe themselves as Army officers . . .[33]

Promptly upon receipt of this letter General Richardson acknowledged it, stating his regrets and announcing that the matter was beyond his control and that he was "reluctant to believe that such calls could have been made by Army personnel."

However, on August 29, 1943, a "restricted" order was issued by General Richardson which recited:

The department commander wishes most emphatically to bring to the attention of the command that the proceedings in question are of a judicial nature. . . .

It is therefore enjoined upon all members of this command that they refrain from injecting into the proceedings any personal feeling if such be the case and from any criticisms of the personalities involved if such is taking place.

The general's "restricted" order had the desired effect and the federal court was relieved of the attention of "intoxicated zealots."

The Army courts-martial *Manual* gives rather careful instructions on what should be done upon the issuance of a writ of habeas corpus. The purpose of the writ is accurately stated:

To bring the person seeking the benefit of it before the court or judge to determine whether or not he is illegally restrained of his liberty . . . If a party thus held be illegally imprisoned it is for the courts or the judicial officers of the United States and those courts or officers alone to grant him release.[34]

Having described the purpose of the writ, the *Manual* then gives

[33] Letter, Judge Delbert E. Metzger to Lieutenant General Robert C. Richardson, Jr., August 27, 1943.
[34] A Manual for Courts-Martial, U.S. Army 192 (1936).

precise directions on what to do when an Army officer having a prisoner in his custody is served:

The officer upon whom such writ is served will at once report the fact of such service by telegraphic direction to the Adjutant General . . . stating briefly the grounds on which the release of the party is sought. The person alleged to be illegally restrained of his liberty will be taken before the court from which the writ has issued and a writ made setting forth the reasons for his restraint.[35]

The *Manual* does not limit the instructions to peacetime nor does it say that the instructions are inapplicable where the privilege of the writ has been suspended. In such circumstances the commanding general is obliged to rely upon his counsel for advice.

It is difficult to see how counsel could have advised the use of force to prevent service of process. Obstructing a federal officer attempting to serve process of a United States court is a rather serious offense.[36] Neither the issuance of General Orders No. 31 nor the use of force was necessary to maintain General Richardson's position. Had he followed the book and had the ruling of the District Court been adverse, an appeal could have been taken to the Circuit Court of Appeals, and probably the Supreme Court of the United States would have entertained the cause on certiorari before judgment in the Circuit Court of Appeals. If the refusal to produce the body of the prisoner at the time of filing the return was considered essential by the Army, that issue could have been litigated and determined before a hearing on the merits of the petition.

As might be expected, the issuance of this order caused a breach between the court and the general. The court was powerless to act in face of the order. General Richardson, unfortunately, was placed in the position of refusing to obey the process of a federal court, countenancing the physical abuse of United States Deputy Marshal Bruns, and finally by written order threatening the public in general and Judge Metzger in particular with the provost court if they had any part in a habeas corpus proceeding. This may sound like a comic opera, but the collision between two arms of the federal government in the persons of a federal judge and a commanding general was anything but humorous.

The cause engaged the attention of the Departments of War, Interior, and Justice in Washington. Edward J. Ennis, Special Assistant to the Attorney General, was dispatched to Hawaii under instruc-

[35] A Manual for Courts-Martial, U.S. Army 193 (1936).
[36] Crimes and Criminal Procedure, Title 18, U.S.C. Sec. 111, 1501.

tions from the Solicitor General, Charles Fahy, together with a representative from the War Department to get the case back on the track.

The final chapter of these cases, so far as the District Court of Hawaii is concerned, was written on October 21, 1943. At this time motions to dismiss the two habeas corpus cases were presented upon the ground that they had become moot by reason of the removal[37] of Seifert and Glockner from the jurisdiction and who by order of the commanding general were set free upon their departure from the Territory. At the same time a motion was filed on behalf of the general to vacate the finding of contempt theretofore entered. At the hearing it appeared that General Orders No. 31, which was issued August 25, 1943, had been rescinded[38] by General Orders No. 38 on October 14, 1943.

Two grounds were urged in support of the motion: the first, addressed to the discretion of the court, that is, that the general was not in contempt since in failing to produce the bodies of the petitioners he was acting under instructions from his superior officer, General George C. Marshall, Chief of Staff, and the second, that where the executive has attempted to suspend the privilege of the writ of habeas corpus as a matter of law the bodies need not be produced.

Judge Metzger dismissed the cases as moot and concluded that the removal of the petitioners from Hawaii was no affront to the court since petitioners were set free, which was all that any court could have done for them in habeas corpus had they been successful. He then called attention to the fact that it was unfortunate that General Richardson had said in his return given to the newspapers[39] but not filed in court that the petitioners were dangerous to the "public peace and safety of the United States if released from his custody and internment and allowed to remain at large."

The court next observed that General Orders No. 31, directed to the judge of the court by name and all other persons in Hawaii, was rescinded but concluded that the motion to vacate the court's finding of contempt should be denied, and finally that in view of the fact that the general was acting under orders from his superior officers, the fine of $5,000 should be reduced to $100. The court stated:

It now appears that the aspects of the circumstance that brought about the heavy fine imposed on General Richardson did not fully portray all

[37] Pursuant to 56 Stat. 173 (1942) ; 18 U.S.C. Sec. 97(a).
[38] General Orders No. 38, although in terms effective October 14, was not published until a week later ; Honolulu Advertiser, October 22, 1943. This is not unusual ; frequently orders were issued effective forthwith but published at a later date. The order read: "General Orders No. 31, this office, 25 August 1943, hereby is rescinded."
[39] Honolulu Advertiser, August 27, 1943.

the surrounding facts. At the time he was cited for contempt he had a mitigating defense, but it was not presented to the court because, it appears that his advisors were bent on following a different course.

. . . While I cannot wholly absolve him from following the views of General Marshall or others in disregard of federal law concerning civilian rights before a court when to follow such course was clearly known to him to be an obstruction to the administration of justice, I feel that the sentence of fine heretofore imposed should be modified . . .[40]

The removal of Messrs. Glockner and Seifert from Hawaii, thus rendering their cases moot, prevented a final determination on the status of the writ. Had the case gone to final judgment, in all likelihood it would have been appealed and perhaps it would have been passed on by the Supreme Court.

It is understandable that the local press, puzzled by the turn in events, first announced that the privilege of the writ of habeas corpus was restored. This, no doubt, was because of the rescission of General Orders No. 31 by General Orders No. 38. If the writ remained lawfully suspended under the proclamation of February 8, 1943, and the factual situation existed at the time the suspension was challenged in court, no military order could affect its legal status. In other words, neither of these orders had any legal effect upon the status of the writ of habeas corpus; the former had the practical effect of deterring the courts from action by force so long as it was outstanding, while the latter served only to confuse the public when it rescinded General Orders No. 31.

A statement to the press[41] by Edward J. Ennis, Special Assistant to the Attorney General, clarified the situation by pointing out that the recent proceeding did not conclude the issue and that the "position" of the Department of Justice was that the writ was lawfully suspended in cases of detention for military reasons. This was a departure from the previous view[42] of the Office of the Military Governor that the writ was suspended in all cases whether related or unrelated to military security. It would seem clear that, although the proclamation of December 7 suspended the privilege of the writ in general terms, it would be rather absurd to include cases involving custody of minors or others not held under military authority.

Martial law, correctly understood, applied in time of war is nothing more or less than an exercise of the war powers—the national right of self-defense—the particular exercise of which in any given case

[40] Transcript, United States v. Richardson, *supra*, note 20.
[41] Honolulu Star-Bulletin, October 22, 1943.
[42] Cf. G.O. 57, G.O. 2, *supra*, note 9, and G.O. 31, *supra*, note 21.

must stand or fall on the presence or absence of military necessity to justify it. Every act then under martial law, whether it be the detention of an individual, the seizure of his property, or his trial before a military tribunal, if challenged in the courts, presents for judicial inquiry the justification of the act in question. Some acts are clearly supportable; others may not be defended upon any accepted standard of justification, and between the two extremes lie the situations that cannot be pigeonholed in advance as lying on either one side or the other side of the line.[43]

The line itself can only be determined by the process of inclusion and exclusion. For example, in the matter of detention of an individual a bright line exists between the case of a person held for reasons of military security and all other cases of detention. Similarly, there is a substantial difference between the detention of an individual for a reasonable period for reasons of military security and the trial and conviction of a civilian before a military tribunal.

The disposition of Messrs. Glockner and Seifert by their removal to San Francisco and their liberation there settled their individual cases, but established no determination as to the validity or invalidity of the military government program except one rather important thing; that was the right of the United States marshal to serve the process of the federal court upon the commanding general. The military government continued to function, meting out fines and jail sentences to violators of military orders in the provost courts. The principal business of the provost courts at this period was the enforcement of the military control of labor. However, under the proclamation of February 8, 1943, the military governor had retained a general jurisdiction to promulgate military orders and enforce them in his own provost courts.

DUNCAN V. KAHANAMOKU[44]

On February 24, 1944, Duncan, a civilian ship fitter employed at Pearl Harbor, reported to work. He engaged in a quarrel with two marine sentries stationed at the gate, was arrested, taken into custody, and released the following morning. On March 2, 1944, he

[43] Willoughby in his able discussion of the Milligan case says: "The better doctrine, then, is, not for the court to attempt to determine in advance with respect to any one element, what does, and what does not create a necessity for martial law, but, as in all other cases of the exercise of official authority, to test the legality of an act by its special circumstances. Certainly the fact that the courts are open and undisturbed will in all cases furnish a powerful presumption that there is no necessity for a resort to martial law, but it should not furnish an irrebuttable presumption." 3 Willoughby, The Constitutional Law of the United States (2d ed. 1929), 1602.
[44] 327 U.S. 304 (1946).

was brought before the provost court at Pearl Harbor presided over by a naval officer and there tried and convicted of the offense of assault and battery against military personnel. He was sentenced to imprisonment of six months in the Honolulu county jail.

On March 14, 1944, he petitioned the United States District Court for the Territory of Hawaii for a writ of habeas corpus, alleging that his conviction and imprisonment were unlawful and unconstitutional; that martial law did not lawfully exist in Hawaii and that regardless of the existence of martial law, there was no military necessity for the trial of civilians by a military tribunal. The petition was served on Duke P. Kahanamoku, sheriff of the City and County of Honolulu. The Department of Justice appeared for the sheriff. Again Mr. Ennis was sent to Hawaii by the Attorney General in defense of the military authorities.

The return and answer admitted that the duly constituted federal and Territorial criminal courts and civil courts were functioning; denied that petitioner's trial and conviction were unlawful or unconstitutional; alleged that the proclamation of the governor of February 8, 1943, continued a state of martial law and the suspension of the privilege of the writ of habeas corpus; alleged that Hawaii at all times since December 7, 1941, had been in imminent danger of attack, and that the public safety required the continuance of martial law and the suspension of the privilege of the writ; and alleged finally that the provost courts were necessary "for the successful prosecution of the war" and were established in good faith and in the honest belief that military necessity required them. Upon the hearing on the return to the order to show cause, the petitioner was released on bond pending a hearing on the merits.

At the trial a full record was made which amply demonstrated the absence of civil strife, the functioning of Territorial and federal courts, and the lack of necessity for military trials of civilians.

After examining the testimony of Admiral Nimitz and General Richardson, the trial court found that they "agreed that an invasion by enemy troops is now practically impossible" and that "no part of the island of Oahu in the Territory of Hawaii is a battlefield today nor has it been for over two years . . ." With respect to the compromise reached by the cabinet officers the trial court said:

Congress may give the Territory of Hawaii any form of government it may see fit, conformable to Constitutional provisions, but no one in the War Department has such lawful power.[45]

[45] Ex parte Duncan, 66 F. Supp. 976, 980 (D. Haw. 1944).

The court also found that the

regularly constituted civil government was either in efficient operation or fully capable of such operation in all of its branches and ordinary departments and was sufficiently equipped, capable and willing to perform all functions for which it was created.[46]

As a result of these findings the trial court concluded that martial law did not lawfully exist in Hawaii; that the office of military governor was without lawful creation, and that the provost court possessed no lawful authority to try the petitioner; accordingly, the court sustained the writ and ordered the prisoner discharged.

WHITE V. STEERE

The day after the decision of Judge Metzger in the *Duncan* case, a petition was filed by one White, a civilian stockbroker who had been tried, sentenced, and convicted before a provost court on August 25, 1942, of the crime of embezzlement. White had been orally informed of the charge against him, appeared in the provost court by counsel who demanded trial by jury, which was promptly denied. He asked for time to prepare his defense, which was likewise denied. The provost court sentenced him to five years' imprisonment. White was discharged on a writ of habeas corpus by the district court on May 2, 1944.[47]

THE OPINIONS OF THE CIRCUIT COURT OF APPEALS

The *Duncan* and *White* cases were appealed to the Court of Appeals for the Ninth Circuit, which disposed of them *en banc*[48] on November 1, 1944, with three opinions reversing the District Court. The opinion of the court by Circuit Judge Healy concluded that the writ was available to test the validity of the military trials; that what was established in Hawaii was "nothing less than total military government"; that the presence of a large Oriental population "posed a continuous threat to public security"; that "the summary punishment of criminal offenders of every sort might conceivably serve to discourage the commission of offenses immediately endangering the general security"; that at the time of the trial of White "the civil

---

[46] *Id.* at 981.

[47] Ex parte White, 66 F. Supp. 982 (D. Haw. 1944).

[48] The court that heard the cases consisted of Circuit Judges Wilbur, Garrecht, Denman, Matthews, and Stephens. It was stipulated that Circuit Judge Healy (who was absent) could participate in the decision. The opinion of the court by Healy, J., concluded with the statement, "Stephens, Circuit Judge, did not participate in the decision of these cases." Ex parte Duncan, 146 F.2d 576, 591 (CCA 9 1944).

courts were disabled from functioning" and that "the situation neces-
sitated his trial by the military."

In the *Duncan* case the Circuit Court of Appeals had more difficulty. It was confronted with a proclamation which substantially
restored civil authority. The court observed, however, that under
the criminal statutes of Hawaii the act of assaulting a military person was not the subject of a specific crime punishable in the civil
courts (which were not authorized to enforce military orders). Reasoning from this premise, the court held:

. . . the power to punish infractions of military regulations of this type
must of necessity reside somewhere. If it has not by legislation or municipal ordinance been delegated to the ordinary courts or made subject to
the authority of the civil police, the power must perforce exist in the
military arm of the government acting through the medium of commissions or like tribunals.[49]

The reasoning is obviously circular. It proceeded upon the assumption that military orders proscribing certain acts of civilians as
crimes were valid and since they were not made specifically enforceable
in the courts ordained by law they must of necessity be enforceable
somewhere and therefore were enforceable in military tribunals. This
assumes the very issue involved, i.e., the validity of the orders. If
the military orders were valid that would be the end of the case. Obviously if one assumes them to be valid, a logical conclusion upholding
the trials presents no problem.

Circuit Judges Wilbur and Matthews evidently had some mis-
giving as to the validity of the military trial of a civilian and preferred
to state an additional ground to support the reversal of the trial court,
namely, that the writ having been suspended by the President, it was
not available to test the validity of the petitioner's trial and "without
a finding of implied fraud on the part of the governor and the military authorities the decision cannot be sustained."[50]

The separate opinion of Judge Denman, who concurred in the
reversal, placed the case upon the ground that the petitions "show no
facts invoking the jurisdiction or power of the District Court to issue
the writs."[51] It is somewhat difficult to understand this opinion since
the petition alleged imprisonment after conviction by a tribunal

[49] Ex parte Duncan, 146 F.2d 576, 584. The argument that there was a void in
the federal and Territorial law making assault and battery a crime because it punished
the wrongful act generally but did not make assault and battery against military personnel a specific crime is reminiscent of the remark attributed to Judge Bean, who is
said to have ruled that he could find nothing in the criminal code of Texas that made
the killing of a Chinaman a murder.
[50] *Id.* at 589.   [51] *Id.* at 590.

whose jurisdiction was challenged both on statutory and constitutional grounds. Apart from the fact that the courts have shown great liberality in the technical aspects of petitions for writs of habeas corpus, the petitions in these cases squarely challenged the validity of the restraint of the prisoners.[52]

The *per curiam* reversal of the lower court by the Court of Appeals in *Ex parte Spurlock*[53] (a companion to *Duncan* and *White*) sheds light on the basis of the appellate court's opinion in the latter cases. At the hearing on Spurlock's petition for a writ of habeas corpus in the United States District Court Judge McLaughlin found "that Spurlock did not plead guilty to the March 28 charge, but was, without trial, found guilty and disposed of accordingly . . ."[54]

The court pointed out that even a person subject to military law is entitled to due process and that Spurlock, having been convicted and imprisoned without trial, was denied his constitutional rights under the Fifth Amendment. The *per curiam* reversal in the *Spurlock* case holds that during time of war, when the privilege of the writ of habeas corpus has been suspended, a civilian may be charged in a military tribunal, found guilty without trial, and sentenced to imprisonment, and that the action of the military authorities is not subject to judicial inquiry.

Spurlock petitioned for a writ of certiorari in the Supreme Court on January 13, 1945. The Department of Justice, evidently not desiring to defend the decision of the Court of Appeals, on February 15, 1945, filed a "suggestion that the cause has become moot," the suggestion being based upon a pardon filed by Lieutenant General Robert C. Richardson, Jr., reciting that

. . . it appears to the best interest of the United States that the execution of so much of the sentence of the said Frederick L. Spurlock as remains unexecuted on this 3 February 1945 be remitted so that he may engage in work that will promote the national defense of the United States.[55]

Spurlock had been imprisoned by the military government of Hawaii from March 28, 1942, to February 3, 1945, without trial upon the charge of having committed a misdemeanor.

[52] Cf. Holiday v. Johnston, 313 U.S. 342, 350 (1941).
[53] 66 F. Supp. 997 (D. Haw. 1944), rev'd *per curiam en banc sub nom.* Steere v. Spurlock, 146 F. 2d 652 (CCA 9 1944).
[54] Ex parte Spurlock, 66 F. Supp. 997, 1001 (D. Haw. 1944).
[55] *Id.* at 1006; under Section 66 of the Hawaiian Organic Act, 31 Stat. 153 (1900), as amended, 48 U.S.C. Sec. 531 (1940), the pardoning power is in the governor and the President; assuming the invalidity of the trial, the commanding general's exercise of the pardoning power presented no problem.

The record of the Department of Justice in mooting cases involving martial law in Hawaii to prevent a determination of the issue in the Supreme Court is impressive. There were, in all, six cases which challenged martial law by habeas corpus proceedings. Four of them were rendered moot and thus avoided a judicial review. In *Zimmerman v. Walker* the petition for certiorari was filed on March 13, 1943; promptly thereafter the Solicitor General filed a memorandum which recited that the case had become moot by reason of the release of the petitioner on or about March 12, 1943.[56] *Ex parte Glockner* and *Ex parte Seifert* were mooted after the undignified clash between General Richardson and the United States District Court and *Ex parte Spurlock* similarly disposed the day his petition for certiorari was filed in the Supreme Court.

The War Department would have been better advised to have pressed for a prompt decision in the Supreme Court in the *Zimmerman* case in early 1942. The strategic advantage of such a course seemed clearly indicated for two reasons: (1) the war had not progressed to a point where victory was in sight, and (2) the case involved internment for military security and not the validity of a military trial. Although there is little to choose between being imprisoned for security reasons without a trial and being imprisoned after a trial by a court that has no jurisdiction (except for the stigma that exists in the former case), it is far easier to find a legal justification in the former case than it is in the latter.

THE OPINION OF THE SUPREME COURT

Certiorari was granted in the *Duncan* and *White* cases and they were argued in the Supreme Court on December 7, 1945, four years after Pearl Harbor.[56a] In the meantime the President by proclamation effective October 24, 1944, had formally terminated the state of martial law and restored the privilege of the writ of habeas corpus.[57]

---

[56] Zimmerman v. Walker, 132 F. 2d 442 (CCA 9 1942), cert. denied "on the ground that the cause is moot, it appearing that Hans Zimmerman on whose behalf the petition is filed, has been released from respondent's custody." 319 U.S. 744 (1943). Ex parte Glockner (D. Haw. 1943, No. 295) (dismissed by the district court as moot by reason of the removal of prisoner and his release in California). Ex parte Seifert (D. Haw. 1943, No. 296) (dismissed by the district court as moot by reason of the removal of prisoner and his release in California). Steere v. Spurlock, 146 F. 2d 652 (CCA 9 1944), cert. denied "on the ground that the cause is moot." 324 U.S. 868 (1945).

[56a] The Duncan case was decided in the Court of Appeals on November 1, 1944. Petition for certiorari was filed on January 13, 1945, and granted on February 12, 1945. The delay in argument was on request of the Solicitor General, J. Howard McGrath.

[57] Proclamation 2627, 9 Fed. Reg. 12831 (1944).

Restoration of the privilege of the writ by presidential proclamation prompted the government in the Supreme Court to recede from its position denying the jurisdiction of the District Court to entertain the petitions for writs of habeas corpus.[58] With the issues thus narrowed the convictions in the provost court were challenged upon three grounds: (1) that Section 67 of the Hawaiian Organic Act did not authorize the trial of civilians before military tribunals; (2) that if Section 67 authorized the trial of civilians before military tribunals, it was unconstitutional; and (3) that if Section 67 was constitutional and authorized the trial of civilians before military tribunals, the factual situation existing on March 14, 1944, did not warrant this extreme application of martial law.

Four opinions were delivered, Justice Black writing the opinion of the court, Chief Justice Stone and Justice Murphy writing concurring opinions, and Justice Burton writing a dissent in which Justice Frankfurter joined. Justice Black did not find it necessary to pass upon the constitutional issue involved, since the first question, namely, whether the Organic Act authorized the trial and punishment of civilians by the military was decisive. In examining Section 67 of the Organic Act, Justice Black stated first that Congress did not attempt a definition of the term "martial law" and that the Constitution makes no reference to it, from which he concluded:

The language of Section 67 thus fails to define adequately the scope

---

[58] Duncan v. Kahanamoku, 327 U.S. 304, 312 (1946). The Supreme Court did not pass on the issue whether the suspension was a general one or limited to cases which the public safety required. Petitioner took the position that the suspension both under the Constitution and Section 67 of the Organic Act was limited to the class of persons hostile to the government and that the writ was available in all other cases—e.g., abduction or any other unlawful detention including detention as a result of conviction by a tribunal that had no jurisdiction. Historically, the suspension of the privilege of the writ was confined to enemies of the state. This is clear from the legislative suspensions in England, see 18 Geo. III, c. 1 (1778); and although it is not clearly recorded in the debates, there can be little doubt that the framers of the Constitution had the precedents of British legislative suspensions in mind when Art. I, Sec. 9, cl. 2 was adopted, see 2 Farrand, Records of the Federal Constitutional Convention, 438 (1911), 3 *id.* at 149; Hurd, A Treatise on the Right of Personal Liberty and the Writ of Habeas Corpus, 116 (2d, 1876). The Civil War suspensions by President Lincoln were likewise limited; see Proclamation of May 10, 1861 (authorizing the military commander in Florida to suspend the writ "and to remove . . . dangerous or suspected persons"), 6 Richardson, Messages and Papers of the Presidents 16 (1898); Proclamation of September 24, 1862, 13 Stat. 730 (1862) (authorizing the detention of persons "guilty of any disloyal practice"); Proclamation No. 7 of September 15, 1863, 13 Stat. 734 (1863) (after statutory sanction of the suspension authorizing the detention of certain persons as "aiders or abetters of the enemy"). Horace Binney, an advocate of executive suspension during the Civil War, held the view that the Constitution permitted only a limited suspension as to persons hostile to the government, see Binney, The Privilege of the Writ of Habeas Corpus under the Constitution, 19 (2d ed. 1862).

of the power given to the military and to show whether the Organic Act provides that courts of law be supplanted by military tribunals.[59]

This conclusion discounts the fact that prior judicial decisions had given content to the term "martial law."

Justice Black next considered the argument that the language of Section 67 was adopted by Congress from the Constitution of the Republic of Hawaii and that in *In re Kalanianaole*[60] the Supreme Court of Hawaii had construed Article 31 of the Constitution of the Republic to authorize the trial of civilians before military tribunals. Justice Black pointed out in passing that the defendants there involved were insurrectionists taking part in the very uprising which the military were to suppress, while here the petitioners had no connection with any organized resistance to the armed forces or the established government.[61]

Not, however, content with this distinction, Justice Black speaking for the court rejected the contention that the *Kalanianaole* decision was any guide to the meaning of Section 67 of the Organic Act:

. . . we are certain that Congress did not wish to make that case part of the Organic Act. For that case did not merely uphold military trials of civilians but also held that courts were to interfere only when there was an obvious abuse of discretion which resulted in cruel and inhuman practices or the establishment of military rule for the personal gain of the President and the armed forces. But courts were not to review whether the President's action, no matter how unjustifiable, was necessary for the public safety.[62]

The conclusion that the term "martial law" as used by Congress in Section 67 of the Hawaiian Organic Act is virtually meaningless is not too persuasive historically. Section 67 of the Organic Act was taken verbatim from Article 31 of the Constitution of the Republic. The Organic Act was adopted in 1900. Five years prior to its adoption the Supreme Court of the Republic of Hawaii had decided the *Kalanianaole* case, which held that a military commission was authorized by Article 31 of the Constitution of the Republic. Chief Justice Frear, the author of the opinion, was also a member of the Hawaiian Annexation Commission and appeared before Congress on the adoption of the Organic Act. It would be strange if Commissioner Frear in 1900 thought that Section 67 had any different meaning from that given the same language by the court of which he was chief justice five years earlier.

The important distinction, however, between the *Kalanianaole*

---

[59] 327 U.S. 304, 315–16 (1946).   [60] 10 Haw. 29 (1895).
[61] 327 U.S. 304, 316 (1946).   [62] *Id.* at 317.

case and *Duncan v. Kahanamoku* is that the accused in *Duncan v. Kahanamoku* was not opposed to the government. Moreover at the time of the trial of the *Kalanianaole* case, the civil courts were open and exercising their statutory criminal and civil jurisdiction.[63] In no instance during the state of martial law did military tribunals assert any jurisdiction except as to those who were charged with disloyal acts. There is one further point of difference: namely, in the *Kalanianaole* case, Article 31 of the Constitution was implemented by legislation which authorized the trial of disloyal persons before military commissions, and although this was not mentioned in the opinion of the court in *In re Kalanianaole*, it is nonetheless significant.[64] In face of this history it would seem that the term "martial law" was intended to permit the trial by a military commission of civilians charged with disloyal conduct, to which category the petitioners Duncan and White did not belong.

This poses two constitutional issues. Assuming Section 67 permitted military trials of civilians, (1) Was the section valid on its face? (2) If so, were the military trials in question required by the public safety and hence unassailable? The opinion of the court did not reach the constitutional issues since the court found that the words of the statute do not include such trials. While as a matter of the legal history of Hawaii this interpretation of the section may be questionable, it should be remembered that the Constitution of the Republic of Hawaii did not contain the crisp language of the Fifth and Sixth Amendments guaranteeing the rights of due process, indictment by a grand jury, and trial by a jury. At the time Article 31 was drafted and when *In re Kalanianaole* was decided, the Constitution of the Republic did not unequivocally guarantee a trial by jury.[65]

The government in the *Duncan* case argued that Section 5 of the Organic Act, in which Congress provided "that the Constitution . . . shall have the same force and effect within the said Territory as elsewhere in the United States,"[66] extended the Constitution only to a limited extent and specifically as circumscribed by Section 67 and the judicial construction placed thereon by the *Kalanianaole* case. This tenuous view had earlier been put forth in support of the military

[63] This was specifically provided in the Proclamation of President Dole of January 7, 1895; see In re Kalanianaole, 10 Haw. 29, 45 (1895).
[64] See Acts of the Republic of Hawaii, 1895; Act 18 of February 8, 1895, authorizing the execution of sentences of military commissions; Acts 20 and 24 of March 15, 1895, ratifying and granting immunity.
[65] Constitution of the Republic of Hawaii (1894), Art. 6, Sec. 1. "No person shall be subject to punishment for any offense except on due and legal conviction thereof by a tribunal having jurisdiction of the case."
[66] 31 Stat. 141 (1900); 48 U.S.C. Sec. 495 (1940).

regime in Hawaii in an article which confessed that a similar course would be unconstitutional within the continental limits of the United States.[67] Never before since the annexation of the Islands had the application of the federal Constitution in Hawaii been seriously challenged. In fact, an unbroken line[68] of decisions had indicated that the Constitution (and specifically the Bill of Rights) protects the rights of residents in the Territory to the same extent that it protects those of residents in the several states. The opinion of Mr. Justice Black puts that issue at rest:

It follows that civilians in Hawaii are entitled to the constitutional guarantee of a fair trial to the same extent as those who live in any other part of our country. . . . For here Congress did not in the Organic Act exercise whatever power it might have had to limit the application of the constitution. Cf. *Hawaii v. Mankichi*, 190 U.S. 197. The people of Hawaii are therefore entitled to constitutional protection to the same extent as the inhabitants of the 48 states.[69]

It should be noted that the opinion of the court leaves open the question as to the power of Congress to limit the application of the Constitution to an organized territory. Although that issue was not necessary to a decision it has generally been believed that the extension of the federal Constitution to an organized territory, once made, is irrevocable.[70]

Since the Organic Act, according to the opinion of the court, gives no clue to the scope and meaning of "martial law," Justice Black found it necessary to turn to the history of our institutions to interpret the expression, pointing out the profound distrust which Anglo-American peoples have traditionally had of the exercise of military power. Quoting with approval the court's historic admonition in *Dow v. Johnson*,[71] that "the military should always be kept in subjection to the laws of the country to which it belongs, and . . . he is no friend to the Republic who advocates the contrary," Justice Black concluded that Section 67 afforded no authority for the trial and conviction of the petitioners:

We believe that when Congress passed the Hawaiian Organic Act and authorized the establishment of "martial law" it had in mind and

[67] King, The Legality of Martial Law in Hawaii, 30 Calif. L. Rev. 599, 632 (1942).
[68] Farrington v. Tokushige, 273 U.S. 284 (1927); Hawaii v. Mankichi, 190 U.S. 197 (1903); cf. Inter-Island Co. v. Hawaii, 305 U.S. 306 (1938); Dorr v. United States, 195 U.S. 138 (1904); Binns v. United States, 194 U.S. 486 (1904); Mormon Church v. United States, 136 U.S. 1 (1890). For the status of an unincorporated territory, see Balzac v. Puerto Rico, 258 U.S. 298 (1922).
[69] 327 U.S. 304, 318–19 (1946).
[70] Murphy v. Ramsey, 114 U.S. 15, 44 (1885).
[71] 100 U.S. 158, 169 (1879).

did not wish to exceed the boundaries between military and civilian power, in which our people have always believed, which responsible military and executive officers had heeded, and which had become part of our political philosophy and institutions prior to the time Congress passed the Organic Act. The phrase "martial law" as employed in that Act, therefore, while intended to authorize the military to act vigorously for the defense of the Islands against actual or threatened rebellion or invasion, was not intended to authorize the supplanting of courts by military tribunals.[72]

As already noted, in the view of the court Section 67 of the Hawaiian Organic Act gave no clue to the meaning of "martial law." Justice Black's opinion says that the language "fails to define adequately the scope of the power given to the military and to show whether the Organic Act provides that courts of law be supplanted by military tribunals."[73]

The expression "martial law," however indefinite it was in 1857 when Caleb Cushing wrote his opinion[74] on the subject, had gathered form through the passage of years. Text writers and the courts had reached the conclusion that martial law is nothing more than the exercise of executive power which is necessary to cope with a given emergency. Thus it had been held in *Moyer v. Peabody* that during times of strife after a declaration of martial law it is competent for the executive to detain persons connected with the current strife and such detention during the period of the exigency is not a denial of due process of law.[75] The court in that case had before it the narrow issue whether the temporary restraint during the existence of martial law was justified. The Supreme Court held that it was. Some however have been misled by the rhetoric of Justice Holmes into the mistaken view that the case stands for the proposition that under any circumstances "a decision by the head of the state upon a matter involving its life" is final and not reviewable by the courts.

Reflection upon this proposition reveals its invalidity in a system of government based on the separation of powers. If we reach the conclusion that in a given circumstance the acts of the executive branch are not reviewable in the courts, then it follows that the executive branch is supreme over either the legislative or judicial branch of government. To be specific, if the executive by an appropriate find-

---

[72] 327 U.S. 304, 324 (1946).   [73] *Id.* at 316.
[74] 8 Ops. Att'y Gen. 365 (1857).

[75] 212 U.S. 78 (1909). Dictum in the opinion of the court written by Justice Holmes is frequently cited for more than the proposition which the case actually holds. Justice Holmes said: "When it comes to a decision by the head of the state upon a matter involving its life, the ordinary rights of individuals must yield to what he deems the necessities of the moment." *Id.* at 85.

ing says that in a particular circumstance the life of the state is at
stake, then irrespective of the existence of legislation or the avail-
ability of judicial review, the acts of the executive are final. Thus
the historic doctrine of the separation of powers is completely nullified.

Fortunately for the law of the subject, the generality of the language used by Justice Holmes has been limited in an opinion by a
unanimous court involving the declaration of martial law by the
governor of Texas. The Supreme Court, holding acts of the executive
reviewable in the courts, said:

If this extreme position could be deemed to be well taken, it is mani-
fest that the fiat of a state governor, and not the Constitution of the United
States, would be the supreme law of the land . . .[76]

The court also said:

There is no such avenue of escape from the paramount authority of
the Federal Constitution . . .
What are the allowable limits of military discretion, and whether or
not they have been overstepped in a particular case, are judicial questions.[77]

It should be noted that the court in reaching the conclusion in
the case just referred to found an "appropriate answer in . . . *Ex
parte Milligan.* . . ."[78] In other words, the exercise of martial law
powers by a state governor in time of domestic disturbance within
the state is to be measured by the same standard applicable to the
exercise of martial law powers by the military authorities in time of
civil war.

It has been suggested that the powers exercised by the nation in
time of a war of survival are different in kind from those required
in time of civil strife falling short of a national or civil war. This
has a ring of validity. No one will dispute the proposition that our
government should not and must not be curtailed in the prosecution of
war. The Constitution gives the government, through its legislative
and executive branches, the power to wage war and, as Chief Justice
Hughes once said, "the power to wage war is the power to wage war
successfully."[79]

The difficulty with the apologists for the exercise of military power
is that the rule which they advocate means that the executive in times
of great exigency may do anything which he in his unreviewable
determination concludes is necessary or proper for the advancement

[76] Sterling v. Constantin, 287 U.S. 378, 397 (1932).
[77] *Id.* at 398, 401.   [78] *Id.* at 402.
[79] Hughes, War Powers under the Constitution, Sen. Doc. No. 105, 65th Cong.,
1st Sess. 7 (1917) ; 47 A.B.A. Rep. 232, 238 (1917).

of the military program. This view is really not as desirable from the military standpoint as it might appear, even wholly apart from its unconstitutionality. The executive alone cannot raise armies or levy taxes, or at least he cannot perform these tasks effectively and comprehensively unless we are prepared for a complete surrender to a totalitarian state. Under our frame of government the power to wage war is vested jointly in the executive and legislative branches.[80]

Obviously, neither the executive nor the legislative branch may wage war successfully alone; the joint action of both is essential in order that the full force of our power may be exerted. There is no reason to assume that the Congress would be less desirous of victory than the executive nor to suppose that it would withhold any needed power from the executive. The role of the judiciary in time of war is essentially no different from what it is in time of peace since our system is designed to function in war and in peace under the same pattern. This does not mean, however, that the exertion of either executive or legislative power which might be doubtful in time of peace would not be upheld in time of war.[81]

There is a wide difference between the exercise of executive power pursuant to an act of Congress and the unilateral action of the executive.[82] At the outset of World War II, Congress and the executive by joint action concluded that the safety of the nation required the removal of persons of Japanese ancestry from the West Coast. In *Korematsu v. United States*, this exercise of the war powers was affirmed by a divided court.[83]

Although the *Korematsu* decision has been sharply criticized,[84] irrespective of one's views on the results reached by the court it must be remembered that the court was confronted with a *fait accompli* and that an adverse decision would have meant endless complications in the midst of war. The fact that an opposite result would have posed an extremely difficult domestic problem at the time when a united effort was most needed is not too solid a basis for a constitutional decision but it is not without precedent in our constitutional

[80] Ex parte Quirin, 317 U.S. 1, 28 (1942).
[81] Bloch v. Hirsh, 256 U.S. 135 (1921) (upholding rent control in the District of Columbia in World War I) ; Hamilton v. Kentucky Distilleries Co., 251 U.S. 146 (1919) (upholding wartime prohibition by legislative action in World War I).
[82] The recurring argument over the power of the President to act without statutory authority probably has been put to rest by the decision of the court invalidating President Truman's seizure of the steel industry, Youngstown Sheet & Tube Co. v. Sawyer, 343 U.S. 579 (1952).
[83] 323 U.S. 214 (1944).
[84] Rostow, The Japanese-American Cases—a Disaster, 54 Yale L.J. 489 (1945).

history.[85] It must be remembered that the Supreme Court is only one of the branches of government and that the power it exerts is largely negative. It is not an instrument for either the initiation or administration of governmental programs in war or in peace.

THE CONCURRING OPINION OF JUSTICE MURPHY

Justice Murphy concurred in the opinion of the court in the *Duncan* case, holding that military trials were not authorized under Section 67 of the Organic Act, but he felt obliged to state separately his reasons why "the usurpation of civil power by the military is so great in this instance as to warrant this Court's complete and outright repudiation of the action."[86]

While it might be thought that Justice Murphy's concurring opinion is not in keeping with the judicial tradition against passing upon more than what is necessary to the disposition of a particular case, nevertheless in the light of the government's argument and the inadequacies of the dissenting opinion, the reasons for Justice Murphy's separate concurrence become apparent.[87] He examined the government's arguments seriatim.

First: The notion that a state of martial law is an "all or nothing" concept and that anything that is done after a declaration is not reviewable in the courts is palpably untenable. Because Hawaii, subsequent to the original raid of December 7, 1941, may have been subject to the threat of subsequent raids is certainly no reason for upholding military orders not required by the public safety, which were issued several years later. Granting the existence of the danger of a subsequent attack Justice Murphy said:

> But it does not follow from these assumptions that the military was free under the Constitution to close the civil courts or to strip them of their criminal jurisdiction, especially after the initial shock of the sudden Japanese attack had been dissipated.[88]

Second: The argument that the civil courts were not swift enough to meet the needs of the commanding general, who could not brook a delay,[89] is hardly a justification for scrapping the Bill of Rights.

---

[85] Cf. Norman v. B. & O. R.R., 294 U.S. 240 (1935); Perry v. United States, 294 U.S. 330 (1935).

[86] Duncan v. Kahanamoku, 327 U.S. 304, 325 (1946).

[87] The opinion of the court, like the separate opinion of Justice Murphy, goes beyond the minimum holding necessary for the disposition of the case. Thus the situation presented in Ex parte Milligan, 4 Wall. 2 (U.S. 1866), was repeated for the same reasons.

[88] 327 U.S. 304, 330 (1946).

[89] Lieutenant General Robert C. Richardson, Jr., admitted on cross-examination

This becomes clear once it is conceded that what the public safety requires and not what a particular general desires is the standard.

Third: The argument that the military commander should have a tribunal at his disposal to enforce his orders is simply an argument for dictatorship:

Moreover, the mere fact that it may be more expedient and convenient for the military to try violators of its own orders before its own tribunals does not and should not afford a constitutional basis for the jurisdiction of such tribunals when civil courts are in fact functioning or are capable of functioning.[90]

Fourth: Obviously untenable is the argument that the military area statute,[91] which vested in the military arm broad powers to promulgate regulations in designated areas but required their enforcement in the federal courts, was inadequate because the regulations were enforceable only in federal courts:

That the military refrained from using the statutory framework which Congress erected affords no constitutional justification for the creation of military tribunals to try such violators.[92]

It is for Congress to decide this issue, not the executive.

Fifth: Another argument in support of the military trials was advanced by the government on the basis of the testimony of General Richardson to whom the civil courts were obnoxious because, as he testified, they were subject to "all sorts of influences, political and otherwise." The natural preference of a military commander for tribunals which will do precisely what he commands is hardly equivalent to a finding that military trials are essential to the public safety. In fact such a preference does not even meet the test of reasonable judgment laid down in *Hirabayashi v. United States*[93] where the court was passing on formal legislative action—not military fiat standing alone. "This," according to Justice Murphy, "is merely a military criticism of the proposition that in this nation the military is subordinate to the civil authority. It does not qualify as a recognizable reason for closing the civil courts to criminal cases."[94]

Sixth: The feeble argument that attendance at jury trials would interrupt war work was readily disposed of by the observation that

that he had no basis for his testimony as to delays in the courts of Hawaii. Record, p. 1051.

[90] 327 U.S. 304, 332 (1946).
[91] 56 Stat. 173 (1942), 18 U.S. Sec. 97(a) (Supp. 1946).
[92] 327 U.S. 304, 332 (1946).
[93] 320 U.S. 81, 95 (1943).
[94] 327 U.S. 304, 332 (1946).

war workers could be excused from jury service.[95] This was the very thing that the circuit judge, Albert M. Cristy, in Honolulu had proposed to the military authorities immediately after the outbreak of war.

Seventh: The last reason advanced by the government in support of military trials was the character of the population of Hawaii and the presence of those of Japanese ancestry. This red herring was injected into the case by the return and answer of the government.[96] How this could have been seriously urged in the light of the conduct of the inhabitants of Hawaii and specifically that of the Americans of Japanese ancestry is difficult to understand[97] except on the theory that it might have struck a responsive chord on the bench.[98] The record in the *Duncan* case contained a demonstration of the loyalty of all elements of the Hawaiian population. No contention was advanced that the Americans of Japanese ancestry were anything but law-abiding, loyal citizens; the government's theory evidently was, however, that they might be otherwise, and that therefore the military should have military tribunals to administer criminal punishment to the entire community. As stated by Colonel Kendall J. Fielder, in charge of military intelligence in Hawaii during the period, no act of sabotage or espionage was known to have been committed by persons of Japanese descent in Hawaii either on or subsequent to December 7, 1941.[99]

THE CONCURRING OPINION OF CHIEF JUSTICE STONE

The concurring opinion of Chief Justice Stone follows the dogma of the court in deciding a case on the narrowest issue necessary for

[95] A. M. Cristy, then senior circuit judge, testified: ". . . on the morning after the so-called blitz, the Judges assembled . . . Shortly after that, and during that week or the following week, several conferences were had with officers delegated from the Military Governor's office as to the contribution that the Judges of the Court could make toward assisting and anything that would be necessary in curtailing their activity for a time being until things were settled down . . . And suggestions were made as to how the Judges could conduct their business, both as to continuances and as to setting of cases so as to make the least disturbance or necessity for popular gathering around the Courthouse but carry on the business of the Court. But we got nowhere for quite awhile." Record, pp. 600–601.

[96] The government's return and answer in the Duncan case cover 356 pages in the printed record. Record, pp. 25–381.

[97] See Lind, Hawaii's Japanese, An Experiment in Democracy (1946).

[98] No member of the court accepted this argument, which had no basis in the record; but see the opinion of the Court of Appeals, 146 F. 2d 576, 580 (CCA 9 1944).

[99] Record, p. 687. Admiral Chester W. Nimitz, testifying before the House Committee on Public Lands, said: "Before World War II, I entertained some doubts as to the loyalty of the American citizens of Japanese ancestry in the event of war with Japan. From my observation during World War II, I no longer have that doubt." Hearings before Committee on Public Lands on H.R. 49, 80th Cong., 1st Sess. 63 (1947), and see the unanimous report of the Committee reporting favorably on H.R. 49 (Hawaii Statehood Bill), H.R. Rep. No. 194, 80th Cong., 1st Sess. (1947).

its disposition.[100] Had there been but one opinion in the case, his would have adequately disposed of the litigation with a minimum of rhetoric. The Chief Justice did not agree that the term "martial law" as used in Section 67 of the Hawaiian Organic Act is "devoid of meaning."[101] His succinct definition of "martial law" is a distillation of the previous decisions of the court on the subject:

It is a law of necessity to be prescribed and administered by the executive power. Its object, the preservation of the public safety and good order, defines its scope, which will vary with the circumstances and the necessities of the case. The exercise of the power may not extend beyond what is required by the exigency which calls it forth.[102]

The Chief Justice conceded broad discretion in the determination of the necessity of martial law and its exercise.

But executive action is not proof of its own necessity, and the military's judgment here is not conclusive that every action taken pursuant to the declaration of martial law was justified by the exigency.[103]

This terse statement was an acute comment on the government's position, namely, that whenever an order was issued by a military commander, the fact of the issuance of the order alone was proof of its necessity and that judges who thought otherwise were invading the hallowed ground of military strategy. If this extreme view of executive power were to be accepted it would be an end of liberty under the law. Whether the public safety demands the suppression of the civil courts is not a question on which the military have any superior knowledge.

Willing to assume that the Constitution permits the substitution of trials by military tribunals for trials in civil courts if the public safety requires it, Chief Justice Stone then observed that the "invasion" of December 7 had ended long prior to the military trials in question. Furthermore, the fact that places of amusement were opened on December 24, 1941, and that bars were opened on February 4, 1942, was cogent evidence that the public safety did not require the closing of the courts, for "trials of petitioners in the civil courts no more endangered the public safety than the gathering of the population in saloons and places of amusement, which was authorized by military order."[104] Thus, in the words of the Chief Justice:

The military authorities themselves testified and advanced no reason which has any bearing on public safety or good order for closing the civil

---

[100] Adherence to judicial self-restraint is a characteristic of the late Chief Justice's opinions. See his dissent in United States v. Butler, 297 U.S. 1, 79 (1936).
[101] 327 U.S. 304, 335 (1946).
[102] *Ibid.*   [103] 327 U.S. 304, 336 (1946).   [104] *Id.* at 337.

courts to the trial of these petitioners, or for trying them in military courts. I can only conclude that the trials and convictions upon which petitioners are now detained, were unauthorized by the statute, and without lawful authority.[105]

THE DISSENTING OPINION OF JUSTICE BURTON

Justice Burton began his dissenting opinion with the sentence, "With the rest of this Court I subscribe unreservedly to the Bill of Rights." Thereafter he apparently conceded (counter to the main argument of the government) that the federal Constitution applies in Hawaii in full force and effect as elsewhere in the United States. The dissent, in which Justice Frankfurter concurred, then proceeded with a detailed examination of the military situation not only in Hawaii but in the Central Pacific, Southwest Pacific, and European theaters. This analysis bore little or no relation to what the public safety in Hawaii required, which, as the Chief Justice pointed out, is the key to any judicial review of executive action after the declaration of martial law.

Parenthetically it is observed that a declaration of martial law by the executive does not mean that all executive acts (subsequent to the declaration) are required by the public safety. What is in fact required is a judicial question and is reviewable in the courts. Justice Burton quite properly observed that in the field of military action in time of war the executive has wide discretion and that "it seems clear that at least on an active battlefield, the executive discretion to determine policy is there intended by the Constitution to be supreme."[106]

He then posed the question, "What is a battlefield and how long does it remain one after the first barrage?"[107] To answer this question he first observed that courts have power to review "the outer limits" of the jurisdiction of the military authorities but that this requires a court to put itself in the position of the executive; that to recreate the emergency is impossible and the court should be reluctant to judge military action "too closely by the inapplicable standards of judicial or even military hindsight."

What Justice Burton overlooked was the difference between acts of a military commander such as taking possession of a building or a beach or requiring certain fortifications to be built or even interning suspicious characters and the creation by the military commander of a system of military tribunals for the trial of civilians. In the one

---

[105] Duncan v. Kahanamoku, 327 U.S. 337.
[106] *Id.* at 342.
[107] *Ibid.*

category the acts of the military commander for all practical purposes are conclusive.

The reason the courts will not review or, to speak more accurately, are reluctant to review the actual exertion of force by a military commander after a declaration of martial law is precisely what Justice Burton had in mind when he talked about the difficulty of recreating the emergency and judging action by judicial or military hindsight, for in such instances the commander acts *in extremis*. He may be right or he may be wrong, but act he must. Warfare could not be conducted upon any other basis. Therefore, his judgment is conclusive. The trial and punishment of persons charged with crime, however, take place under no such stress. Even a military tribunal presumably undertakes a deliberative[108] process with an avowed effort on the part of the provost court to give the accused some measure of due process. It is not something that has to be done on the spur of the moment lest the fate of the nation be imperiled. Clearly the trials of *Duncan* and *White* were not dictated by any consideration of the public safety.

The standard to be applied is far different in this field (military trials of civilians) from the standard to be applied in judging the exertion of force such as evacuating civilians from a shoreline. The dissent is unrealistic in concluding that, because Pearl Harbor was under attack for several hours on December 7, 1941, and in that sense could be considered a battlefield, it therefore was a battlefield in March 1944 when our forces were knocking at the inner ring of the Japanese defenses.

The dissent is inaccurate in stating the President "supported" the action of the governor in turning over his functions and those of judicial officers to the commanding general. After quoting the proclamation of the governor turning over the government to the commanding general the opinion states: "This action was communicated by him to the President . . ."[109] That action was never communicated by the governor to the President and hence the President never passed on the question whether the governor should or was authorized to turn over his statutory powers and those of judicial officers to the commanding general.

Beyond this inaccuracy, however, there is a deeper defect, namely, that neither Section 67 nor any other statute authorizes such a delegation of power. In other words, assuming a valid declaration of

---

[108] The picture of meting out rough and swift justice "amidst great social disorder" discussed by Birkheimer, Military Government and Martial Law, 492 (1892), had no factual resemblance to Hawaii following December 7, 1941.

[109] 327 U.S. 304 at 308.

martial law, there is no escaping from the conclusion that the act of Congress contemplates that the governor and not a general or an admiral or anyone else would be the administrator of the martial law proclaimed.

It is of interest to note that the theory of the government's defense, that the powers of the military were derivative from the governor, was an innovation of the Department of Justice; it was not the operating theory of the Army in Hawaii. The Army's position was that after the declaration of martial law and the suspension of the privilege of the writ the power of the military was supreme in all branches of the Hawaiian government. The "supersession," as it was called, was complete, including the governor himself as well as the courts, the legislature of Hawaii, and the Congress. Thus, when restoration took place by proclamation on February 8, 1943, two proclamations were issued, one by the governor which had legal standing and effect under Section 67 of the Organic Act and the other by the commanding general, in which he announced:

1. Full jurisdiction and authority are hereby relinquished by the Commanding General to the Governor and other officers of the Territory of Hawaii, to the courts of that territory, to the city and county of Honolulu, to other counties, to all other officers of the territory or other persons acting under its authority, to the United States District Court for Hawaii, and to the appropriate officers of the United States, to exercise such powers as may now or hereafter be vested in them respectively by law over the following matters and others necessarily related thereto.[110]

The proclamation of the commanding general purporting to give back powers that he never held was without statutory basis but is significant in demonstrating the military view of its supremacy over the civil power.

Justice Burton seems to have been of the view that the military proceeded to relax controls as and when the exigencies of the situation permitted. This is unsupported by the record, which disclosed that the original restoration by the proclamation of February 8, 1943 (effective March 10, 1943), was accomplished only after protracted negotiations in Washington and that thereafter not a single step was taken to relax the controls despite the fact that the President in approving the compromise had expressed this request.[111] The dissent disregards the facts as to what the public safety required and the find-

---

[110] Record, p. 77.

[111] On the relaxation of military control after March 10, 1943, the governor testified, "Nothing has been relinquished as far as I know, and we have taken no action." Record, p. 892.

ings of the trial court as to the absence of civil strife or obstruction of the courts in their ordinary functions. It should be remembered that at the time of the trial of the *Duncan* case (March 1944) the criminal as well as the civil courts were in the full exercise of their powers, trying cases regularly. No reason was suggested in the dissent why the civil courts which were actually trying cases involving major crimes, could not enforce any regulations that were promulgated by the general pursuant to the act of Congress authorizing them. The military authorities were adamant in clinging to the last degree to their assumed powers.

The holding of the Supreme Court may be summarized as follows:

1. The federal Constitution and particularly the Bill of Rights apply in the Territory of Hawaii as elsewhere in the United States; whether Congress can in any way limit their Territorial application remains, technically, an open question.

2. Section 67 of the Hawaiian Organic Act does not authorize the trial of civilians before military tribunals.

3. After a declaration of martial law every act of the military commander in pursuance of the declaration does not automatically become lawful simply because the military commander has ordered it done. Lawfulness of such a military act is reviewable in the courts and is judged by whether or not the particular act in question was required by the public safety.

A month after the decision of the Supreme Court the Secretary of War, prompted by radio broadcasts involving the exercise of military authority in Hawaii, wrote a letter of explanation to Representative Walter G. Andrews, dated March 25, 1946, which the Representative inserted in the *Congressional Record*. Secretary Patterson in his letter said:

The Army did not in any sense oust or overthrow the civil government of the Territory. The civil authorities of the Territory continued for the most part to function as before, their authority supported and assured by martial law.[112]

[112] 92 Cong. Rec. A1699 (1946); but see the statement of a better-informed observer, District Judge J. Frank McLaughlin, 92 Cong. Rec. A4930-4 (1946): "Did the Army in good faith truly believe in the legality, the constitutionality of its acts? Did it really wish an ultimate ruling from the Supreme Court? Or was it bluffing, stalling, threatening, dodging and evading while it ground your rights and mine under the butt of a gun? The record speaks for itself . . . The Supreme Court's decision is as I have said, a victory for the Constitution . . . If what they did here was right, it could be done at any time in any other part of the United States. You may not realize how close to a military dictatorship we came. If you do not, read the Supreme Court's dissenting opinion."

The Secretary went on to state, "The War Department, of course, accepts as settled law the decision of the Supreme Court in the *Duncan* and *White* cases and will follow it with circumspection." In his letter the Secretary, in defense of the Army's actions in Hawaii, quotes at length from the opinion of the Court of Appeals in the *Zimmerman* case, which was mooted by a release of the prisoner simultaneously with the filing of the petition for certiorari in the Supreme Court.[113] Secretary Patterson does not quote from the decision of the Supreme Court in the *Duncan* case, and his statements that "the Army did not in any sense oust or overthrow the civil government" and that "the civil authorities of the territory continued for the most part to function as before" disclose a lack of knowledge of the facts and, what is even more remarkable for an able lawyer, a lack of familiarity with the opinion of the Supreme Court which he quoted.

It probably will be years before the historian of the future can clearly appraise the motives and causes that led the Army to pursue the course it did in Hawaii. It is inconceivable that those in high places in the War Department were not cognizant of the fact that the regime erected in Hawaii superseding the civil government was not only illegal but contrary to our most cherished traditions of the supremacy of the law. It is readily understandable that military personnel not familiar with the mixed peoples of Hawaii should have had misgivings concerning them. However, the conduct of the populace on December 7 and thereafter should have put these military doubts at rest. To be sure it took some time for the military authorities to assure themselves that the civil population was all that it seemed—a loyal American community. What is not understandable is why the military government was continued after several years had elapsed and the fears of the most suspicious had been allayed.

After bases which the Japanese held several thousand miles west of Hawaii were captured by our forces, it was clear that there could be no invasion of Hawaii. Why then was the regime continued? A possible explanation may have been military fears that, having assumed a fictitious title of military governor[114] and having erected a military government without legal sanction, the Army would lose prestige if it were to admit its error.

A military government is essentially like any other form of bureaucracy. Its tendency is to expand, not liquidate. In the matter of rank, for example, if a military government has sufficient subordinate

[113] Zimmerman v. Walker, 319 U.S. 744 (1943).
[114] The title "military governor" was dropped on the eve of President Roosevelt's visit to Hawaii. See General Orders No. 63, July 21, 1944.

personnel, then of course it can justify the creation of a certain number of lieutenants, captains, majors, colonels, and generals. On the other hand, if the activity should decline with declining need, that would require a reduction of personnel and rank. The reluctance of the military governor's office to reduce its size and power is not peculiar to the military. However, there is one important difference between a civil and a military bureaucracy. If the action of a civil official is too arbitrary or too wide a departure from either statutory or regulatory authority, it can be checked in the courts, whereas in the case of a military government, as Justice Black pointed out, all power is centered in one person, and the individual affected by the operation of such a government is powerless to have his case reviewed by anyone since he must turn to the very person he claims as his oppressor and ask for relief from the oppression.

On March 1, 1946, *nunc pro tunc* as of November 1, 1944, Circuit Judge Stephens filed a dissenting opinion in the *Duncan* case.[115] In a preliminary statement, Judge Stephens explained that he had reached the conclusion that the judgment should be affirmed and had distributed an opinion to his colleagues on the Court of Appeals, but because the war was still in progress he had concluded that a dissenting opinion held more possibility of harm than of good and had accordingly withheld it. The opinion contains an exhaustive discussion of the problems presented and it is only to be regretted that his dissent was not made known when the case was disposed of in the Court of Appeals. Surely we are sufficiently strong as a nation to sustain the impact of a judicial opinion even though it be critical of the military arm of our government during time of war.

Even though a particular decision may be considered ill-founded as a matter of law or unfortunate as a matter of policy it would be far more unfortunate to suppress conflicts among members of our courts. Justices Murphy and Rutledge did not hesitate to express themselves in the *Yamashita* case.[116] There are some who hold the view that dissenting opinions shake the confidence of the people in the judicial system and who long for the return to the days when dissenting opinions were less frequent and unanimity appeared to be a prime judicial objective. Although it may be desirable from some standpoints that dissents be kept to a minimum, it does not appear desirable where large issues are at stake that a dissent should be avoided simply to portray a solidarity of judicial opinion which is unreal.

[115] Ex parte Duncan, 153 F. 2d 943 (CCA 9 1946).
[116] In re Yamashita, 327 U.S. 1, 26, 41 (1946).

The phase of martial law passed on by the Supreme Court involves the most extreme exercise of martial law powers—the supplanting of the civil courts and the trial of civilians by military tribunals. This is the ultimate in the exercise of such powers. At the other end of the scale lie invasions of personal and property rights whose justification must also depend on judicial balancing of the invaded rights against the acuteness of the emergency which is alleged to require their sacrifices.

The decision of the court was a salutary one. While it is of particular interest to lawyers, political scientists, and historians, it is of general interest to every thoughtful citizen who believes that the constitutional safeguards of civil liberties are as important in time of war as in time of peace.[117]

The safeguarding of our civil liberties in time of war is more important and incidentally far more difficult than in less troublesome times.[118] Ordinarily in time of peace one is not imprisoned without a trial or convicted otherwise than in conformity with the Bill of Rights. Moreover, the Supreme Court in recent years has shown an increasing willingness to review criminal cases in which real or fancied miscarriages of justice have occurred. Yet in time of war there will always be zealous and well-meaning souls who would rashly abandon the civil liberties of the individual under the guise of aiding the war effort. Such efforts usually have the approval of the crowd and sometimes the courts.[119] This decision, coming as we enter the threshold of the atomic age with the realization of the revolutionary methods of modern warfare, is significant. It may serve as a warning for the future that the seizure of civil government by the military authorities in the absence of invasion or rebellion will not receive the sanction of the highest court in the land.

[117] The problem presented is discussed in the following: Anthony, Hawaiian Martial Law in the Supreme Court, 57 Yale L.J. 27 (1947); Fairman, The Supreme Court on Military Jurisdiction: Martial Rule in Hawaii and the Yamashita Case, 59 Harv. L. Rev. 833 (1946); Frank, Ex parte Milligan v. The Five Companies: Martial Law in Hawaii, 44 Col. L. Rev. 639 (1944); Rankin, Hawaii under Martial Law, 5 Jour. Politics 270 (1943); Armstrong, Martial Law in Hawaii, 29 A.B.A.J. 698 (1943); Radin, Martial Law in Hawaii, 30 Calif. L. Rev. 599 (1942); Fairman, Law of Martial Rule, 55 Harv. L. Rev. 1253 (1942).

[118] In Ex parte Quirin, 317 U.S. 1, 19 (1942), Chief Justice Stone recognized that "the duty . . . rests on the courts, in time of war as well as in time of peace, to preserve unimpaired the constitutional safeguards of civil liberty . . ."

[119] Chafee, Free Speech in the United States, IX (1941): "When war begins, all thinking stops."

Chapter Five

TERMINATION OF MARTIAL LAW

*T*HE case of *Duncan v. Kahanamoku* was submitted to the
Court of Appeals on July 1, 1944, and decided on November 1, 1944.
It is of interest that the administration took pains to have a formal
proclamation terminating[1] martial law signed by the President on
October 19, 1944, a few weeks before the decision of the Court of
Appeals. The termination was timed so that an affirmance of the
District Court would have little public effect since the President had
already ended martial law. The Court of Appeals, however, reversed
the District Court, but the case did not become moot upon the issuance
of the President's proclamation since the reversal required the petitioner to serve out the balance of his sentence ordered by the provost
court. The fact that martial law was terminated did not have the
effect of automatically vacating sentences that had been imposed by
the military authorities. This could only be accomplished by pardoning the prisoners whose cases were before the court or by the filing
of a confession of error. At this point a fatal error in strategy was
made by the Department of Justice acting, no doubt, upon instructions
of the War Department. After receiving the blessing of the Court
of Appeals upholding military trials in Hawaii, a generous and wise
course would have been to release all provost court prisoners. It is
difficult to believe that the Department of Justice would not have
welcomed this solution. In his "memorandum for the United States"
presented to the court when the petition for certiorari was filed, the
Solicitor General, while not unequivocally opposing the petition,
sought to minimize the importance of the case by pointing out that
martial law had ended by the President's proclamation and further
that there were at that date, January 1945, only sixteen persons serving unexpired sentences of the provost courts.[2]

[1] Proclamation No. 2627, 9 Fed. Reg. 12831.
[2] See Memorandum for the United States, p. 21; Record, Duncan v. Kahanamoku,
327 U.S. 304.

In addition to this there lurked in the background the pending litigation against Generals Richardson, Green, and Short. Whatever the reason, it was error in determination which was indeed fortunate for the future of the law on the subject.

Simultaneously with the issuance of the proclamation terminating martial law, the President signed an Executive Order[3] which authorized the Secretary of War to designate the commanding general, United States Army Forces, Pacific Ocean Areas, as the military commander within the meaning of the act of March 21, 1942, and authorized the military commander to designate the Territory of Hawaii as a military area from which persons could be excluded and to regulate the conduct of persons within the prescribed area.

This order authorized the military commander "whenever military necessity therefor exists and the military commander so finds" to establish blackout and curfew periods; establish air raid precautions; to regulate the conduct of enemy aliens; to evacuate or exclude persons from Hawaii to prevent espionage or sabotage; to prohibit the use of firearms; to regulate ports and harbors; to regulate travel within the military area and to regulate the publication of newspapers "published in a foreign or in dual languages." Thus on October 24, 1944, the government finally got around to utilizing the ample powers that Congress had provided for the protection of the nation and the prosecution of the war. This had been advocated as early as 1942 by the attorney general of Hawaii, but the military authorities had not seen fit to use the framework established by Congress since it involved the enforcement of military regulations in the United States District Court and did not authorize the establishment of provost courts.

Immediately following the executive order of the President, Lieutenant General Robert C. Richardson, Jr., issued Public Proclamation No. 1, pursuant to the direction of the Secretary of War which designated Hawaii as a military area and provided for Security Orders Nos. 1 to 7. These related to enemy aliens, air raids, curfew, identification, travel, censorship, and ports and harbors. It will be recalled that General Richardson had testified in the *Duncan* case that one of the reasons why he could not bring himself to terminate martial law was the possibility of a conflict in authority between himself and the governor on the matter of curfew or blackout. He must have known that Congress had afforded the machinery for just such orders.

[3] Executive Order No. 9489, 9 Fed. Reg. 12831.

It was under this same statute that the whole evacuation program of the West Coast had been conducted in 1942.

Simultaneously with the formal termination of martial law he issued Security Order No. 3, which related to the curfew and blackout, which prohibited all civilians excepting those granted special privileges from being "on the streets and highways, in parks and on beaches either on foot or in vehicles during the hours of curfew," and the hours of curfew were from 10:00 P.M. to 5:30 A.M. It will be remembered that at the time this order was issued our forces were knocking at the inner ring of the Japanese defenses. The finding that such an order was dictated by necessity at this time was difficult if not impossible to sustain. The people of Hawaii had never complained about any security regulation, however lacking in real necessity. The challenges to military authority were confined to convictions in the provost courts and to unlawful detentions.

The curfew and blackout were maintained until July 11, 1945, when they were lifted by Security Order No. 10, which rescinded Security Order No. 3. The way in which General Richardson took this step was interesting. The public had finally begun to be vocal about the needless imposition of the curfew, which was particularly burdensome on the defense workers residing in Civilian Housing Area No. 3, near Pearl Harbor. When the pressure became such that it could no longer be ignored, the general took steps to ascertain the views of the public on March 18, 1945. He wrote to H. P. Faye, president of the Honolulu Chamber of Commerce, in regard to the matter:

> The curfew is no longer primarily necessary for security but its extension in part or lifting will bring about many problems which the community itself, and especially the businessmen, must solve. . . .
>
> Before taking any action in this matter I request that the Chamber of Commerce give me an expression of opinion as representative of the community, as an extension or lifting of the curfew now is a community matter.[4]

A committee of the Honolulu Chamber of Commerce, in response to the request of General Richardson, held a meeting which resulted in the unanimous opinion that the curfew should remain at 10:00 P.M., and accordingly advised the general against lifting it.

Executive Order No. 9489 of the President of the United States had authorized the military commander "whenever military necessity therefor exists and the military commander so finds" to establish a

---

[4] University of Hawaii War Records Depository.

curfew. This language was unequivocal. It authorized the military commander to establish a curfew whenever he found that military necessity for it existed. The general was perfectly satisfied at least as early as March 18, 1945, that the curfew was indefensible on the basis of military necessity—"the curfew is no longer primarily necessary for security but . . . will bring about . . . problems which . . . businessmen must solve."

Having made this determination on March 18, 1945, his duty under the proclamation issued by the commander in chief was clear. It should have been lifted forthwith. The commanding general, however, still visualized himself as the guardian of the conduct of the people and of what was good for the community apart from what was necessary as a matter of military security. Probably this was the reason that prompted him to ask the advice of the Chamber of Commerce. Certainly it was not to make the military judgment required by the President's Executive Order. His determination that no military necessity existed for the curfew, however, was not made public until July 2, 1945, at a press conference in which he said:

> As commanding general, I can no longer defend the curfew as justi-
> fied as a military necessity. I have felt that way for many months.
> I have informed the governor and the Honolulu Chamber of Com-
> merce that I was ready to rescind the curfew at any time . . .
> If the curfew is rescinded, it means that the cafés and restaurants
> will stay open longer. That means additional manpower, additional trans-
> portation, additional police work.[5]

As one defense worker writing the editor of the *Honolulu Adver-tiser* put it:

> Now comes General Richardson with a naïve assumption that because
> we have not been pestering him we must like the curfew. The Chamber
> of Commerce and Governor Stainback like it, he explains. And what
> have they to do with it . . . American workmen do not have to be locked
> by night like galley slaves to keep them fit for their jobs . . . There is
> no question of modifying the curfew to another hour. Ten o'clock is as
> good or as bad as any hour. The curfew is either right or wrong. I say
> it is wrong. No curfew will be tolerated without military necessity . . .[6]

And another writing to the same paper:

> I am an American and was raised to believe that Americans do not
> need a policeman to put them to bed. . . . General Richardson says he
> thinks we want a curfew because we haven't said we didn't. He never
> asked us working plugs who don't belong to the Chamber of Commerce.[7]

  [5] Honolulu Star-Bulletin, July 2, 1945, p. 1.
  [6] Honolulu Advertiser, July 4, 1945.
  [7] Honolulu Advertiser, July 4, 1945.

In the same edition of the paper, the *Honolulu Advertiser* reached the conclusion that it might be a good thing to extend the curfew from ten to midnight. It stated:

I believe a midnight curfew, for BOTH CIVILIAN AND SERVICE PARTIES, should be even more rigidly enforced than the present 10 o'clock curfew. Midnight is late enough to meet all the requirements of the services and of the community for an occasional party. . . .[8]

Letters to the newspapers protesting the curfew reached a climax on July 5, 1945, with the expression of a legal opinion that in the absence of military necessity the curfew was invalid.[9] Two days later, on July 7, 1945, General Richardson issued Security Order No. 10, rescinding the curfew. Certain members of the public had become so accustomed to rule by a military commander they completely overlooked the fact that whether or not the continuance of the curfew best served their own particular ends was immaterial under the President's proclamation.

THE REACTION OF THE CIVIL COMMUNITY
TO MILITARY GOVERNMENT

One might have expected a widespread criticism of the military regime in Hawaii. This, however, was not the case. While any generalization on this subject must be accepted with reservations it must be said that a large number of persons holding positions of importance in the community were little disturbed by the invasion of their civil liberties. When the newly elected delegate to Congress, Joseph R. Farrington, made a statement from Washington in December 1942 that it was his purpose to secure a modification of the strict martial law that obtained in the Islands and said that the regime was without precedent in our history, he not only failed to received the backing of important business groups but on the contrary was met with positive opposition. On December 27, 1942, acting on the press reports from Washington as to the activities of the delegate, the governor, and the attorney general of Hawaii, in regard to prosecuting their requests for a return of civil government before the appropriate authorities in the capital, the Chamber of Commerce of Honolulu wired the President, the Attorney General of the United States, the Secretary of the Interior, the Secretary of War, and the Secretary of the United States Chamber of Commerce a sharp protest against the course pursued by the officials of the Territory in Washington.

[8] Honolulu Advertiser, July 4, 1945.
[9] Honolulu Star-Bulletin, July 5, 1945, p. 1.

The exchange of communications has been referred to in an earlier chapter; the wire concluded with the plea:

WE FEEL THAT GENERAL EMMONS, OUR MILITARY GOVERNOR, HAS BEEN EMINENTLY FAIR AND CONSIDERATE OF OUR CIVIL RIGHTS THIS PAST YEAR AND WE HAVE EVERY CONFIDENCE THAT HE WILL CONTINUE TO EXERCISE THIS CONSIDERATION.[10]

As already observed, this was but the expression of the directors of the Chamber of Commerce, and not the result of a poll of the membership. The authors of the message were aware of the operations of the provost courts in Hawaii, the fact that thousands of persons were convicted in these tribunals, some with trials, some without trials, and that sentences were imposed without regard to the limitations of law for the offenses involved; that persons found guilty of traffic violations were given prison terms up to five years; that persons were held without bail; were obliged to purchase war bonds and donate blood in expiation of their sins.

The Chamber of Commerce also asked Delegate Farrington to advise them "specifically what functions of civil government you favor now having returned to civil jurisdiction" to which the delegate replied:

THE RESPONSIBILITY FOR DETERMINING WHAT FUNCTIONS OF GOVERNMENT . . . SHOULD BE RETURNED TO CIVIL CONTROL HAS BEEN PLACED BY THE PRESIDENT WITH A COMMITTEE OF HIGH OFFICERS REPRESENTING THE EXECUTIVE DEPARTMENTS CONCERNED.[11]

The delegate was obviously disturbed at the attitude of the Chamber of Commerce, but the organization elected to stand on the position they had taken "without apology." While it may be safe to assume that the attitude expressed by the Chamber of Commerce represented the views of the business community, it certainly did not represent the feeling of the war workers or of labor. The reasons for the resentment of labor to the regime were not so much because of a conviction that their civil liberties had been flagrantly invaded, but rather because of the fact that they were frozen to their jobs and were not free to move about the community as they wished.

An example of the businessman's attitude toward the problem is found in the statements given before the Army–Pearl Harbor Board inquiring into the causes of Pearl Harbor. The proceedings before the board were held in the latter part of 1944, and included state-

[10] University of Hawaii War Records Depository.
[11] *Id.*

ments of civilians in Hawaii who gave their views on the matter. The proceedings, of course, were a top secret and the witnesses naïvely assumed that their testimony would remain in the secret file. Walter F. Dillingham appeared before the board and gave his views on the conduct of Admiral Kimmel and General Short, in which he said:

> If, as I assume, a message was sent out to be alerted for any emergency and Admiral Kimmel and General Short knew of this background . . . I think they were very derelict in their duty.[12]

Mr. Dillingham was asked in the course of his testimony whether there was any indication that businessmen were inclined not to cooperate with the military authorities, to which Mr. Dillingham replied:

> I do not think that the businessmen have reached that point even in their own minds. I think that this little community was solidly behind whatever was necessary in the judgment of our military leaders to be done. Just as if they were all in uniform and drilled to support them . . . The exception to the rule was when politics entered into the thing and there was a feeling amongst some of our legal fraternity and colleagues that we ought to say, "By God, we ought to maintain the rights of American citizens," and all that sort of hooey that nobody cared a damn about.
>
> We were perfectly willing to go to bed at 10 o'clock and 8 o'clock and go without lights and all the rest of it, and nobody wanted any change. Irrespective of what was said, that was the truth . . . they felt that if there was any lurking in the minds of the Japanese . . . they . . . were a darned sight safer as American citizens under that kind of military control, when the fear of immediate punishment was facing the violator of military law, as against cases dragged along in the courts . . .[13]

To this General Grunert inquired: "Wouldn't that be good government on the part of the city or county to have put that in of their own accord?" Mr. Dillingham replied, "No, it is the fear of punishment, General. It was the teeth in the military control that made people feel comfortable here."

When the statements of Hawaii's citizens were made public as the result of the Pearl Harbor investigation, as might be expected there was considerable consternation among the witnesses who had appeared before the Army board and bared their innermost thoughts in the proceeding which they erroneously assumed would be held confidential, as they were advised by the Army board. However, what the willing confessors failed to realize was that on an issue of this magnitude, involving as it did the public interest of the whole nation,

[12] Hearings, Joint Committee on the Investigation of the Pearl Harbor Attack, 79th Cong., S. Con. Res. 27, Part 28, p. 1444.
[13] *Id.*

it was not within the competence of any Army board or any official
of the United States to maintain the seal of secrecy over the testimony. All of us from the highest to the lowest are under the law and
when the Congress of the United States acts within the field of its
investigatory powers no testimony can be suppressed.

An example of one civilian's point of view is found in the testimony of Frank H. Locey who, after testifying that he was president
of the Board of Agriculture and Forestry, gave as his opinion "that
General Short was a saviour to this country on December 7,"[14] and
when questioned about the character of the local population, proceeded
to pay his respects to the statehood movement and particularly the
Japanese population, admitting however that he was in the great
minority in the community and stated that he hoped it was not for
publication. He was assured by General Grunert, "All this is secret
but whoever digs out the secret record has to have authority to do so,
but it is not for publication."

Mr. Locey: I am interested here. It's not becoming of me, really, to
talk this way against the community and this territory.[15]

One reason for the complacent acceptance of the regime was undoubtedly the fact that civilians in Hawaii throughout the war lived
off the fat of the land. The Army saw to it that Hawaii was well
stocked and overstocked with food supplies and other materials that
fellow Americans on the mainland were denied. Throughout the
entire period of the war no rationing program existed in Hawaii with
the single exception of the military rationing of liquor and gasoline,
and with the thousands of military and naval personnel stationed in
the Islands with access to both commodities, there was no occasion
for anyone in Hawaii to do without either if he chose to obtain it.
In short, the Army deprived the citizen of his most cherished possession—the inheritance of free men—which the founders of this
country had waged bloody battles to secure, and these were supinely
exchanged for meat, butter, Kleenex, and liquor.

Throughout the history of Anglo-American peoples the groups
that have traditionally stood for freedom of conscience and civil liberties have been the legal profession, the clergy, and the press, and yet
in this period representatives of these groups who held true to their
best traditions were rare. However, those who experienced the press
of the provost courts became overnight converts to an appreciation
of the meaning of the American tradition.

[14] Hearings, Joint Committee on the Investigation of the Pearl Harbor Attack,
79th Cong., Part 28, p. 1454.   [15] *Id.* at 1457.

REACTION OF THE PRESS TO MARTIAL LAW

One interesting aspect of the regime of martial law in Hawaii was the attitude of the press both in Hawaii and on continental United States. In Hawaii the two leading newspapers took opposite stands on the issue. The *Honolulu Star-Bulletin* at an early date recognized the threat to Hawaii inherent in the continuance of the military government. This position was in accord with the position of Joseph R. Farrington, the publisher of the paper who was elected delegate to Congress from Hawaii in November 1942.

The *Honolulu Advertiser*, on the other hand, for the most part stoutly defended the military regime, which course was dictated both by editorial preference as well as by the rivalry existing between the two newspapers.

The press on the mainland by and large was critical of the military regime in Hawaii and particularly the supersession of the civil authorities by the Army. The first written protest of martial law appeared not in a newspaper, but in a sober law journal[16] which questioned the validity of the trial of civilians in military tribunals. This article was quoted from extensively in the Honolulu newspapers[17] as well as in the *New York Times*.

Lieutenant General Delos C. Emmons, who was then commander of the Hawaiian Department, gave a statement in the press in reply to an article appearing in the *California Law Review*:

> Academic discussion regarding the legal technicalities involved in martial law is, of course, the inherent right of a free and independent people . . .
> No doubt the history and operation of martial law in Hawaii will be the subject of many interesting legal debates in years to come, . . .
> It is, I believe, sufficient to say that in this theater of operations we are not going to question the wisdom of our Congress in passing the Organic Act nor question the judgment of our President in approving the declaration of martial law by the civil governor.[18]

No one had questioned the wisdom of Congress in passing the Organic Act or the judgment of the governor in declaring martial law on December 7, 1941, nor the judgment of the President in approving the declaration of martial law and the suspension of the writ of habeas corpus. What was questioned was the right of military

---

[16] Martial Law in Hawaii, 30 Calif. L. Rev. 371.

[17] Honolulu Advertiser, May 15, 1942; Honolulu Star-Bulletin, May 16, 1942; see also New York Times, May 17, 1942.

[18] Honolulu Advertiser, May 16, 1942.

tribunals to try civilians for offenses unrelated to military security. This could hardly be called a "legal technicality."

The statement of General Emmons was first released to a bilingual newspaper published in Hawaii, the *Nippu Jiji*.[19] This newspaper had originally been suppressed by military order, but later was permitted to publish under Army supervision.

One weekly newspaper which has had a precarious existence characterized the articles appearing in the *California Law Review* as "untimely" and added that "it was embarrassing to the military government."[20]

On September 4, 1942, the *Honolulu Advertiser*, commenting on martial law, said:

Hawaii has been a test tube and a guinea pig for what might happen on the mainland. It does not mind this role. It is proud that it has had the opportunity to serve in this humble way.

For just about nine months it has followed obligingly the dictates of a military rule—a rule as firm or firmer than any to be found in combat zones elsewhere . . .

The public has accepted military rule as a fact that is to be with us for no short time. It does not ask its abolition or that Washington turn over all of the duties of the military in government to civilian authority.[21]

This view however by no means reflected the sentiments of the ordinary man in the street or of persons who had the misfortune to run afoul of the provost courts. The Democratic party had a somewhat different view of the military regime from that expressed by the *Honolulu Advertiser*. The convention adopted a platform which stated:

We have the utmost confidence in the civil judicial system of the Territory of Hawaii, and firmly believe that the civil courts should be open and allowed to function under civilian administration in all matters where the military effort is not involved.

Further, we believe that all criminal offenses which are in no way related to the military effort should be administered by the civilian courts, and the right of a jury trial in criminal cases should be restored immediately.

We deplore a system of government whereby the citizens of the Territory of Hawaii can be arrested and held for investigation, without bail, for offenses that have nothing to do with the operations of the military establishment.

We deplore the exercise of public authorities who are making unlawful searches and seizures in the homes of the people of the Territory of Hawaii without a search warrant . . .

[19] Nippu Jiji, May 15, 1942.
[20] Hawaii Sentinel, May 14, 1942.
[21] Honolulu Advertiser, September 4, 1942.

We deplore the continued existence of the suspension of the writ of habeas corpus . . .[22]

The platform of the Republican party for the Territory by sharp contrast ignored completely the fact that the government of Hawaii had been taken over by the Army.[23]

When the first major step toward the restoration of civil government in Hawaii took place under the proclamations of February 8, 1943, the leading newspapers of Honolulu met the restoration with wide publicity as well as editorial comment.

The *Honolulu Star-Bulletin* of February 9, 1943, met the return of civil government with great acclaim in its editorial "Restoration and Its Meaning." This newspaper said:

The dominant principle observed throughout the formula announced Monday is the principle that on American soil not invaded or occupied by foreign troops or forces and not set aside as military or naval reservations for specific military or naval occupancy and use, civil authority shall be prevalent and paramount . . .

For the people of Hawaii generally, we have every right to be deeply proud that The White House, the Interior Department, the Justice Department, the War Department, the Navy Department—all participating in this plan of restoration—have said in effect, "You have proved your right to direct the affairs of local government in our American outpost territory."[24]

The *Honolulu Advertiser* greeted the restoration with a less cordial note. The editor voiced a wishful note that possibly military necessity might require a restoration of the military regime and reminded the public of Hawaii:

Now that conditions are such that certain civil responsibilities safely can be relinquished they have been returned to the civil authorities to handle until such time, if any, as military necessity may dictate otherwise.[25]

The filing of petitions for writs of habeas corpus in the *Glockner* and *Seifert* cases, the evasion by General Richardson of the United States marshal and his subsequent citation for contempt in the federal court provoked editorial comment both in Hawaii and on the mainland. After General Richardson had defied the process of the court and had been cited for contempt the case was ultimately disposed of by the military sending the interned individuals out of the

[22] Honolulu Star-Bulletin, September 21, 1942.
[23] Honolulu Star-Bulletin, October 2, 1942.
[24] Honolulu Star-Bulletin, February 9, 1943.
[25] Honolulu Advertiser, February 9, 1943.

Territory and liberating them on the mainland. This rendered the cases moot and the issue of the suspension of the writ could not then be passed on. The *Honolulu Advertiser said*:

Inevitably, the territory will be regarded in many uninformed quarters as having kicked up a deterrent row while the war is on. The nation is not now very greatly concerned about the legal rights and wrongs of a community as was shown by its attitude when the constitutional rights of Americans of Japanese ancestry were set aside in California, and it cannot be expected to consider the fine points at issue here.[26]

The *Honolulu Star-Bulletin*, on the other hand, recognized the seriousness of the situation and in an editorial said:

The question is whether suspects kept in a military internment camp can be held indefinitely without trial—at a time when no imminent danger of serious enemy attack is apparent, and when, in fact, martial law has been substantially modified by a large scale restoration of civil rights . . .
What the judge has said, in effect, is that these prisoners are being denied fundamental rights to which they are entitled under the American Constitution, and that the military situation in the Pacific is no justification for this.[27]

The spectacle of a commanding general in the United States Army playing hide-and-seek to escape the clutches of a United States marshal had its humorous aspects. The *Buffalo Courier* of August 27, 1943, said:

If times weren't so serious—and the basic issue so important to a people fighting for democracy—there would be Gilbert-and-Sullivanesque material in the clash between Lieut. Gen. Robert C. Richardson, Jr., . . . and United States Judge Delbert E. Metzger, . . .

The *Birmingham Age-Herald*, writing on the incident under the caption "A Modern Major General," said:

There is nothing new in a run-in between military and civil authorities during a war. That has happened before. But the writ of habeas corpus is too precious a thing to be left to the discretion solely of a lieutenant general. If conditions in Hawaii are so touchy as to warrant making a military area of the whole place, with all civil rights and laws suspended, why has the need for this measure been overlooked until now, why was strict military control ever allowed to lapse.

Governor Stainback in his report to the Secretary of the Interior in 1944 reviewed the events of the prior year and noted that the restoration of civil authority in Hawaii was the "most important

26 Honolulu Advertiser, August 19, 1943.
27 Honolulu Star-Bulletin, August 17, 1943.

political event" of the year. The accuracy of his observation could hardly be questioned since it involved a partial restoration of civil government and the reopening of the courts for the exercise of their jurisdiction. The *Honolulu Advertiser* stated editorially:

> If the *Advertiser* knows anything about the community sentiment throughout the Territory of Hawaii, and we believe we do, we will be willing to gamble that a vote of confidence by the public in behalf of the opinions of Admiral Nimitz and General Richardson as contrasted to that of Governor Stainback, would show better than a 95% backing of those men upon whose shoulders rests the responsibility of conducting the Pacific war . . . It is time that Governor Stainback started being Governor of Hawaii, instead of Chief Clerk for Secretary Harold L. Ickes. . . . The fact that he and his Chief Clerk are not willing to subordinate their personal desire for power and control, to the honestly expressed serious needs of the Army and Navy, in the midst of the most difficult war the nation has ever faced, has created an intolerable situation. . . .[28]

This editorial was fairly typical of the newspaper's attitude toward the efforts of Territorial officers to restore civil authority. Those who made these attempts were criticized upon the ground that their activities were interfering with the war effort.

The *Maui News* (a small country newspaper) on April 15, 1944, in an editorial "Is December 7, 1941, Forgotten So Quickly?" attacked everyone who challenged the unconstitutional military regime in Hawaii. This followed the decision of the District Court in *Duncan v. Kahanamoku*. The *News* said:

> . . . whatever complaints against martial law that have been uttered in Hawaii, have emanated from a small, noisy group, the leadership of which has sprung from the legal fraternity whose income has been vastly reduced due to the natural restrictions placed on their activities by military rule . . .
>
> Is it logical, then, to ask why the time and thoughts of two men (Admiral Nimitz and General Richardson) responsible for this miraculous change have been diverted from their primary function to that of defendants in a petty court trial, the importance of which has been grossly magnified by counsel for the plaintiff? . . . If martial law is believed to be necessary in the minds of these military leaders, Hawaii has but one course to follow, that being to accept their opinion as fact, and to do its full share of pulling the load at home. The sooner this realization is reached, the quicker will be the end of that which is such an anathema to Mr. Anthony and his cohorts.

The same newspaper circulated a ballot among the citizenry of the island of Maui to vote Yes or No on the question whether to

---

[28] Honolulu Advertiser, April 23, 1944.

retain or abolish martial law. The ballot contained a space for the name, address, and occupation of the voter and also the statement, "Your vote will be held strictly confidential by the *Maui News.* Servicemen are requested not to vote," and at the foot of the ballot was the admonition, "Vote only once."

The Maui Sugar Planters Association financed the distribution of 5,000 copies of this editorial, which was circulated among the newspapers on the mainland and also to members of Congress. The newspaper, however, never got around to giving any final result of its poll.

The *Honolulu Advertiser* on April 20, 1944, after the decision of the District Court in *Duncan v. Kahanamoku,* adhered to its pro-military government position, saying:

. . . there was and is no popular demand—no mandate from the public— for a relaxation of martial law here. By and large the people of Hawaii have been satisfied with martial law. . . . Labor conditions have been generally stable and the record of absenteeism compares most favorably with the best the Mainland has to offer. . . .

The editorial failed to point out that the "stable" labor conditions were based upon the fact that workers were frozen to their jobs and those who disobeyed the order were punished by fine or jail sentences in the provost courts. It continued:

Hawaii also has been remarkably well cared for in civilian supplies. Food has been abundant, and with almost as much variety as in peace.

Here the editor was referring to the situation of which many residents of Hawaii were not particularly proud, the fact that our fellow citizens on the mainland were burdened with the OPA rationing program while Hawaii, under the guise of being "a theater of operations," was not.

The *Honolulu Star-Bulletin* of April 17, 1944, praised the attitude of Edward J. Ennis, the attorney from the Department of Justice who represented the government in opposition to the writs of habeas corpus in *Duncan v. Kahanamoku,* as well as the earlier *Glockner* and *Seifert* cases. Commenting on Mr. Ennis' statement that the Department of Justice considered the bringing of the petition in court "a helpful thing" and "commendable," this newspaper said:

This statement from the government's own attorney, is quoted for the information of those who may think the bringing up of this issue of the legality of martial law and the provost courts in Hawaii is unwise or inexpedient.

Mr. Ennis' attitude in this as in other matters which have given this community acquaintance with him, is that there is no impropriety in discussing and debating an issue of American government.

One article, attacking those who questioned the necessity for the continuance of martial law as late as 1944, appeared in *Hawaii*, a magazine (now defunct) which for several years had been subsidized by the Hawaiian Sugar Planters Association. The editor wrote:

It is difficult to see what good purpose is to be served by the continual baiting of local military authority and the persistent attempt to supplant martial law with complete civilian control of territorial affairs. The military has a much too important job to do to be continually distracted by petty annoyances of court contests and political maneuverings. Whatever the merits of the habeas corpus case now being tried in the local courts, the fact of the case being tried is being used as an opportunity to renew the attack on military government and martial law in Hawaii. . . .

This editor was apparently disturbed by the fact that the busy military people were bothered with a court case which might result in their relinquishment of civil government and becoming more busily occupied with military rather than civilian affairs. He failed to see that if the military confined themselves to military matters, leaving civilians to run the civilian government, the time of military personnel would be conserved for the performance of military duties.

The situation was particularly trying for those who believed it was important in a free society to wage war successfully and at the same time preserve the constitutional liberties of the individual. It is always easy to accuse such persons of interfering with the war effort, if not of being outright traitors. This editorial came on the heels of the decision of Judge Metzger in *Duncan v. Kahanamoku*, in which the federal court found that there was no necessity for continuance of martial law in Hawaii.

Three days later the *Honolulu Star-Bulletin* published an editorial in which it charged:

A studious attempt seems to be under way in certain quarters to discredit civil government in order to praise and indorse military government in Hawaii . . . The support for restoration of civil law has never been opposition to the military task and mission.

It has been, and is, based on the constitutional question of validity of martial law in an American community neither invaded by an enemy nor disorganized by insurrection within its borders.[29]

At this time there were rumors to the effect that legislation would be introduced in the Congress designed to put Hawaii under the control of the Navy.

In Washington, Benjamin F. Thoron, Director of the Division of

[29] Honolulu Star-Bulletin, April 26, 1944.

Territories of the Interior Department, appeared before the House Appropriations Committee and was interrogated by Representative Jed Johnson (D. Okla.), who expressed amazement at the continuation of martial law in Hawaii at such a late date. Mr. Thoron testified before the committee: "I feel that its continuance is unnecessary under conditions as they exist now and that complete restoration of civil authority would be justified."[30]

Upon receipt of this dispatch the *Honolulu Advertiser* wrote an editorial entitled, "The Department of Interior's Recipe for Beating Japan!" The editorial summarized the testimony of the Director of the Division of Territories as follows:

To hell with General Richardson and Admiral Nimitz and what *they* think is vitally necessary in Hawaii. The Department of the Interior, with the help of Governor Stainback (under the guise of the inalienable rights guaranteed every citizen by the American Constitution) *must be* in a position to tell Admiral Nimitz and General Richardson to what extent, when, where, and how, the Navy or Army can control any situation which might arise in Hawaii, . . .[31]

The meteoric rise of Thomas H. Green of the United States Army from the rank of lieutenant colonel in 1941 to that of major general has already been noted. He was the principal architect of the military government of Hawaii and as such was cognizant of the abuses occurring at the height of the regime of martial law. When pressure became so great that the War Department felt obliged to remove him from the Hawaiian area he was assigned to duty in Washington, D.C., as assistant judge advocate general on April 14, 1943, and later promoted to the rank of major general and became the judge advocate general of the United States Army on December 1, 1945, one of the most highly prized posts in the military establishment.

When General Green's name was sent to the Senate for confirmation of his appointment as Judge Advocate General of the Army it received no publicity. Not until after the Senate had acted did the public in Hawaii realize that his name was under consideration. James L. Coke, former chief justice of the Supreme Court, wrote to Senator Pat McCarran, chairman of the Judiciary Committee, expressing the view "that General Green is not fit for the position in view of his record in Hawaii." Judge Coke was also quoted as saying that he had been advised by Senator Morse "that General Green's appointment slipped through in a block of military appointments."[32]

[30] Honolulu Star-Bulletin, April 26, 1944.
[31] Honolulu Advertiser, April 27, 1944.
[32] Honolulu Star-Bulletin, January 25, 1946.

The decision of the Supreme Court on February 25, 1946, holding invalid the military trials in Hawaii, as would be expected, received wide attention in the press in Honolulu. The matter had been a subject of constant discussion after December 7, 1941. The *Honolulu Star-Bulletin*, commenting on the decision, stated:

> War does not authorize or excuse the military arm of government in operating counter to the Constitution of the United States.
> That principle written into the laws of a free people has again been upheld by the highest tribunal in the land.

Dealing with the government's argument that the Constitution applied to only a limited extent in Hawaii, this newspaper said:

> Not the least significant feature of this decision is that it settles the question whether the Constitution of the United States applies fully to Hawaii.
> The Supreme Court says that it does so apply . . . Not even Congress can take that right away—it would require a revision of the Constitution![33]

The *New York Times* said:

> The Supreme Court decision holding unconstitutional the trial of civilians by military courts in Honolulu during the war reaffirms the historic attitude of the court and of this country's leaders. . . .
> Military rule of Honolulu, and especially the operation of the military courts, was a sore point with the residents of Hawaii all through the war. They felt they were being deprived of constitutional rights for no good reason. After the battle of Midway, June 4–6, 1942, the Hawaiian Islands were never again even remotely in danger of a Japanese attack. But their pleas for relief went unheeded. What was regarded as an often capricious operation of justice in the Provost Marshal's Court built up a bitterness against the Army that may long remain.[34]

The *Washington Post* editorially remarked that "the court is very tardy" but that "it is heartening to have the constitutional rights of citizens upheld and the rule of law resustained over and above military dictation."[35]

The *Honolulu Advertiser* noted:

> Hawaii has been something of a proving ground for better application of democracy. Dark and anxious days that followed the outbreak of war . . . became a period of trial and error. From it we have learned what can and what cannot be done under martial law . . . The military in their sometimes stern, sometimes harsh judicial manner, in their overall

[33] Honolulu Star-Bulletin, February 26, 1942.
[34] New York Times, February 27, 1946.
[35] Washington Post, February 27, 1946.

assumption of power of civilian courts might be excused on the ground of expediency and lack of precedent to follow.[36]

United States District Judge J. Frank McLaughlin, who had some knowledge of the facts, was prompted to express his views as the result of an editorial appearing in the *Honolulu Advertiser* on March 16, 1946. The editorial asserted that the community in Hawaii liked what the Army did even if the Supreme Court found it unlawful. "They did it—and we liked it."

Judge McLaughlin outlined how it was done, pointing out that the proclamation of martial law was prepared by the Army months in advance of December 7, 1941, and noted that the proclamation "was in the hands of publishers for printing that afternoon some substantial period of time before the governor's proclamation was signed and received for publication."[37] Commenting on Secretary Patterson's letter to Representative Andrews and a public statement by General Richardson on the same subject, Judge McLaughlin said:

. . . They did not, of course, mention that the Army went back on its word to the Hawaiian legislature. They did not tell you that it had said one thing while preparing to do another thing. They did not tell you that they prepared Governor Poindexter's proclamation for him and induced him to sign it, reluctantly. They did not tell you either that he finally agreed to do as they asked with the understanding that the effect of the proclamation would be for maybe 30 days. . . .[38]

Judge McLaughlin concluded:

Yes "they did it." They did it intentionally. They did it with design aforethought. They did it in knowing disregard of the Constitution. They did it because Hawaii is not a State. They did it because they did not have faith that Americanism transcends race, class and creed.

[36] Honolulu Advertiser, February 28, 1946.
[37] Cong. Rec. Appendix, July 31, 1946, A4931.
[38] *Ibid.*

Chapter Six

CONCLUSION

$\mathcal{E}$VEN the sharpest critics of the military rule in Hawaii do not go to the extent of contending that the military regime was a plot to overthrow the government. What General Green did undoubtedly was done in the honest belief that it was best for the security of the nation, yet as Lincoln once said, this is the profession of every tyrant.

You will find all the arguments in favor of kingcraft were of this class; they always bestrode the necks of the people—that they didn't want to do it, but that the people were better off for being ridden.[1]

Objectively, it does not make much difference if our liberties are subverted by overzealous or ignorant patriots or by citizens who have fallen under the spell of the totalitarian philosophy of a foreign power. The end result, namely, the loss of liberty, is the same in both instances.

The problem posed by a genuine military emergency presents an issue of the first order to any democratic government. When the life of the nation is at stake, the executive is bound to take whatever action is necessary for its preservation. If the executive or the military commander on the spot in such instances transgresses constitutional limitations, then redress should be granted by the legislature. The executive, in the case of a genuine emergency, is bound to act and cannot await legislative authorization. In the absence of bad faith and upon establishment of a genuine emergency the action of the executive will be sustained by the judicial branch of government.

The difficulty lies not in the statement of the theory as an abstract principle but in its application to specific facts. Any executive, of course, can distinguish between acts which are dictated by the immediacy of the situation and other acts which do not require an "on the spot" determination but which might await legislation. For

---

[1] Stern, The Life and Writings of Abraham Lincoln, 69.

example, upon a declaration of martial law, assuming a valid emergency existed, no one could successfully deny to the military commander the most ample powers over genuine security matters, such as the movement of people, establishment of curfews and blackouts, and the occupation by the military forces of places deemed of strategic importance. In all such matters, of course, the commander's judgment must be final. It would seem that the internment of suspected individuals should be in the same category, however great the hardship may be on the individual wrongfully detained.

A problem of a different order, however, is presented where the military under a state of martial law purports to change the existing laws for the punishment of individuals against the general laws of the state or nation for violations not connected with security matters. In time of a genuine emergency, a military court could function no better than a civilian court. If the emergency is great enough the military commander might very well detain persons arrested for violation of civil law, but there seems to be no good reason why he should erect a system of courts to try such offenders. The very personnel engaged in such procedure might more profitably be employed, notwithstanding the assault of the enemy.

At the moment there are those who contend that the present clash between the democracies of the West and the materialism of the Soviet Union presents a genuine national emergency which justifies strong measures almost akin to those justifiable only in a genuine military emergency. On the one hand, we have the view that the country must be rid of communism, and the way to do that is to outlaw it or deport those professing that philosophy. At the other end of the scale is the extreme liberal who, although opposed to the basic tenets of communism, believes that the best way to dissipate its false doctrines is to leave it undisturbed but exposed to the searching light of publicity. These persons believe that no regulation should be attempted since it is vain to undertake regulation in the field of ideas. There is danger in both extremes. To follow the former would mean an end of liberty under law. To follow the latter would expose us to the same danger if a Communist minority were ever able to seize the reins of government.

In an organized society man must have rules to govern his conduct. The absence of rules means anarchy and the liberty of no one would survive.

If men were angels, no government would be necessary. If angels were to govern men, neither external nor internal control on government would be necessary. In framing a government which is to be administered by men over men, the great difficulty lies in this: you must first enable the government to control the governed; and in the next place oblige it to control itself.[2]

The question is a most profound one in any democratic form of government. It was this that prompted Lincoln's classic statement in the Second Inaugural: "Must a government of necessity be too *strong* for the liberties of its people, or too weak to maintain its own existence?"

The fact that this dilemma recurs throughout our history is evidence of the vitality of our institutions but the problem remains how to "promote the general welfare and secure the blessings of liberty to ourselves and our posterity."

The conflict between military and civil authorities described in these pages illustrates the validity of the familiar expression that "eternal vigilance is the price of liberty" which perhaps is repeated so often that the words lose meaning. It sheds some light on the more subtle invasion of democratic processes which may take place in a comparatively free community with the approval of a majority of the people. Upon the happening of a great catastrophe we are inclined to accept the invasion of traditional and hard-won liberties in the face of danger with little inquiry into the need or little thought of the probable consequences. It is only natural in time of war that the general populace will look to the professionally trained military men for leadership, direction, and command. However, there is danger in overlooking the necessity of keeping the military subordinate to the civil power. The danger in the situation is that the military mind is a specialist in military affairs and rarely has any fundamental grasp of government, politics, or our whole economy. The training of the professional soldier of necessity involves unswerving obedience to the command of his superior. In other fields, whether it be science, politics or philosophy, the basic tenet of the discipline is a steadfast adherence to the attitude of what Professor Chafee once called "the inquiring mind." Although this is not accepted among military men, it appears to the layman that perhaps even the professionally trained soldier would advance his profession and its objectives if he were surrounded by intelligent subordinates who were free to give an informed criticism of the judgments and commands of their superiors without fear of reprisals. Possibly Clemenceau had this in mind when he said, "War is too serious a business to be left to the generals."

[2] Madison, The Federalist, No. 51.

Perhaps one of the reasons why martial law in Hawaii was allowed to continue for years without correction from the War Department in Washington lies in the application to the situation in Hawaii of the precept that the judgment of the military commander in the field should not be disturbed, a principle valid enough at or near the battle-field, but dangerous when applied generally. No one likes to admit error. It is only human to defend a position once it is publicly asserted. However, in the face of convincing proof most people will give way. In the military system this would be looked upon as a sign of weak-ness. Once a decision is reached by a military commander, change will be resisted even in the face of almost conclusive evidence of error.

It was the application of this principle that led General Richard-son (without the knowledge of the War Department) to promulgate the notorious General Orders No. 31, which threatened the two fed-eral judges in Hawaii with swift and certain punishment in the pro-vost courts if they dared to entertain habeas corpus proceedings in the United States District Court for Hawaii. Once issued, the War Department stood by the order to maintain the prestige of the com-manding general in the field. No doubt General Marshall, who had to turn from his duties as Chief of Staff to take personal charge of the incident, appreciated the blunder of his subordinate in Hawaii. For here was an American general threatening an American judge with a drumhead court-martial if the judge should attempt to carry out his sworn duty to carry out the command of Congress as contained in the Habeas Corpus Act. Nevertheless, General Marshall, whose devotion to the nation as well as his military proficiency is generally accepted, would not correct the error since it might damage the pres-tige of a general. It took Charles Fahy, Solicitor General of the United States, and Edward J. Ennis, Assistant Attorney General from the Justice Department, to bring General Richardson to a final acceptance that he and every other person in the land was under the law, a fundamental lesson in our polity that goes back to the historic clash between Lord Coke and James I.

Despite the profound mistrust of military rule which we have inherited and which dates back to the founding of the nation, in the wake of the recent war there seems to be abroad a notion that because one has excelled in the arts of war he therefore will excel in the arts of peace or in the arts of government. Hence we find posts in our government which require the highest qualities of statesmanship filled by persons whose chief recommendation for elevation is their proficiency in military affairs. This tendency, if unchecked, may work a gradual but radical change in our form of government.

We are now in a head-on conflict with Communist materialism. It is too much to believe that this conflict will ever be resolved either by the force of arms or the enactment of laws. Only when men of good will come to the universal understanding and belief that man is answerable to a Supreme Being and that no government or force can be a barrier between man and his God will we have set our course on the way to a solution of the riddle.

APPENDIXES

APPENDIX A

APPENDIX B

APPENDIX C

APPENDIX D

APPENDIX E

TERRITORY OF HAWAII

A PROCLAMATION

WHEREAS, it is provided by Section 67 of the Organic Act of the Territory of Hawaii, approved April 30, 1900, that, whenever it becomes necessary, the Governor of that territory may call upon the commander of the military forces of the United States in that territory to prevent invasion; and

WHEREAS, it is further provided by the said section that the governor may in case of invasion or imminent danger thereof, when the public safety requires it, suspend the privilege of the writ of habeas corpus and place the territory under martial law; and

WHEREAS, the armed forces of the Empire of Japan have this day attacked and invaded the shores of the Hawaiian Islands; and

WHEREAS, it has become necessary to repel such attack and invasion; and

WHEREAS, the public safety requires;

NOW, THEREFORE, I, J. B. POINDEXTER, Governor of the Territory of Hawaii, do hereby announce that, pursuant to said section, I have called upon the Commanding General, Hawaiian Department, to prevent such invasion;

And, pursuant to the same section, I do hereby suspend the privilege of the writ of habeas corpus until further notice;

And, pursuant to the same section, I do hereby place the said territory under martial law;

And I do hereby authorize and request the Commanding General, Hawaiian Department, during the present emergency and until the danger of invasion is removed, to exercise all the powers normally exercised by me as Governor;

And I do further authorize and request the said Commanding General, Hawaiian Department, and those subordinate military personnel to whom he may delegate such authority, during the present emergency and until the danger of invasion is removed, to exercise the powers normally exercised by judicial officers and employees of this territory and of the counties and cities therein, and such other and further powers as the emergency may require;

And I do require all good citizens of the United States and all other persons within the Territory of Hawaii to obey promptly and fully, in letter and in spirit, such proclamations, rules, regulations and orders, as the Commanding General, Hawaiian Department, or his subordinates, may issue during the present emergency.

IN WITNESS WHEREOF, I have hereunto set my hand and caused the seal of the Territory of Hawaii to be affixed.

DONE at Honolulu, Territory of Hawaii, this 7th day of December, 1941.

(SEAL OF THE TERRITORY OF HAWAII)

J. B. POINDEXTER,
Governor of the Territory of Hawaii.

PROCLAMATION

UNITED STATES ARMY

Headquarters Hawaiian Department
Fort Shafter, 7 December 1941.

To the People of Hawaii:

The military and naval forces of the Empire of Japan have attacked and attempted to invade these islands.

Pursuant to section 67 of the Organic Act of the Territory of Hawaii, approved April 30, 1900, the Governor of Hawaii has called upon me, as commander of the military forces of the United States in Hawaii, to prevent such invasion; has suspended the privilege of the writ of habeas corpus; has placed the Territory under martial law; has authorized and requested me and my subordinates to exercise the powers normally exercised by the governor and by subordinate civil officers; and has required all persons within the Territory to obey such proclamations, orders, and regulations as I may issue during the present emergency.

I announce to the people of Hawaii, that, in compliance with the above requests of the Governor of Hawaii, I have this day assumed the position of military governor of Hawaii, and have taken charge of the government of the Territory, of the preservation of order therein, and of putting these islands in a proper state of defense.

All persons within the Territory of Hawaii, whether residents thereof or not, whether citizens of the United States or not, of no matter what race or nationality, are warned that by reason of their presence here they owe during their stay at least a temporary duty of obedience to the United States, and that they are bound to refrain from giving, by word or deed, any aid or comfort to the enemies of the United States. Any violation of this duty is treason, and will be punished by the severest penalties.

The troops under my command, in putting down any disorder or rebellion and in preventing any aid to the invader, will act with such firmness and vigor and will use such arms as the accomplishment of their task may require.

The imminence of attack by the enemy and the possibility of invasion make necessary a stricter control of your actions than would be necessary or proper at other times. I shall therefore shortly publish ordinances governing the conduct of the people of the Territory with respect to the showing of lights, circulation, meetings, censorship, possession of arms, ammunition, and explosives, the sale of intoxicating liquors and other subjects.

In order to assist in repelling the threatened invasion of our island home, good citizens will cheerfully obey this proclamation and the ordinances to be published; others will be required to do so. Offenders will be severely punished by military tribunals or will be held in custody until such time as the civil courts are able to function.

Pending further instructions from this headquarters the Hawaii Defense Act and the Proclamation of the Governor of Hawaii heretofore issued thereunder shall continue in full force and effect.

> Walter C. Short,
> Lieutenant General, U. S. Army
> Commanding.
> Military Governor of Hawaii.

DEC 7 1941

THE PRESIDENT
THE WHITE HOUSE
WASHINGTON DC

I HAVE TODAY DECLARED MARTIAL LAW THROUGHOUT THE TERRITORY OF HAWAII AND HAVE SUSPENDED THE PRIVILEGE OF THE WRIT OF HABEAS CORPUS PERIOD YOUR ATTENTION IS CALLED TO SECTION SIXTY SEVEN OF THE HAWAIIAN ORGANIC ACT FOR YOUR DECISION ON MY ACTION

> POINDEXTER

DEC 9 1941

HONORABLE JOSEPH B POINDEXTER
GOVERNOR TERRITORY OF HAWAII
HONOLULU HAWAII

YOUR TELEGRAM OF DECEMBER SEVENTH RECEIVED AND YOUR ACTION IN SUSPENDING THE WRIT OF HABEAS CORPUS AND PLACING THE TERRITORY OF HAWAII UNDER MARTIAL LAW IN ACCORDANCE WITH USC TITLE 48 SECTION 532 HAS MY APPROVAL

> FRANKLIN D ROOSEVELT

PROCLAMATION

WHEREAS a Proclamation by Joseph B. Poindexter, Governor of the Territory of Hawaii, dated December 7, 1941, reciting that "the armed forces of the Empire of Japan have this day attacked and invaded the shores of the Hawaiian Islands" and that "the public safety requires" the acts set forth in the said Proclamation, declared martial law and authorized and requested the Commanding General, Hawaiian Department, to exercise the powers normally exercised by judicial officers and employees of this Territory and of the counties and cities therein; and

WHEREAS the Commanding General, Hawaiian Department, has since determined that it is no longer impossible for the judicial officers and employees of this Territory and of the counties and cities therein to function, within limits set forth in various orders;

NOW, THEREFORE, I, INGRAM M. STAINBACK, hereby proclaim that after the date of this Proclamation the powers normally exercised by judicial officers and employees of this Territory and of the counties and cities therein shall be exercised by such officers and employees, subject to such limitations and restrictions as may be imposed by military authority. The Proclamation of December 7, 1941, above cited, is amended accordingly.

> IN WITNESS WHEREOF, I have hereunto set my hand and caused the seal of the Territory of Hawaii to be affixed.
>
> DONE at Honolulu, Territory of Hawaii, this 2nd day of September, 1942.

(SEAL)

INGRAM M. STAINBACK
Governor of the Territory of Hawaii

By the Governor of Hawaii

A PROCLAMATION

WHEREAS, the Governor of Hawaii by his proclamation of December 7, 1941, placed the Territory of Hawaii under martial law, in exercise of his powers under section 67 of the Organic Act, which action was confirmed by the President of the United States on December 8, 1941; and

WHEREAS, a state of martial law remains in effect and the privilege of the writ of habeas corpus remains suspended;

NOW, THEREFORE, I, INGRAM M. STAINBACK, Governor of Hawaii, under the authority given by section 67 of the Organic Act, do hereby proclaim:

1. The Governor of Hawaii and the other civilian officers and agencies of the federal, the territorial and the local governments, will resume on the thirtieth day hereafter their respective jurisdictions, functions and powers, according to law, with respect to the following matters, and others necessarily related thereto:

(a) Control of prices
(b) Rationing of commodities among the civilian population
(c) Control of hospitals, medical personnel, and medical supplies
(d) Food production by and distribution of food among the civilian population
(e) Control of rents
(f) Control of transportation and traffic by land, except the movement of troops,

military supplies and equipment, and except that the Commanding General may prescribe rules for the traffic during blackout hours

(g) Public Health, sanitation, and prevention of disease among civilians

(h) Licensing of businesses, regulation of hours of business, and types of forbidden occupations

(i) Judicial proceedings, both criminal and civil, except:

(1) Criminal prosecutions against members of the armed forces. Members of auxiliary armed forces shall be included within the term "armed forces" after induction into the service and also before induction in respect of any act or omission certified by the Commanding General to be in the line of duty.

(2) Civil suits against members of the armed forces, as defined in subparagraph (1), in respect of any act or omission certified by the Commanding General to be in the line of duty.

(3) Criminal prosecutions for violations of military orders.

The Commanding General may waive the above exception with respect to any particular prosecution or suit, or any class of prosecutions or suits, thereby permitting such prosecutions or suits to be tried in the appropriate court of the Territory or in the United States District Court for Hawaii, as the case may be.

(j) Control of imports for civilian consumption and exports by civilians within allotments of tonnage made by the Commanding General

(k) Censorship of mail from civilians in the Territory

(l) Control of liquor and narcotics

(m) Schools and children

(n) The custody of alien property

(o) Collection and disposition of garbage, ashes, and other waste

(p) Banking, currency, and securities, provided that the Commanding General may prescribe the measures to be taken to prevent the enemy from obtaining securities or money or realizing upon them if he should obtain them

(q) Civilian defense activities, except that the Commanding General shall have jurisdiction to prescribe the duties of the Civilian Defense Corps, and to regulate and inspect their training

(r) Control of the supply, employment, hours, wages, and working conditions of labor, except as to (1) employees of the United States under the War Department or the Navy Department, (2) workers employed on construction and other projects under the War Department or the Navy Department, (3) stevedores and other workers employed on docks and dock facilities, and (4) employees of public utilities. It is contemplated that the Commanding General and the Governor of Hawaii by mutual agreement will appoint a joint advisory committee which shall from time to time consult and advise with each of them with reference to labor matters in their respective fields.

2. For the purposes of the defense of the Hawaiian Islands and for their preparation for use as a base for offensive operations, the Commanding General shall continue so far as he deems the military security of the Territory to require, to exercise full jurisdiction over all matters over which he now has jurisdiction except such as are resumed by civil authorities pursuant to paragraph 1 of this proclamation.

3. Whenever the Commanding General, in the light of an existing military emergency or in anticipation of any military emergency, considers it necessary for the security of the islands or their use as a military or naval base, he shall have power, upon a written declaration of the existence or the anticipation of a military emergency, to exercise such of the functions and jurisdictions as are hereby or may hereafter be resumed by the civil authorities, or to issue such additional military orders, after consultation with the Governor of the Territory where civilian rights and the administration of the civilian government are affected, directing such action as in the judgment of the Commanding General may be required for the military security of the Territory.

4. Nothing in this proclamation shall operate to invalidate any conviction, or any application of military orders to persons or activities, or any other action, which occurred or shall occur prior to the thirtieth day hereafter.

5. I call upon all good citizens of the United States and all other persons within the Territory of Hawaii to obey promptly and fully, in letter and spirit, such orders as the

Commanding General may issue under this proclamation and during the continuance of the state of martial law.

DONE at Honolulu, Territory of Hawaii, this 8th day of February, 1943.

(SEAL OF THE TERRITORY OF HAWAII)

INGRAM M. STAINBACK
Governor of Hawaii

PROCLAMATION

U. S. ARMY

Headquarters, Hawaiian Department.
Honolulu, Feb. 8, 1943.

TO THE PEOPLE OF HAWAII:

I, DELOS C. EMMONS, LIEUTENANT GENERAL, UNITED STATES ARMY, as Commanding General, Hawaiian Department, and as Military Governor of Hawaii, do hereby proclaim:

1. Full jurisdiction and authority are hereby relinquished by the Commanding General to the Governor and other officers of the Territory of Hawaii, to the courts of that territory, to the city and county of Honolulu, to other counties, to all other officers of the territory or other persons acting under its authority, to the United States District Court for Hawaii, and to the appropriate officers of the United States, to exercise such powers as may now or hereafter be vested in them respectively by law over the following matters and others necessarily related thereto:

(a) Control of prices

(b) Rationing of commodities among the civilian population

(c) Control of hospitals, medical personnel, and medical supplies

(d) Food production by and distribution of food among the civilian population

(e) Control of rents

(f) Control of transportation and traffic by land, except the movement of troops, military supplies and equipment, and except that the Commanding General may prescribe rules for the traffic during blackout hours

(g) Public health, sanitation, and prevention of disease among civilians

(h) Licensing of businesses, regulation of hours of business, and types of forbidden occupations

(j) Judicial proceedings, both criminal and civil, except:

(1) Criminal prosecutions against members of the armed forces. Members of auxiliary armed forces shall be included within the term "armed forces" after induction into the service and also before induction in respect of any act or omission certified by the Commanding General to be in the line of duty.

(2) Civil suits against members of the armed forces, as defined in subparagraph (1), in respect of any act or omission certified by the Commanding General to be in the line of duty.

(3) Criminal prosecutions for violations of military orders.

The Commanding General may waive the above exception with respect to any particular prosecution or suit, or any class of prosecutions or suits, thereby permitting such prosecutions or suits to be tried in the appropriate court of the territory or in the United States District Court for Hawaii, as the case may be.

(j) Control of imports for civilian consumption and exports by civilians within allotments of tonnage made by the Commanding General

(k) Censorship of mail from civilians in the territory
(l) Control of liquor and narcotics
(m) Schools and children
(n) The custody of alien property
(o) Collection and disposition of garbage, ashes, and other waste
(p) Banking, currency, and securities, provided that the Commanding General may prescribe the measures to be taken to prevent the enemy from obtaining securities or money or realizing upon them if he should obtain them

(q) Civilian defense activities, except that the Commanding General shall have jurisdiction to prescribe the duties of the Civilian Defense Corps, and to regulate and inspect their training

(r) Control of the supply, employment, hours, wages, and working conditions of labor, except as to (1) employees of the United States under the War Department or the Navy Department, (2) workers employed on construction and other projects under the War Department or the Navy Department, (3) stevedores and other workers employed on docks and dock facilities, and (4) employees of public utilities. It is contemplated that the Commanding General and the Governor of Hawaii by mutual agreement will appoint a joint advisory committee, which shall from time to time consult and advise with each of them with reference to labor matters in their respective fields.

2. The Commanding General, Hawaiian Department, is charged with responsibility for the defense of the Hawaiian Islands and for their preparation for use as a base for offensive operations. For such purposes he shall continue, so far as he deems the military security of the territory to require, to exercise full jurisdiction over all matters over which he now has jurisdiction except such as are transferred to civil authorities pursuant to paragraph 1 of this proclamation.

3. Whenever the Commanding General, in the light of an existing military emergency or in anticipation of any military emergency, considers it necessary for the security of the islands or their use as a military or naval base, he shall have power, upon a written declaration of the existence or the anticipation of a military emergency, to resume such of the functions and jurisdictions as are hereby or may hereafter be transferred to the civil authorities, or to issue such additional military orders, after consultation with the Governor of the territory where civilian rights and the administration of the civilian government are affected, directing such action as in the judgment of the Commanding General may be required for the military security of the territory.

4. Neither this proclamation nor the revocation of orders announced in paragraph 5 hereof shall operate to invalidate any conviction, or any application of military orders to persons or activities, or any other action, which occurred prior to the effective date of this proclamation or such revocation.

5. This proclamation shall take effect thirty days after its date. Those parts of all military orders affecting the subjects enumerated in paragraph 1 hereof are hereby revoked effective thirty days after the date hereof.

Delos C. Emmons
Lieutenant General, U. S. Army,
Commanding.
Military Governor of Hawaii.

133

Territory of Hawaii

OFFICE OF THE MILITARY GOVERNOR
Iolani Palace
HONOLULU, T. H.

1 June, 1943.

PROCLAMATION

TO THE PEOPLE OF THE TERRITORY OF HAWAII:

WHEREAS the Governor of the Territory of Hawaii by his proclamation of December 7, 1941, placed the Territory of Hawaii under martial law in the exercise of his powers under Section 67 of the Organic Act of the Territory of Hawaii and called upon Walter C. Short, Lieutenant General, United States Army, The Commanding General, Hawaiian Department, as commander of the military forces of the United States in said Territory of Hawaii, to prevent invasion thereof; and whereas on said date the said Walter C. Short, Lieutenant General, United States Army, The Commanding General, Hawaiian Department, assumed the position of Military Governor of the Territory of Hawaii; and,

WHEREAS the said Walter C. Short, Lieutenant General, United States Army, on December 17, 1941, relinquished command of the Hawaiian Department and his position as Military Governor of the Territory of Hawaii; and,

WHEREAS I, Delos C. Emmons, Lieutenant General, United States Army, thereafter on said December 17, 1941, assumed command of the Hawaiian Department in accordance with War Department orders and thereafter on said date assumed the position of Military Governor of the Territory of Hawaii; and,

WHEREAS I have this day relinquished command of the Hawaiian Department in accordance with War Department orders;

NOW, THEREFORE, I, Delos C. Emmons, Lieutenant General, United States Army, hereby do relinquish my position as Military Governor of the Territory of Hawaii.

DELOS C. EMMONS,
Lieutenant General, United States Army,
Military Governor of the Territory of Hawaii.

---

1 June, 1943.

PROCLAMATION

TO THE PEOPLE OF THE TERRITORY OF HAWAII:

WHEREAS the Governor of the Territory of Hawaii by his proclamation of December 7, 1941, placed the Territory of Hawaii under martial law in the exercise of his powers under Section 67 of the Organic Act of the Territory of Hawaii and called upon Walter C. Short, Lieutenant General, United States Army, The Commanding General, Hawaiian Department, as commander of the military forces of the United States in said Territory of Hawaii, to prevent invasion thereof; and whereas on said date the said Walter C. Short, Lieutenant General, United States Army, The Commanding General, Hawaiian Department, assumed the position of Military Governor of the Territory of Hawaii; and,

WHEREAS the said Walter C. Short, Lieutenant General, United States Army, on December 17, 1941, relinquished command of the Hawaiian Department and his position as Military Governor of the Territory of Hawaii; and,

WHEREAS, Delos C. Emmons, Lieutenant General, United States Army. thereafter on said December 17, 1941, assumed command of the Hawaiian Department in accordance with War Department orders and thereafter on said date assumed the position of Military Governor of the Territory of Hawaii; and,

WHEREAS the said Delos C. Emmons, Lieutenant General, United States Army, on this June 1, 1943, has relinquished command of the Hawaiian Department in accordance with War Department orders and has relinquished his position as Military Governor of the Territory of Hawaii; and,

WHEREAS, I, Robert C. Richardson, jr, Lieutenant General, United States Army, have on this date assumed command of the Hawaiian Department in accordance with War Department orders; and,

WHEREAS a state of martial law remains in effect within the Territory of Hawaii and the privilege of the writ of habeas corpus remains suspended therein;

NOW, THEREFORE, I, Robert C. Richardson. jr., Lieutenant General, United States Army, and The Commanding General, Hawaiian Department, by virtue of the premises aforesaid, on this day hereby assume the position of Military Governor of the Territory of Hawaii, and, as such Military Governor of the Territory of Hawaii, I hereby assume all the powers and duties held, possessed, assumed, imposed upon, and exercised by the said Delos C. Emmons, Lieutenant General, United States Army, as Military Governor of the Territory of Hawaii, at the time that he, as aforesaid, relinquished the command of the Hawaiian Department and the said position of Military Governor of the Territory of Hawaii; and I, as Military Governor of the Territory of Hawaii, hereby adopt and ratify the existing orders issued by the said Delos C. Emmons, Lieutenant General, United States Army, as Military Governor as aforesaid.

ROBERT C. RICHARDSON, JR.,
Lieutenant General, United States Army,
Commanding General, Hawaiian Department,
Military Governor of the Territory of Hawaii.

EXECUTIVE ORDER No. 9489

AUTHORIZING AND DIRECTING THE SECRETARY OF WAR TO DESIGNATE A MILITARY COMMANDER FOR THE TERRITORY OF HAWAII AND AUTHORIZING THE MILITARY COMMANDER TO PRESCRIBE SAID TERRITORY, OR ANY PART THEREOF, AS A MILITARY AREA, AND FOR OTHER PURPOSES

WHEREAS the defense of the Territory of Hawaii and the successful prosecutuion of the war require every possible protection against espionage and sabotage, the maintenance of internal security, and the efficient utilization of available facilities in that territory:

NOW, THEREFORE, by virtue of the authority vested in me by the Constitution, the laws of the United States, including the act of March 21, 1942, c. 191, 56 Stat. 173 (18 U. S. C. 97a), and Title III of the Second War Powers Act, 1942, and as Commander in Chief of the Army and Navy and as President of the United States, I order as follows:

1. I hereby authorize and direct the Secretary of War to designate the Commanding General, United States Army Forces, Pacific Ocean Areas, as the military commander within the meaning of the act of March 21, 1942. The military commander may prescribe the Territory of Hawaii or any part thereof as a military area, from which any and all persons may be excluded and with respect to which the right of any person to enter, remain in, or leave shall be subject to whatever restrictions or orders the said military commander may impose as hereinafter authorized.

2. In the military area prescribed under the authority of this order, the military commander may, whenever military necessity therefor exists and the military commander so finds:

    a. Establish blackout and curfew periods and restrict and regulate the actions of all persons during such period.

    b. Establish air raid precautions.

    c. Regulate the conduct of enemy aliens.

    d. Evacuate or exclude, and detain incident thereto, any or all persons from the military area or from any part thereof, whenever the evacuation or exclusion, or the detention incident thereto, is necessary to prevent espionage or sabotage, and the military commander so finds.

    e. Regulate or prohibit possession or use of firearms or other weapons.

    f. Define, for the purposes of this order, what shall constitute military service with the armed forces of nations other than the United States and require all persons who have had such military service with the armed forces of nations other than the United States to register such military service.

    g. Issue regulations to assure adequate protection of the following: ports and harbors, dockage and stevedoring, barges, tugs and floating equipment, transportation of ship cargoes and passengers, and disposition of all cargoes until removed from dock areas at docks and wharves.

    h. Regulate, restrict, or prohibit travel within, into, or from the military area whenever such regulation, restriction, or prohibition is necessary for military security, and the military commander so finds.

    i. Whenever necessary to prevent espionage or sabotage, and the military commander so finds, regulate the publication of any newspapers and periodicals that are published in a foreign language or in dual languages, regulate, restrict, or prohibit the possession or use of radio transmission sets or the transmission of information (by any means other than newspapers) between the military area and points outside of the said area, and between the islands within the said military area.

3. Whenever the military commander finds it to be in the interests of national defense and the successful prosecution of the war, he may, to the extent that he deems it necessary to carry out the purposes of this order, perform the functions and exercise power and authority conferred on the President by Title III of the Second War Powers Act, 1942 (50 U. S. C., app. 633) insofar as they relate to priorities and allocation of the following in the Territory of Hawaii: Ports and harbors, dockage and stevedoring, barges, tugs, floating equipment and all travel facilities; and fixing of over-all quotas to vessels of all commercial cargo.

4. Nothing in this order shall be construed to modify or revoke any of the provisions of Executive Order No. 9066, dated February 19, 1942. Any designation of the military commander and of the Territory of Hawaii or any part thereof as a military area under paragraph 1 hereof shall constitute designation of such military commander as the military commander, and of such Territory or such part thereof as a military area for the purposes of the said Executive Order No. 9066, and shall vest the military commander with the powers provided in that order.

5. Unless sooner terminated, the authority herein conferred shall expire thirty days after the cessation of hostilities between the Empire of Japan and the United States.

6. All prior Executive orders, insofar as they are in conflict herewith, are amended accordingly.

7. This order shall become effective on October 24th, 1944.

FRANKLIN D. ROOSEVELT

THE WHITE HOUSE,
    October 18, 1944.

PROCLAMATION 2627

TERMINATION OF MARTIAL LAW IN THE TERRITORY OF HAWAII

BY THE PRESIDENT OF THE UNITED STATES OF AMERICA—A PROCLAMATION

WHEREAS the armed forces of the Empire of Japan having attacked and invaded the Territory of Hawaii, and the public safety requiring it, the Governor of the Territory of Hawaii, acting under the authority vested in him by section 67 of the act of April 30, 1900, 31 Stat. 153 (48 U. S. C. 532), did, by proclamation dated December 7, 1941, suspend the privilege of the writ of habeas corpus and did place the said Territory under martial law until communication could be had with the President and his decision thereon made known; and

WHEREAS communication was had with the President and his decision approving the said action of the Governor of the Territory of Hawaii was made known to the Governor on December 9, 1941; and

WHEREAS the public safety no longer requires that the privilege of the writ of habeas corpus remain suspended or that martial law continue in the said Territory:

NOW, THEREFORE, I, FRANKLIN D. ROOSEVELT, President of the United States of America, acting under and by virtue of the authority vested in me by the said act of April 30, 1900, do proclaim that the privilege of the writ of habeas corpus is hereby restored and that martial law is hereby terminated in the Territory of Hawaii, and I do hereby direct the Governor of the Territory of Hawaii so to proclaim to the people of the Territory of Hawaii.

This Proclamation shall become effective October 24, 1944.

IN WITNESS WHEREOF, I have hereunto set my hand and caused the seal of the United States of America to be affixed.

DONE at the City of Washington this 19th day of October in the year of our Lord nineteen hundred and forty-four, and of the Independence of the United States of America the one hundred and sixty-ninth.

FRANKLIN D. ROOSEVELT

By the President:
CORDELL HULL,
Secretary of State.

BY THE GOVERNOR OF HAWAII—A PROCLAMATION

WHEREAS the Governor of Hawaii by proclamation of December 7, 1941, in the exercise of his powers under Section 67 of the act of April 30, 1900, 31 Stat. 153 (48 U. S. C. 532), suspended the privilege of the writ of habeas corpus and placed the Territory of Hawaii under martial law, which action was approved by the President of the United States of America on December 9, 1941; and

WHEREAS by proclamation dated October 18, 1944, the President of the United States of America makes known that the public safety no longer requires that the privilege of the writ of habeas corpus remain suspended or that martial law continue in the Territory of Hawaii, and proclaims that the privilege of the writ of habeas corpus is restored and that martial law is terminated in the Territory of Hawaii:

NOW, THEREFORE, I, Ingram M. Stainback, Governor of Hawaii, do hereby proclaim to the people of the Territory of Hawaii that the privilege of the writ of habeas corpus is restored and that martial law is terminated throughout the Territory of Hawaii.

DONE at Iolani Palace, Honolulu, Territory of Hawaii, this 24th day of October, 1944.

INGRAM M. STAINBACK.

WAR DEPARTMENT,
WASHINGTON, D. C., 24 October 1944.
Lieutenant General ROBERT C. RICHARDSON, Jr.,
Commanding General, United States
Army Forces, Pacific Ocean Areas.

DEAR GENERAL RICHARDSON: In accordance with the authority conferred on me by Executive Order No. 9489, dated October 18, 1944, issued pursuant to the provisions of the Act of Congress approved March 21, 1942 (Ch. 191, 56 Stat. 173, 18 U. S. C., Sec. 97a), I hereby designate you as the Military Commander of the Territory of Hawaii, with full power to prescribe the Territory of Hawaii or any part thereof a military area within the meaning of the Act of Congress and the Executive Order above referred to, and to exercise therein any and all of the powers conferred by that Act and the said Executive Order.

Sincerely yours,
(S) HENRY L. STIMSON,
Secretary of War.

PUBLIC PROCLAMATION NUMBER ONE

24 OCTOBER 1944.
To: The People Within The Territory of Hawaii, And To The Public Generally:

WHEREAS, national-defense material, national-defense premises, and national-defense utilities, as defined by Section 4, Act of April 20, 1918, Chapter 59, 40 Stat. 533, as amended by the Act of November 30, 1940, Chapter 926, 54 Stat. 1220, and the Act of August 21, 1941, Chapter 388, 55 Stat. 655 (USC, Title 50, Section 104), are located within the Territory of Hawaii, are subject to attack by the armed forces of the Empire of Japan with which the United States is at war and are subject to espionage and acts of sabotage; and,

WHEREAS, by Executive Order No. 9489 dated October 18, 1944, the President of the United States authorized and directed the Secretary of War to designate The Commanding General, United States Army Forces, Pacific Ocean Areas, as the Military Commander within the meaning of the Act of March 21, 1942, Chapter 191, 56 Stat. 173, USC, Title 18, Section 97a, and provided that the said Military Commander may prescribe the Territory of Hawaii or any part thereof as a military area within the meaning of the said Act from which any and all persons may be excluded and with respect to which the right of any person to enter, to remain in or leave shall be subject to whatever restrictions or orders the said Military Commander may impose as authorized in said Executive Order; and,

WHEREAS, the Secretary of War on 24 October 1944 designated the undersigned, The Commanding General, United States Army Forces, Pacific Ocean Areas, as the Military Commander to carry out the functions, duties and powers imposed by the said Executive Order; and,

WHEREAS, in order to secure every possible protection for said national-defense material, national-defense premises, and national-defense utilities against espionage and sabotage, to secure the maintenance of military and internal security, the efficient utilization of available facilities in the Territory of Hawaii, and to successfully prosecute the war, it is required by military necessity that the Territory of Hawaii be prescribed a military area within the meaning of the said Executive Order and the said Act of March 21, 1942, Chapter 191, 56 Stat. 173, USC, Title 18, Section 97a, and that the security orders hereinafter set forth be issued and made applicable to the said military area prescribed herein:

NOW, THEREFORE, I, ROBERT C. RICHARDSON, JR., Lieutenant General, United States Army, by virtue of the authority vested in me by the President of the United States and by the Secretary of War and my powers and prerogatives as Commanding General, Pacific Ocean Areas, do hereby declare and proclaim that:

1. The present situation requires as a matter of military necessity the establishment of the Territory of Hawaii as a military area, and, based upon the findings above set forth and for

the purposes aforesaid, I hereby prescribe the Territory of Hawaii as a military area to be designated and known as the Territory of Hawaii Military Area.

2. The right of any person to enter, remain in, or leave the Territory of Hawaii Military Area or any part thereof designated hereafter in this Proclamation or any subsequent Proclamation shall be subject to the provisions of this Proclamation No. 1 and Security Orders Nos. 1 to 7 inclusive as hereinafter set forth which are hereby promulgated and declared effective from the date of this Proclamation, and shall be further subject to the provisions of any subsequent Proclamations, restrictions, orders, rules, regulations, or instructions which may hereafter be promulgated by undersigned Military Commander.

In addition thereto, any person who fails to comply with or violates any provisions of any Proclamations, restrictions, orders, rules, regulations or instructions issued or adopted by the undersigned Military Commander, Territory of Hawaii Military Area, pursuant to the authority cited in the preamble of this Proclamation, applicable to the whole or any part of the Territory of Hawaii Military Area, including any district, or restricted area thereof, is subject to the penalties provided by Public Law No. 503 of the 77th Congress approved March 21, 1942, entitled "An Act to Provide a Penalty for Violation of Restrictions or Orders with respect to persons entering, remaining in, leaving, or committing any act in Military Areas or Zones," providing therein a fine of not to exceed $5,000.00, or to imprisonment for not more than one year, or both, for each offense.

If two or more persons conspire to violate Public Law No. 503 and one or more do any act to effect the object of such conspiracy, each of the parties will be subject to the penalties provided by Title 18, Section 88, United States Code.

Whoever shall knowingly and willfully falsify or conceal or cover up by any trick, scheme, or device a material fact, or make or cause to be made any false or fraudulent statements or representations in any matter within the jurisdiction of the Military Commander of the Territory of Hawaii Military Area shall be subject to the penalties provided by Title 18, Section 80, United States Code.

In the case of an alien enemy, such persons will in addition be subject to immediate apprehension and internment.

3. Any or all persons will be ordered excluded or evacuated from the Territory of Hawaii Military Area or from any part thereof by the undersigned Military Commander whenever such evacuation or exclusion is necessary to prevent espionage or sabotage. Incident to such exclusion or evacuation such persons will be subject to detention. No person who has been ordered excluded or evacuated from the Territory of Hawaii Military Area or from any part thereof by the undersigned Military Commander, in accordance with the provisions of this paragraph, shall enter, or remain in the Territory of Hawaii Military Area or in such part thereof.

4. Nothing contained herein shall be construed as limiting or modifying the rights, powers, duties and responsibilities of the undersigned Military Commander as Commanding General, Pacific Ocean Areas, to prescribe regulations for the conduct and control of alien enemies, and the apprehension and internment of such alien enemies as are subject to apprehension and internment in the judgment of the undersigned Military Commander as Commanding General, Pacific Ocean Areas, duly authorized by the Secretary of War and pursuant to the Proclamations of the President of the United States dated December 7, 1941 and December 8, 1941.

5. It shall be the duty of every person found within the Territory of Hawaii Military Area or any part thereof, to familiarize himself with the terms of this Proclamation and the restrictions, orders, rules, regulations and instructions hereinafter contained and which may hereafter be issued and promulgated by the undersigned Military Commander.

6. The Executive of the Military Commander, Territory of Hawaii Military Area, is hereby designated, authorized and empowered to issue the orders of the Military Commander relative to all matters relating or pertaining to functions, powers, duties and responsibilities of the said Military Commander under Executive Order No. 9489, dated October 18, 1944.

7. Unless otherwise clearly indicated in the Proclamation, restriction, order, rule, regulation or instruction in which used, the term "person" as used in any Proclamations, restrictions, orders, rules, regulations or instructions of the undersigned Military Commander shall include and hereby is defined to mean, any natural person or persons, firms, associations, trusts, corporation or corporations, or any agent, servant, employee, or representative of any of the foregoing.

ROBERT C. RICHARDSON, Jr.,
Lieutenant General, United States Army; Commanding General, United States Army Forces, Pacific Ocean Areas; Military Commander, Territory of Hawaii Military Area.

TERRITORY OF HAWAII
OFFICE OF THE MILITARY GOVERNOR
FORT SHAFTER, T.H.

11 December 1941

GENERAL ORDERS)
NO. 1)   CORRECTED COPY
           (Destroy all previous copies)

By virtue of the power vested in me as Military Governor,
I hereby appoint the following persons:

Governor J. B. Poindexter.
Mr. Charles M. Hite.
Major Lester Petrie.
Mr. Charles F. Hemenway.
Mr. Frank E. Locey.
Acting Attorney General Ernest K. Kai.

as an Advisory Committee to the Military Governor:

By order of the Military Governor

(Signed) Thomas H. Green
THOMAS H. GREEN,
Lt. Col., J.A.G.D.,
Executive.

A TRUE COPY:

James F. Hanley

JAMES F. HANLEY,
Major, J.A.G.D.

TERRITORY OF HAWAII
OFFICE OF THE MILITARY GOVERNOR
FORT SHAFTER, T.H.

7 December 1941

GENERAL ORDERS)
NO. 3)

1. By virtue of the power vested in me as Military Governor, a
Military Commission is appointed to meet at Honolulu, Territory of Hawaii,
to meet at the call of the president thereof, for the trial of such persons
as may be properly brought before it.

James L. Coke, President and Law Member
Alva E. Steadman
Lieutenant Colonel E. F. Ely, F. D.
Lieutenant Colonel Hyatt F. Newell, I. G. D.
Lieutenant Colonel V. J. Allen, A. G. D.
Angus Taylor, Trial Judge Advocate
Major R. M. Coppin, A. G. D., Defense Counsel

2. By virtue of the power vested in me as Military Governor, Major
Henry Du Proo, A.G.D., is appointed as a Provost Court to meet at Schofield
Barracks, Territory of Hawaii, for the trial of such persons as may be
properly brought before it.

3. By virtue of the power vested in me as Military Governor,
Lieutenant Colonel Neal D. Franklin, J.A.G.D., is appointed as a Provost
Court to meet at Honolulu, Territory of Hawaii, for the trial of such persons
as may be properly brought before it.

By order of the Military Governor.

(Signed) Thomas H. Green

THOMAS H. GREEN
Lt. Col, J.A.G.D.
Executive

A TRUE COPY:

(s) James F. Hanley
Major, J.A.G.D.

TERRITORY OF HAWAII
OFFICE OF THE MILITARY GOVERNOR
FORT SHAFTER, T. H.

7 December 1941

GENERAL ORDERS)
NO. 2)

1. All saloons will close immediately.

2. All dealers in intoxicating liquor, wine o.
beer will immediately stop sale or disposition thereof,
either by drink or in any other quantity.

3. This order will remain in force until further
notice.

By order of the Military Governor.

(Signed) Thomas H. Green
THOMAS H. GREEN

Lieutenant Colonel, J.A.G.D.
Executive Officer

A TRUE COPY:

(s) JAMES F. HANLEY
Major, J.A.G.D.

TERRITORY OF HAWAII
OFFICE OF THE MILITARY GOVERNOR
FORT SHAFTER, T.H.

7 December 1941

GENERAL ORDERS)
No. 4)

By virtue of the power vested in me as Military Governor, the following
policy governing the trial of civilians by Military Commission and Provost
Courts is announced for the information and guidance of all concerned:

1. Military commissions and provost courts shall have power to try
and determine any case involving an offense committed against the
laws of the United States, the laws of the Territory of Hawaii or
the rules, regulations, orders or policies of the military
authorities. The jurisdiction thus given does not include the
right to try commissioned and enlisted personnel of the United
States Army and Navy. Such persons shall be turned over to their
respective services for disposition.

2. Military commissions and provost courts will adjudge sentences
commensurate with the offense committed. Ordinarily, the sentence
will not exceed the limit of punishment prescribed for similar
offenses by the laws of the United States or the Territory of Hawaii.
However, the courts may adjudge an appropriate sentence.

3. The record of trial in cases before military commissions will be
substantially similar to that required in a special court-martial.
The record of trial in cases before provost courts will be substantially similar to that in the case of a Summary Court-Martial.

4. The procedure in trials before military commissions and provost
courts will follow, so far as it is applicable, the procedure
required for Special and Summary Courts-Martial respectively.

5. The records of trial in all cases will be forwarded to the
Department Judge Advocate. The sentences adjudged by provost
courts shall become effective immediately. The sentence adjudged
by a military commission shall not become effective until it shall
have been approved by the Military Governor.

6. All charges against civilian prisoners shall be preferred by the
Department Provost Marshall or one of his assistants.

7. The Provost Marshall is responsible for the prompt trial of all
civilian prisoners and for carrying out the sentence adjudged by
the court.

138

8. Charges involving all major offenses shall be referred to a military commission for trial. Other cases of lesser degree shall be referred to provost courts. The maximum punishment which a provost court may adjudge is confinement for a period of five years, and a fine of not to exceed $5,000. Military commissions may adjudge punishment commensurate with the offense committed and may adjudge the death penalty in appropriate cases.

9. In adjudging sentences, provost courts and military commissions will be guided by, but not limited to the penalties authorized by the courts-martial manual, the laws of the United States, the Territory of Hawaii, the District of Columbia, and the customs of laws in like cases.

By order of the Military Governor:

(Signed) Thomas H. Green
THOMAS H. GREEN
Lt. Col, J.A.G.D.
Executive Officer

A TRUE COPY:

(s) James F. Hanley,
Major, J.A.G.D.

TERRITORY OF HAWAII
OFFICE OF THE MILITARY GOVERNOR
FORT SHAFTER, T. H.

8 December 1941

GENERAL ORDERS)
NO. 7)

1. The office of the Military Governor has been established in the office of the Department Judge Advocate, Headquarters Hawaiian Department, (Building No. 18, Fort Shafter, T.H.) Telephone 8531, local 217.

2. There has been established in the office of the Attorney General, Territory of Hawaii (second floor, Iolani Palace) a branch of the Office of the Military Governor. Telephone Honolulu 6321.

3. All civilians having business with the Military Governor will communicate with him through the Executive to the Military Governor at the Iolani Palace.

By order of the Military Governor.

(Signed) Thomas H. Green
THOMAS H. GREEN
Lt. Col., J.A.G.D.
Executive.

A TRUE COPY:

(Signed) JAMES F. HANLEY
Major, J.A.G.D.

TERRITORY OF HAWAII
OFFICE OF THE MILITARY GOVERNOR
Fort Shafter, T.H.

GENERAL ORDERS)
NO. 6)

8 December 1941

By virtue of the authority vested in me as Military Governor of the Territory of Hawaii, all schools, public and private, on all the islands in the Territory, will be closed until further notice.

By order of the Military Governor:

(Signed) THOMAS H. GREEN,
Lt. Col., J.A.G.D.,
Executive.

OFFICIAL COPY
HEADQUARTERS HAWAIIAN DEPARTMENT · FORT SHAFTER T.H.

For the information of the Staff
Office of Civilian Defense

TERRITORY OF HAWAII
OFFICE OF THE MILITARY GOVERNOR
FORT SHAFTER, T. H.

10 December 1941.

GENERAL ORDERS)
No. 14)

PRESS, RADIO CENSORSHIP

By virtue of the authority vested in me as Military Governor, I hereby order and prohibit, effective at 8:00 A. M. December 12, 1941, the publication, printing, or circulation of all newspapers, magazines, periodicals, the dissemination of news or information by means of any unauthorized printed matter, or by wireless, radio, or press association, except as follows:

1. Newspapers. Until further notice the following newspapers may, if they so desire, continue to be published and circulated under such conditions and regulations as shall be prescribed from time to time by the Military Governor:

NEWSPAPER	LOCATION
Honolulu Star-Bulletin	Oahu
Honolulu Advertiser	Oahu
Hilo Tribune-Herald	Hawaii
Hawaii Press	Hawaii
Maui News	Maui
Garden Island	Kauai

2. Radio Stations. Until further notice the following radio stations may, if they so desire, continue to broadcast under such conditions and regulations as shall be prescribed from time to time by the Military Governor:

RADIO STATION	LOCATION
KGU	Oahu
KGMB	Oahu
KTOH	Kauai
KHBC	Hawaii

3. Press Associations. Until further notice the following press associations may continue to operate under such conditions and regulations as shall be prescribed from time to time by the Military Governor:

PRESS ASSOCIATIONS
Associated Press
United Press
International News Service
Transradio Press

By order of the Military Governor:

(Signed) THOMAS H. GREEN,
Lt. Col., J.A.G.D.,
Executive.

A TRUE COPY:
W.R.C. MORRISON,
Major, J.A.G.D.

TERRITORY OF HAWAII
OFFICE OF THE MILITARY GOVERNOR
FORT SHAFTER, T.H.

11 December 1941

GENERAL ORDERS)
NO.   17   )

    Judge Ingram M. Stainback is announced as
legal advisor to the Military Governor, Territory of
Hawaii.

    By order of the Military Governor:

                (signed) Thomas H. Green
                THOMAS H. GREEN,
                Lt. Col. J.A.G.D.,
                Executive

A TRUE COPY:

William R C Morrison
WILLIAM R. C. MORRISON
Major, J. A. G. D.

TERRITORY OF HAWAII
OFFICE OF THE MILITARY GOVERNOR
FORT SHAFTER, T.H.

14 December 1941

GENERAL ORDERS)
NO.   24   )

    By virtue of the authority vested in me as Military
Governor of the Territory of Hawaii, the following is published for the information and guidance of all concerned:

    1. All organizations, retail stores, physicians,
dentists, and veterinarians, desiring to purchase medical
supplies will submit a list in triplicate to the office of
Controller of Civilian Medical Supply at the Hawaiian Medical
Depot, Fort Shafter, T.H., before 10:00 A.M. daily for
supplies they desire delivered on the following day. This
list will show all items desired and amount of each item
with the name of the wholesaler from whom the merchandise
is to be purchased. Official permission is NOT required for
individuals making normal purchases at retail stores for
family or personal use. For example: a few aspirin tablets,
a spool of adhesive tape, etc.

    2. After processing, requisitions will be forwarded
direct to the wholesaler designated.

    3. After filling orders as approved by the Controller,
the wholesaler will complete the triplicate copy to show
amount actually delivered and return it to the controller.

    4. If purchases from more than one wholesaler are to
be made on any one day, a separate order will be prepared
for EACH wholesaler. In order to speed up the processing,
the following will be grouped on separate sheets:

        Patent Medicines
        Spiritus liquor for medicinal use
        Narcotics
        Poisons - all types

    5. The sale of the following products to retail stores
is absolutely prohibited unless specific clearance is given
by the Controller each instance:

TERRITORY OF HAWAII
OFFICE OF THE MILITARY GOVERNOR
FORT SHAFTER, T.H.

13 December 1941.

GENERAL ORDERS)
No. . . . . 21)

    By virtue of the power vested in me as Military
Governor, Territory of Hawaii, the following directive is
published, effective this date:

    1. Section 9 of Ordinance 941 of the City and County
of Honolulu, T.H., is hereby suspended until further notice.

    2. The Rent Control Commission created under authority
of Ordinance No. 941 is hereby empowered, subject to approval
of the Provost Marshal in each case, to issue writs of possession to any Sheriff or Police Officer to remove persons from
housing accommodations under the following conditions:

    (a) For committing a nuisance or using the housing
accommodations for immoral or illegal purposes.

    (b) For non-payment of rent, unless the inability
of tenant to pay the rent is caused by emergency conditions beyond his control.

    By Order of the Military Governor:

            (Signed) Thomas H. Green
              THOMAS H. GREEN
              Lt. Col., J.A.G.D.,
              Executive.

A TRUE COPY:

James F. Hanley
JAMES F. HANLEY
Major, J.A.G.D.

(GO No. 24 OMG, 1941)

        1. All products containing Vitamin A
        2. Benzedrine in any form
        3. Sulfonamide derivatives
        4. Biological products
        5. Suprarenal products (Adrenalin, Etc.)
        6. Poisons in any form
        7. Spiritus liquor for medicinal use
        8. Narcotics
        9. Herbiturates and similar products

    6. The retail sale of drugs previously controlled
by Territorial Law, which required a doctor's prescription,
will continue to be dispensed as before.

    7. Wholesalers will report in writing to the Controller
by 10:00 A.M. daily all medical supplies received by them
during the previous 24 hours.

    By order of the Military Governor:

            (signed) Thomas H. Green
              THOMAS H. GREEN,
              Lt. Col., J.A.G.D.,
              Executive.

A TRUE COPY:

James F. Hanley
JAMES F. HANLEY,
Major, J.A.G.D.

TERRITORY OF HAWAII
OFFICE OF THE MILITARY GOVERNOR
FORT SHAFTER, T. H.

14 December 1941

GENERAL ORDERS)
NO. 25   )

1. Paragraph 1, General Orders No. 3, Office of the Military Governor, Fort Shafter, T. H., dated 7 December 1941, is revoked.

2. A Military Commission is hereby appointed to meet at Honolulu, Territory of Hawaii, at 9:00 AM, 17 December 1941, or as soon thereafter as practicable, for the trial of such persons as may be properly brought before it:

Major General James A. Woodruff, U. S. A.,
    President and Law Member.
Colonel John S. Pratt, C. A. C.
Lieutenant Colonel Leighton N. Smith, F. D.
Lieutenant Colonel Virgil G. Allen, Inf.,
Lieutenant Colonel Hyatt F. Newell, Inf.,
Major Ray O. Welch, Q. M. C.
Lieutenant Colonel Neal D. Franklin, J. A. G. D.,
    Trial Judge Advocate.
Major Harrison M. Coppin, A. G. D.,
    Defense Counsel.

By Order of the Military Governor:

                    Thomas H. Green,
        (sgd)   THOMAS H. GREEN,
                    Lt. Col., J. A. G. D.,
                    Executive

A TRUE COPY:
    James F. Hanley
    JAMES F. HANLEY,
    Major, J.A.G.D.

TERRITORY OF HAWAII
OFFICE OF THE MILITARY GOVERNOR
FORT SHAFTER, T. H.

15 December 1941

GENERAL ORDERS)
NO. 28   )

By virtue of the authority vested in me as Military Governor of the Territory of Hawaii, I do authorize the Governor of the Territory of Hawaii to continue to call out the territorial militia and place so much of it in the active service of the Territory as may be determined and selected by the Adjutant General of the Territory of Hawaii.

Further, I do authorize the Governor of the Territory of Hawaii, and said Adjutant General to continue to organize and constitute a Territorial Home Guard from such of the Militia as may volunteer for service and enlist therein, and immediately upon the organization of the Territorial Home Guard, or any unit thereof, to place it in the active service of the Territory.

By order of the Military Governor:

                    (signed) Thomas H. Green,
                    THOMAS H. GREEN,
                    Lt. Col., J.A.G.D.
                    Executive.

A TRUE COPY:
    James F. Hanley
    JAMES F. HANLEY,
    Major, J.A.G.D.

TERRITORY OF HAWAII
OFFICE OF THE MILITARY GOVERNOR
FORT SHAFTER, T. H.

GENERAL ORDERS)
NO. 29   )   16 December 1941.

WHEREAS, pursuant to the proclamation of Martial Law in the Territory of Hawaii the operation of the civil courts in the Territory of Hawaii has been suspended,

NOW, THEREFORE, by virtue of the authority vested in me as Military Governor, and for the purpose of more effectively carrying out the duties of such Military Governor, IT IS HEREBY ORDERED that all courts in the Territory of Hawaii are hereby authorized to exercise the following powers normally exercised by them during the existence of civil government:

1. The United States District Court for the Territory of Hawaii is hereby authorized to receive and file all petitions for the condemnation of land in the Territory of Hawaii, under any statutes and laws of the United States authorizing condemnation, needed by the Army or Navy of the United States; to receive and file deposits of checks into the Registry of said court, certificates of the clerk of said court and the Declarations of Taking; to make and enter orders on the Declaration of Taking, and orders of Immediate Possession; and to file and enter notices of pendency of action, with reference to such condemnations.

2. The Supreme Court of the Territory of Hawaii may make and enter all orders necessary for the preservation of the rights of litigants in all pending appeals or appeals which may be perfected to said court, and may hear and determine all such appeals, and make such further orders as may be necessary to carry out or enforce said orders, or any of them.

3. The circuit courts of the Territory of Hawaii and the several divisions thereof are hereby authorized to exercise the following of their normal powers under the civil laws applicable thereto:

PROBATE: To hear and determine all probate matters, provided, however, that no contested matter may be heard or entertained save by consent of the parties and which does not involve the subpoenaing of witnesses.

G.O. 29, O.M.G., 1941.

EQUITY: To hear and determine all matters involving trusts, trust accounts, bills of instructions and similar matters, provided, however, that no writs of habeas corpus, prohibition, mandamus, injunction or specific performance shall be issued or granted by any circuit judge, and further provided that no matter shall be heard or entertained which involves the subpoenaing of witnesses.

ACTIONS AT LAW: To hear and determine all pending matters not involving jury trials where the subpoenaing of witnesses is not required; to hear and determine all appeals heretofore or hereafter perfected for the district courts; to make and enter all orders or judgments necessary to facilitate the immediate taking of land under condemnation proceedings by the Territorial, City and County, or county officers, orders of possession and details required therewith which do not involve the subpoenaing of witnesses or compulsory process.

DIVISION OF DOMESTIC RELATIONS AND JUVENILE COURT: To hear and determine all matters either pending or to be brought for the support and maintenance of women and minor children or other dependents; to hear and determine all probate, guardianship and adoption matters as are exclusively under the jurisdiction of the Division of Domestic Relations; to hear all matters properly coming before the Juvenile Court.

CRIMINAL CASES ON APPEAL: To hear and determine all pending appeals in criminal cases to the circuit courts of the Territory from district magistrates which do not involve jury trials.

LAND COURT: To hear and determine all pending matters not requiring the subpoenaing of witnesses; all formal matters connected with subdivisions; all normal minor petitions for the purpose of notation of marriage, death, divorce and other matters required to be noted on transfer certificates of title; proceedings for substitution of lost certificates of title; recording of conveyances; issuance of transfer certificates of title; notations of encumbrances; ex parte petitions not involving the subpoenaing of witnesses; and the maintaining of the Office of the Registrar of the Land Court for the purpose of facilitating searching of records and certificates of transfers.

DISTRICT COURTS: Finish all pending matters where the subpoenaing of witnesses is not required:

-2-

G.O. 29, O.M.G., 1941.

ALL COURTS: All courts authorized under the civil law to do so may perpetuate testimony or take depositions of witnesses and may make and enter all necessary orders to enable litigants to perfect appeals.

By order of the Military Governor:

/s/ Thomas H. Green,
THOMAS H. GREEN,
Lt. Col., J.A.G.D.,
Executive.

A TRUE COPY:

William R C Morrison
WILLIAM R. C. MORRISON
Major, J.A.G.D.

TERRITORY OF HAWAII
OFFICE OF THE MILITARY GOVERNOR
FORT SHAFTER, T.H.

GENERAL ORDERS)
NO. 38   )   20 December 1941

The following policy governing the employment and use of labor in the Territory of Hawaii is announced for the information and guidance of all concerned:

1. All wage rates to be frozen as of December 7, 1941, for all employees on the Island of Oahu, so long as they remain in the same classification.

2. All employees of Federal Government and its contractors now actively deriving support from Federal funds, to be frozen to their respective employer as of December 7, 1941. This is to include the City and County of Honolulu, Territorial agencies, their contractors and subcontractors and utilities and sources of supply controlled by the Army and Navy. All the above workers who have separated from their employment since December 7, 1941, are to return to the job held as of that date.

3. Army and Navy will continue their established agencies for recruiting directly the workers required for their respective activities.

4. The normal working day shall be 8 hours, and all hours worked in excess of 8 hours will be paid at the rate of 1½ times the regular rate.

5. Terms of labor contracts between individuals and contractors, and other agencies of the Federal Government, which restrict or specify the nature of work to be performed are hereby suspended.

6. Men employed hereafter must report to the job for which they are ordered by the Military Governor.

By order of the Military Governor:

(Signed) Thomas H. Green
THOMAS H. GREEN,
Lt. Col., J.A.G.D.,
Executive.

TRUE COPY: *William R C Morrison*
WILLIAM R. C. MORRISON,
Major, J.A.G.D.

TERRITORY OF HAWAII
OFFICE OF THE MILITARY GOVERNOR
FORT SHAFTER, T. H.

20 December 1941.

GENERAL ORDERS)
NO. 37   )

1. It is directed that all dealers, handlers, brokers, and dispensers of intoxicating liquor, wine and beer will submit to the Office of the Military Governor, NOT LATER THAN 12:00 noon, 24 December 1941, a complete inventory of all intoxicating liquor, wine and beer on hand as of the date of this order.

2. All persons or firms required by this order to submit an inventory failing to do so shall be subject to a fine or imprisonment, or both, by the Provost Court and any stock of intoxicating liquor, wine and beer found in their possession will be seized and forfeited.

By order of the Military Governor:

(signed) Thomas H. Green
THOMAS H. GREEN,
Lt.Col., J.A.G.D.,
Executive.

A TRUE COPY:

James F. Hanley
JAMES F. HANLEY,
Major, J.A.G.D.

TERRITORY OF HAWAII
OFFICE OF THE MILITARY GOVERNOR
FORT SHAFTER, T. H.

22 December 1941.

GENERAL ORDERS)
NO. 40   )

1. Paragraph 1, General Orders No. 14, this office, 10 December 1941, is changed as follows:

DELETE:

Nippu Jiji	Oahu
Hochi	Oahu

ADD:

Valley Isle Chronicle	Maui
Hawaiian Church Chronicle	Oahu
Catholic Herald	Oahu
Show Parade	Oahu
Hawaii Sentinel	Oahu

2. The following new paragraphs are added to General Orders No. 14, this office, 10 December 1941:

"4. Magazines. Until further notice the following magazines may, if they so desire, continue to be published and circulated under such conditions and regulations as shall be prescribed from time to time by the Military Governor:

Magazine	Location
Paradise of the Pacific	Oahu
The Load Builder	Oahu
Sales Builder	Oahu
Hawaii Educational Review	Oahu
Rizal Journal	Oahu

Over

1

G. O. No. 40, O.M.G.

"5. Until further notice the publishers of Thrum's Hawaiian Annual and Standard Guide may, if they so desire, continue to publish and circulate that publication under such conditions and regulations as shall be prescribed from time to time by the Military Governor."

By order of the Military Governor:

(Signed) Thomas H. Green
THOMAS H. GREEN,
Lt. Col., J.A.G.D.,
Executive.

A TRUE COPY:

James F. Hanley
JAMES F. HANLEY,
Major, J.A.G.D.

G. O. No. 42, O. M. G., 1941.

6. In no place of amusement shall any speech be made, words uttered, gestures made, songs sung, music played, plays performed, pictures, banners, or placards exhibited expressing hostility or disrespect to the United States or the Territory of Hawaii, their armed forces or any member thereof, or the Military Governor or the civil Governor of the Territory of Hawaii, or any member of their staffs.

7. Any place of amusement violating any Territorial or local law or any regulation issued by properly constituted authority during the present emergency will be closed.

8. With respect to shooting galleries, they will remain closed until further notice and owners or proprietors thereof will report in to the nearest police station all rifles and other shooting devices and ammunition therefor. The police will then collect such rifles and other shooting devices and ammunition from the shooting gallery, and all articles collected shall remain in the custody of the authorities until such time as shooting galleries are permitted to open.

By order of the Military Governor:

(signed) Thomas H. Green,
THOMAS H. GREEN,
Lt. Col., J.A.G.D.,
Executive.

A TRUE COPY:

James F. Hanley
JAMES F. HANLEY,
Major, J.A.G.D.

TERRITORY OF HAWAII
OFFICE OF THE MILITARY GOVERNOR
FORT SHAFTER, T.H.

24 December 1941

GENERAL ORDERS)
NO. 42)

All places of amusement, except shooting galleries, located on the Island of Oahu, may open for business this date and remain open until further notice, subject to the following regulations:

1. Such places may be open between the hours of 9:00 a.m. and 4:00 p.m. daily except Sunday. On Sundays such places may be open from 12:00 o'clock noon to 4:00 p.m.

2. The owner or operator of each place of amusement covered by this order desiring to remain open will file, by mail, in the Office of the Military Governor, Honolulu, T. H., as soon as practicable, a statement containing the following information:

a. The name of the place and its location.

b. Name of the owner, his address and citizenship.

c. The type or types of amusement afforded the public

d. Statement of necessity for its opening.

3. Upon the filing of the information required in paragraph 2 above, consideration will be given to the issuance of a permit for the operation of such place of amusement. All places of amusement not receiving a permit by January 15, 1942, will close effective at 12:01 a.m. that day, and remain closed until a permit is received.

4. No motion pictures having dialogue in other than the English language will be shown in any motion picture house without a special permit from the Military Governor, granted upon written application.

5. No intoxicating liquor, wine or beer will be sold or offered for sale or otherwise disposed of in any place of amusement

TERRITORY OF HAWAII
OFFICE OF THE MILITARY GOVERNOR
FORT SHAFTER, T.H.

2 January 1942

GENERAL ORDERS)
NO. 48)

Section I. PROVOST COURTS.—1. All provost courts heretofore or hereafter appointed by the Military Governor of the Territory of Hawaii shall have power, and hereby are authorized and empowered, to try and punish commissioned or enlisted personnel of the Army of the United States or of the United States Navy, for violations, whether heretofore or hereafter committed, of any statute of the Territory of Hawaii, or of any ordinance, resolution, by-law, regulation, or rule of any city, town, or other municipal corporation of the Territory of Hawaii, or of any order, rule, or regulation of the Military Governor of the Territory of Hawaii, regulating or relating to vehicular or pedestrian traffic.

2. The concurrent jurisdiction of the Army of the United States or of the United States Navy to court-martial or otherwise discipline commissioned or enlisted personnel of their respective services for such offenses is not withdrawn by anything herein contained.

3. Any and all parts, portions, or provisions of any General Order of the Military Governor heretofore made, in conflict with the provisions of this Section, hereby are revoked and rescinded to the extent of any such conflict herewith out to the extent of such conflict only and no more.

Section II. AMENDING GENERAL ORDERS NO. 16.—Paragraph 10 of General Orders No. 16, this office, 11 December 1941, is amended to add to the list of streets upon which no parking will be permitted day or night, the following streets:

"Sumner Street
Ewilei Street
Pacific Street
Prison Road"

By order of the Military Governor:

(signed) Thomas H. Green,
THOMAS H. GREEN,
Colonel, J.A.G.D.,
Executive.

A TRUE COPY:

James F. Hanley
JAMES F. HANLEY,
Major, J.A.G.D.

TERRITORY OF HAWAII
OFFICE OF THE MILITARY GOVERNOR
FORT SHAFTER, T.H.

6 January 1942

GENERAL ORDERS)
NO. 49   )

Section I. RESCISSION OF GENERAL ORDERS.- General Orders No. 16, this office, 11 December 1941 (Corrected Copy); General Orders No. 43, this office, 24 December 1941, and Section II, General Orders No. 48, this office, 2 January 1942, relating to blackout restrictions and to certain traffic control, is hereby rescinded. (See Section II of this General Order.)

Section II. BLACKOUT RESTRICTIONS AND TRAFFIC CONTROL RESTRICTIONS.-1. No person shall be on the streets and highways, or in parks or on beaches, either on foot or in vehicles, between 6:00 PM and 6:00 A M, except:

a. Military and Naval personnel on duty or proceeding to and from duty.

b. Law enforcement officers.

c. Civilian personnel required to be on the streets and highways during such hours because of their employment on defense work, by public utilities, in civilian defense activities, or by the government, or while directly proceeding to and from work.

d. Doctors on call.

e. Those holding Police passes issued since December 7, 1941.

f. Those holding special passes issued or approved by the Provost Marshal, Military Police or Civilian Police.

Except as hereinafter provided, the existing laws, regulations, and ordinances of the Civilian government, and any of its subdivisions, pertaining to traffic, shall continue in full force and effect.

-1-

G. O. No. 49, O. M. G., 1942.

4. Any person stopped by Civil or Military Police will identify himself promptly. All persons required to be on the streets during blackout hours should carry some sort of identification or pass, letter from your employer, or badge.

5. Operation of motor or other vehicles, except as authorized by the Civil or Military Police, at a speed in excess of 20 miles per hour during dark hours is prohibited.

6. In the event of an air raid alarm only the following vehicles and persons are allowed to proceed:

a. Army and Navy.
    (1) All Army and Navy vehicles on duty.
    (2) Army and Navy personnel in uniform when proceeding to their posts of duty.

b. Police Department.
    (1) Police on duty.
    (2) Police called to report at their stations.

c. Fire Department.
    (1) Fire engines.
    (2) Trucks designated as auxiliary fire fighting equipment when on duty or proceeding to posts for duty.
    (3) Official Fire Chief cars.
    (4) Firemen called in and proceeding to their stations.

d. Medical Groups.
    (1) Doctors on call.
    (2) Members of First-Aid Units called and proceeding to their posts.
    (3) Employees and volunteers serving the Emergency Hospital, if on duty.
    (4) Ambulances, and trucks loaned as ambulances.

-3-

G. O. No. 49, O. M. G., 1942.

2. All motor vehicles, as above authorized, operated between the hours of 6:00 PM and 6:00 AM shall have lights conforming to the following specifications:

Headlights to be painted all black with exception of a two and one-half inch circle, slightly below the center of the headlight lens - which circle will be painted with Moss Blackout Blue paint (quick drying) or equivalent; tail lights to be painted all blue.

3. The following paint shops and garages are equipped to paint lenses:

Honolulu: Automotive Service Company
             Aloha Paint Shop
             Eddie Lem's
             Auto Service Garage
             Murphy Motors
             Wong's Auto Top Shop
             Frias Paint Shop
             Funasaki Fender Shop
             Mclins
             Universal Motors
             Von Hamm Young
             Schumann Carriage
             Hamsens Auto Paint Shop
             Hawaiian Pineapple Company
Country: Nambo Service Station, Pearl City
             Honolulu Plantation
             Kuroda Service Station, Aiea
             Waipahu Plantation
             Waipahu Motors
             S. Kuranaka Garage, Honouliuli
             Ewa Plantation
             Waianae Plantation, Waianae
             Wahiawa Motors, Wahiawa
             Castner Garage, Wahiawa
             Service Garage, Wahiawa
             Kaialua Service, Waialua
             Kahuku Plantation, Kahuku
             S. Tanaka, Kahuku
             Soeda Garage, Kaneohe
             Dates Service Station, Kailua
             Waimanalo Plantation, Waimanalo

It is not necessary that the painting be done at one of the above named garages. It may be done by anyone, provided it meets with the specifications stated above.

-2-

G. O. No. 49, O. M. G., 1942.

e. Civilian Defense.
    (1) Chairmen and Executives of important committes of Civilian Defense when on duty or proceeding to posts for duty.
    (2) Messengers, if telephone system is cut.

f. Utilities.
    (1) Key men of the various utilities when designated by utility.
    (2) Necessary repair trucks of utilities.

g. Others.

    Persons or vehicles allowed to proceed by the Civil or Military Police.

All other persons must leave the street or highway and seek the nearest best available shelter. All other vehicles must immediately be driven to the side of the street or highway and stopped and must remain there until the "All Clear" signal is given or until the police (Civil or Military) authorizes the same to move. The occupants of the vehicle must leave the vehicle and seek the nearest best available shelter.

7. No parking on any public thoroughfare will be permitted after dark.

8. No parking on the following streets, day or night:

School Street	Pacific Street
Lusitania Street	Sumner Street
Beretania Street	Watkins Road
King Street	Reserve Road
Waialae Avenue	Queen Street on makai side
Dillingham Boulevard	between Iwilei Road and
Middle Street	Fort Street.
Nuuanu Avenue	Fort Street from Queen
Alapai Street, between	Street to Ala Moana.
Lusitania & Beretania	Ala Moana on makai side from
Iwilei Road	Fort Street to Immigration
Prison Road	Station.

-4-

G. O. No. 49, O. M. G., 1942.

9. The following streets are changed from one-way streets to two-way streets, effective this date:

River Street, from King Street to
Beretania Street
Fort Street, from Queen Street to
Halekauwila Street.
Bethel Street

10. The carrying of lighted cigarettes, cigars and pipes, and the striking of matches, lighters, etc., in the open during the hours of blackout is prohibited. All flashlights shall be printed or otherwise fixed so as to give off a blue light. The excessive use of flashlights or other means of illumination during the period of the blackout is also prohibited.

11. Enforcement of the above directives, and all motor vehicle traffic, is vested exclusively in the Military Police and the Civil Police.

12. Saving Clause. - The provisions of this section shall take effect upon the date of this General Order, but shall not apply to any offense heretofore committed. Any such prior offense shall be punishable in the same manner and to the same effect, as if this Section had not been published.

Section III. AMENDMENT TO GENERAL ORDERS NO. 21. - Paragraph 2, General Orders No. 21, this office, 13 December 1941, setting out the conditions under which the Rent Control Commission may issue, subject to the approval of the Provost Marshal, writs of possession, is amended by adding thereto a new subsection as follows:

(c) Where the landlord seeks in good faith to recover possession of his property for his immediate and personal use and occupancy as a dwelling and the Commission finds that the landlord and his family would be subjected to undue hardship if possession was not awarded to him.

Section IV. NEWSPAPERS AUTHORIZED TO RESUME PUBLICATION. - Paragraph 1, General Orders No. 14, this office, 10 December 1941, as amended, authorizing certain newspapers to continue

-5-

TERRITORY OF HAWAII
OFFICE OF THE MILITARY GOVERNOR
FORT SHAFTER, T.H.

9 January 1942

GENERAL ORDERS)
NO. 50   )

Section I. LOCATION OF OFFICE OF THE MILITARY GOVERNOR.-- 1. General Orders No. 7, this office, dated 8 December 1941, is rescinded.

2. The Office of the Military Governor is located in Iolani Palace, Honolulu, T. H.

3. All civilians having business will communicate with him through the Executive to the Military Governor at the Iolani Palace.

4.. The business hours of the Office of the Military Governor will be from 8:00 A.M. to 5:00 P.M.

Section II. BUSINESS SCHOOLS.--1. The following schools are authorized to resume business on 11 January 1942:

Cannon's School of Business
Margaret Dinty Commercial School
Gallery School of Business
Honolulu Business College
Phillips Commercial School
Hawaii Trade School, Limited
Wolfe School of Costume Designing

2. Such schools may conduct classes of instruction between the hours of 8:00 A.M. and 5:00 P.M. on all days except Sunday and holidays.

Section III. CHANGE IN GENERAL ORDERS NO. 42.-- Paragraph 1, General Orders No. 42, this office, 24 December 1941, is amended by changing "12:00 o'clock Noon" to read "10:00 a.m." thereby permitting places of amusement to open at 10:00 a.m. each Sunday.

Section IV. PINBALL MACHINES AND OTHER SIMILAR GAMES OF SKILL.-- Pinball machines and other similar games of skill are considered "places of amusement" within the meaning of General Order No. 42, this office, 24 December 1941, and accordingly the operation of such machines before 10:00 A.M. and after 4:30 P.M.
9:00

-1-

G. O. No. 49, O. M. G., 1942.

publication, is amended by adding the following:

Nippu Jiji   Oahu
Hawaii Hochi   Oahu

By order of the Military Governor:

(signed) Thomas H. Green,
(signed) THOMAS H. GREEN,
Colonel, J.A.G.D.,
Executive.

A TRUE COPY:

James F. Hanley
JAMES F. HANLEY,
Major, J.A.G.D.

G. O. No. 50, O.M.G., 1942.

on week days and before 10:00 A.M. and after 4:30 P.M. on Sundays is prohibited and any person permitting the operation of such machines at other times than between these periods will be punished and his permit to operate such a "place of amusement" will be revoked.

By order of the Military Governor:

(signed) Thomas H. Green,
THOMAS H. GREEN,
Colonel, J.A.G.D.,
Executive.

A TRUE COPY:

James F. Hanley
JAMES F. HANLEY,
Major, J.A.G.D.

-2-

TERRITORY OF HAWAII
OFFICE OF THE MILITARY GOVERNOR
IOLANI PALACE
HONOLULU, T.H.

9 January 1942

GENERAL ORDERS}
NO. 51 }

The following order is published, effective January 12, 1942, governing the withdrawal and possession of currency by persons in the Territory of Hawaii:

1. **Definitions.** As used herein:

(a) The term "individual" means a natural person, and includes a natural person acting by or through any other person. For the purpose hereof, husband and wife living together within the Territory of Hawaii shall be deemed to be one individual.

(b) The term "person" means an individual, partnership, association, corporation, or other organization.

(c) The term "currency" means coin, government notes, and bank notes of all denominations, but does not include bonds, stamps, or other obligations of the United States Government not circulating as money.

(d) The term "deposit in a bank or trust company" means any payment to a bank or trust company, but does not include a deposit in a safe deposit box.

(e) The term "bank" means any bank as defined in Section 6501 of the Revised Laws of Hawaii 1935, and every national bank engaged in business in the Territory of Hawaii.

(f) The term "trust company" means any trust company as defined in Section 6900 of the Revised Laws of Hawaii 1935.

(g) The term "building and loan association" means any building and loan association as defined in Section 6650 of the Revised Laws of Hawaii 1935.

(h) The term "fiduciary company" includes any fiduciary company as defined in Section 6758 of the Revised Laws of Hawaii 1935, as amended.

-1-

G. O. No. 51, O. M. G., 1942.

(i) The term "loan company" means any industrial loan company as defined in Section 6782A of the Revised Laws of Hawaii 1935, as amended.

2. **Withdrawal of currency.** No person shall, except as otherwise hereinafter provided, withdraw or receive from any bank, trust company, building and loan association, fiduciary company, loan company, or other financial institution currency in excess of an aggregate sum of $200.00 in any one calendar month if such person is an individual, or in excess of an aggregate sum of $500.00 in any one calendar month if such person is a partnership, association, corporation or other organization. The withdrawal or receipt of currency by an agent, trustee, or other fiduciary for the account of any principal or beneficiary shall be deemed to be a withdrawal or receipt of such currency by each such principal or beneficiary. No bank, trust company, building and loan association, fiduciary company, loan company, or other financial institution shall be obligated to pay out or deliver currency in excess of the amounts permitted to be withdrawn or received under this order.

3. **Possession of currency.** No person shall at any time, except as otherwise hereinafter provided, directly or indirectly retain in his possession, custody, or control any currency in excess of the sum of $200.00 if such person is an individual, or in excess of the sum of $500.00 if such person is a partnership, association, corporation or other organization. Currency located in a safe deposit box in the Territory of Hawaii shall be deemed to be in the possession, custody, or control of the lessee or lessees of such box. Any person having or at any time hereafter obtaining possession, custody, or control of any currency in excess of the sum permitted by this order shall, not later than the third day after the effective date of this order, or not later than the third day after the receipt of such currency, divest himself of possession, custody, and control of all such currency in excess of the sum permitted by this order by a bona fide payment thereof to another person or by a deposit in a bank or trust company; PROVIDED, HOWEVER, that any person who is for any reason unable so to divest himself of such possession, custody, and control shall, within the period of time specified above, file with the Military Governor a report in triplicate stating: (1) The amount and location of all currency directly or indirectly in his possession, custody, and control; (2) The name and address of each person having any interest of any nature whatsoever, direct or indirect, in such currency; (3) The source of all such currency; and (4) The reason why he is unable to divest himself of possession, custody, and control of such currency as required above. Such person shall, as soon thereafter as he is able, divest himself of possession, custody, and control of such currency as provided above.

- 2 -

G. O. No. 51, O. M. G., 1942.

4. **Currency for payrolls.** Nothing contained in this order shall be deemed to forbid the withdrawal or the possession, custody, or control by any person of the amount of currency required for the payment within three days of the receipt of such currency of wages of bona fide employees of such person, provided that prior to any withdrawal or receipt of such currency such person shall present to the bank, trust company, building and loan association, fiduciary company, loan company or other financial institution from which such currency is sought to be withdrawn a certificate executed by such person or his or its authorized agent certifying that the currency sought to be withdrawn is to be used solely and immediately for wage purposes. Any certificate accepted in good faith by such bank, trust company, building and loan association, fiduciary company, loan company or other financial institution as genuine shall constitute an authority to make payment in accordance with such certificate.

5. **Exceptions.** The provisions of Sections 2 and 3 of this order shall not be deemed to apply to any of the following or to any authorized officer or agent thereof acting on behalf of any of the following:

(a) The United States Government, the Government of the Territory of Hawaii, or any political subdivision, agency, or instrumentality thereof;

(b) Post exchanges and ship stores;

(c) Banks;

(d) Trust companies;

(e) Building and loan associations;

(f) Finance companies, fiduciary companies, loan companies and other financial institutions subject to the examination of the Territorial Bank Examiner;

(g) Any person authorized by the Military Governor to retain or withdraw currency in an amount greater than that permitted under Section 2 or 3 of this order.

6. **Investigation.** Any agency designated by the Military Governor may upon finding that there is a reasonable suspicion of a violation of this order, investigate the suspected violation. Such agency shall have free access to all relevant books and papers and may summon witnesses, administer oaths or affirmations, and receive testimony in the course of its investigation. Any person who shall wilfully refuse to produce relevant books or records, wilfully refuse or fail to attend and testify when summoned, knowingly testify falsely with respect to any matter material to such

- 3 -

G. O. No. 51, O. M. G., 1942.

an investigation, or refuse to give full and truthful information in response to any relevant question directed to him in the course of such an investigation, shall, upon conviction, be subject to the penalties provided in Section 7 of this order.

7. **Penalties.** Whoever is found guilty of wilfully violating any of the provisions of this order shall, upon conviction, be fined not more than five thousand dollars ($5,000.00), or if a natural person, may be imprisoned for not more than five (5) years, or both; and any officer, director or agent of any corporation who knowingly participates in such a violation may be punished by a like fine, imprisonment, or both.

8. **Freezing Order.** Nothing contained in this order shall be deemed to authorize any transaction prohibited under Executive Order No. 8389 of April 10, 1940, as amended, or any regulations issued thereunder.

By order of the Military Governor:

(signed) Thomas H. Green,
THOMAS H. GREEN,
Colonel, J.A.G.D.,
Executive.

A TRUE COPY:

James F. Hanley
JAMES F. HANLEY,
Major, J.A.G.D.

TERRITORY OF HAWAII
OFFICE OF THE MILITARY GOVERNOR
IOLANI PALACE
HONOLULU, T.H.

14 January 1942

GENERAL ORDERS)
NO. 52)

SECTION I. LABOR ON SUNDAYS.
SECTION II. SOLICITORS.

SECTION I. LABOR ON SUNDAY.-- The provisions of Section 6211, Revised Laws of Hawaii, 1935, as amended, prohibiting labor on Sunday, is suspended until further notice, and all places of business, professional offices, etc., may operate on Sundays from 9:00 a.m. to 5:00 p.m. except that this shall not apply to places of business, professional offices, etc., which are now permitted to operate longer hours by the laws or regulations of the Territory of Hawaii or of the Military Governor, nor shall it apply to any business forbidden to operate by order of the Military Governor.

SECTION II. SOLICITORS.-- 1. No person shall engage in, transact or conduct business as a solicitor hereinafter defined before he shall have complied with the provisions of this Order.

2. Definition. A solicitor within the meaning of this Order is defined to be any person who goes from house to house or from place to place selling or taking orders or offering to sell or take orders for goods, wares, merchandise, or memberships to any group, club, or society, who demands, accepts or receives payment or deposit of money for such sale, order or membership.

3. Any person desiring to engage in, transact or conduct business as a solicitor as defined in Section 2 of this Order shall apply to the Executive Section, Office of the Military Governor for a permit to engage in, transact or conduct such business.

4. Before the permit is authorized, the applicant shall submit to the Office of the Military Governor the following information: (1) General description and manner in which such business shall be conducted; (2) Business address and telephone number, home address and telephone number of each employee; (3) Number of employees; (4) Amount of profit; (5) The period of time between the taking of such order for goods, wares or merchandise and the delivery date of such goods, wares or merchandise. Such period of time shall not exceed thirty (30) days; (6) Evi-

-1-

G. O. No. 52, O. M. G., 1942.

dence that he has complied with the Territorial Statutes pertaining to business, vendor and gross income tax licenses, and (7) Evidence that he has obtained a police personal identification card for each employee engaged in such business. Such investigation as is deemed necessary will be conducted by the Executive Section, Office of the Military Governor.

By order of the Military Governor:

(signed) Thomas H. Green,
THOMAS H. GREEN,
Colonel, J.A.G.D.,
Executive.

A TRUE COPY:

James F. Hanley

JAMES F. HANLEY,
Major, J.A.G.D.

-2-

TERRITORY OF HAWAII
OFFICE OF THE MILITARY GOVERNOR
IOLANI PALACE
HONOLULU, T.H.

20 January 1942

GENERAL ORDERS)
NO. 54)

SECTION I. ISSUE OF GAS MASKS TO CIVILIANS
SECTION II. TRAFFIC DURING AIR RAID ALARMS
SECTION III. TRIAL JUDGE ADVOCATE, MILITARY COMMISSION
SECTION IV. DOGS
SECTION V. CLOSING HOURS OF BUSINESS ESTABLISHMENTS ON WEEKDAYS

SECTION I. ISSUE OF GAS MASKS TO CIVILIANS.--1. Gas masks for civilians residing in the Island of Oahu are now available for issue. These masks are furnished by the Chemical Warfare Service, U. S. Army, and will be issued from the various Civilian First Aid Stations throughout the Island of Oahu. Masks available for issue at this time are of universal size and will fit the average person of 14 years of age or older. Gas masks for babies and small children are not immediately available but have been ordered and will be issued as soon as received.

2. Colonel GEORGE F. UNMACHT, C. W. S., Department Chemical Officer, is hereby designated Coordinator of Gas Defense for the Island of Oahu and empowered with authority to regulate and coordinate existing territorial civilian personnel having to do with Civil Defense matters pertaining to gas protection.

3. To obtain a gas mask, each individual will report to the First Aid Station nearest their home and upon presentation of the recently issued Identification Certificate of the Territory of Hawaii the mask will be issued. At the time of issue each individual will receipt for the mask received.

4. Gas masks have already been issued to some civilian defense workers and other key civilians and these masks are the same as masks now being issued to the general public. Any civilian already having a mask in his possession will not obtain an additional mask.

5. Although the gas masks will be issued to the public free of charge they remain Government property and it must be borne in mind that the masks were obtained after considerable expense to the Government. Every effort must be made to protect the mask against loss or damage. Any person who wilfully loses, destroys or damages his or any other person's mask will be subject to trial and punishment.

-1-

G. O. No. 54, O. M. G., 1942

Section II. TRAFFIC DURING AIR RAID ALARMS.--1. Paragraph 6 of General Orders No. 49, this office, dated 6 January 1942, is rescinded.

2. When an air raid alarm is sounded, the Military and Civil Police will direct all unofficial motor traffic away from the water front and business sections, toward the hills, at fast speed. When this traffic has cleared the congested area and reached areas where cover is available, cars should stop off the roadway, dispersed as much as possible. Cars must not block the roadways, Occupants should seek the best cover and protection that is immediately available and remain stationary until the "All Clear" signal is sounded. They should avoid attracting the attention of an enemy aviator by movement, and avoid offering him a tempting target by assembling in groups. The best available protection against both bombing and machine gun attack is a narrow slit trench. If no trench is near that they can use, they should lie down taking advantage of any concealing and protecting cover, that may be available. By so doing they reduce materially the probability of their being hit by bomb fragments and machine gun bullets. There is also a definite danger from falling fragments of friendly anti-aircraft projectiles and machine gun bullets and many such fragments may fall in and around Honolulu. When anti-aircraft is in action adequate protection must include overhead cover. Lacking a strong roof, or other suitable overhead cover, the branches of a tree will afford some protection. Civilians will be provided with steel helmets as soon as they can be obtained. In the meantime, they should use those which may be in their possession for their own protection.

3. While complying with the preceding paragraph, the Military and Civil Police will exercise care that the unofficial traffic does not impede the rapid progress of official traffic of the following classes:

    a. Army and Navy;

    b. Police Department;

    c. Fire Department;

    d. Medical Services;

    e. Civilian Defense Authorities;

    f. Operating and repair personnel for public utilities.

-2-

G. O. No. 54, O. M. G., 1942

SECTION III. TRIAL JUDGE ADVOCATE, MILITARY COMMISSION.--
1. Lieutenant Colonel Neal D. Franklin, J.A.G.D., is relieved
as Trial Judge Advocate of the Military Commission appointed
by Paragraph 2, General Orders No. 25, this office, 14 December
1941.

2. Captain Eugene V. Slattery, J.A.G.D., is appointed
Trial Judge Advocate of the Military Commission appointed by
Paragraph 2, General Orders No. 25, this office, 14 December 1941.

SECTION IV. DOGS.--1. All dogs will be confined during the
hours of blackout.

2. All dogs will wear at all times except when actually
confined, license tags issued by the proper authorities.

3. All dogs found at large during the hours of blackout,
or found without their license tags will be impounded in the dog
pound and the owner will be subject to a fine of not more than
fifty dollars.

SECTION V. CLOSING HOURS OF BUSINESS ESTABLISHMENTS ON
WEEKDAYS.--1. All business establishments, including places of
amusement may remain open until 5:00 p.m. on weekdays.

2. Paragraph 2, Rule No. 4, Hawaii Defense Act, and
Paragraph 1, General Orders No. 42, this office, 24 December 1941,
as amended by Section IV, General Orders No. 45, this office, 27
December 1941, closing business establishments at 4:30 p.m. are
modified accordingly.

By order of the Military Governor:

(Signed) Thomas H. Green,
THOMAS H. GREEN,
Colonel, J.A.G.D.,
Executive.

A TRUE COPY:

James F. Hanley
JAMES F. HANLEY,
Major, J.A.G.D.

-3-

G. O. No. 56, O. M. G., 1942.

5. Any person who shall fail to register as required by paragraphs
1 and 2 hereof, or any private employer or the responsible official of any
public employer, who shall fail to notify as required by paragraph 3 hereof,
shall upon conviction, be fined not more than One Thousand Dollars ($1000.00),
or be imprisoned for not more than one (1) year, or both.

SECTION II. REGULATING SALE OF AGRICULTURAL SEEDS ON THE ISLAND OF
OAHU.--1. All varieties of agricultural seeds in the hands of dealers on
Oahu may be sold without order or permit to purchasers for planting on Oahu.

2. Purchases for shipment from Oahu will be released for sale only on
permit issued by the Office of the Military Governor.

3. Any rule or regulation contrary hereto is hereby rescinded.

SECTION III. ORGANIZATION OF OFFICE OF THE MILITARY GOVERNOR.--1.
Executive Section for the Military Governor. a. The Executive Section shall
function on behalf of the Military Governor in carrying out all policies
and operations of martial law. The Executive Section will have the coordinating control of military commissions and provost courts, and alien property.
The Executive Section will act as a final clearing house in establishing policies for the Coordinating Sections, viz: Civilian Defense, Food Control,
Labor Control, Material and Supply Control, Cargo and Passenger Control and
Land Transportation Control.

The following sections function directly under the Executive Section
and have no direct connection with the Coordinating Sections:

ADVISORY COMMITTEE
LAW ENFORCEMENT
    MILITARY COMMISSION
    PROVOST COURTS
LEGAL ADVISOR
    SPECIAL CONSULTANTS
ALIEN PROPERTY CONTROLLER
PUBLIC INFORMATION
PERSONNEL
FINANCE
MORALE

The functions of these sections are as follows:

b. Advisory Committee.--This committee, when requested to do so,
shall consult with and advise the Military Governor on all matters of general
policy.

c. Law Enforcement.--The military commissions and the provost courts
shall carry out designated functions as prescribed by law and by orders of
the Military Governor.

-2-

TERRITORY OF HAWAII
OFFICE OF THE MILITARY GOVERNOR
IOLANI PALACE
HONOLULU, T.H.

26 January 1942

GENERAL ORDERS)
NO. 56)

SECTION I. REGISTRATION OF ABLE-BODIED MEN
SECTION II. REGULATING SALE OF AGRICULTURAL SEEDS ON THE ISLAND OF OAHU
SECTION III. ORGANIZATION OF OFFICE OF THE MILITARY GOVERNOR

SECTION I. REGISTRATION OF ABLE-BODIED MEN.--1. Every able-bodied male
person, now in the Territory of Hawaii, who, as of the date hereof, shall
have reached his eighteenth birthday and is not gainfully occupied,
beginning February 2, 1942 and prior to February 12, 1942, present himself
to the nearest office of the United States Employment Service where he shall
be registered.

2. In the event any such person is now gainfully occupied but hereafter
shall cease to be gainfully occupied, he shall within 72 hours from the time
he ceases to be gainfully occupied present himself to the nearest office of
the United States Employment Service there he shall be registered, or re-
registered.

3. After February 1, 1942, every public employer, including the United
States of America, the Territory of Hawaii, city and county or municipality,
or of any of their respective departments, bureaus, agencies, instrumentalities,
and every private employer doing business in the Territory of Hawaii shall
notify the nearest office of the United States Employment Service within 48
hours, on forms prescribed by the United States Employment Service, of any
employee, added to or dropped from such employer's payroll, regardless of
whether or not such employee is covered by Paragraph 1 or 2 hereof.

4. The United States Employment Service is hereby designated as the
central employment agency for the procurement and distribution of civilian
labor hereby required to register, and shall allocate labor in the fulfillment of employers' requisitions in accordance with the plans and priorities
to be hereafter established by the Director of Plans and Priorities through
the office of Director of Labor Control, Office of the Military Governor;
subject, however, to the following provisions:

(a) The United States Army and its associated contractors, the
United States Navy and its associated contractors, may maintain their own
labor recruiting facilities but shall inform the United States Employment
Service of placements from both local and mainland sources and of releases
from their employ.

(b) Whenever any governmental agency is required by any Civil Service law or regulation to recruit employees in a prescribed manner or from a
prescribed group or through prescribed channels, such agency shall not be
affected by the provisions of this section.

-1-

G. O. No. 56, O. M. G., 1942

d. Legal Advisor.--The legal advisor shall render legal advice to
the Military Governor and the Executive Section.

e. Alien Property Controller.--The Temporary Military Alien Property
Controller shall perform the duties set out in General Order No. 39 of this
office, until such time as an alien property custodian is appointed under
Federal authority.

f. Public Information.--This section shall issue such press releases
and other information to the public as ordered from time to time by the Military Governor.

g. Personnel.--This section shall procure the necessary personnel
for the office operation of the Military Governor.

h. Finance.--This section shall handle all matters of finance connected with the office of the Military Governor.

i. Morale.--All matters involving the public morale shall be referred
to this section for handling.

2. Planning and Priorities.--a. Director of Planning and Priorities.
Under the direction of the Military Governor, the Director of Planning and
Priorities will control, coordinate and supervise the activities of the six
Directors hereinafter provided for or establish priorities in all matters
coming under their supervision.

The Director of Planning and Priorities will be assisted by an Advisory Board consisting of the six Directors hereinafter provided for, together with a representative appointed by the Commandant of the 14th Naval
District.

b. Director of Civilian Defense.--The Director of Civilian Defense
shall recommend to the Military Governor, such rules and regulations as he
shall deem necessary and proper, and when so directed by the Military Governor
shall administer such regulations as may be published.

The Director of Civilian Defense shall to the extent directed by the
Military Governor:

(1) Supervise and coordinate the civilian defense corps, consisting of fire wardens, air raid wardens, rescue and demolition squads,
gas wardens and such other wardens services as may from time to time be approved.

(2) Supervise housing and billeting, emergency feeding, clothing
and relief of civilian evacuees, evacuated to points within the Territory
and such military evacuees within the Territory as he may be requested by
the military authorities.

(3) Supervise emergency medical and ambulance services, first
aid stations, emergency hospitals (other than those established by the City
and County of Honolulu or by military authorities) and the procurement of
medical supplies and equipment for the same and the management of blood and
plasma banks.

-3-

G. O. No. 56, O. M. G., 1942

(4) Make adequate provision for public air raid and bomb-proof shelters and trenches on the Island of Oahu, and to disseminate information relative to the protection of persons and property against air raids, bombardment and gas attacks by the enemy.

(5) Coordinate and assist all City and County and Territorial functions referred to in the Hawaii Defense Act.

c. Director of Food Control.--The Director of Food Control shall recommend to the Military Governor, such rules and regulations as he shall deem necessary and proper and when directed by the Military Governor shall administer such regulations.

The Director of Food Control shall to the extent directed by the Military Governor:

(1) Supervise and coordinate the production, storage, distribution, price and sale of foods throughout the Territory, exclusive of foods consigned to or by Army and Navy Supply services. The word "foods" as used in this Order shall include, without prejudice to the generality of the foregoing, livestock, poultry, livestock and poultry feeds and agriculture seeds.

(2) Supervise and coordinate the importation and exportation of foods, exclusive of foods consigned to or by Army and Navy supply services, into and out of the Territory, subject to the allocation of cargo space by the Military Governor.

d. Director of Labor Control.--The Director of Labor Control shall recommend to the Military Governor, such rules and regulations as he shall deem necessary and proper and when so directed by the Military Governor administer such regulations.

The Director of Labor shall, to the extent directed by the Military Governor:

(1) Make plans for procurement, augmentation and distribution of labor available within the Territory.

(2) Investigate and mediate such labor disputes as are referred to him by the Military Governor.

e. Director of Materials and Supplies Control.--The Director of Materials and Supplies Control will recommend to the Military Governor, such rules and regulations as he shall deem necessary and proper and when so directed by the Military Governor shall administer such regulations as may be published.

The Director of Materials and Supplies Control shall to the extent directed by the Military Governor supervise and coordinate the importation, exportation, distribution and sale of all commodities the supervision of which is not otherwise specifically designated herein, exclusive of supplies consigned to Army and Navy supply services.

-4-

G. O. No. 56, O. M. G., 1942

f. Director of Cargo and Passenger Control.--The Director of Cargo and Passenger Control shall recommend to the Military Governor, such rules and regulations as he shall deem necessary and proper and when so directed by the Military Governor shall administer such regulations.

The Director of Cargo and Passenger Control shall to the extent directed by the Military Governor:

(1) Supervise and coordinate dockage, stevedoring and other facilities necessary to expedite the handling of cargo and passengers at the docks.

(2) Supervise the disposition of all cargo until removed from the docks.

g. Director of Land Transportation Control.--The Director of Land Transportation Control shall recommend to the Military Governor, such rules and regulations as he shall deem necessary and proper and when so directed by the Military Governor shall administer such regulations as may be published.

The Director of Land Transportation Control shall to the extent directed by the Military Governor:

(1) Coordinate rail and motor transportation on the Island Of Oahu make recommendations to the Military Governor relative to priorities in the use thereof.

(2) Supervise and coordinate the operation of all common carriers, taxi cabs and other vehicles carrying passengers for hire on Oahu.

(3) Perform the duties of this office set forth in Section IV, General Orders No. 53, and Section III, General Orders No. 55.

3. Supervision and Coordination of Cold Storage.--Section I, General Order No. 44, this office, 26 December 1941, is amended to read: "Colonel William R. White, Quartermaster Corps, is hereby designated, authorized and directed to supervise and coordinate cold storage operations in the Territory Of Hawaii and to recommend to the Military Governor such rules and regulations as he shall deem proper".

4. Sale and Distribution of Cloth in Bolts.--Section II, General Order No. 44, this office, 26 December 1941, is amended to read: "Colonel William R. White, Quartermaster Corps, is hereby designated, authorized and directed to supervise the sale and distribution of cloth in bolts by wholesalers within the Territory of Hawaii, and to recommend to the Military Governor such regulations relative thereto as he shall deem proper".

5. Appointments.--The following appointments to the offices indicated are hereby made:

Lt. Col. B. F. Hayford   Director of Planning and Priorities
Mr. Frank Locey   Director of Civilian Defense

-5-

Col. William R. White   Director of Food Control
Mr. Douglas Bond   Director of Labor Control
Mr. Alexander Budge   Director of Materials and Supplies Control
Mr. Stanley Kennedy   Ass't Director of Materials and Supplies Control
Comdr. Ernest Gray   Director of Cargo and Passenger Control
Mr. A. E. Kirk   Director of Land Transportation Control

By order of the Military Governor:

(signed) Thomas H. Green,
THOMAS H. GREEN,
Colonel, J.A.G.D.,
Executive.

A TRUE COPY:

James F. Hanley
JAMES F. HANLEY,
Major, J.A.G.D.

-6-

TERRITORY OF HAWAII
OFFICE OF THE MILITARY GOVERNOR
IOLANI PALACE
HONOLULU, T.H.

27 January 1942

GENERAL ORDERS)
NO. 57)

SECTION I. REGULATING IMPORTS TO TERRITORY OF HAWAII
SECTION II. CIVIL COURTS

SECTION I. REGULATING IMPORTS TO TERRITORY OF HAWAII.--
1. In order to provide the civilian population of the Territory of Hawaii with an adequate diet composed of items to which consumers are accustomed, and to assure a flow of supplies sufficient for current needs and to provide a six month's reserve of those items that will keep for such period, the following instructions are published for the information of all and strict compliance by all concerned:

a. The Federal Surplus Commodities Corporation will be the sole procuring agency and importer for the following list of basic foods:

(1) Rice
(2) Wheat flour
(3) White Potatoes
(4) Onions, dried
(5) Citrus fruits, fresh
(6) Canned evaporated milk
(7) Canned beef, corned and other
(8) Canned salmon
(9) Canned sardines
(10) Canned Peas
(11) Canned Baked beans, or Pork and beans
(12) Canned Peaches
(13) Canned Tomato Juice

No merchant, broker, importer or other commercial agency will be permitted to place an order on the Mainland for any article appearing in the above list. All orders for the above basic foods must be placed with the Director of Food Control, Office of the Military Governor. Name brands, desired by local merchants, will be furnished by the F. S. C. C. insofar as possible, consistent with inventories on hand. Future orders for the above basic foods will specify to the F. S. C. C. in San Francisco, name brands desired, which will be obtained from local merchants.

b. The procurement, storage and distribution to the retail trade, of all foods not shown in the list of basic foods, paragraph a. above, is delegated to local wholesalers, importers,

-1-

G. O. No. 57, O. M. G., 1942.

manufacturer's agents, brokers, etc., in accordance with the following policies:

(1) All orders for this class of foods will be submitted to the Office of the Director of Food Control, Office of the Military Governor for clearance and priority shipping number. The mainland shipper then simply offers to the carrier proof that his shipment carried a clearance from the Territory by displaying the stamped copy of his order. Failure to obtain clearance will result in refusal to permit shipment.

(2) In the event shipping facilities become more or less acute during any period, arrangements will be made to have these shipments included in the shipments of foods for the F. S. C. C.

(3) In the event the shipping situation becomes too acute it may become necessary to deny permits for importing relatively unimportant items.

(4) In order to conserve shipping space merchants will confine their orders to normal size containers and types of products for which they have had a relatively steady demand.

(5) Merchants will maintain as heavy a stock of non-basic commodities as their capital and storage facilities will permit except that the purchase of long-term, speculative stocks will not be cleared for shipment.

(6) Failure of merchants to provide stocks as indicated in (5) above will result in moving to the basic food list those items which the dealer could not or would not stock.

2. Wholesalers, Importers, Brokers, etc., who have long term or large contracts on the mainland for articles of food appearing in the basic food list, paragraph 1 a, will submit a statement thereof in detail to the Director of Food Control, Office of the Military Governor, showing amounts, terms of the contract, shipping instructions, etc.

3. Providing the civilian population with a flow of foods in general of types to which they are accustomed, and at the same time accumulating as much as a six month's supply for any eventuality that might happen, is the primary function of the Director of Food Control, Office of the Military Governor. Under present conditions supply must be assured and the above plan will insure the same with the least disruption to normal business. When present stocks of basic foods on hand are consumed and name brands are secured, merchants may then purchase their particular brands without ordering these items from the mainland.

-2-

G. O. No. 57, O. M. G., 1942.

as a witness of any person so engaged or employed.

All prior orders inconsistent herewith are hereby repealed.

By order of the Military Governor:

(signed) Thomas H. Green,
THOMAS H. GREEN,
Colonel, J.A.G.D.,
Executive.

A TRUE COPY:

James F. Hanley
JAMES F. HANLEY,
Major, J.A.G.D.

-4-

G. O. No. 57, O. M. G., 1942

SECTION II. CIVIL COURTS.--WHEREAS, pursuant to the proclamation of martial law in the Territory of Hawaii the operation of the civil courts in the Territory of Hawaii was suspended; and

WHEREAS, by General Orders No. 29, dated December 16, 1941, the courts in said Territory were authorized to exercise certain of the powers normally exercised by them during the existence of civil government; and

WHEREAS, it is now advisable, that said courts be authorized to exercise certain other of their said powers,

NOW, THEREFORE, the United States District Court for the Territory of Hawaii, the Supreme Court of said Territory, and the justices thereof, the circuit courts, circuit judges at chambers, land court, juvenile court, tax appeal court, and the district magistrates are hereby authorized, as agents of the Military Governor, to exercise their respective functions according to law, as it existed immediately prior to the declaration of martial law, except in the following respects:

1. No trial by jury shall be had, no session of the grand jury shall be held, nor shall any writ of habeas corpus be issued;

2. No circuit court or district magistrate shall exercise criminal jurisdiction except: Subject to the limitations prescribed by Section 4 in respect to the subpoening of witnesses, the circuit and district courts may dispose of cases pending on December 7, 1941, either upon plea or by trial whenever the intervention of a jury is not necessary or by order of nolle prosequi or dismissal on proper motion;

3. No suit, action or other proceeding shall be permitted against any member of the armed forces of the United States for any act done in line of or under color of duty; nor shall any suit, action or other proceeding be maintained against any person employed or engaged in any occupation, business or activity under the direction of the Military Governor or essential to the national defense for any act done within the scope of such employment;

4. No judgment by default shall be entered against any party except upon proof by affidavit or otherwise that the party is not engaged in military service nor employed or engaged in any occupation, business or activity under the direction of the Military Governor, or otherwise, essential to the national defense; nor shall any subpoena issue to require the attendance

-3-

TERRITORY OF HAWAII
OFFICE OF THE MILITARY GOVERNOR
IOLANI PALACE
HONOLULU, T.H.

29 January 1942

GENERAL ORDERS)
NO. 59)

SECTION I. NEWSPAPERS
SECTION II. MAGAZINES

SECTION I. NEWSPAPERS.--Paragraph 1, General Orders No. 14, as amended by paragraph 1, General Orders No. 40 and Section IV, General Orders No. 49, is hereby revoked and the following substituted therefor:

Newspapers. Until further notice the following newspapers may, if they so desire, continue to be published and circulated under such conditions and regulations as shall be prescribed from time to time by the Military Governor:

Newspaper	Location
Honolulu Star-Bulletin	Oahu
Honolulu Advertiser	Oahu
Nippu Jiji	Oahu
Hawaii Hochi	Oahu
Hilo Tribune-Herald	Hawaii
Hawaii Press	Hawaii
Maui News	Maui
Garden Island	Kauai
Valley Isle Chronicle	Maui
Hawaiian Church Chronicle	Oahu
Catholic Herald	Oahu
Snow Parade	Oahu
Hawaii Sentinel	Oahu
The United Chinese News	Oahu
The New China Press	Oahu
The Liberty News	Oahu
The Hawaii Chinese Journal	Oahu
Ti Silaw	Oahu
The Korean National Herald and	
The Korean Pacific Weekly	Oahu
The Filipino News	Kauai
Ka Hoku O Red Hill	Oahu
The Native Son	Oahu
The Friend	Oahu
Ka Hoaloha	Oahu
The Kalendar	Oahu
The Herald	Oahu

-1-

G. O. No. 59, O. M. G., 1942.

SECTION II. MAGAZINES.--Paragraph 4, General Orders No. 14, as set out in Paragraph 2, General Orders No. 40, is hereby revoked and the following substituted therefor:

Magazines. Until further notice the following magazines may, if they so desire, continue to be published and circulated under such conditions and regulations as shall be prescribed from time to time by the Military Governor:

Magazine	Location
Paradise of the Pacific	Oahu
The Land Builder	Oahu
Sales Builder	Oahu
Hawaii Educational Review	Oahu
Rizal Journal	Oahu
Hawaii	Oahu
The Army-Navy Review	Oahu
Current Hawaiiana	Oahu
Paaheo Press	Oahu
Elepaio	Oahu
The Councillor	Oahu
Honolulu Academy of Arts Publications	Oahu
Looking at Honolulu	Oahu
The Boxing Program	Oahu
Ke Keclikolani	Oahu
The Hawaii Health Messenger	Oahu
University of Hawaii Administration Publications	Oahu
Ti Mananginpadanang	Oahu
Wailuku Sugar Company's Plantation Hi-Lites	Maui
Hawaiian Commercial and Sugar Company Puunene Echo	Maui
Maui Agricultural Company's MACO Breeze	Maui
Maui High School's Hi-Notes	Maui
Baldwin High School's Baldwin Courier	Maui
Hawaiian Association of Social Workers Bulletin	Oahu

By order of the Military Governor:

(signed) Thomas H. Green,
THOMAS H. GREEN,
Colonel, J.A.G.D.,
Executive.

A TRUE COPY: *James F. Hanley*
JAMES F. HANLEY,
Major, J.A.G.D.

-2-

TERRITORY OF HAWAII
OFFICE OF THE MILITARY GOVERNOR
IOLANI PALACE
HONOLULU, T.H.

3 February 1942

GENERAL ORDERS)
NO. 65)

CURFEW

1. All persons, except enemy aliens, are permitted to be on the streets, as pedestrians, until 8:00 P.M.

2. Blackout regulations now in effect, such as the prohibition against lighted cigarettes, limited use of flashlights, etc., will be enforced.

3. Present restrictions on the use of motor vehicles will remain in force.

By order of the Military Governor:

(Signed) Thomas H. Green,
THOMAS H. GREEN,
Colonel, J.A.G.D.,
Executive.

A TRUE COPY: *James F. Hanley*
JAMES F. HANLEY,
Major, J.A.G.D.

TERRITORY OF HAWAII
OFFICE OF THE MILITARY GOVERNOR
IOLANI PALACE
HONOLULU, T. H.

1 February 1942

GENERAL ORDERS)
NO. 62   )

AMENDMENT OF GENERAL ORDER NO. 39--MILITARY ALIEN PROPERTY CONTROLLER.

General Orders Number 39 is amended by deleting paragraph 1 and substituting the following therefor:

"1. MR. ALFRED E. TREE of the Treasury Department is appointed as Military Alien Property Controller for the Territory of Hawaii to serve in such capacity under the Office of the Military Governor."

By order of the Military Governor:

(Signed) Thomas H. Green
THOMAS H. GREEN,
Colonel, J.A.G.D.,
Executive

A TRUE COPY:

William R. C. Morrison
WILLIAM R. C. MORRISON
Major, J.A.G.D.

TERRITORY OF HAWAII
OFFICE OF THE MILITARY GOVERNOR
IOLANI PALACE
HONOLULU, T.H.

3 February 1942

GENERAL ORDERS)
NO. 66)

SECTION I.   DAYLIGHT SAVING TIME
SECTION II.   BLACKOUT HOURS
SECTION III. CURFEW
SECTION IV.   OPENING AND CLOSING HOURS FOR PLACES OF BUSINESS AND AMUSEMENT

SECTION I. DAYLIGHT SAVING TIME.--1. Effective 2:00 A.M. 9 February 1942, "Daylight Saving Time" will be effective for the Territory of Hawaii.

2. At that time all clocks will be set ahead one hour to 3:00 A.M.

SECTION II. BLACKOUT HOURS.--The hours for blackout previously announced in Section II, General Orders No. 49, are amended, effective 9 February 1942, so that the blackout period begins at 7:30 P.M. and extends until 7:00 A.M.

SECTION III. CURFEW.--The curfew for pedestrians is hereby extended, effective 9 February 1942, to 9:00 P.M.

SECTION IV. OPENING AND CLOSING HOURS FOR PLACES OF BUSINESS AND AMUSEMENT.--1. All previous orders regarding the opening and closing hours of places of business and amusement are rescinded effective 9 February 1942, and the following substituted therefor:

2. Places of Business.--Places of business shall close not later than 6:00 P.M.

3. Places of Amusement.--Places of amusement may open at 9:00 A.M. on week days and 10:00 A.M. on Sundays and close not later than 6:00 P.M.

4. Exemptions from closing hour regulation.--The following types of business establishments are specifically exempted from the closing hours set out herein, provided they comply with all blackout regulations:

-1-

G. O. No. 66, O. M. G., 1942

a. Government offices.
b. Harbor facilities.
c. Hospitals.
d. Dairies.
e. Freight transportation.
f. Public utilities.
g. Radio
h. Newspapers.
i. Hotels and rooming establishments.
j. And such establishments as have been or may
hereafter be authorized to remain open by the Military Police.

5. Restaurants may open at 4:30 A.M. and close not
later than 9:00 P.M., except for such restaurants as are
permitted to remain open for longer periods by the Office of
the Military Governor.

By order of the Military Governor:

(Signed) Thomas H. Green,
THOMAS H. GREEN,
Colonel, J.A.G.D.,
Executive.

A TRUE COPY:

James F. Hanley
JAMES F. HANLEY,
Major, J.A.G.D.

-2-

TERRITORY OF HAWAII
OFFICE OF THE MILITARY GOVERNOR
IOLANI PALACE
HONOLULU, T.H.

4 February 1942

GENERAL ORDERS)
NO. 68)

INTOXICATING LIQUORS.--1. General Orders No. 2, this office,
7 December 1941, is hereby suspended.

2. Chapter 82 (Sections 2570-2642), Revised Laws of Hawaii, 1935,
as amended, shall be given full force and effect except insofar as it is
contrary to the provisions of this General Order.

3. From and after 24 February 1942, persons, firms, corporations,
clubs, and other associations holding licenses on 7 December 1941, under
Chapter 82, Revised Laws of Hawaii, 1935, as amended, and obtaining a permit
as herein provided, will be permitted to operate according to the existing
Territorial Laws and the regulations herein set forth. Nothing herein
contained shall be construed as granting the holders of licenses obtained
under Section 82, Revised Laws of Hawaii, 1935, as amended, any types of
licenses other than those held on 7 December 1941. No new licenses shall
be issued, nor shall any transfer of an existing license be made without the
consent of the Military Governor, or his duly authorized representative.

4. Regulations.--a. There shall be two types of permits, namely:
seller's permits and purchaser's permits. Seller's permits and purchaser's
permits will be issued by the Liquor Commission of the respective counties
of the Territory of Hawaii.

b. Seller's Permit.--(1) Seller's permits shall be issued only
when approved by the Military Governor or his duly authorized representatives. Seller's permit will be issued upon application to any holder of
a manufacturer's license, agent's license, wholesale dealer's license,
retail dealer's license, dispenser's license, or club license, under Chapter
82, Revised Laws of Hawaii, 1935, as amended, by the Liquor Commission of
the county which issued the license, at a cost of ten dollars ($10.00).
No seller's permit will be issued to holders of vessel licenses, nor to
"Class 8", Section 2580, Revised Laws of Hawaii, 1935, as amended. Such
applications and permits will be in the form prescribed by the Military
Governor.

(2) No seller's permit will be issued to any enemy alien,
nor to any company, corporation, association, or partnership, twenty-five
per centum (25%) or more of whose stock or interest therein is owned or
controlled by enemy aliens. No transfer of stock in any company, corporation or association or interest in any copartnership shall be made to
avoid this provision.

-1-

G. O. No. 68, O. M. G., 1942.

(3) The fees collected under the provisions of this sub-
paragraph shall be deposited by the respective Liquor Commissions in
special funds and a report thereof made to the Finance Officer, Office
of the Military Governor.

c. Purchaser's Permit.--(1) A permit to buy liquor in the
original package from retail dealers, holding seller's permits, may be
obtained upon application from the Liquor Commission of the county in
which the applicant resides by any individual at a cost of one dollar
($1.00). Under no circumstances will such permits be issued to minors.
Only one permit will be issued to any person. Persons who desire to
purchase liquor by the drink are not required to obtain a purchaser's
permit. Such applications and permits will be in the form prescribed
by the Military Governor.

(2) Purchaser's permits shall be valid for a period of
sixty (60) days from the issuance thereof. A new permit which shall
likewise be valid for a period of sixty (60) days shall be issued upon
application if the old permit is surrendered and a fee of fifty (50)
cents is paid.

(3) No purchaser's permit will be issued to any enemy
alien.

(4) When a purchase is made under a purchaser's permit,
the retail dealer making the sale will indicate in ink, on the space
provided therefor on the permit, the information required thereon. The
retail dealer will execute a sales slip, in triplicate, at the time of
sale, showing the date of sale, the name of the retail dealer and his
seller's permit number, the name of purchaser and number of his purchaser's
permit and the quantity of liquor sold and the price thereof. The original
of such sales slip will be affixed, with glue or similar substance, to
the bottle or original package. It shall be illegal to remove such sales
slip. Where there is more than one bottle or package a separate sales
slip will be made for each. The duplicate of all sales slips will be
sent to the Liquor Commission of the county in which the sale is made
within seven days after the sale and the triplicate will be retained by
the retailer dealer.

(5) The fees collected under the provisions of this sub-
paragraph will be deposited by the respective Liquor Commissions in a
special fund and a report thereof made to the Finance Officer, Office of
the Military Governor.

(6) Any person having obtained a purchaser's permit will
be permitted to purchase from a licensed retail dealer not to exceed one
(1) standard quart, or fifth, of liquor (except wine and beer), in the
original package, per week, or one (1) case of beer in the original
package per week, or three (3) quarts of wine per week. The weekly
allowance is not cumulative. If the allowance is not purchased in any

-2-

G. O. No. 68, O.M.G., 1942.

week, the right to purchase for that week expires. No liquor may be
purchased in advance or on credit.

d. Manufacturers, agents, and wholesale dealers who have
obtained a seller's permit may operate during the normal business hours
on all days of the week except Sundays. Retail dealers, dispensers and
clubs may receive deliveries of liquor during normal business hours on
6 days of the week except Sundays.

e. Retail dealers, dispensers and clubs who have obtained a
seller's permit may operate between the hours of 10:00 a.m., and 5:00 p.m.
daily except Sundays.

f. Dispensers and clubs who have obtained a seller's permit
may dispense only beer between the hours of 2:00 p.m. and 5:00 p.m. on
Sundays.

g. No retail dealer, dispenser or club shall employ any enemy
alien in their business as bartender, waiter, waitress, or in any other
position involving the serving or selling of liquor.

h. No intoxicating liquor shall be consumed on any street,
highway, river, stream, road, lane, park, beach, alley, or pathway, nor
from or in any automobile or other public or private carrier of freight
or passengers, nor from any horse-or-man-drawn vehicle, nor from or in
any trench, dug-out or similar cover, nor shall any package liquor be
consumed in any public place.

i. The regulations herein prescribed shall not be applicable
to military and naval reservations.

j. No liquor in package form shall be sold to any member of
the armed forces of the United States while in uniform.

k. Prices.--Prices charged shall not exceed those in effect on
6 December 1941, except upon specific authority of the Military Governor,
or his duly authorized representative.

l. Penalties.-- (1) Any holder of a seller's permit who shall
violate any of these regulations may have his permit revoked and shall be
subject to a fine of not more than $5,000.00 and imprisoned for not more
than five years, or both.

(2) Any holder of a seller's permit who permits any person
to become drunk on his premises may have his seller's permit suspended or
revoked and shall be subject to a fine of not to exceed $1,000.00.

(3) Any applicant for a seller's or a purchaser's
permit, who shall make a false statement on the application for such permit
shall have such permit revoked if it has been issued, or refused if such
permit has not been issued, and shall be subject to a fine of not more than
$500.00 or imprisonment for not more than six months, or both. Further,

-3-

G. O. No. 68, O. M. G., 1942.

such applicant will be precluded from obtaining either type of permit thereafter.

(4). Any person granted a purchaser's permit who shall purchase liquor, beer, or wine on behalf of another person on such permit or any person holding a purchaser's permit who shall purchase more than the quantity of liquor authorized in any one week or any person permitting another to use his purchaser's permit to purchase liquor, or any person who shall be convicted of drunkenness, shall forfeit such permit, shall not be granted another such permit for a period of six months and shall be subject to a fine not to exceed $500.00, or imprisonment for not more than six months, or both.

(5) Any person who makes a purchase of liquor, using as his authority therefor a purchaser's permit issued to another person, shall forfeit his permit, if one has been issued; shall in any event be granted a purchaser's permit for a period of 6 months; and shall be subject to a fine not to exceed $100.00 or imprisonment for not more than 2 months, or both.

(6) Any person who shall forge in any manner or make reproductions of a seller's permit or a purchaser's permit issued under the authority of this General Order without the permission of the Military Governor, shall be subject to a fine not to exceed $1,000 or imprisonment not to exceed one year, or both, and if such person has received for his use either type of permit, such permit shall be forfeited and a new permit shall in no event be issued to him for one year.

(7) Any person who engages in bootlegging or conspires to engage in bootlegging; or any person who purchases liquor from a bootlegger or in any manner not otherwise covered by this General Order; or who manufactures liquor in his home, place of business, or any other place in excess of that provided by the Federal and Territorial law in effect on 6 December 1941, or conspires to engage in such manufacture, shall be subject to a fine of not in excess of $5,000.00, or imprisonment for not to exceed five years, or both, and further any and all liquor owned by such person or in the process of manufacture or any ingredients thereof belonging to such person shall forthwith be forfeited and shall be disposed of in the manner prescribed by the Military Governor.

m. In the event of the loss of his purchaser's permit, the person to which it was issued will advise the Liquor Commission of the county issuing the same without delay.

n. Under the supervision of the Military Governor the Liquor Commission of the City and County of Honolulu will operate as provided for by law and will administer the provisions of this General Order. The Liquor Commissions of the Counties of Hawaii, Maui, and Kauai, respectively, will do likewise under the supervision of the District Commanders of the Military Districts of Hawaii, Maui, and Kauai, respectively.

-4-

G. O. No. 68, O. M. G., 1942.

o. Persons not granted seller's permits under the provisions of this General Order, and persons who are granted seller's permits under this General Order, who may desire to dispose of liquor stocks owned by them may, with the approval of the Office of the Military Governor, sell such stocks to any person, firm, etc., having a seller's permit.

p. Manufacturers, agents and wholesale dealers who have been issued seller's permits will limit their sales of liquor to other wholesale dealers, or retail dealers, dispensers or clubs who hold seller's permits except on special authorization from the Military Governor. This does not apply to sales made to the Federal Government, the Territorial Government, and instrumentalities of either.

By order of the Military Governor:

(Signed) Thomas H. Green
THOMAS H. GREEN
Colonel, J.A.G.D.,
Executive.

A TRUE COPY:
James F. Hanley
JAMES F. HANLEY,
Major, J.A.G.D.,

-5-

TERRITORY OF HAWAII
OFFICE OF THE MILITARY GOVERNOR
IOLANI PALACE
HONOLULU, T.H.

7 February 1942

GENERAL ORDERS)
NO. 71)

SECTION I.   AMENDING GENERAL ORDERS NO. 67 (EVACUATION)
SECTION II.   CHILDREN
SECTION III. WORKERS GOING TO WORK IN MORNING
SECTION IV.   BLACKOUT OF PIERS, ETC.
SECTION V.   CHANGES IN ONE-WAY STREETS AND "LEFT TURN" SIGNS
SECTION VI.   STICKERS, ETC.
SECTION VII. CONTROL OF EPIDEMIC DISEASE

SECTION I. AMENDING GENERAL ORDERS NO. 67 (EVACUATION).--1. Paragraph 1, General Orders No. 67, this office, 4 February 1942, is amended to read as follows: "1. In order that residents of greatest danger areas be prepared to evacuate should such an eventuality become necessary, all women, girls, and those boys under 15 years of age living in that part of Honolulu Makai of the line (toward the sea or between the line formed by these streets and the seashore): Middle Street--King Street--Houghtailing Street--Vineyard Street--Liliha Street--School Street--Lusitana Street--Auwaiolimu Street--Pensacola Street--Wilder Avenue--Punahou Street--Beretania Street--Waialae Avenue--Kapahulu Avenue--Campbell Avenue--Hayden Street--Eleventh Avenue--Kaimuki Avenue--Oili Road and Kahala Avenue; should provide themselves at once with an evacuation kit containing the following:

a. Four days supply of non-perishable food, already cooked and including special foods for small children where necessary (tinned foods preferable).

b. Two blankets.

c. One raincoat--waterproof garment may be substituted.

d. Warm clothing.

e. Gas mask.

f. Miscellaneous articles: can opener, toilet articles, soap, towels, flashlights.

Most of the daily newspapers have published a map which clarifies the line described above and all persons are advised to cut out the map from the newspapers and keep it for future reference.

SECTION II. CHILDREN.--Effective 9 February 1942, children under the age of sixteen years will not be permitted on the streets between the hours of 7:30 p.m. and 9:00 a.m. unless accompanied by one of their parents or an adult person.

-1-

G. O. No. 71, O. M. G., 1942.

SECTION III. WORKERS GOING TO WORK IN MORNING.--The following regulations relating to workers going to work on and after 9 February 1942, are published for the information and guidance of those concerned:

1. Men and women who must leave their homes before 7:00 a.m. in order to reach their places of employment between the hours of 7:00 a.m. and 8:00 a.m., respectively, will be permitted to proceed on the streets and highways of the City and County of Honolulu in motor vehicles or on foot after 5:30 a.m. in the morning. Such workers should leave their homes as late as possible.

2. Between the hours of 5:30 a.m. and 7:00 a.m., all blackout restrictions as prescribed in Section II, General Orders No. 49, this office, 6 January 1942, must be observed. Each motor vehicle must proceed with all caution necessary with safety. The maximum speed authorized is thirty miles an hour, except in those areas where a lesser speed is prescribed for daytime travel, the lesser speed will be observed.

3. The permission to proceed to work before 7:00 a.m. is not to be interpreted as authorizing lights or other illumination of any kind in homes, etc., before 7:00 a.m. except under blackout conditions. All violators will be subject to the same penalties as violators during other hours of blackout.

4. Enemy aliens will not be permitted on the streets or highways between the hours of 5:30 a.m. and 7:00 a.m. unless they have the special permission of the Provost Marshal or his duly authorized representative.

5. Children under the age of 16 years will not be permitted on the streets or highways between the hours of 5:30 a.m. and 7:00 a.m., unless accompanied by one of their parents or some other adult person, and unless their travel is directly connected with their parents or guardians proceeding to work.

SECTION IV. BLACKOUT OF PIERS, ETC.--1. Where piers, factories and other facilities have been given special permission to work during the hours of blackout, the maximum blackout consistent with the work will be observed. Windows will be painted or otherwise blacked-out, doors and other openings will be opened only to the extent necessary, and the minimum illumination consistent with efficient operation will be used. In the event the pier, or factory, etc., is not completely enclosed, all lights will be shaded so as not to be visible from the air, or outside, insofar as possible, that is, they will be shaded so as to throw the illumination only downward.

2. The control of blackout and the decision of the sufficiency and effectiveness of the blackout effort is vested in the Provost Marshal.

3. Applications for special permission to operate piers, factories, etc., during the hours of blackout will be filed with the Provost Marshal for approval.

-2-

G. O. No. 71, O. M. G., 1942.

SECTION V. CHANGES IN ONE-WAY STREETS AND "LEFT TURN" SIGNS.--1. Effective February 9, 1942, the following changes in one-way streets are made:

a. Fort Street, between King and Kukui Streets, will be one-way in the Mauka direction.

b. Queen Street, between Fort and Punchbowl Streets, will be a two-way street.

2. All "No Left Turn" signs, except those posted at signalized intersections will be removed from the streets of the City of Honolulu. If and when it becomes necessary to prohibit left turns, portable "No Left Turn" signs will be placed in the intersection temporarily.

SECTION VI. STICKERS, ETC.--1. Effective February 15, 1942, no sticker, emblem, poster, marker or similar device will be displayed on the windshield or other part of any motor vehicle operating on the Island of Oahu, visible to the public unless such sticker, emblem, poster, marker or similar device has been registered with the Honolulu Police Department and its use authorized by the Office of the Military Governor.

2. The person or organization authorized to issue a marker, or similar device shall maintain an alphabetical record of persons or organizations to whom such stickers have been issued, which record will be available to the military authorities and the Honolulu Police Department for consultation. Copies of any rules or regulations prescribed by the issuing agency for the use of authorized stickers, emblems, poster, marker, or similar device will be furnished the Office of the Military Governor and the Honolulu Police Department.

3. No sticker, emblem, poster, marker or similar device covered by this section will exceed 4 inches by 5 inches, placed at the lower right hand corner of windshield, nor will it be displayed on any part of the windshield, or other part of motor vehicle, when such motor vehicle is not engaged in the mission for which the sticker, emblem, poster, marker or similar device is authorized.

4. Any person or organization violating this section will be punished by a fine of not more than fifty dollars, or confined at hard labor for not more than thirty days, or both.

SECTION VII. CONTROL OF EPIDEMIC DISEASE.--1. In the interest of the public safety and for the common good of those citizens who may have to go inland to camps or villages in the event of enemy action, it is directed that all persons living in the area on the seaward (makai) side of a line from Keena Point on the North Shore through Puu Iki to Lae O Kaoio Point on the windward shore of Oahu be protected at once against smallpox and against typhoid and the para-typhoid fevers by vaccination, under the following provisions:

-3-

G. O. No. 71, O. M. G., 1942.

a. Vaccinations will be given without charge at places accessible to the citizens by the Medical Department of the Office of Civilian Defense and/or the Medical Department of the Army.

b. Those who are acutely ill, infirm or aged may be registered with the doctors of the Office of Civilian Defense for vaccination at a later date and may be delayed at this time. Exemption by reason of having attained the age of forty-five is not applicable under existing conditions.

c. Vaccination against smallpox will be given to all persons over the age of six months who have not been vaccinated since 1 January 1941, unless, in the opinion of the doctor in charge at that point they show definite evidence of having had smallpox or of reason for delay as provided in 1 b above. Vaccination of infants under six months is advised but is not made compulsory at this time. In order to secure a certificate of vaccination, it will be necessary for each person vaccinated to report back that the doctors may see the results of the vaccination. This must be done at the time and place specified.

d. Vaccination against typhoid and para-typhoid fevers will be given to all persons who have passed their third birthday unless they show evidence of having had this immunization since 1 January 1941 or have definite cause for delay by reason of ill health or infirmity. This vaccination requires three doses administered within strict time limits and all concerned are directed to report at the time and place named for each of the three doses in order to complete their treatment properly and to avoid the necessity of starting the course over again. Children weighing less than fifty pounds will receive one-half the adult dosage.

e. Careful rosters of vaccinations will be maintained by all doctors and upon completion of vaccination a certificate showing the record of doses and results of the smallpox vaccination will be furnished each person, or in the case of children, the parent or guardian. These should be kept with care and carried by those persons who find it necessary to go inland for safety. They will be accepted as proof of vaccination and avoid the need of further vaccination in the camps or villages to which they may go.

2. All persons affected by this order may be assured that the vaccinations directed are safe and are not likely to cause them much inconvenience. Children usually have very little discomfort. Men, women, and children of families connected with the Army and Navy have taken these protective treatments during many years. The protection afforded has proven of the greatest value in saving lives and averting illness.

By order of the Military Governor:

(signed) Thomas H. Green,
THOMAS H. GREEN,
Colonel, J.A.G.D.,
Executive.

A TRUE COPY: *James F. Hanley*
JAMES F. HANLEY,
Major, J.A.G.D.

-4-

TERRITORY OF HAWAII
OFFICE OF THE MILITARY GOVERNOR
IOLANI PALACE
HONOLULU, T.H.

10 February 1942

GENERAL ORDERS)
NO. 72   )

SECTION I. PAYMENT AND REFUND OF RENT
SECTION II. APPOINTMENT OF PROVOST COURT NO. 2, HONOLULU, T.H.

SECTION I. PAYMENT AND REFUND OF RENT.--1. No person, firm, or corporation shall institute, maintain, or prosecute any action, suit or other proceeding in any circuit or district court in the City and County of Honolulu, Territory of Hawaii, to recover the possession of any premises used for housing accommodations as defined in Section 1, Ordinance 941 of the City and County of Honolulu, Territory of Hawaii, without first having obtained an order of the Rent Control Commission of said City and County of Honolulu that said plaintiff or plaintiffs is or are entitled to the possession of said premises, and no such suit, action, or other proceeding shall be instituted, maintained, or prosecuted for the purpose aforesaid in any such said circuit or district court without such order having been first obtained by the said plaintiff or plaintiffs in such suit, action, or other said proceeding.

2. This order shall be retroactive and shall be deemed to have been in full force and effect as of and after January 27, 1942, and shall be retroactive and applicable to any such action, suit, or proceedings, now pending in said circuit and district courts as well as to those hereafter instituted, maintained, or prosecuted in said circuit and district courts.

3. Payments of rent shall continue to be made at the dates the rent becomes due on all housing accommodations in accordance with the agreement or procedure previously effected by the parties thereto. Landlords shall refund any unused portion of rent paid in advance to any tenants who are duly evacuated from the Territory of Hawaii.

SECTION II. APPOINTMENT OF PROVOST COURT NO. 2, HONOLULU, T.H.-- Lieutenant Colonel John R. Hermann, Infantry, is appointed as a Provost Court and is assigned to duty as Provost Court No. 2, at Honolulu, Territory of Hawaii, for the trial of such persons as may be properly brought before it.

By order of the Military Governor:

(signed) Thomas H. Green,
THOMAS H. GREEN,
Colonel, J.A.G.D.,
Executive.

A TRUE COPY: *James F. Hanley*
JAMES F. HANLEY,
Major, J.A.G.D.

TERRITORY OF HAWAII
OFFICE OF THE MILITARY GOVERNOR
IOLANI PALACE
HONOLULU, T.H.

26 February 1942

GENERAL ORDERS)
NO. 78   )

CIVILIAN DEFENSE ADVISOR TO MILITARY GOVERNOR.--Mr. Benjamin W. Thoron is announced as Civilian Defense Advisor to the Military Governor, Territory of Hawaii.

By order of the Military Governor:

(signed) Thomas H. Green,
THOMAS H. GREEN,
Colonel, J.A.G.D.,
Executive.

A TRUE COPY: *James F. Hanley*
JAMES F. HANLEY,
Major, J.A.G.D.

TERRITORY OF HAWAII
OFFICE OF THE MILITARY GOVERNOR
IOLANI PALACE
HONOLULU, T.H.

28 February 1942

GENERAL ORDERS)
NO. 81)

LIVESTOCK AND POULTRY CENSUS.--1. Every poultry farm, dairy farm, hog farm and stable in the Territory of Hawaii shall submit to the Office of Food Control of the County or City and County in which his flock, herd or stable is located, an accurate census of birds or animals in his flock, herd, or stable as defined below. This census will be as of February 28, 1942, to be in the hands of the Office of Food Control of the respective Counties not later than March 5, 1942 and monthly thereafter as of the last day of each calendar month, to be in the hands of the Office of Food Control by the fifth day of the month next following, until further notice.

2. The basis for census enumeration by individual flocks, herds or stables shall be:

a. Poultry farms. Every poultry farm having one hundred (100) birds three (3) months old and older shall submit a census showing the number of birds three (3) months old or older.

b. Dairy farms. Every dairy farm milking ten (10) or more cows shall submit a census showing the number of barn fed and/or pen fed mature dairy cattle and the number of heifer calves one (1) to eight (8) months old.

c. Hog farms. Every hog farm having twenty-five (25) or more swine of all descriptions shall submit a census showing the number of mature breeding pigs; the number of pigs three (3) weeks to three (3) months old; the number of pigs, other than breeding pigs, which are over three (3) months old divided into the following weight classes: under one hundred and fifty (150) pounds; over one hundred and fifty (150) pounds.

d. Stables. Every feeder of riding or working horses and/or mules shall submit a census showing the number of draft horses and/or mules; the number of riding horses and/or mules; the number of pack horses and/or mules.

3. Census forms for the above described enumeration may be obtained from the Office of the Director of Food Control, Office of the Military Governor, Iolani Palace, Honolulu, T. H., and from the offices of the Food Administrators of the Counties of Maui, Hawaii and Kauai, respectively. These forms may also be obtained from the Agricultural Extension Agent in each district.

By order of the Military Governor:

(signed) Thomas H. Green,
THOMAS H. GREEN,
Colonel, J.A.G.D.,
Executive.

A TRUE COPY:

James F. Hanley
JAMES F. HANLEY,
Major, J.A.G.D.

TERRITORY OF HAWAII
OFFICE OF THE MILITARY GOVERNOR
IOLANI PALACE
HONOLULU, T.H.

11 March 1942

GENERAL ORDERS,
NO. 84)

SECTION I.   CARRIAGE OF INFORMATION TO MAINLAND
SECTION II. PROCEDURE FOR RESIGNATION OF NURSES
SECTION III. PIGEONS.
SECTION IV. AMENDMENT TO GENERAL ORDERS NO. 59

SECTION I. CARRIAGE OF INFORMATION TO MAINLAND.--1. It is illegal for any person to carry to the mainland, or elsewhere for transmission to the mainland, by clipper, ship, or otherwise, any written or printed matter whatsoever, or any photographs, sketches or drawings intended for publication in newspapers, magazines, etc., which have not been censored and so marked by a duly authorised censor.

2. Any person violating this section shall be subject to a fine of not more than five hundred dollars ($500.00) or imprisonment for not to exceed six (6) months, or both.

SECTION II. PROCEDURE FOR RESIGNATION OF NURSES.--1. The resignation by a nurse employed in a hospital, other than Army and Navy Hospitals, or in a First-Aid Station shall be submitted in writing to the Superintendent of Nurses in the hospital or to the doctor or official in charge of the First-Aid Station, as the case may be, who will refer such resignation with approval or disapproval to the Supervisor of Nursing Activities of Oahu, Office of Civilian Defense, who will in turn submit the resignation with recommendation to the Director of Labor Control, Office of the Military Governor, for approval or disapproval. Any nurse desiring a personal hearing may apply therefor to the Director of Labor Control.

2. In instances where the Superintendent of Nurses, or doctor or official in charge has disapproved the resignation and the Director of Labor Control has approved the resignation, the nurse will not be released until the Superintendent of Nurses, or doctor or official in charge concerned has been notified of the action taken.

3. Mrs. David Y. K. Akana, is designated Supervisor of Nursing Activities for Oahu, Office of Civilian Defense, with offices at Kaunamanu School, where she may be contacted between the hours of 10:00 a.m. and 2:00 p.m. daily, except Sundays. Telephone number 1317.

SECTION III. PIGEONS.--1. All persons, whether citizens or aliens, having any number of pigeons of any type in their possession, custody or under their control, shall report such fact to the Office of the Military Governor, not later than 25 March 1942, giving the number of birds, address

-1-

TERRITORY OF HAWAII
OFFICE OF THE MILITARY GOVERNOR
IOLANI PALACE
HONOLULU, T.H.

10 March 1942

GENERAL ORDERS)
NO. 83)

AMENDING GENERAL ORDERS NO. 35.--General Orders No. 35, this office, 19 December 1941, relating to the evacuation of the Iwilei area, is hereby amended by adding thereto two new paragraphs reading as follows:

"4. No suit or action shall be instituted or maintained in any court within the Territory of Hawaii for the collection of rent or ejection of any tenant in the Iwilei area, or for cancellation of any lease by reason of non-payment of rent, taxes, or breach of any covenant or condition of such lease of any of the above described area during the period that such area shall be evacuated under the terms of this Order.

"5. Paragraph 4 above shall not apply to any premises in the Iwilei area which is actually in use or occupation by a tenant and where the tenant has not been deprived of the reasonable intended use thereof by General Orders No. 35."

By order of the Military Governor:

(signed) Thomas H. Green,
THOMAS H. GREEN,
Colonel, J.A.G.D.,
Executive.

A TRUE COPY:

James F. Hanley
JAMES F. HANLEY,
Major, J.A.G.D.

G. O. No. 84, O. M. G., 1942

of cote or place such birds are kept, registered numbers or letters of the individual leg bands, if any, and reason for keeping such birds.

2. All homing or carrier pigeons will be equipped with individual leg bands if not now so equipped and will be registered with the Office of the Military Governor.

3. It shall be unlawful to transport, carry, or deliver any type of pigeon from one place to another within the Territory of Hawaii without the permission of the Military Governor.

4. It shall be unlawful to send any message, writing or code by carrier or homing or other pigeon within the Territory of Hawaii.

5. Any person finding a homing or carrier pigeon at large will immediately turn such bird in to the Military Police, Honolulu Police Station.

6. This order does not apply to the armed forces of the United States.

7. Any person violating any provision of this section shall be subject to a fine of not more than five hundred dollars ($500.00), or imprisonment for not to exceed six (6) months, or both.

SECTION IV. AMENDMENT TO GENERAL ORDERS NO. 59.--1. Section I, General Orders No. 59, this office, 29 January 1942, is amended by adding thereto the following newspapers:

Ka Huku O Hawaii	Hawaii
Ka Punahou	Oahu
The Daily Pinion	Oahu
The Hawaii Farm and Home	Oahu
The St. Louis Collegian	Oahu
Ka Leo O Hawaii	Oahu

2. Section II, General Orders No. 59, this office, 29 January 1942, is amended by adding thereto the following magazines:

Ka Moi	Oahu
Hawaii Vocational Rehab Bulletin	Oahu
The Hawaii Public Employe	Oahu
HEA Newsflash	Oahu
Washington Hi-Lights	Oahu
Knispeak	Oahu
Ka Pokou Hana Hookupu	Oahu
The Governor	Oahu
Ke Kiaaina	Oahu

-2-

G. O. No. 84, O. M. G., 1942

The Leahi Bulletin	Oahu
The Helemano Flash	Oahu
The Rough Rider & Roundup	Oahu
Ka Alii	Oahu
Hawaii Medical Journal	Oahu
Allied Youth Post Bulletin	Oahu
Farrington High School Alumni Bulletin	Oahu

By order of the Military Governor:

(signed) Thomas H. Green,
THOMAS H. GREEN,
Colonel, J.A.G.D.,
Executive.

A TRUE COPY:

James F. Hanley

JAMES F. HANLEY,
Major, J.A.G.D.

TERRITORY OF HAWAII
OFFICE OF THE MILITARY GOVERNOR
IOLANI PALACE
HONOLULU, T.H.

31 March 1942

GENERAL ORDERS)
NO. 91   )

LABOR.--1. General Orders No. 38, Office of the Military Governor, 20 December 1941, is revoked as of 31 March 1942.

2. The following policy, effective 1 April 1942, governing wages, hours of work, overtime, the employment and use of labor in the Territory of Hawaii, is announced for the information and guidance of all concerned. Nothing herein shall be construed as superseding or in conflict with the provisions of the Fair Labor Standards Act of 1938, or the Walsh Healey Public Contracts Act.

a. Wages.--(1) Revised Wage Schedule No. 9, U. S. Navy Contractors, Pacific Naval Air Bases, effective 1 December 1941, is hereby designated as the standard wage scale for workers engaged in work for Army and Navy agencies, their contractors and subcontractors. No person seeking employment with the above mentioned employers shall be employed at a rate less than or in excess of the standard rate for the job as listed in Revised Wage Schedule No. 9, and as same may be revised from time to time, as approved by the Military Governor.

(2) The above provision, relative to wages, shall not apply to Federal or Territorial, and City and County of Honolulu Civil Service employees.

b. Hours of Work and Overtime.--(1) Normal work-week on war projects in the Territory of Hawaii shall be six (6) days of eight (8) hours each.

(2) Overtime at the rate of one and one-half the regular rate will be paid for overtime in excess of forty-four (44) hours, or in excess of eight (8) hours in any one day. The maximum hours worked in any seven (7) consecutive days shall not exceed fifty-six (56), except in cases of emergencies and with the approval of the Chief of Military or Naval Service concerned.

TERRITORY OF HAWAII
OFFICE OF THE MILITARY GOVERNOR
IOLANI PALACE
HONOLULU, T.H.

19 March 1942

GENERAL ORDERS)
NO. 88   )

Slaughtering of Hogs. To prevent the slaughter of immature hogs on Oahu as well as sows suitable for breeding, the following regulations are hereby made effective:

1. No hog shall be killed on Oahu for marketing which shall have a dressed weight of less than one hundred and forty (140) pounds.

2. No sow suitable for breeding shall be killed on Oahu for marketing without a permit issued by the Director of Food Control, Office of the Military Governor, through one of the following authorized agents:

Paul A. Gantt	Office of Food Control
Dr. S. H. Work	University of Hawaii
Frank G. Sutherland	University of Hawaii
Edwin Chun	County Agent, South Oahu
F. Okamura	County Agent, West Oahu
M. Riley	County Agent, East Oahu
Dr. E. H. Willers	Territorial Veterinarian
Dr. R. W. Pinfold	Territorial Veterinarian
Dr. L. C. Hoss	Licensed Veterinarian
Dr. Y. Yamashiro	Licensed Veterinarian
Dr. Paul Nomura	Licensed Veterinarian

3. Any violation of the above regulations shall be punishable by a fine of not to exceed two hundred dollars ($200.00) or imprisonment for not more than thirty (30) days or both for each conviction.

By order of the Military Governor:

(signed) Thomas H. Green,
THOMAS H. GREEN,
Colonel, J.A.G.D.,
Executive.

A TRUE COPY:

James F. Hanley

JAMES F. HANLEY,
Major, J.A.G.D.

G. O. No. 91, O. M. G., 1942

(3) Work shall be so scheduled that all workers will receive one (1) day off in seven (7). This day is to be in lieu of Sunday, and Sunday work per se shall not be considered overtime, and no overtime shall be paid for Sunday except when it is worked consecutively in excess of six (6) days. It is the intent of this provision to make it possible for work on war projects to be carried on seven (7) days per week, and at the same time provide that all war workers shall have one (1) day of rest out of seven (7) for the purpose of recreation and to attend to personal business.

(4) The provisions relative to hours of work and overtime shall not apply to: (a) Federal, Territorial or City and County of Honolulu civil service employees; (b) Employees of employers mentioned in paragraph 2a above, who are in a supervisory capacity on a monthly salary basis.

(5) The provisions of any contract with individual employees, labor unions, etc., in conflict with the provisions of this order are hereby suspended.

c. Employment.--(1) No Army or Navy agencies, their contractors or subcontractors, Federal agencies, Territorial agencies, City and County of Honolulu agencies, their contractors or subcontractors, hospitals, public utilities, stevedoring companies and sources of supply controlled by the Army and/or the Navy, shall employ or offer to employ, any individual formerly or now in the employment of the above mentioned employers unless and until such individual shall have presented to the employing agency a bona fide release without prejudice, in writing, from his last previous employer.

(2) Any individual who is or has been employed by any employer, as above described, who presents himself to any other such agency and secures or attempts to secure employment without having a bona fide release without prejudice from his last previous employer, or in any way misrepresents his employment status with regard to such release, shall, upon conviction, be fined not more than Two Hundred Dollars ($200.00) or be imprisoned for not more than two (2) months, or both.

d. Use of Labor.--(1) Terms of labor contracts between individuals and agencies of the Army and Navy, their contractors and subcontractors, which restrict or specify the nature of work to be performed, are hereby suspended.

(2) Persons employed now or hereafter employed by employers mentioned in paragraph 2c(1) must report, within a reasonable time thereafter, to the job to which they are ordered by their employer.

- 2 -

G. O. No. 91, O. M. G., 1942

(3) Any individual now or hereafter employed by employers mentioned in paragraph 2c(1) who fails to report, within a reasonable time thereafter, to the job to which he is ordered by his employer, shall, upon conviction, be fined not more than Two Hundred Dollars ($200.00) or be imprisoned for not more than two (2) months, or both.

3. Appeal Agency.--a. Persons discharged with prejudice from employment with employers mentioned in paragraph 2c(1) may appeal their cases to the Appeal Agency, Office of the Director of Labor Control, for decision as to whether or not they may be allowed to continue work with another employer.

b. The Chief Administrator, Office of the Director of Labor Control, is hereby designated as the Appeal Agency for persons discharged with prejudice by employers mentioned in paragraph 2c(1). Any complainant not satisfied with the decision of the Appeal Agency may further appeal his case to the Advisory Council to the Director of Labor Control.

By order of the Military Governor:

(Signed) Thomas H. Green,
THOMAS H. GREEN,
Colonel, J.A.C.D.,
Executive.

A TRUE COPY: *James F. Hanley*
JAMES F. HANLEY,
Major, J.A.G.D.

- 3 -

G. O. No. 92, O. M. G., 1942

SECTION IV. AIR RAID SHELTERS.--1. The entrance or use of public air raid shelters for any purpose other than protection during air raids is prohibited.

2. Any person causing damage in any way to any public air raid shelter, splinter-proof shelter, splinter-proof trench, or any other public structure intended for use as protection during an air raid, or using such place for any purpose other than protection during an air raid, shall be subject to a fine of not to exceed five hundred dollars ($500.00) or imprisonment not in excess of six (6) months, or both, and shall be required to pay for any damage such person may have caused and to put such place in the same condition as it was before such person committed the act prohibited by this section.

3. This is not intended as preventing persons entering such places for purposes of inspection or if in a public building, the normal intended use of the premises.

SECTION V. GENERAL ORDERS NO. 49, AMENDED.--Paragraph 8, General Orders No. 49, this office, 6 January 1942, enumerating streets upon which no parking will be permitted, is amended as follows:

a. Change "Lusitana Street" to read Lusitana Street, between School Street and Alapai Street".

b. Add thereto:

"Kapiolani Boulevard".
"Harding Avenue, from Kapiolani Boulevard to 16th Avenue".
"16th Avenue, from Waialae Avenue to Fort Ruger".

By order of the Military Governor:

(signed) Thomas H. Green,
THOMAS H. GREEN,
Colonel, J.A.C.D.,
Executive.

A TRUE COPY: *James F. Hanley*
JAMES F. HANLEY,
Major, J.A.G.D.

-2-

TERRITORY OF HAWAII
OFFICE OF THE MILITARY GOVERNOR
IOLANI PALACE
HONOLULU, T.H.

GENERAL ORDERS)
NO. 92)

APR 1 1942

SECTION I. GAS ALARM SIGNALS
SECTION II. REGISTRATION OF GRADUATE NURSES
SECTION III. SPEED LIMITS IN THE TERRITORY OF HAWAII
SECTION IV. AIR RAID SHELTERS
SECTION V. GENERAL ORDERS NO. 49, AMENDED

SECTION I. GAS ALARM SIGNALS.--1. Signals for sounding of gas alarms been placed throughout the Island of Oahu. These signals have been marked to indicate the use for which they are installed. The public is warned to refrain from sounding gas alarms. Only members of the Honolulu Police Department, Air Raid Wardens, Businessmen's Training Corps, Hawaiian Territorial Guard Reserve, Teacher Gas Sentries, members of the armed forces and other specifically authorized persons may sound the alarm.

2. Any unauthorized person who sounds a gas alarm or damages in any manner a gas alarm shall be subject to a fine not in excess of five hundred dollars ($500.00) or imprisonment for not to exceed six (6) months, or both.

SECTION II. REGISTRATION OF GRADUATE NURSES.--1. In order to better handle any emergency situation which may arise, all graduate nurses in the Territory of Hawaii, except those in the armed forces, shall register, on or before April 15, 1942.

2. Registration on the Island of Oahu will be conducted at the Mabel L. Smythe Memorial Building, 510 South Beretania Street, Honolulu, T. H. Registration on the other islands will be conducted at the times and places to be designated by the Commanding Officer of the Service Command of each of the islands, respectively.

SECTION III. SPEED LIMITS IN THE TERRITORY OF HAWAII.--1. In conformity with the recent directive of the President of the United States that speed limits be reduced, it is ordered that the following maximum speed for motor vehicles in the Territory of Hawaii be observed:

a. Trucks and buses of 1½ tons or over (except fire apparatus) - 30 miles per hour.

b. All other motor vehicles - 40 miles per hour.

-1-

TERRITORY OF HAWAII
OFFICE OF THE MILITARY GOVERNOR
IOLANI PALACE
HONOLULU, T.H.

4 April 1942

GENERAL ORDERS)
NO. 94)

INTOXICATING LIQUORS.--1. Paragraph 4 g (6), General Orders No. 68, this office, 4 February 1942, is amended to read:

"Any person having obtained a purchaser's permit will be permitted to purchase from a licensed retail dealer not to exceed one (1) standard quart or fifth of liquor (except wine and beer) in the original package per week or one (1) case of beer in the original package per week, or one (1) gallon of wine per week. Same for the purposes of this paragraph is considered as "wine". The weekly allowance is not cumulative. If the allowance is not purchased in any week the right to purchase for that week expires. No liquor may be purchased in advance or on credit."

2. Paragraph 4 g, General Orders No. 68, is amended to read:

"Dispensers, clubs and retail dealers who have obtained a seller's permit may open for business not earlier than 10:00 a.m. each day except Sunday. Dispensers and clubs must close not later than 5:00 p.m. Retail dealers must close not later than 5:00 p.m. except on Tuesday and Thursday when such dealers may remain open until 6:30 p.m.

3. Paragraph 4 i, General Orders No. 68, is amended by adding at the end thereof the following new sub-paragraph:

"(8) Any person or firm violating or permitting the violation on his or its premises of any limitation or restriction prescribed by this general order which is not otherwise punishable by the provisions of paragraph 4 i, shall upon conviction be subject to a fine not to exceed five hundred dollars ($500.00) or imprisonment for not more than six (6) months or both."

By order of the Military Governor:

(signed) Thomas H. Green,
THOMAS H. GREEN,
Colonel, J.A.G.D.,
Executive.

A TRUE COPY: *James F. Hanley*
JAMES F. HANLEY,
Major, J.A.G.D.

TERRITORY OF HAWAII
OFFICE OF THE MILITARY GOVERNOR
IOLANI PALACE
HONOLULU, T.H.

GENERAL ORDERS)
NO. 101)   30 April 1942

SECTION I.   TRAVEL CONTROL BUREAU
SECTION II.   SPEED LIMITS IN THE TERRITORY OF HAWAII
SECTION III. LOADING ZONE
SECTION IV.   RESCISSION OF GENERAL ORDERS
SECTION V.   BLACKOUT HOURS
SECTION VI.   CURFEW
SECTION VII. CHILDREN
SECTION VIII. ESTABLISHMENT OF CIVILIAN HOSPITAL CONTROL OFFICE

SECTION I.   TRAVEL CONTROL BUREAU.-- For the purpose of carrying out the provisions of the President's Proclamations of December 7 and 8, 1941, and the provisions of General Orders No. 32, this office, 18 December 1941, with respect to inter-island travel by enemy aliens, and for the purpose of controlling and regulating inter-island travel by air with a view to conservation of facilities for necessary and important traffic, there is established in each County a Travel Control Bureau.

2.   The Travel Control Bureau in the City and County of Honolulu will function as a section of the Contact Office, Office of the Assistant Chief of Staff, G-2, Headquarters Hawaiian Department, and in each of the other counties than Oahu the bureau will be under the control of the District Commander thereof.

3.   a.   An officer from the Contact Office, Office of the Assistant Chief of Staff, G-2, Headquarters Hawaiian Department, will be detailed to the office of the Hawaiian Airlines, Limited, Honolulu, T. H., for the purpose of examining applications for such travel.

b.   The Commanding General of the District concerned (Hawaii, Maui, Kauai) or an officer designated by him, will examine each application for travel originating in that district.

c.   On the Island of Molokai examination of such travel applications will be made by an officer detailed for that purpose by the Commanding General of the Maui District.

4.   The following regulations are prescribed for the control of travel by enemy aliens, and travel by air:

a.   No enemy alien will be allowed to travel on any airplane, Governmental or commercial, except in cases of extreme emergency when such travel may be authorized by the Travel Control Bureau after proper precautions and safeguards have been taken. "Extreme emergency" is limited to persons dangerously ill or in need of medical treatment not available in their immediate location, when possible, such persons will be accompanied by a trusted physician, nurse, or attendant. In any event, when the travel of an enemy alien is allowed, the crew of the airplane will be so advised in order that they may be able to keep the passenger under close surveillance at all times.

- 1 -

G. O. No. 101, O. M. G., 1942

b.   All other persons desiring to travel by airplane between the islands in the Territory of Hawaii must show reason and necessity for such travel and establish proof of their identity in submitting their application. Proof of citizenship must be furnished to the satisfaction of the officer in charge.

c.   Any person desiring inter-island transportation by air and any enemy alien desiring inter-island transportation will submit an application for travel on the form prescribed by the Military Governor. The application will be made in quadruplicate. The following disposition will be made:

(1)   The original -- Returned to applicant. If approved it will be surrendered to the carrier at the time passage is purchased.

(2)   The duplicate -- Sent to Contact Office, Office of the Assistant Chief of Staff, G-2, Headquarters Hawaiian Department, 214 Dillingham Building, Honolulu, T. H., at the close of each day.

(3)   The triplicate -- Sent to G-2, Office of the District Commander of the County to which travel is to be made.

(4)   The quadruplicate -- Retained in office of the Travel Control Bureau for record.

d.   No passage on any aircraft will be sold except to a holder of an approved application for travel by air.

SECTION II.   SPEED LIMITS IN THE TERRITORY OF HAWAII.--1. Section III, General Orders No. 92, Office of the Military Governor, 1 April 1942, is rescinded.

2.   In conformity with the recent directive of the President of the United States that speed limits be reduced, it is ordered that the maximum speed for motor vehicles in the Territory of Hawaii is forty (40) miles per hour.

SECTION III.   LOADING ZONE.--1. The loading zone on Queen Street, in the rear of the Star-Bulletin Office, is eliminated and a loading zone of the same size is established on Merchant Street in front of the Star-Bulletin Office.

SECTION IV.   RESCISSION OF GENERAL ORDERS.--Paragraph 1, General Orders No. 18, this office, 11 December 1941, is rescinded. (See paragraph 6, General Orders No. 74, this office, 16 February 1942.)

SECTION V.   BLACKOUT HOURS.--Effective 6 May 1942, the hours of blackout as announced in paragraph 1, Section II, General Orders No. 49, this office, 6 January 1942, as amended, are further extended so that the blackout period begins at 8:00 P.M. and extends to 6:15 A.M.

SECTION VI.   CURFEW.--The curfew for pedestrians, as announced in General Orders No. 68, this office, 3 February 1942, as amended, is further amended so that the curfew is hereby extended, effective 6 May 1942, to 10:00 P.M.

- 2 -

G. O. No. 101, O. M. G., 1942

SECTION VII.   CHILDREN.--1. Section II, General Orders No. 71, this office, 7 February 1942, is rescinded.

2.   Children under the age of sixteen years will not be permitted on the streets as pedestrians during the blackout hours and before curfew unless accompanied by one of their parents or an adult person. After curfew, children will not be permitted on the streets during blackout hours, except as provided in paragraph 5, Section III, General Orders No. 71, this office, 7 February 1942.

3.   Carriers of morning newspapers, having special passes, will be permitted to be on the streets during the hours of blackout as provided on such passes.

SECTION VIII.   ESTABLISHMENT OF CIVILIAN HOSPITAL CONTROL OFFICE.--1. A recent survey of the patient capacity of civilian hospitals on the Island of Oahu indicates that some hospitals are filled to capacity, that others are crowded, while still others have available facilities to accommodate additional patients. To alleviate this condition, it is necessary to provide a suitable regulation of the receiving of patients.

2.   Major C. C. Gill, Medical Corps, is hereby appointed Civilian Hospital Control Officer, with authority to regulate and control the admission of patients to all civilian hospitals on the Island of Oahu and will comply with the regulations and orders of the Civilian Hospital Control Officer in this connection.

3.   The Civilian Hospital Control Officer will immediately survey the patient capacity of all civilian hospitals on the Island of Oahu and will maintain a Civilian Hospital Control Office on a twenty-four hour basis for the purpose of expediting and assisting hospitals and doctors in securing adequate hospital patient facilities.

4.   Until further notice, the Civilian Hospital Control Office will be located at Farrington High School, phone number 3564, or phone number 8531, Locals 490, 563, or 676.

By order of the Military Governor:

(signed) Thomas H. Green,
THOMAS H. GREEN,
Colonel, J.A.G.D.,
Executive.

A TRUE COPY:

James F. Hanley
JAMES F. HANLEY,
Major, J.A.G.D.

- 3 -

TERRITORY OF HAWAII
OFFICE OF THE MILITARY GOVERNOR
IOLANI PALACE
HONOLULU, T.H.

6 May 1942

GENERAL ORDERS)
NO. 102)

SECTION I.   AMENDMENT OF GENERAL ORDERS NO. (LABOR) 91
SECTION II.   FLASHLIGHTS

SECTION I.   AMENDMENT OF GENERAL ORDERS NO. (LABOR) 91.-- Paragraph 2 a (1), General Orders No. 91, this office, 31 March 1942, is amended to read as follows:

"a.   Wages.--(1) Revised Wage Schedule No. 9, dated 3 May 1942 and effective at the beginning of the first payroll period after 3 May 1942, is hereby designated as the standard wage scale for workers engaged in work for Army and Navy agencies, their contractors and subcontractors. No person seeking employment with the above mentioned employers shall be employed at a rate less than, or in excess of the standard rate for the job as listed in Revised Wage Schedule No. 9, and as same may be revised from time to time, as approved by the Military Governor."

SECTION II.   FLASHLIGHTS.--1. Military Police and members of the Civilian Police Department on night duty are authorized to use orange or red cellophane, paint, or other material, on the lense of their flashlights.

2.   All other flashlights will conform to the provisions of Paragraph 10, General Orders No. 49, this office, 6 January 1942, requiring them to be painted or otherwise fixed to give off a blue light.

By order of the Military Governor:

(signed) Thomas H. Green,
THOMAS H. GREEN,
Colonel, J.A.G.D.,
Executive.

A TRUE COPY:

James F. Hanley
JAMES F. HANLEY,
Major, J.A.G.D.

TERRITORY OF HAWAII
OFFICE OF THE MILITARY GOVERNOR
IOLANI PALACE
HONOLULU, T.H.

29 May 1942

GENERAL ORDERS)
NO. 108)

PRICE CONTROL.--1. Regulation of Maximum Prices.--a. No person shall, regardless of any contract, agreement or other obligation heretofore or hereafter entered into, sell or deliver any commodity or in the course of trade or business buy or receive any commodity or otherwise do or omit to do any act in violation of any maximum price regulation, order, or price schedule which may hereafter be issued by the Military Governor, or offer, solicit or attempt to agree to do any of the foregoing.

b. In order to effectuate the purposes of this paragraph and of any maximum price regulation, order or price schedule issued hereunder, the Military Governor may by such maximum price regulation, order or price schedule require of any person or persons subject to any such maximum price regulation, order or price schedule a license as a condition of selling any commodity or commodities with respect to which such maximum price regulation, order or price schedule is applicable.

2. Price Control Section.--a. There is hereby created a Price Control Section in the Office of the Military Governor.

b. The principal office of said Price Control Section shall be at Iolani Palace, Honolulu, T. H.

c. The Price Control Section is authorized to administer and enforce such maximum price regulations, orders or price schedules as may hereafter be issued pursuant to this order, and to hear and determine applications for adjustment or exception to such maximum prices as may be established hereby.

3. Advisory Appeal Board.--a. The Military Governor will hereafter by regulation issued hereunder create an Advisory Appeal Board. Such Advisory Appeal Board shall advise the Military Governor with respect to the determination of applications for adjustment or exception to maximum prices made to the Price Control Section; and shall have such other powers and perform such other functions as the Military Governor may designate by regulation issued hereunder.

b. The Military Governor will hereafter by regulation issued hereunder create Island Advisory Appeal Boards for each of the Islands of Hawaii, Maui, Molokai, and Kauai. Such Island Advisory Appeal Boards shall hear and determine applications for adjustment or exceptions to such maximum prices as may be established by maximum price regulation,

---

G. O. No. 108, O. M. G., 1942

orders or price schedules as may be issued hereunder, subject to review by the Military Governor. The Island Advisory Appeal Boards shall not have power to grant exceptions or adjustments with respect to said maximum prices for periods in excess of thirty (30) days. The Island Advisory Appeal Boards shall have such other powers and perform such other functions as the Military Governor may designate by regulation issued hereunder.

4. Freedom From Civil Liability.--No person shall be held liable for damages or penalties in any court on any grounds for or in respect of anything done or omitted to be done in good faith pursuant to any provision of this order or any maximum price regulation, order or price schedule issued hereunder, notwithstanding that subsequently such provisions, regulation, order or price schedule may be modified, rescinded or determined to be invalid. In any suit or action wherein a party relies on grounds of relief or defense upon this order or any regulation order or price schedule thereunder the court having jurisdiction of such suit or action shall certify such fact to the Military Governor.

5. Suspension of Licenses.--If any person wilfully violates any provision of a maximum price regulation, order or price schedule issued hereunder, any license issued pursuant to such maximum price regulation, order or price schedule may be suspended by the Military Governor for a period not to exceed one year to the extent that it authorizes such person to sell the commodity or commodities in connection with which such violation occurred or to the extent that it authorizes such person to sell any commodity or commodities with respect to which a maximum price regulation, order or price schedule issued hereunder is applicable.

6. Penalty for Violations.--Any person, corporation, partnership or other association who wilfully violates any provision of such maximum price regulation, order or price schedule as may be issued hereunder shall upon conviction be subject to a fine of not more than $5,000, or imprisonment of not more than one year, or to both such fine and imprisonment.

By Order of the Military Governor:

(Signed) Thomas H. Green
THOMAS H. GREEN
Brigadier General, A.U.S.
Executive

A TRUE COPY:

James F. Hanley
JAMES F. HANLEY,
Lieut. Colonel, J.A.G.D.

TERRITORY OF HAWAII
OFFICE OF THE MILITARY GOVERNOR
IOLANI PALACE
HONOLULU, T.H.

5 June 1942

GENERAL ORDERS)
NO. 113)

SECTION I. REMOVAL OF KEYS FROM PARKED CARS
SECTION II. CHILD LABOR

SECTION I. REMOVAL OF KEYS FROM PARKED CARS.--1. All operators of motor vehicles are requested to move ignition keys therefrom whenever such vehicles are left unattended.

2. Any person failing to comply with this section shall be subjected to a fine not to exceed one hundred dollars ($100) or to imprisonment for not in excess of thirty (30) days, or both.

SECTION II. CHILD LABOR.--Section I, General Orders No. 103, this office, 14 May 1942, is amended by adding at the end thereof a new paragraph to read as follows:

"3. Employers mentioned in paragraph 1 may employ minors between twelve (12) and sixteen (16) years of age, when not legally required to attend school, provided that such minors shall not be permitted to work

a. More than six consecutive days in any one week;

b. More than eight hours in any one day;

c. Before 7 a.m. or after 6 p.m.;

d. More than 40 hours in any one week;

e. More than 5 hours continuously without at least a 30-minute lunch period;

f. In a factory or gainful occupation otherwise prohibited by law;

g. In, about or in connection with power driven machinery."

By order of the Military Governor:

(signed) Thomas H. Green,
THOMAS H. GREEN,
Brigadier General, A.U.S.,
Executive.

A TRUE COPY:

James F. Hanley
JAMES F. HANLEY,
Lt. Col., J.A.G.D.

TERRITORY OF HAWAII
OFFICE OF THE MILITARY GOVERNOR
IOLANI PALACE
HONOLULU, T. H.

20 June 1942

GENERAL ORDERS)
NO. 117)

SECTION I.   BLACKOUT HOURS.
SECTION II.   OPENING AND CLOSING HOURS FOR RESTAURANTS.
SECTION III. BOWLING ALLEYS AND NEIGHBORHOOD MOTION PICTURE THEATRES.
SECTION IV.   CIVILIAN HOSPITAL CONTROL OFFICER.

SECTION I. BLACKOUT HOURS.--Effective 20 June 1942, the hours of blackout as announced in paragraph 1, Section II, General Orders No. 49, this office, 6 January 1942, as amended, are further extended so that the blackout period begins at 8:15 P.M. and extends to 6:00 A.M.

SECTION II. OPENING AND CLOSING HOURS FOR RESTAURANTS.--Effective 20 June 1942, the closing hour for restaurants, as announced in paragraph 5, Section IV, General Orders No. 66, this office, 3 February 1942, is extended to 9:30 P.M., except for such restaurants as are permitted to remain open for longer periods by the Office of the Military Governor.

SECTION III. BOWLING ALLEYS AND NEIGHBORHOOD MOTION PICTURE THEATRES. Bowling alleys and neighborhood motion picture theatres may remain open until 9:00 P.M., each evening, providing they comply with blackout requirements when operated during blackout hours.

SECTION IV. CIVILIAN HOSPITAL CONTROL OFFICER.--Colonel E. G. Colby, Medical Corps, is appointed Civilian Hospital Control Officer, vice Major C. C. Gill, Medical Corps, relieved. (See Sec. VIII, G.O. 101, this office, 30 April 1942.)

By order of the Military Governor:

(signed) Thomas H. Green,
THOMAS H. GREEN,
Brigadier General, A.U.S.,
Executive.

A TRUE COPY:

James F. Hanley
JAMES F. HANLEY,
Lt. Col., J.A.G.D.

TERRITORY OF HAWAII
OFFICE OF THE MILITARY GOVERNOR
IOLANI PALACE
HONOLULU, T.H.

25 June 1942

GENERAL ORDERS)
NO. 119)

SECTION I. DEPUTY DIRECTOR OF LABOR CONTROL.
SECTION II. AMENDING GENERAL ORDERS NO. 91.

SECTION I. DEPUTY DIRECTOR OF LABOR CONTROL.--Mr. John R. Mead is hereby appointed the Deputy Director of Labor Control, Office of the Military Governor, Territory of Hawaii.

SECTION II. AMENDING GENERAL ORDERS NO. 91.--Paragraph 3. b., General Orders No. 91, this Office, 31 March 1942, is amended to read as follows:

"b. The Deputy Director of Labor Control, Office of the Military Governor, is hereby designated as the Appeal Agency for persons discharged with prejudice by employers mentioned in paragraph 2 c (1). Any complainant not satisfied with the decision of the Appeal Agency may further appeal his case to the Advisory Council to the Director of Labor Control."

By Order of the Military Governor:

(Signed) Thomas H. Green
THOMAS H. GREEN
Brigadier General, A.U.S.,
Executive.

A TRUE COPY:

James F. Hanley
JAMES F. HANLEY,
Lt. Col., J.A.G.D.

TERRITORY OF HAWAII
OFFICE OF THE MILITARY GOVERNOR
IOLANI PALACE
HONOLULU, T.H.

24 July 1942

GENERAL ORDERS)
NO. 128)

KNIVES.--The sale of any hunting knife, sheath knife, dagger, or dirk, or any pocket knife with a blade in excess of four inches in length is hereby prohibited except as specifically authorized by the Military Governor.

By order of the Military Governor:

(Signed) Thomas H. Green
THOMAS H. GREEN
Brigadier General, A.U.S.
Executive

A TRUE COPY:

James F. Hanley
JAMES F. HANLEY,
Lt. Col., J.A.G.D.

TERRITORY OF HAWAII
OFFICE OF THE MILITARY GOVERNOR
IOLANI PALACE
HONOLULU, T.H.

26 June 1942

GENERAL ORDERS)
NO. 120)

AMENDMENT TO GENERAL ORDERS NO. 91.--General Orders No. 91, this office, 31 March 1942, is hereby amended by adding thereto one new paragraph reading as follows:

"4. Holidays.--a. All legal holidays, both Federal and Territorial, are hereby suspended.

b. No premium pay shall be paid for regular work performed on days mentioned in sub-paragraph a, above.

c. The above provisions, relative to holidays and holiday pay, shall not apply to Federal, Territorial and City and County of Honolulu Civil Service Employees."

By order of the Military Governor:

(signed) Thomas H. Green,
THOMAS H. GREEN,
Brigadier General, A.U.S.,
Executive.

A TRUE COPY:

James F. Hanley
JAMES F. HANLEY,
Lt. Col., J.A.G.D.

TERRITORY OF HAWAII
OFFICE OF THE MILITARY GOVERNOR
IOLANI PALACE
HONOLULU, T.H.

31 August 1942

GENERAL ORDERS)
NO. 133)

SECTION I. DECLARATION AND FINDING.
SECTION II. OPERATION OF THE CIVIL COURTS.
SECTION III. FUTURE MODIFICATION OF THIS ORDER.

SECTION I. DECLARATION AND FINDING.--Hawaii constitutes the main Pacific outpost of the United States, and accordingly must be regarded as a fortress to whose defense the entire population of the Islands is committed. Its man power and its economic resources must be subject to a single ultimate control. Martial law has been declared and the emergency which called it forth still prevails. The privilege of the writ of habeas corpus has been suspended and remains suspended. For all this there is authority in Section 67 of the Organic Act. The measures of military control have from time to time been modified in the light of experience and as changes in conditions have dictated. By General Orders No. 29 of December 16, 1941, the civil courts were reopened, subject to certain restrictions. It is now consistent with the public safety and the national defense that they be permitted more fully to exercise the powers normally exercised by them. They cannot, however, be allowed to interfere with the measures required by military security. It is to be understood that the relaxation herein specified is intended to return to the courts criminal prosecutions and civil litigation to the extent that war conditions permit. However, this action is experimental in nature and the Military Governor reserves the right further to limit the jurisdiction of the courts or to close them entirely, if that course shall be necessary.

SECTION II. OPERATION OF THE CIVIL COURTS.--In accordance with the above declaration and finding, the civil courts are now authorized to exercise their normal jurisdiction, subject, nevertheless, to the following restrictions and limitations:

1. The privilege of the writ of habeas corpus has been and remains suspended.

2. No criminal proceedings shall be maintained against any member of the armed forces of the United States or any person employed or engaged in any occupation, business, or defense activity under the direction of the Army, the Navy, or the Military Governor.

3. No civil suit, action or other proceeding shall be maintained against any member of the armed forces of the United States or any person employed or engaged in any occupation, business, or defense activity under the direction of the Army, the Navy, or the Military Governor for any act done within the scope of such employment.

- 1 -

G.O. NO.133, O.M.G., 1942.

4. (a) No judgment by default shall be entered against any person who is in the Army, Navy, Marine Corps, or Coast Guard of the United States. No judgment by default shall be entered against any person employed or engaged in any occupation, business, or activity under the supervision or direction of the Military Governor, or otherwise essential to the national defense, until seven (7) days shall have elapsed after the return day provided in the summons or by the statutes of the Territory of Hawaii. A default judgment hereafter entered shall be set aside upon the mere request of the defendant or his attorney, made either orally or in writing, to the court, or clerk thereof, in which the case was pending at the time of the entry of such judgment, if such request be so made within fifteen days after entry of such default judgment. Leave to appear or answer shall be allowed or extended for a like period of fifteen days after such default judgment shall have been set aside. In the event the defendant, after having been allowed to so appear or answer as aforesaid, shall fail to so appear or answer as aforesaid within said period of fifteen days, the court again may enter or cause to be entered the default of the defendant and enter or order entered judgment by default against such defendant. A defendant shall have no right upon his mere request to have a default judgment set aside a second time in the same case.

(b) The provisions contained in this paragraph shall apply to pending cases as well as to cases hereafter commenced or instituted.

(c) A verbatim copy of the contents of this paragraph shall be attached to the summons and served upon the defendant or defendants in cases hereinafter commenced or instituted.

5. No person referred to in paragraphs 2 and 3 of this section, with respect to whom a certificate of exemption is issued by the Military Governor or under his authority, shall be selected or listed by any jury commission as a trial juror or grand juror and no subpoena issued to require the attendance of any such person in such courts shall be valid. Based upon the requirements for labor in the National Defense, the Military Governor will from time to time prescribe the maximum number of persons who may be summoned or held for jury service.

6. (a) No person, firm, or corporation shall institute, maintain, or prosecute any action, suit or other proceeding in any circuit or district court in the City and County of Honolulu, Territory of Hawaii, to recover the possession of any premises used for housing accommodations as defined in Section 1, Ordinance 941 of the City and County of Honolulu, Territory of Hawaii, without first having obtained an order of the Rent Control Commission of said City and County of Honolulu that said plaintiff or plaintiffs is or are entitled to the possession of said premises, and no such suit, action, or other proceeding shall be instituted, maintained, or prosecuted for the purpose aforesaid in any such said circuit or district court without such order having been first obtained by the said plaintiff or plaintiffs in such suit, action, or other said proceeding.

- 2 -

TERRITORY OF HAWAII
OFFICE OF THE MILITARY GOVERNOR
IOLANI PALACE
HONOLULU, T.H

1 September 1942

GENERAL ORDERS)
NO. 134)

SECTION I.   RESCISSION OF GENERAL ORDERS.
SECTION II.   BLACKOUT HOURS.
SECTION III. PEDESTRIAN TRAFFIC DURING BLACKOUT.
SECTION IV.   VEHICULAR TRAFFIC DURING BLACKOUT.
SECTION V.   INTER ISLAND-TRAVEL.
SECTION VI.   GENERAL IDENTIFICATION BUREAU.
SECTION VII. INTOXICATING LIQUORS.
SECTION VIII. GAMBLING DEVICES.

SECTION I. RESCISSION OF GENERAL ORDERS.—The following General Orders and parts of General Orders of this office are rescinded:

Paragraph 4, Section III, General Orders No. 32.
Paragraphs 1, 4, 5, 7 and 10, Section II, General Orders No. 49.
General Orders No. 65.
Sections II and III, General Orders No. 66.
Section I, General Orders No. 89.
Sections I, V and VI, General Orders No. 101.
Section II, General Orders No. 102.
Section III, General Orders No. 107.
Section II, General Orders No. 117.
Section II, General Orders No. 125.

SECTION II. BLACKOUT HOURS.—1. Effective 1 September 1942, the hours of blackout are as follows:

City and County of Honolulu: 7:45 p.m. to 6:30 a.m.
Hawaii District: 7:30 p.m. to 6:15 a.m.
Maui District: 7:45 p.m. to 6:30 a.m.
Kauai District: 7:45 p.m. to 6:30 a.m.

2. During the hours of blackout the use of exterior lights, or of interior lights which are visible on the outside of houses, buildings, etc., except as authorized by the provisions of Section I, General Orders No. 129, this office, 28 July 1942, is forbidden.

3. Except as otherwise provided in General Orders, during the hours of blackout, no person shall be on the streets and highways, or in parks or on beaches, either on foot or in vehicles, except:

a. Military and Naval personnel on duty or proceeding to and from duty.

b. Law enforcement officers.

- 1 -

G.O. NO.133, O.M.G., 1942.

(b) This section shall be retroactive and shall be deemed to have been in full force and effect as of and after January 27, 1942, and shall be retroactive and applicable to any such action, suit, or proceeding, now pending in said circuit and district courts as well as to those hereafter instituted, maintained, or prosecuted in said circuit and district courts.

(c) Payments of rent shall continue to be made at the dates the rent becomes due on all housing accommodations in accordance with the agreement or procedure previously effected by the parties thereto. Landlords shall refund any unused portions of rent paid in advance to any tenants who are duly evacuated from the Territory of Hawaii.

7. Violations of the laws of war or of proclamations, regulations, or orders of the Military Governor now in force or hereafter issued will continue to be triable by Military Commissions or Provost Courts.

8. The Military Governor may waive any restriction or limitation established by the foregoing paragraphs, with respect to any person, case, or matter, or class of persons, cases, or matters.

SECTION III. FUTURE MODIFICATION OF THIS ORDER.—This order shall be subject to modification, or revocation, by the Military Governor whenever in his judgment such action is necessary.

All prior orders inconsistent herewith are hereby revoked.

SECTION IV. EFFECTIVE DATE.—This General Order is effective 12:00 noon, 2 September 1942.

By order of the Military Governor:

(signed) THOMAS H. GREEN,
THOMAS H. GREEN,
Brigadier General, A.U.S.
Executive

A TRUE COPY:

James F Hanley
JAMES F. HANLEY,
Lieut. Colonel, J.A.G.D.

G.O. NO. 134, O.M.G., 1942.

c. Civilian personnel required to be on the streets and highways during such hours because of their employment on defense work, by public utilities, in civilian defense activities, or by the government, or while directly proceeding to and from work.

d. Doctors on call.

e. Those holding Police passes issued since 7 December 1941.

f. Those holding special passes issued or approved by the Provost Marshal, Military Police or Civilian Police.

4. Any person stopped by Civil Police or Military Police will identify himself promptly. All persons required to be on the streets during blackout hours in motor vehicles after 8:00 p.m. or on foot after 10 p.m. should carry some sort of identification or pass, letter from their employer, or badge evidencing their right to be on the streets.

5. Operation of motor or other vehicles, except as authorized by the Civil or Military Police, at a speed in excess of 20 miles per hour during the hours of blackout is prohibited.

6. No parking on any public thoroughfare will be permitted during the hours of blackout.

7. The carrying of lighted cigarettes, cigars and pipes, and the striking of matches, lighters, etc., in the open during the hours of blackout is prohibited.

8. a. All flashlights shall be painted or otherwise fixed so as to give off a blue light. The excessive use of flashlights or other means of illumination during the hours of blackout is also prohibited.

b. Military Police and members of the Civilian Police Department on night duty are authorized to use orange or red cellophane, paint, or other material, on the lens of their flashlights.

9. Saving Clause. The provisions of this section shall take effect upon the date of this General Order, but shall not apply to any offense heretofore committed. Any such prior offense shall be punishable in the same manner and to the same effect, as if this section had not been published.

SECTION III. PEDESTRIAN TRAFFIC DURING BLACKOUT. —1. All persons except enemy aliens are permitted to be on the streets and highways as pedestrians until 10:00 p.m.

2. After 10:00 p.m., pedestrians are prohibited from being on the streets and highways without special authority (Sec.II, G.O.134).

3. Pedestrians will comply with applicable blackout regulations as published in General Orders.

- 2 -

G.O. NO. 134, O.M.G., 1942.

SECTION IV. VEHICULAR TRAFFIC DURING BLACKOUT.—1. Motor vehicles are permitted to operate on the streets and highways until 8:00 p.m. provided motor vehicles operating on the streets and highways during the hours of blackout conform to all other blackout regulations and more particularly those set forth in Section II, General Orders No. 132, this office, 17 August 1942.

SECTION V. INTER-ISLAND TRAVEL—1. Travel Control Bureau. a. For the purpose of carrying out the provisions of the President's Proclamations of December 7 and 8, 1941, and the provisions of this section, with respect to inter-island travel by enemy aliens, and for the purpose of controlling and regulating inter-island travel by air with a view to conservation of facilities for necessary and important traffic, a Travel Control Bureau is established in each County.

b. (1) The Travel Control Bureau in the City and County of Honolulu will function as a section of the Contact Office, Office of the Assistant Chief of Staff, G-2, Headquarters Hawaiian Department, and in each of the other counties, the bureau will be under the control of the District Commander thereof.

(2) An officer from the Contact Office, Office of the Assistant Chief of Staff, G-2, Headquarters Hawaiian Department, will be detailed to the office of the Hawaiian Airlines, Limited, Honolulu, T. H., for the purpose of examining applications for such travel.

(3) The Commanding General of the District concerned (Hawaii, Maui, Kauai), or an officer designated by him, will examine each application for travel originating in that district.

(4) On the Island of Molokai, examination of such travel applications will be made by an officer detailed for that purpose by the Commanding General of the Maui District.

2. Priorities for Air Travel. a. Transportation priorities shall be provided in the following order:

(1) Military personnel (Army, Navy, Marine Corps and Coast Guard) travelling under official orders.

(2) Army and Navy equipment, ammunition, supplies, and materials essential to the war effort ordered for air movement.

(3) Personnel of government departments and agencies and personnel whose activities are essential to the war effort, other than military personnel, travelling on official business which is necessary to the successful prosecution of the war effort.

(4) Persons other than those mentioned above travelling on business.

(5) Other persons.

- 3 -

G.O. NO. 134, O.M.G., 1942.

a. All passengers travelling on priority will have their tickets stamped with the class of "Priority" at the time the ticket is purchased to insure proper handling at stopovers or return from other Districts.

5. a. Baggage and persons will be searched only when it is deemed advisable to make such search.

b. No written or printed matter in any language other than English will be taken aboard any commercial aircraft without prior approval by local Military Intelligence officials.

c. No maps, charts or blueprints will be transported except by authorized persons.

d. No photographs or negatives showing any of the beaches, shoreline, panoramic views from a high point, or military or naval installations will be transported. Under no circumstances will any (except Official) undeveloped film be transported.

SECTION VI. CENTRAL IDENTIFICATION BUREAU.—1. Effective 1 September 1942, the Central Identification Bureau will operate as a bureau of the Office of the Military Governor.

2. The purpose of the Central Identification Bureau is the issuance of identification to persons who are required to have such identification before they gain access to various military and naval reservations, and other restricted areas.

3. Any person desiring a C.I.B. identification badge must present themselves at the Central Identification Bureau's office. It is required that all applicants present a "CIB-2" form signed by their employer, whose signature must have been previously presented and approved. It is required that all applicants prepare a "Personal History Declaration" prior to the time that they present themselves for their badge. The employer should assist and supervise the preparation of the "Personal History Declaration" on all of his employees who desire identification badges.

4. Major General JAMES A. WOODRUFF, U.S.A., is designated as the Director of the Central Identification Bureau.

SECTION VII. INTOXICATING LIQUORS.—1. Paragraph 4 D, General Orders No. 68, this office, 4 February 1942, is amended to read:

"D. In the event of the loss of his purchaser's permit, the person to whom it was issued will advise the Liquor Commission of the county issuing the same without delay. At the expiration of the 60 day period for which such lost permit was issued a new permit may be issued to replace it at a cost of one dollar ($1.00)."

- 5 -

G.O. NO. 134, O.M.G., 1942.

b. Clearing of space for passengers or cargo of higher priority classifications than those mentioned in paragraph 2a (3), (4), and (5) may require displacement of passengers in those classifications.

3. Enemy Aliens. a. No enemy alien shall undertake an air flight or ascend into the air in any aircraft, balloon, or flying machine of any sort, whether owned governmentally, commercially, or privately, except upon written authority of the Contact Office, Office of the Assistant Chief of Staff, G-2, Headquarters Hawaiian Department.

b. No enemy alien will be allowed to travel on any airplane, Governmental or commercial, except in cases of extreme emergency when such travel may be authorized by the Travel Control Bureau after proper precautions and safeguards have been taken. "Extreme emergency" is limited to persons dangerously ill or in need of medical treatment not available in their immediate location. When possible, such persons will be accompanied by a trusted physician, nurse, or attendant. In any event, when the travel of an enemy alien is allowed, the crew of the airplane will be so advised in order that they may be able to keep the passenger under close surveillance at all times.

4. Applications for Air Travel. a. All persons requiring air transportation will report in person at the local office of the transportation company and/or other designated place and fill out the required application form. The travel control officer will pass on each application and grant the priority authorized. Tickets may be sold only after the application has been approved by the travel control officer. The office from which it is proposed to purchase transportation should be contacted as soon as possible.

b. All persons desiring to travel by airplane between the islands in the Territory of Hawaii must show reason and necessity for such travel and establish proof of their identity in submitting their application. Proof of citizenship must be furnished to the satisfaction of the travel control officer.

c. The application for travel will be submitted on the form prescribed by the Military Governor. The application will be made in quadruplicate. The following disposition of the application will be made:

(1) The original — returned to applicant. If approved it will be surrendered to the carrier at the time passage is purchased.

(2) The duplicate — sent to Contact Office, Office of the Assistant Chief of Staff, G-2, Headquarters Hawaiian Department, 214 Dillingham Building, Honolulu, T. H., at the close of each day.

(3) The triplicate — sent to G-2, Office of the District Commander of the County to which travel is to be made.

(4) The quadruplicate — retained in office of the Travel Control Bureau for record.

- 4 -

G.O. NO. 134, O.M.G., 1942.

SECTION VIII. GAMBLING DEVICES.—1. No person, corporation, firm or other association in the Territory of Hawaii shall buy and/or sell or attempt to buy and/or sell for any purpose whatsoever any marked playing cards; loaded, magnetic or prepared dice; roulette wheels; banking layouts; contrivance, device, apparatus, artifice, trick or token that can or could be used to cheat, deceive or defraud others of their money or property in lotteries or games that involve the risk of chance.

2. Every person, corporation, firm or other association violating such section shall be punished upon conviction by a fine of not more than $1,000.00 or by imprisonment at hard labor not exceeding one year, or both.

By order of the Military Governor:

(signed) THOMAS H. GREEN,
THOMAS H. GREEN,
Brigadier General, A.U.S.
Executive

A TRUE COPY:

James F. Hanley
JAMES F. HANLEY,
Lieut. Colonel, J.A.G.D.

- 6 -

TERRITORY OF HAWAII
OFFICE OF THE MILITARY GOVERNOR
IOLANI PALACE
HONOLULU, T.H.

4 September 1942

GENERAL ORDERS)
NO. 135)

JURISDICTION OF COURTS.--1. Criminal Jurisdiction: General. This General Order I issued to define the criminal jurisdiction to be exercised by the Federal and Territorial courts and the courts established by the Military Governor, in accordance with General Orders No. 133, this office, 31 August 1942.

2. Jurisdiction of Federal Courts. The United States District Court for the Territory of Hawaii shall not exercise jurisdiction over the following crimes and offenses:

a. 10 USCA Section 1393 (Protection of uniform of the Army, Navy, Marine Corps, etc); 18 USCA Sections 1 to 17 inclusive (Offenses against the existence of the Government); 18 USCA Section 76a and 76b (Prohibiting reproduction of official badges, identification cards, and other insignia); 18 USCA Sections 94 to 98 inclusive (Offenses against the operations of the Government, such as enticing desertion from the Army or Navy, etc); 50 USCA Sections 31 to 36 inclusive (Espionage); 50 USCA Sections 45 to 45d inclusive (Photographing, etc., defensive installations); 50 USCA Sections 101 to 106 inclusive (Wilful destruction, etc., of war or national defense material); Violations of the Selective Training and Service Act of 1940; and Federal statutes relating to Prostitution;

b. All other Federal Statutes heretofore enacted, although not hereinabove enumerated, and all other Federal Statutes hereafter enacted of the class of criminal offenses herein set forth, or relating to offenses directed against the Government, or violations in connection with the war effort;

c. Violations of the laws of war or of proclamations, regulations, or orders of the Military Governor now in force or hereafter issued;

d. Instigations, conspiracies and attempts to commit the criminal offenses hereinabove referred to.

3. Jurisdiction of Territorial Courts. All courts of the Territory of Hawaii shall not exercise jurisdiction over the following crimes and offenses:

a. Chapter 163, R.L.H. 1935 (Anarchistic Publications and Criminal Syndicalism); Chapter 178, R.L.H. 1935 (Disloyalty and desecration of flag); Chapter 180, R.L.H. 1935 (Disorderly House and Drunkenness); Chapter 199, R.L.H. 1935 (Military organizations); Chapter 205, R.L.H. 1935 (Riots, unlawful assemblies); Chapter 208, R.L.H. 1935 (Secret Associations); Chapter 214, R.L.H. 1935 (Vagrants, Disorderly persons, Loitering); Section 5710, R.L.H. 1935 (Places of Prostitution, etc.); Violations of any law, rule or regulation of the Territory or ordinance of any county or city and county relating to public health; assault or assault and battery on police officers or other law enforcement officers in violation of Section 5657, R.L.H. 1935; Act 123, S.L.H. 1937

- 1 -

G. O. No. 135, O. M. G., 1942,

(Carrying Deadly Weapons); Act 82, S.L.H. 1941 (Sabotage); Violations of traffic ordinances of any county or city and county relating to drunken driving; Violations of territorial traffic laws or traffic ordinances of any county or city and county during blackout hours as established by the Military Governor or during periods of alert as announced by the Military Governor;

b. All other Territorial statutes county or city and county ordinances, rules and regulations heretofore enacted, or promulgated although not hereinabove enumerated, and all other Territorial statutes hereafter enacted or promulgated of the class of criminal offenses herein set forth, or relating to offenses directed against the Federal or Territorial Governments, or relating to offenses in connection with the war effort;

c. Violations of the laws of war or of proclamations, regulations, or orders of the Military Governor now in force or hereafter issued;

d. Instigations, conspiracies and attempts to commit the criminal offenses hereinabove referred to.

4. Jurisdiction over Persons. The Federal and Territorial courts shall not assume criminal jurisdiction over the following persons except when authority to do so is first obtained from the Military Governor:

a. Members of the armed forces of the United States;

b. Persons employed or engaged in any occupation, business, or defense activity under the direction of the Army, Navy or Military Governor where the offense is committed within the scope of their employment. The determination of the status of such persons, and whether an offense is committed within the scope of employment shall rest with the Military Governor whose decision shall be final.

5. Jurisdiction of Military Commissions and Provost Courts Retained. Military Commissions and Provost Courts shall retain and exercise all jurisdiction and powers heretofore granted them by the Military Governor except as otherwise provided herein.

6. Determination of Jurisdiction where Questioned. Whenever the jurisdiction of the Federal or Territorial Courts, or Military Commissions or Provost Courts, to hear and determine any case shall in any manner or for any reason be questioned, then in every such case, the issue of jurisdiction shall be determined by the Military Governor whose decision shall be final; and, notwithstanding any other provision of this or any other order of the Military Governor, the Federal or Territorial Court, or Military Commission or Provost Court, as the case may be, shall take, have and exercise jurisdiction in accordance with such determination and decision.

- 2 -

G.O. NO. 135, O.M.G., 1942.

7. Special Cases. Notwithstanding any provision of this or any other order of the Military Governor to the contrary, the Military Governor may, whenever in his opinion such action be necessary in the public interest, exercise jurisdiction at any time over any crime or offense or person, and direct that the same be tried before a Military Commission or Provost Court.

8. Future Modification of this Order. This order shall be subject to modification or revocation, by the Military Governor whenever in his judgment such action is necessary.

9. Effective Date. This order shall take effect forthwith. Criminal cases pending before the Provost Courts and Military Commission of the class which is within the jurisdiction herein given to the Federal and Territorial courts and in which no plea has been entered shall be tried and determined by the Federal or Territorial court, as the case may be.

By order of the Military Governor:

(signed) THOMAS H. GREEN,
THOMAS H. GREEN,
Brigadier General, A.U.S.
Executive

A TRUE COPY:

James F. Hanley
JAMES F. HANLEY,
Lieut. Colonel, J.A.G.D.

- 3 -

TERRITORY OF HAWAII
OFFICE OF THE MILITARY GOVERNOR
IOLANI PALACE
HONOLULU, T.H.

9 September 1942

GENERAL ORDERS)
NO. 136)

HOUSE NUMBERING --1. For the purpose of quickly locating any building in the City of Honolulu and in the areas of Kailua, Lanikai, Wahiawa, and Pearl City in case of fire, attack or any emergency, it is ordered that all owners of buildings fronting on any street, road, or lane, public or private, in these areas, who have not previously obtained correct numbers from the City authorities, call at Room 202 in the City Hall in Honolulu during the period specified in the Table in Paragraph 4 below, and obtain a certificate designating the correct number or numbers applicable to such building or buildings. Such owner, at his own expense, shall then install such designated number or numbers on such building or buildings within said period, in accordance with Section 3033, Revised Laws of Hawaii 1935, which reads as follows:

"Sec. 3033. Numbers placed how. All numbers shall be placed in such a manner as to be readily seen from the street, road or lane; shall be of a different color from the background on which they are placed, and shall be at least two inches in height. The numbers shall be placed in a substantial and permanent manner, chalk or other easily effaceable material not being permitted."

2. The Air Raid Warden Division of the Office of Civilian Defense shall cooperate with the owners in carrying out the provisions of this order. Owners may contact local block wardens for information and assistance.

3. Any owner of a building in the areas referred to in Paragraph 1 above, who neglects to number such building as herein provided, or who shall place, maintain or allow to remain thereon any number other than that as designated in accordance herewith, shall upon conviction be punished by a fine not in excess of thirty dollars ($30.00) or imprisonment for a period not to exceed thirty (30) days, or both.

4. TABLE

AREA AFFECTED	DATE AND PERIOD ASSIGNED
Kailua, Lanikai, Pearl City, and Wahiawa	Sept.15 to Sept.30, 1942
Zone One, District of Honolulu	Oct. 1 to Oct. 15, 1942
Zone Two, District of Honolulu	Oct. 16 to Oct. 31, 1942
Zone Three, District of Honolulu	Nov. 1 to Nov. 15, 1942
Zone Five, District of Honolulu	Nov. 16 to Nov. 30, 1942

-1-

G.O. NO. 136, O.M.G., 1942

Zones referred to above are those which have been established by the Air Raid Warden Division of the Office of Civilian Defense and maps showing these zones will be republished from time to time during the periods shown above.

By order of the Military Governor:

(signed) THOMAS H. GREEN,
THOMAS H. GREEN,
Brigadier General, A.U.S.
Executive

A TRUE COPY:

William R. C. Morrison
WILLIAM R. C. MORRISON,
Lieut. Colonel, J.A.G.D.

-2-

G. O. No. 139, O. M. G., 1942

2. Between the hours of 5:30 a.m. and the termination of the hours of blackout, all blackout restrictions must be observed. Each motor vehicle must proceed with all caution necessary with safety. The maximum speed authorized is twenty miles an hour.

3. The permission to proceed to work before the termination of the hours of blackout is not to be interpreted as authorizing lights or other illumination of any kind in homes, etc., during the hours of blackout except under blackout conditions. All violators will be subject to the same penalties as violators during other hours of blackout.

4. Enemy aliens will not be permitted on the streets or highways between the hours of 5:30 a.m. and the termination of the hours of blackout, unless they have the special permission of the Provost Marshal or his duly authorized representative.

5. Children under the age of 16 years will not be permitted on the streets or highways between the hours of 5:30 a.m. and the termination of the hours of blackout, unless accompanied by one of their parents or some other adult person, and unless their travel is directly connected with their parents or guardians proceeding to work.

SECTION V. PROCUREMENT AND USE OF IDENTIFICATION BADGES.--1. Swearing Falsely to a Personal History Declaration. Any person who knowingly swears falsely to a Personal History Declaration and presents same to the Central Identification Bureau, Honolulu, T. H., for purpose of obtaining an identification badge, shall be subject to a fine not to exceed two hundred fifty dollars ($250.00), or imprisonment for not longer than one month, or both.

2. Securing Badge under False Pretenses. Any person who attempts to secure or does secure any identification badge issued by the Central Identification Bureau under false pretenses, or any person who aids another in attempting to secure any identification badge, under false pretenses, shall be subject to a fine not to exceed two hundred fifty dollars ($250.00), or imprisonment for not longer than one month, or both.

3. Surrendering of Obsolete Badges. Any person who fails to deliver his identification badge issued by the Central Identification Bureau to his employer, or the Central Identification Bureau, within forty-eight (48) hours after the termination of his employment for which said badge was issued, or removes, takes or sends an identification badge issued by the Central Identification Bureau from the Territory of Hawaii, shall be subject to a fine not to exceed two hundred fifty dollars ($250.00), or imprisonment for not longer than one month, or both.

4. Fraudulent Use of Badges. Any person who attempts to commit or commits a fraudulent use of any identification badge issued by the Central Identification Bureau, shall be subject to a fine not to exceed two hundred fifty dollars ($250.00), or imprisonment for not longer than one month, or both.

5. Fraudulent Entry to Restricted Area. Any person who attempts to commit or commits a fraudulent entry to any military or naval reservation

- 2 -

TERRITORY OF HAWAII
OFFICE OF THE MILITARY GOVERNOR
IOLANI PALACE
HONOLULU, T.H.

17 September 1942

GENERAL ORDERS)
NO. 139)

SECTION I.   AMENDMENT TO GENERAL ORDERS NO. 91.
SECTION II.   GENERAL ORDERS NO. 132 AMENDED.
SECTION III. SPEED LIMITS IN THE TERRITORY OF HAWAII.
SECTION IV.   WORKERS GOING TO WORK IN MORNING.
SECTION V.   PROCUREMENT AND USE OF IDENTIFICATION BADGES.
SECTION VI.   RESCISSION OF GENERAL ORDERS.
SECTION VII. RESCISSION OF GENERAL ORDERS.

SECTION I. AMENDMENT TO GENERAL ORDERS NO. 91.--Paragraph 1 c (1), General Orders No. 91, this office, 31 March 1942, is hereby amended to read as follows:

"c. Employment.--(1) No Army or Navy agencies, their contractors or subcontractors, Federal agencies, Territorial agencies, City and County of Honolulu agencies, their contractors or subcontractors, hospitals, public utilities, stevedoring companies, laundries, milk producers and dairy companies and sources of supply controlled by the Army and/or Navy, shall employ or offer to employ any individual formerly or now in the employment of the above mentioned employers unless and until such individual shall have presented to the employing agency a bona fide release without prejudice, in writing, from his last previous employer."

SECTION II. GENERAL ORDERS NO. 132 AMENDED.--The effective date referred to in Sections I and II, General Orders No. 132, this office, 17 August 1942, is changed from "20 September 1942" to "20 October 1942."

SECTION III. SPEED LIMITS IN THE TERRITORY OF HAWAII.--In conformity with the recent proposal of the President of the United States, that speed limits be reduced in order to save tires and gasoline, it is ordered that effective this date the maximum speed for motor vehicles in the Territory of Hawaii is thirty-five (35) miles an hour.

SECTION IV. WORKERS GOING TO WORK IN MORNING.--The following regulations, relating to workers going to work on and after 20 September 1942, are published for the information and guidance of those concerned:

1. Men and women who must leave their homes before the termination of the hours of blackout in order to reach their places of employment between the hours of 7:00 a.m. and 8:00 a.m., respectively, will be permitted to proceed on the streets and highways of the City and County of Honolulu in motor vehicles or on foot after 5:30 a.m. in the morning. Such workers should leave their homes as late as possible.

- 1 -

G. O. No. 139, O. M. G., 1942.

or other restricted area, by use of an identification badge issued by the Central Identification Bureau, shall be subject to a fine not to exceed two hundred fifty dollars ($250.00), or imprisonment for not longer than one month, or both.

6. Duplication of Badges. Any person who attempts to commit or commits a duplication of any identification badge issued by the Central Identification Bureau shall be subject to a fine not to exceed two hundred fifty dollars ($250.00), or imprisonment for not longer than one month, or both.

SECTION VI. RESCISSION OF GENERAL ORDERS.--Section III, General Orders No. 71, this office, 7 February 1942, is rescinded effective 20 September 1942.

SECTION VII. RESCISSION OF GENERAL ORDERS.--Section II, General Orders No. 101, this office, 30 April 1942, is rescinded.

By order of the Military Governor:

(Signed) Thomas H. Green
THOMAS H. GREEN,
Brigadier General, A.U.S.,
Executive

A TRUE COPY:

James F. Hanley
JAMES F. HANLEY,
Lieut. Colonel, J.A.G.D.

TERRITORY OF HAWAII
OFFICE OF THE MILITARY GOVERNOR
IOLANI PALACE
HONOLULU, T.H.

3 October 1942

GENERAL ORDERS)
NO. 143)

SECTION I.   PRICE CONTROL ADVISER TO MILITARY GOVERNOR.
SECTION II. PROHIBITION OF TRANSFER OF USED RUBBER TIRES AND
TUBES.

SECTION I.   PRICE CONTROL ADVISER TO MILITARY GOVERNOR.-- Mr.
Karl Borders is announced as Price Control Adviser to the Military
Governor, Territory of Hawaii, vice Mr. James Hill Palmer.

SECTION II. PROHIBITION OF TRANSFER OF USED RUBBER TIRES AND
TUBES.-- 1. No person shall sell, lease, trade, lend, deliver, or
transfer any used tire or tube, and no person shall accept delivery
of any such used tire or tube, except as authorized by the Military
Governor.

2. No dealer or distributor of tires or automobiles shall
mount any used tire or used tube on any vehicle owned by him or
otherwise subject to his control, except as authorized by the Military
Governor.

3. DEFINITION: For the purpose of this order -

a. "Used Tire" means any rubber tire, capable of being used as
a tire on a vehicle, which has run 1,000 miles or more, excluding
a retreaded or recapped tire which has been run less than 1,000
miles after having been retreaded or recapped.

b. "Used Tube" means any rubber tube, capable of being used as
a tube within a tire casing, which has been run 1,000 miles or more.

By order of the Military Governor:

(Signed) Thomas H. Green,
THOMAS H. GREEN,
Brigadier General, A.U.S.
Executive

A TRUE COPY:

WILLIAM R. C. MORRISON
Lieut. Colonel, J.A.G.D.

TERRITORY OF HAWAII
OFFICE OF THE MILITARY GOVERNOR
IOLANI PALACE
HONOLULU, T.H.

6 November 1942

GENERAL ORDERS)
NO. 153)

SECTION I.   AMENDMENT TO GENERAL ORDERS NO. 71
(BLACKOUT OF PIERS).
SECTION II. DIRECTOR OF FOOD PRODUCTION.

SECTION I.   AMENDMENT TO GENERAL ORDERS NO. 71 (BLACKOUT OF PIERS).--
Section IV, General Orders No. 71, this office, 7 February 1942, is hereby
amended by adding thereto the following new paragraph:

"4. In case of an air raid alarm, or any type of attack, during
the prescribed hours of blackout, all lights will be immediately extinguished and will not be turned on until the 'All Clear' is sounded."

SECTION II. DIRECTOR OF FOOD PRODUCTION.--1. Mr. Walter F.
Dillingham is hereby appointed the Director of Food Production, Office of
the Military Governor, Territory of Hawaii.

2. The Director of Food Production will coordinate and control
all matters pertaining to:

a. fishing in Hawaiian waters;

b. production of livestock and poultry products in the Territory
of Hawaii;

c. production of vegetables and fruits in the Territory of Hawaii
for local consumption and the assembly, transportation and distribution
of all such production.

By order of the Military Governor:

(Signed) Thomas H. Green
THOMAS H. GREEN,
Brigadier General, A.U.S.
Executive

A TRUE COPY:

WILLIAM R. C. MORRISON
Lt. Col. J.A.G.D.

TERRITORY OF HAWAII
OFFICE OF THE MILITARY GOVERNOR
IOLANI PALACE,
HONOLULU, T. H.

5 November 1942

GENERAL ORDERS)
NO. 152)

REGISTRATION OF WOMEN.-- 1. Every female person in the
Territory of Hawaii who is sixteen years of age or older is
hereby required to register and furnish such information as
to age, occupational history, education and citizenship as is
required to classify such individual for employment purposes.

2. Every person required to register hereunder shall do
so in such manner and at such times as is provided by the Office
of Civilian Defense.

3. From and after the date of registration as above provided, every person required to register hereunder shall notify
the Office of Civilian Defense of any change in status as to
employment or non-employment. Such notification shall be
furnished in accordance with procedures as shall be established
by the Office of Civilian Defense.

4. Every person required to register hereunder who is
gainfully occupied at the time of such registration but thereafter ceases to be gainfully occupied shall, in addition to
notifying the Office of Civilian Defense, as provided in paragraph 3 above, register for employment with the nearest office
of the United States Employment Service, within seventy-two
(72) hours from the time she ceases to be gainfully occupied.

5. Any person who shall fail to register or give notification as required by this order shall upon conviction be fined
not more than One Thousand Dollars ($1000.00), or be imprisoned
for not more than one (1) year, or both.

By order of the Military Governor:

(Signed) Thomas H. Green,
THOMAS H. GREEN,
Brigadier General, A.U.S.
Executive

A TRUE COPY:

WILLIAM R. C. MORRISON
Lt. Col. J.A.G.D.

TERRITORY OF HAWAII
OFFICE OF THE MILITARY GOVERNOR
IOLANI PALACE
HONOLULU, T.H.

9 November 1942

GENERAL ORDERS)
NO. 155)

PUBLIC RELATIONS ADVISER TO MILITARY GOVERNOR.--
Mr. Lorrin P. Thurston is announced as Public Relations
Adviser to the Military Governor, Territory of Hawaii.

By order of the Military Governor:

(Signed) Thomas H. Green,
THOMAS H. GREEN,
Brigadier General, A.U.S.
Executive

A TRUE COPY:

WILLIAM R. C. MORRISON
Lt. Col. J.A.G.D.

TERRITORY OF HAWAII
OFFICE OF THE MILITARY GOVERNOR
IOLANI PALACE
HONOLULU, T.H.

18 November 1942

GENERAL ORDERS)
NO. 158)

APPOINTMENT OF MILITARY COMMISSION.--1. A Military Commission hereby is appointed to meet at Honolulu, Territory of Hawaii, at 9:00 a.m., 23 November 1942, or as soon thereafter as practicable, and at such other places and times within the Territory of Hawaii as the President of said Military Commission may direct, for the trial of such persons as may be properly brought before it:

DETAIL FOR THE MILITARY COMMISSION

Major General James A. Woodruff, United States Army, President and Law Member.
Colonel John H. Howard, United States Army.
Lieutenant Colonel Virgil G. Allen, General Staff Corps.
Lieutenant Colonel Ray O. Welch, Ordnance Department.
Lieutenant Colonel Moe D. Baroff, Infantry.
Major Eugene V. Slattery, The Judge Advocate General's Department, Trial Judge Advocate.
Lieutenant Colonel Harrison M. Coppin, The Adjutant General's Department, Defense Counsel.
Captain Sam B. Thomas, Corps of Military Police, Assistant Defense Counsel.

2. All unarraigned cases referred for trial to Major Eugene V. Slattery, The Judge Advocate General's Department, Trial Judge Advocate, and to the Military Commission, appointed by Paragraph 2, General Orders Number 25, Office of the Military Governor, Fort Shafter, T. H., dated 14 December 1941, as amended by Paragraphs 1 and 2, Section III, General Orders Number 54, Office of the Military Governor, Iolani Palace, Honolulu, T. H., dated 20 January 1942, will be brought to trial before and be tried and determined by the Military Commission appointed by these General Orders.

By order of the Military Governor:

(signed) Thomas H. Green,
THOMAS H. GREEN,
Brigadier General, A.U.S.
Executive

A TRUE COPY:

William R. C. Morrison
WILLIAM R. C. MORRISON,
Lt. Col., J.A.G.D.

TERRITORY OF HAWAII
OFFICE OF THE MILITARY GOVERNOR
IOLANI PALACE
HONOLULU, T. H.

22 November 1942

GENERAL ORDERS)
NO. 159)

SECTION I. DIRECTOR OF FOOD CONTROL.
SECTION II. DIRECTOR OF PRICE CONTROL.

SECTION I. DIRECTOR OF FOOD CONTROL.— Mr. Alexander Walker is hereby appointed as Director of Food Control, Office of the Military Governor, Territory of Hawaii.

SECTION II. DIRECTOR OF PRICE CONTROL.— Mr. Karl Borders is hereby appointed Director of Price Control, Office of the Military Governor, Territory of Hawaii.

(Signed) Thomas H. Green,
THOMAS H. GREEN,
Brigadier General, A.U.S.
Executive

A TRUE COPY:

WILLIAM R. C. MORRISON
Lt. Col., J.A.G.D.

TERRITORY OF HAWAII
OFFICE OF THE MILITARY GOVERNOR
IOLANI PALACE
HONOLULU, T.H.

30 November 1942

GENERAL ORDERS)
NO. 161)

SECTION I. RECISSION OF GENERAL ORDERS (BLACKOUT HOURS).
SECTION II. BLACKOUT HOUR SCHEDULE.

SECTION I. RECISSION OF GENERAL ORDERS (BLACKOUT HOURS).— Effective 15 December 1942, the following General Orders and parts of General Orders of this office are rescinded:

Paragraph 4, Section II, General Orders No. 134, 1 September 1942;
Section V, General Orders No. 137, 11 September 1942;
General Orders No. 139, 13 September 1942;
Section IV, General Orders No. 142, 28 September 1942;
Section I, General Orders No. 145, 10 October 1942; and
General Orders No. 156, 10 November 1942.

SECTION II. BLACKOUT HOUR SCHEDULE.—1. On and after 15 December 1942, the hours of blackout for the City and County of Honolulu, Maui District, and Kauai District shall be as stated in the following blackout schedule showing the effective dates and hours for the ensuing year:

DATES From	Through	HOURS From	To
15 December 1942	14 January 1943	7:00 p.m.	7:15 a.m.
15 January 1943	9 February 1943	7:15 p.m.	7:15 a.m.
10 February 1943	28 February 1943	7:30 p.m.	7:15 a.m.
1 March 1943	14 March 1943	7:30 p.m.	7:00 a.m.
15 March 1943	31 March 1943	7:45 p.m.	6:45 a.m.
1 April 1943	14 April 1943	7:45 p.m.	6:30 a.m.
15 April 1943	30 April 1943	7:45 p.m.	6:15 a.m.
1 May 1943	31 May 1943	8:00 p.m.	6:00 a.m.
1 June 1943	31 July 1943	8:15 p.m.	6:00 a.m.
1 August 1943	31 August 1943	8:00 p.m.	6:15 a.m.
1 September 1943	14 September 1943	7:45 p.m.	6:15 a.m.
15 September 1943	30 September 1943	7:30 p.m.	6:30 a.m.
1 October 1943	14 October 1943	7:15 p.m.	6:30 a.m.
15 October 1943	31 October 1943	7:00 p.m.	6:30 a.m.
1 November 1943	14 November 1943	7:00 p.m.	6:45 a.m.

-1-

G. O. No. 161, O. M. G., 1942

DATES From	Through	HOURS From	To
15 November 1943	14 December 1943	6:45 p.m.	7:00 a.m.
15 December 1943	14 January 1944	7:00 p.m.	7:15 a.m.

2. On and after 15 December 1942, the hours of blackout for the Hawaii District shall be as stated in the following blackout schedule showing the effective dates and hours for the ensuing year:

DATES From	Through	HOURS From	To
15 December 1942	14 January 1943	6:45 p.m.	7:00 a.m.
15 January 1943	9 February 1943	7:00 p.m.	7:00 a.m.
10 February 1943	28 February 1943	7:15 p.m.	7:00 a.m.
1 March 1943	14 March 1943	7:15 p.m.	6:45 a.m.
15 March 1943	31 March 1943	7:30 p.m.	6:30 a.m.
1 April 1943	14 April 1943	7:30 p.m.	6:15 a.m.
15 April 1943	30 April 1943	7:30 p.m.	6:00 a.m.
1 May 1943	31 May 1943	7:45 p.m.	5:45 a.m.
1 June 1943	31 July 1943	8:00 p.m.	5:45 a.m.
1 August 1943	31 August 1943	7:45 p.m.	6:00 a.m.
1 September 1943	14 September 1943	7:30 p.m.	6:00 a.m.
15 September 1943	30 September 1943	7:15 p.m.	6:15 a.m.
1 October 1943	14 October 1943	7:00 p.m.	6:15 a.m.
15 October 1943	31 October 1943	6:45 p.m.	6:15 a.m.
1 November 1943	14 November 1943	6:45 p.m.	6:30 a.m.
15 November 1943	14 December 1943	6:30 p.m.	6:45 a.m.
15 December 1943	14 January 1944	6:45 p.m.	7:00 a.m.

By order of the Military Governor:

(Signed) Thomas H. Green
THOMAS H. GREEN,
Brigadier General, A.U.S.
Executive

A TRUE COPY:

William R.C. Morrison
WILLIAM R.C. MORRISON
Lieut. Colonel, J.A.G.D.

166

TERRITORY OF HAWAII
OFFICE OF THE MILITARY GOVERNOR
IOLANI PALACE
HONOLULU, T. H.

30 December 1942

GENERAL ORDERS)
NO. 167)

AUTHORIZING BOWLING-ALLEYS AND MOTION-PICTURE THEATERS TO OPERATE AND REMAIN OPEN UNTIL 9:30 P.M., AND RESCINDING SECTION III, GENERAL ORDERS NO. 117, THIS OFFICE, 20 JUNE 1942.— 1. Bowling-alleys and motion-picture theaters may operate and remain open until 9:30 P.M., but not thereafter during blackout hours, providing that the owners or operators thereof, during that period of the blackout hours that the said bowling-alleys or motion-picture theaters are operated or remain open pursuant to the provisions of this Order, comply with any of the blackout rules and regulations of the Military Governor that are applicable to the said bowling-alleys or motion-picture theaters while the same are operated or remain open as aforesaid. No person, firm, or corporation shall conduct or operate a bowling-alley or motion-picture theater within the Territory of Hawaii at any time during blackout hours after 9:30 P.M., or allow or permit any patron, customer, or guest thereof, to remain in or about such bowling-alley or in such motion-picture theater, at any time during blackout hours after 9:30 P.M.; nor shall any person, firm, or corporation who or which is the owner or operator of a bowling-alley or motion-picture theater, or who or which is engaged in the business of conducting or operating a bowling-alley or motion-picture theater, within the Territory of Hawaii, permit or allow such bowling-alley or motion-picture theater to be operated, or to remain open, for any purpose whatsoever, at any time during blackout hours after 9:30 P.M.

2. Any person, firm or corporation, who or which violates, refuses, fails, or neglects to comply with any of the provisions of this Order, or who or which evades or attempts to evade any of the provisions of this Order, upon conviction thereof, shall be punished by confinement, with or without hard labor not to exceed one (1) year, or by a fine not to exceed one thousand dollars ($1,000.00), or by both such confinement and fine.

3. Section III, General Orders No. 117, this Office, 20 June 1942, hereby is rescinded and repealed.

By order of the Military Governor:

(Signed) Wm. R. C. Morrison
WM. R. C. MORRISON
Lieut. Colonel, J.A.G.D.
Assistant Executive

A TRUE COPY:

Robert B. Griffith
ROBERT B. GRIFFITH
Captain, Infantry

TERRITORY OF HAWAII
OFFICE OF THE MILITARY GOVERNOR
IOLANI PALACE
HONOLULU, T.H.

15 January 1943

GENERAL ORDERS)
NO. 172)

WAR MANPOWER COMMISSION ADVISOR TO MILITARY GOVERNOR.--Mr. Newton R. Holcomb, Territorial Director, War Manpower Commission, is announced as War Manpower Commission Advisor to the Military Governor of the Territory of Hawaii.

By order of the Military Governor:

/S/ Wm. R. C. Morrison
WM. R. C. MORRISON
Lieut. Colonel, J.A.G.D.
Assistant Executive

A TRUE COPY:

Robert B. Griffith
ROBERT B. GRIFFITH
Captain, Infantry

TERRITORY OF HAWAII
OFFICE OF THE MILITARY GOVERNOR
IOLANI PALACE
HONOLULU, T.H.

18 January 1943

GENERAL ORDERS)
NO. 174)

FALSE STATEMENTS TO, OR MISUSING AUTHORIZATIONS GRANTED BY, AGENCIES OF THE MILITARY GOVERNOR.--1. DEFINITIONS:

(a) OFFICE OF THE MILITARY GOVERNOR. The term "Office of the Military Governor," as used herein, shall include, and hereby is defined to mean, any of the following, to wit:

(1) The Military Governor of the Territory of Hawaii;

(2) The agencies, agents, committees, departments, directors, divisions, employees, sections, and all other personnel, included within the organization of the Office of the Military Governor by the provisions of Section III, General Orders No. 58, this office, 26 January 1942; Paragraphs Numbered 2 and 3, General Orders No. 108, this office, 29 May 1942, and Section VI, General Orders No. 134, this office, 1 September 1942;

(3) Any representative of the Military Governor not specifically included or mentioned in subdivision (2) aforesaid; and,

(4) The successor or successors, if any, of any of those included or mentioned within subdivisions (1), (2), and (3) aforesaid.

(b) STATEMENT. The term "statement," as used herein, shall include, and hereby is defined to mean, any of the following, to wit: Account, affidavit, oral or written application, bill, claim, deposition, document, form, instrument, letter, oral or written report, oral or written representation, roll, voucher, or any document, instrument or oral or written statement not specifically mentioned heretofore in this sentence.

- 1 -

G.O.NO.174, O.M.G., 1943

(c) AUTHORIZATION. The term "authorization," as used herein, shall include, and hereby is defined to mean, any approval, certificate, permit, release, license, order, parole, commutation or suspension of sentence, power, privilege, waiver, or other document or instrument, authorized, granted, or issued, or that may be authorized, granted, or issued, by the Office of the Military Governor.

2. No person, firm, or corporation, shall, in any matter within the jurisdiction of the Office of the Military Governor, wilfully falsify, or wrongfully or fraudulently conceal or cover up by any trick, scheme, or by any act or omission or commission, any fact concerning said matter. No person, firm, or corporation, shall make or cause to be made, or present or cause to be presented, to the Office of the Military Governor, any false, fictitious, misleading, evasive, or fraudulent statement, for the purpose of securing, obtaining, or receiving any authorization, payment of money, or any consideration or determination of any matter by the Office of the Military Governor, or for any purpose whatsoever, knowing or having reason to believe such statement to be false, fictitious, misleading, evasive, or fraudulent in whole or in any part, particular, or item thereof, or without having good and substantial reason to believe such statement to be true and correct in whole and in every part, particular, and item thereof.

3. No person, firm, or corporation, shall receive or obtain, or cause to be received or obtained, from the said Office of the Military Governor, any authorization for any purpose or use other than that purpose or use for which it was granted, authorized, issued, or intended by said Office of the Military Governor; and no person, firm, or corporation, who or which shall have received, or obtained, any authorization from the Office of the Military Governor, shall use or employ, or allow, permit, or cause to be used or employed, the authorization so obtained, for any purpose or use other than that for which it was granted, authorized, issued, or intended, by said Office of the Military Governor; and no person, firm, or corporation, who or which shall have obtained any materials, fixtures, goods, wares, merchandise, or any other personal property, by means of or pursuant to any authorization, shall employ, use, or dispose of in any manner whatsoever or allow, permit, or cause to be employed, used, or in any manner whatsoever disposed of, any of the said materials, fixtures, goods, wares, merchandise, or other personal property, for any purpose, use, or disposition, other than that purpose, use, or disposition authorized by the authorization by means of or pursuant to which ownership or possession of said property was obtained or is held by said person, firm, or corporation, unless such person, firm,

-2-

G.O.NO.174, O.M.G., 1943

or corporation is authorized in writing by the Office of the Military Governor to so otherwise use, employ, or dispose of said property.

4. No person, who shall have taken an oath or affirmation in a trial or any proceeding before a provost court or a military commission appointed by the Office of the Military Governor of the Territory of Hawaii, or in connection with any affidavit, deposition, or other instrument or document intended to be used or actually used in any such trial or proceeding, shall wilfully swear or affirm falsely in regard to any matter or thing, whether material or immaterial, during, or concerning which, such trial or other proceeding is being had by said provost court or said military commission, or wilfully swear or affirm falsely in regard to any matter or thing, whether material or immaterial, contained in such affidavit, deposition, or other instrument or document.

5. Any person, firm, or corporation, who or which violates, refuses, fails, or neglects to comply with any of the provisions of this General Orders, or who or which evades or attempts to evade any of the provisions of this General Orders, upon conviction thereof, if a natural person, shall be punished by confinement, with or without hard labor, not to exceed five (5) years, or by a fine not to exceed five thousand dollars ($5,000.00), or by both such confinement and fine, or if a corporation or other than a natural person, by a fine not to exceed five thousand dollars ($5,000.00).

6. Nothing herein contained shall be construed as abrogating, repealing, limiting, amending, or modifying the provisions of any other General Orders. The provisions of this General Orders shall be in addition to any provisions contained in any other General Orders. If any act or acts prohibited by this General Orders also is or are prohibited by or made a violation or violations of any other General Orders, the offender may be convicted or punished, or convicted and punished, for a violation of either this General Orders or such other General Orders.

By order of the Military Governor:

/S/ Wm. R. C. Morrison
WM. R. C. MORRISON
Lieut. Colonel, J.A.G.D.
Assistant Executive

A TRUE COPY: *Robert B. Griffith*
ROBERT B. GRIFFITH
Captain, Infantry

-3-

---

28 January 1943

GENERAL ORDERS)
NO. 177)

REQUIRING SOLICITORS TO OBTAIN A SOLICITOR'S IDENTIFICATION CARD FROM THE CENTRAL IDENTIFICATION BUREAU AND RESCINDING SECTION II, GENERAL ORDERS NO. 52, RELATING TO SOLICITORS.

1. This order is issued in the interests of internal security as additional protection against possible espionage and sabotage.

2. Section II, General Orders No. 52, this office, 14 January 1942, is rescinded as of March 1, 1943.

3. The term "solicitor", as used in this General Orders, shall include, and hereby is defined to mean, any person who, within the Territory of Hawaii, goes from house to house, or from place to place, selling, soliciting, or taking orders for, or offering to sell or take orders for, farm products, goods, wares, merchandise, or memberships, shares, certificates, or similar interests in any group, club, lodge, or society. Insurance salesmen, persons who go from house to house or place to place to deliver newspapers or milk or to collect garbage or to pick up or deliver property of any kind, and agents, employees, or representatives of privately owned public utilities, who go from house to house or place to place, regularly or occasionally during the course of their employment, shall be deemed to be solicitors within the meaning of the provisions of this General Orders. It shall be no defense in the prosecution of any person charged with a violation of any of the provisions of this General Orders that such person did not demand, solicit, accept, or receive payment or deposit of money in connection with any of the aforesaid acts or matters; nor will it be necessary for the accuser or prosecutor to allege or prove, or for the Court to find, in any such

---

TERRITORY OF HAWAII
OFFICE OF THE MILITARY GOVERNOR
IOLANI PALACE
HONOLULU, T.H.

RECEIVED

21 January 1943

JAN 25 2 55 PM 1943

GENERAL ORDERS)
NO. 175)

RESCISSION OF GENERAL ORDERS PROHIBITING THE CARRYING OF LIGHTED CIGARETTES, CIGARS, AND PIPES, AND THE STRIKING OF MATCHES AND LIGHTERS, IN THE OPEN DURING THE HOURS OF BLACKOUT.—1. Paragraph Numbered 7, Section II, General Orders No. 134, this office, 1 September 1942, hereby is rescinded.

2. The carrying of lighted cigarettes, cigars, and pipes in the open and the use of matches and lighters in the open for the purpose of lighting cigarettes, cigars, and pipes, during the hours of blackout, except during air raids, air raid alarms and attacks, hereby is permitted.

3. Nothing herein contained shall be construed as abrogating, repealing, limiting, amending, or modifying the provisions of any other General Orders, except as herein provided.

By order of the Military Governor:

/S/ Wm. R. C. Morrison
WM. R. C. MORRISON
Lieut. Colonel, J.A.G.D.
Assistant Executive

A TRUE COPY: *Robert B. Griffith*
ROBERT B. GRIFFITH
Captain, Infantry

G. O. No. 177, O.M.G., 1943

prosecution that any such person so charged was regularly engaged or employed as a solicitor, but it will be sufficient to establish that such person is a solicitor within the meaning of this General Orders if such person irregularly or occasionally does any of the acts mentioned in the first two sentences of this paragraph.

4. No person shall engage in, transact, or conduct business as, or act as, or do an act as, or be, a solicitor within the Territory of Hawaii after March 1, 1943, without first having obtained a solicitor's identification card from the Central Identification Bureau of the Office of the Military Governor, at Honolulu, T.H. Solicitors shall retain their solicitor's identification card on their person at all times and exhibit such card upon demand by any municipal, territorial, or federal police officer, or upon demand by any duly authorized member of the United States Naval Intelligence or Military Intelligence Division. No person other than the person to whom such solicitor's identification card duly has been issued by the said Central Identification Bureau, shall possess or use in any manner, said solicitor's identification card.

5. None of the provisions of this General Orders shall be applicable to any person under sixteen (16) years of age, nor to any municipal, territorial, or federal employees.

6. Any person who violates, refuses, fails, or neglects to comply with any of the provisions of this General Orders, or who evades, or attempts to evade, any of the provisions of this General Orders, upon conviction thereof, shall be punished by confinement, with or without hard labor, not to exceed six (6) months or by a fine not to exceed Five Hundred Dollars ($500.00); or by both such confinement and fine.

By order of the Military Governor:

/S/ Wm. R. C. Morrison
WM. R. C. MORRISON
Lieut. Colonel, J.A.G.D.
Assistant Executive

A TRUE COPY: *Robert B. Griffith*
ROBERT B. GRIFFITH
Captain, Infantry

GENERAL ORDERS NO. 1

10 March, 1943

1. EXECUTIVE.
1.01. Thomas H. Green, Brigadier, General, A.U.S., hereby is appointed Executive of the Military Governor.
2. ASSISTANT EXECUTIVE.
2.01. William R. C. Morrison, Colonel, J.A.G.D., hereby is appointed Assistant Executive of the Military Governor.

DELOS C. EMMONS
Lieuenant General, United States Army
Commanding General, Hawaiian Department,
Military Governor of the Territory of Hawaii.

GENERAL ORDERS NO. 2

10 March, 1943

COURTS AND COMMISSIONS AND OFFENSES RELATING TO THE ADMINISTRATION OF JUSTICE

1. Martial Law and the Writ of Habeas Corpus.
2. Civil Courts.
3. Provost Courts and Military Commissions.
4. Military Commissions.
5. Provost Courts.
6. Provost Court Commissioner.
7. Attempts and Conspiracies to Violate a General Orders.
8. Interference with Military Police and Personnel.
9. False Statements to, or Misusing Authorizations Granted by, Agencies of the Military Governor.
10. Power of Civilian Police Officer to Make Arrests for Violation of General Orders of the Military Governor.
11. Definition of "Person".
12. Prosecution of Offenses under Rescinded General Orders.

1. MARTIAL LAW AND THE WRIT OF HABEAS CORPUS.

1.01 A state of martial law remains in effect and the privilege of the writ of habeas corpus has been, and remains, suspended.

2. CIVIL COURTS (PURSUANT TO PROCLAMATIONS OF FEBRUARY 8, 1943).

2.01. Civil courts are authorized to exercise their normal jurisdiction as provided by law, except that such courts shall not have jurisdiction of the following:

Criminal prosecutions against members of the armed forces. Members of auxiliary armed forces shall be included within the term "armed forces" after induction into the service and also before induction in respect of any act or omission certified by the Commanding General, Hawaiian Department, to be in the line of duty;

Civil suits against members of the armed forces, as defined above, in respect of any act or omission certified by the Commanding General, Hawaiian Department, to be in the line of duty;

Criminal prosecutions for violations of military orders.

2.02. The Commanding General, Hawaiian Department, may waive the above exception with respect to any particular prosecution or suit, or any class of prosecutions or suits, thereby permitting such prosecutions or suits to be tried in the appropriate court of the territory or in the United States District Court for Hawaii, as the case may be.

3. PROVOST COURTS AND MILITARY COMMISSIONS.

3.01. Provost Courts and Military Commissions shall have jurisdiction and power, and hereby are authorized and empowered, to try and determine any case, matter, or proceeding involving any violation or violations by a civilian or civilians of the rules, regulations, proclamations, or Orders of the Military or Naval authorities, or of the Military Governor of the Territory of Hawaii, or of the laws of war; and, such Provost Courts and Military Commissions, in addition to the power to impose upon or against any person or persons charged or tried in any such case, matter, or proceeding, the penalties, forfeitures, and similar punishment otherwise authorized by the General Orders of the Military Governor, shall have power, and hereby are authorized and empowered, to punish any such person or persons committing such violation or violations, or offense or offenses, by fine or imprisonment with or without hard labor, or by both such fine and imprisonment, as may be ordered or pro-

vided in the General Orders of the Military Governor. Such Provost Courts or Military Commissions shall have jurisdiction and power, and hereby are authorized and empowered, to try and punish members of the Armed Forces of the United States only for violations of any statute of the Territory of Hawaii, or of any ordinance, resolution, by-law, regulation, or rule of any city, city and county, county, or other municipal corporation or political subdivision of the Territory of Hawaii, or of any order, regulation, or rule of the Military or Naval authorities or of the Military Governor of the Territory of Hawaii, regulating or relating to vehicular or pedestrian traffic. The concurrent jurisdiction of the Armed Forces of the United States to court-martial or otherwise discipline commissioned or enlisted personnel of their respective services for such traffic offenses is not withdrawn by anything herein contained.

3.02. Charges involving major offenses shall be referred to a Military Commission for trial and determination, unless otherwise ordered by the Military Governor of the Territory of Hawaii. Other cases involving charges of lesser degree shall be tried and determined by Provost Courts. Military Commissions and Provost Courts will adjudge appropriate sentences commensurate with the offense. In adjudging such sentences, Provost Courts and Military Commissions will be guided by, but not limited to or bound by, the penalties provided by the Courts-Martial Manual, the laws of the United States, the laws of the Territory of Hawaii, the laws of the District of Columbia, county, and city and county ordinances, and the customs of law in like cases. The maximum fine or confinement, or both fine and confinement, which a Provost Court may adjudge as punishment, is confinement with or without hard labor for a period not to exceed five (5) years, or a fine not to exceed five thousand dollars ($5,000.00), or both such confinement and fine. The foregoing limitation on the fine or confinement, or fine and confinement, that a Provost Court may adjudge, shall not restrict the power and authority of such a Provost Court to order and direct the confiscation and destruction of property, the suspension, cancellation, or revocation of licenses, or such other penalties or sentences in addition to such fine or confinement, or both, as may be provided by this or any other General Orders of the Military Governor. Military Commissions may adjudge confinement with or without hard labor for any number of years, or for life, or may adjudge the death penalty, and may impose fines with or without such confinement, in any case tried and determined by a Military Commission. The sentences adjudged by a Provost Court shall become effective immediately. The sentence adjudged by a Military Commission shall not become effective until it shall have been approved by the Military Governor.

3.03. Any person who fails, neglects, or refuses to comply with any subpoena, summons, citation, notice, warrant of arrest, commitment, order of commitment, or other process, issued by a Provost Court, a Military Commission, the Trial Judge Advocate of a Military Commission, or by any duly authorized agent or representative of such a Provost Court or Military Commission, or who uses any menacing words, signs, or gestures in the presence of a Provost Court or Military Commission, or who disturbs the proceedings of a Provost Court or Military Commission by a riot or disorder or in any manner, or who in any manner or way wilfully disobeys any rule or order of a Provost Court or Military Commission, shall be deemed to be guilty of contempt of such Provost Court or Military Commission, and may be tried and punished for such contempt by such Provost Court or Military Commission summarily or as such Provost Court or Military Commission may otherwise determine.

3.04. Provost Courts and Military Commissions, in addition to the power to impose a fine or confinement, or both such fine and confinement, as otherwise authorized in this General Orders or any other General Orders of the Military Governor of the Territory of Hawaii, upon conviction of a person for a violation of a General Orders of the Military Governor or for any offense that may be tried and determined by such Provost Courts or Military Commissions, shall have power and hereby are authorized and empowered to suspend, cancel, or revoke, or direct or order the suspension, cancellation, or revocation of any license, franchise, or permit of a personal nature issued by the Military Governor or any agent or representative thereof to the person so convicted, and also shall have power and hereby are authorized and empowered, upon conviction of any person as

168

aforesaid, to suspend, cancel, or revoke, or order or direct the suspension, cancellation, or revocation of, any license, permit, or franchise of a personal nature issued to such person so convicted by any federal or territorial officer, department, agent or agency, or by any department, officer, agent or agency of any municipal corporation or other political subdivision within the Territory of Hawaii.

3.05. In all cases of violation of any provision of any General Orders of the Military Governor, where no other or different provision for fine or confinement or both is provided by such General Orders, the maximum fine or confinement, or both fine and confinement, that a Provost Court may impose, shall be a fine not to exceed five thousand dollars ($5,000.00), or confinement with or without hard labor not to exceed five (5) years, or both such fine and confinement. The limitations on punishment in any General Orders defining an offense and providing a punishment for such offense shall not be deemed a limitation upon the punishment or sentence that a Military Commission may impose if such offense be tried and determined by a Military Commission rather than by a Provost Court.

3.06. Provost Courts and Military Commissions hereby are authorized and empowered to forfeit or confiscate or to order or direct the forfeiture or confiscation or other disposition of any personal property used, or having for its sole purpose use, in the commission of a violation of any of the provisions of any of the General Orders of the Military Governor now in full force and effect or hereafter enacted or issued.

3.07. Provost Courts hereby are authorized, empowered, and directed, and Military Commissions hereby are authorized and empowered in their discretion, to admit persons arrested for or charged with an offense triable by such Provost Courts or Military Commissions to cash bail, to fix and accept said bail, provided, however, that such bail shall not be excessive, to determine the conditions subject to which such bail may be or is furnished, and to order and direct forfeiture thereof, and the manner in which the said bail may be forfeited. The police departments of any county, or city and county, within the Territory of Hawaii, when authorized, empowered, and directed to do so by the Military Governor of the Territory of Hawaii, may also fix and accept bail for offenses triable by such Provost Courts. Bail may be set by the Provost Court Commissioner.

3.08. The record of trial in cases before Military Commissions will be substantially similar to that required in a general courts-martial. The record of trial in cases before Provost Courts will be substantially similar to that in the case of a summary courts-martial. The procedure in trials before Military Commissions and Provost Courts will follow so far as it is applicable, the procedure required by general and summary courts-martial respectively. The records of trial in all cases will be forwarded to the Office of the Military Governor.

3.09. All charges brought in the Provost Courts or before Military Commissions shall be preferred by either the Provost Marshal, Hawaiian Department, the Provost Marshal of a Military district with said Hawaiian Department, or such deputies or assistants of said Provost Marshals and such other persons as first shall be approved by the Military Governor. The Provost Court Commissioner is responsible for the prompt trial of all prisoners in Provost Courts or before Military Commissions, and the Provost Marshals shall be responsible for carrying out the sentence adjudged by the Court or Commission.

4. MILITARY COMMISSIONS.

4.01. A Military Commission hereby is appointed to meet at such times and places within the Territory of Hawaii as the President of said Military Commission may direct, for the trial of such persons as may be properly brought before it.

4.02. The following persons shall comprise the detail for said Military Commission:

Major General James A. Woodruff, U.S.A., President and Law Member.
Col. John H. Howard, U.S.A.
Lt. Col. Virgil G. Allen, General Staff Corps.
Lt. Col. Ray O. Welch, Ordnance Department.
Lt. Col. Moe D. Baroff, Infantry.
Major Eugene V. Slattery, J.A.G.D., Trial Judge Advocate.
Lt. Col. Harrison M. Coppin, A.G.D., Defense Counsel.

Captain Sam B. Thomas, C.M.P., Assistant Defense Counsel.

4.03. The defendant in any case tried before said Military Commission may retain and introduce individual counsel of his own selection to represent him in said proceedings.

5. PROVOST COURTS.

5.01. Each of the following persons hereby is appointed as a Provost Court, and assigned to duty as such in addition to his other duties, for the trial of such persons as may properly be brought before the court, at the respective places as hereinafter designated, viz.:

At Hilo, Hawaii, T. H.
Col. Arthur C. Huston, Jr., Inf.
Captain William A. E. King, J.A.G.D.
1st Lt. Woolbridge B. Morton, Jr., F.A.
At Honolulu and Kaneohe, Oahu, T. H.
Col. John H. Howard, U.S.A.
Lt. Col. Moe D. Baroff, Inf.
Major Eugene V. Slattery, J.A.G.D.
Captain John F. Wickhem, J.A.G.D.
At Lihue, Kauai, T. H.
Major Charles A. Fisher, Inf.
At Lanai City, Lanai, T. H.
Arthur W. Carlson.
At Wailuku, Maui, T. H.
Major Merryl G. Shaver, J.A.G.D.
At Kaunakakai, Molokai, T. H.
Major Merryl G. Shaver, J.A.G.D.
At Palmyra Island, T. H.
The Commanding Officer, United States Naval Air Station.
At Schofield Barracks and Pearl City, Oahu, T. H.
Lt. Col. Henry DuPree, Inf.

6. PROVOST COURT COMMISSIONER.

6.01. There is hereby created the office of Provost Court Commissioner for the Territory of Hawaii.

6.02. The powers and duties of such Provost Court Commissioner shall be as follows:

To establish a method of process for Provost Courts and Military Commissions and to prepare and recommend rules and regulations of procedure to be promulgated by the Military Governor;

To have charge of and be responsible for, acting under the direction of the Military Governor, the prosecution of all cases before the Provost Courts, and to appear in and prosecute such cases personally or through prosecutors selected from those duly designated and approved pursuant to Paragraph 3.09 of this General Orders No. 2 to prefer charges; provided, however, that the said Provost Court Commissioner may at any time that he elects to do so appear in, take over, and prosecute any case before the Provost Courts at any stage of the proceedings in such case;

To supervise and coordinate the operations and activities of the Provost Courts and Military Commissions, including the assignment of cases and determination of questions of jurisdiction;

To coordinate the operations and activities of such Provost Courts and Military Commissions with the activities of the federal and territorial courts, so that a full, complete and expeditious administration of justice may be had and maintained in the Territory of Hawaii during the present emergency;

To have the power of administering oaths or affirmations and to have all other powers necessary or incidental to an efficacious accomplishment of the foregoing duties;

To perform such other duties and functions and exercise such other powers as may from time to time be directed or authorized by the Military Governor.

6.03. Edward N. Sylva, Captain, J.A.G.D., hereby is appointed the Provost Court Commissioner for the Territory of Hawaii and assigned to duty as such Provost Court Commissioner in addition to his other duties.

7. ATTEMPTS AND CONSPIRACIES TO VIOLATE A GENERAL ORDERS.

7.01. An attempt to commit a violation of a General Orders of the Military Governor or any offense triable by a Provost Court or a Military Commission is some act done towards committing and in part execution of the intent to commit the same. No person, firm, corporation, or other association or group of persons, shall attempt to commit a violation of any provisions of a General Orders of the Military Governor, or attempt to commit any offense triable by a Provost Court or a Military Commission.

7.02. A conspiracy is a wilful or malicious combination or mutual undertaking or concerting together of two or more persons to commit a violation of a General Orders of the Military Governor, or any offense triable by a Provost Court or a Military Commission, or instigate any other person thereto, or to do what plainly and directly tends to excite or occasion such a violation. No person shall conspire to violate any provision of a General Orders of the Military Governor, or attempt to commit any offense triable by a Provost Court or a Military Commission.

7.03. Any person knowingly acceding to and joining in a conspiracy after the same is formed, is a party thereto, no less than the one who originally takes part in forming the same. The act of each party to a conspiracy, in pursuance thereof, is the act of all. It shall not be necessary that the act agreed upon shall be done or attempted in pursuance of the conspiracy, as the conspiracy, itself, constitutes the offense.

8. INTERFERENCE WITH MILITARY POLICE AND PERSONNEL.

8.01. No person shall commit an assault or an assault and battery on any military police, any member of the shore patrol, or other military or naval personnel, with intent to resist, prevent, hinder, or obstruct him in the discharge, execution, or performance of his duty as such, nor shall any person willfully interfere or attempt to interfere with any military police, any member of the shore patrol, or other military or naval personnel in the performance of his official, defined, or required duties as such.

8.02. No person shall commit an assault or an assault and battery on a federal, territorial, or municipal police officer with intent to resist, prevent, hinder, or obstruct said police officer in the arrest of a person violating, or charged with a violation of, any General Orders of the Military Governor, or for any offense that may be tried and determined by a Provost Court or Military Commission, nor shall any person wilfully interfere with any such federal, territorial, or municipal police officer in the performance of any duties imposed upon such police officer, or which the said police officer is authorized or empowered to perform, by any General Orders of the Military Governor.

8.03. No person, who is or has been made prisoner, or now or hereafter is detained, on conviction or charge of any offense defined by any General Orders of the Military Governor, or triable by a Provost Court or Military Commission, shall escape from imprisonment or detention against the will of the officer or person having him in custody or against the will or consent of the Military Governor.

8.04. No person shall, after another person has committed an offense constituting a violation of any of the General Orders of the Military Governor, or a violation that may otherwise be tried and determined by a Provost Court or a Military Commission, harbor, conceal, or aid such other person, with knowledge or having good reason to believe that such other person has committed such offense, and with the intent that such other person may avoid or escape from arrest, trial, conviction, or punishment for such offense.

9. FALSE STATEMENTS TO, OR MISUSING AUTHORIZATIONS GRANTED BY, AGENCIES OF, THE MILITARY GOVERNOR.

9.01. Definition of "Office of the Military Governor". The term "Office of the Military Governor," as used herein shall include, and hereby is defined to mean, any of the following, to wit:

The Military Governor of the Territory of Hawaii;

The agencies, agents, committees, departments, directors, divisions, employees, sections, and all other personnel, included within the organization of the Office of the Military Governor;

Any representative of the Military Governor not specifically included or mentioned in the subdivision immediately above; and,

The successor or successors, if any, of any of those included or mentioned within the three subdivisions immediately above.

9.02. Definition of "Statement." The term "statement," as used herein, shall include, and hereby is defined to mean, any of the following, to wit: Account, affidavit, oral or written application, bill, claim, deposition, document, form, instrument, letter, oral or written report, oral or written representation, roll, voucher, or any document, instrument, or oral or written statement not specifically mentioned heretofore in this sentence.

9.03. Definition of "Authorization." The term "authorization," as used herein, shall include, and hereby is

defined to mean, any approval, certificate, permit, release, license, order, parole, commutation or suspension of sentence, power, privilege, waiver, or other document or instrument, authorized, granted, or issued, or that may be authorized, granted, or issued, by the Office of the Military Governor.

9.04. No person, firm, or corporation, shall, in any matter within the jurisdiction of the Office of the Military Governor, wilfully falsify, or wrongfully or fraudulently conceal or cover up by any trick, scheme, or by any act of omission or commission, any fact concerning said matter. No person, firm, or corporation, shall make or cause to be made, or present or cause to be presented, to the Office of the Military Governor, any false, fictitious, misleading, evasive, or fraudulent statement, for the purpose of securing, obtaining, or receiving any authorization, payment of money, or any consideration or determination of any matter by the Office of the Military Governor, or for any purpose whatsoever, knowing or having reason to believe such statement to be false, fictitious, misleading, evasive, or fraudulent in whole or in any part, particular, or item thereof, or without having good and substantial reason to believe such statement to be true and correct in whole and in every part, particular, and item thereof.

9.05. No person, firm, or corporation, shall receive or obtain, or cause to be received or obtained, from the said Office of the Military Governor, any authorization for any purpose or use other than that purpose or use for which it was granted, authorized, issued, or intended by the said Office of the Military Governor; and no person, firm, or corporation, who or which shall have received or obtained any authorization from the Office of the Military Governor, shall use or employ, or allow, permit, or cause to be used or employed, the authorization so obtained, for any purpose or use other than that for which it was granted, authorized, issued, or intended by said Office of the Military Governor; and no person, firm, or corporation, who or which shall have obtained any materials, fixtures, goods, wares, merchandise, or any other personal property, by means of or pursuant to any authorization, shall employ, use, or dispose of, any of the said materials, fixtures, goods, wares, merchandise, or other personal property, for any purpose, se, or disposition, other than that purpose, use, or disposition authorized by the authorization by means of or pursuant to which ownership or possession of said property was obtained or is held by said person, firm, or corporation, unless such person, firm, or corporation is authorized in writing by the Office of the Military Governor to so otherwise use, employ, or dispose of said property.

9.06. No person, who shall have taken an oath or affirmation in a trial or any proceeding before a Provost Court or a Military Commission appointed by the Office of the Military Governor of the Territory of Hawaii, or in connection with any affidavit, deposition, or other instrument or document intended to be used or actually used in any such trial or proceeding, shall wilfully swear or affirm falsely in regard to any matter or thing, whether material or immaterial, during such trial or other proceeding, or concerning which, such trial or other proceeding is being had by said Provost Court or said Military Commission or wilfully swear or affirm falsely in regard to any matter or thing, whether material or immaterial, contained in such affidavit, deposition, or other instrument or document.

9.07. Any person, firm, or corporation who or which violates, refuses, fails, or neglects to comply with any of the provisions of this Title 9 of this General Orders, or who or which evades or attempts to evade any of the provisions of this Title 9, upon conviction thereof, if a natural person, shall be punished by confinement, with or without hard labor, not to exceed five (5) years, or by a fine not to exceed five thousand dollars ($5,000.00), or by both such confinement and fine, or if a corporation or other than a natural person, by a fine not to exceed five thousand dollars ($5,000.00).

9.08. The provisions of this Title 9 of this General Orders shall be in addition to any provisions contained in any other General Orders. If any act or acts prohibited by this Title 9 also is or are prohibited by or made a violation or violations of any other General Orders, the offender may be convicted or punished, for a violation of either this Title 9 or such other General Orders.

10. POWER OF CIVILIAN POLICE OFFICER TO MAKE ARRESTS.

10.01. All law-enforcement officers of the United States, police officers of the Territory of Hawaii, all police officers of all municipal corporations and other political subdivisions within the Territory of Hawaii, and all other public officers or public employees granted power or authority to make arrests by the laws of the United States, by the laws of the Territory of Hawaii, or by the ordinances, rules, or regulations of any municipal corporation or other political subdivision or department of or within the Territory of Hawaii, hereby are authorized, empowered, directed, and ordered, to forthwith arrest, without warrant of arrest, all persons who, in the presence of such police officers or persons so authorized to arrest, commit any violation of any General Orders of the Military Governor now in full force and effect or hereafter enacted or issued, or any offense triable by a Provost Court or a Military Commission. No cause of action or claim for damages against such police officer or person making such arrest shall accrue in favor of any person arrested as authorized or provided herein, provided, however, that no more force be used by such police officer or person in effecting such arrest than is authorized by law. No person arrested by any of the said law-enforcement officers, police officers, public officers, or public employees, for any violation of any General Orders of the Military Governor now in full force and effect or hereafter enacted or issued, or for any offense triable by a Provost Court or a Military Commission, shall file, commence, institute, maintain, or prosecute any complaint, petition, suit, action, or other proceedings for false arrest, false imprisonment, or for any other cause, reason, or purpose whatsoever, arising out of or because of the fact that such person was arrested by said law-enforcement officers, police officers, public officers, or public employees, for any such violation or offense; nor shall any person allow or permit any complaint, petition, suit, action, or other proceedings for false arrest, false imprisonment or for any other purpose whatsoever arising out of or because of the fact that such person was arrested by said law-enforcement officers, police officers, public officers, or public employees, for any such violation or offense, to be filed, commenced, instituted, maintained, or prosecuted.

11. DEFINITIONS OF "PERSON".

11.01. Unless otherwise clearly indicated in the General Orders in which used, the term "person," as used in any General Orders of the Military Governor, shall include, and hereby is defined to mean, any natural person or persons, firms, associations, trusts, corporation or corporations, or any agent, servant, employee, or representative of any of the foregoing.

12. PROSECUTION OF OFFENSES UNDER RESCINDED GENERAL ORDERS.

12.01. It is expressly provided that no revocation or rescission of General Orders of and by the Military Governor, nor any proclamation issued by the Military Governor, shall operate to invalidate any conviction, or any application of such military orders to persons or activities, and Provost Courts and Military Commissions hereby are expressly authorized and empowered to try and determine any proceeding for violation of a provision of a General Orders of the Military Governor at any time hereafter, notwithstanding any such rescission or revocation, heretofore or hereafter made, for an offense committed while such General Orders remained in full force and effect.

By order of the Military Governor of the Territory of Hawaii:

THOMAS H. GREEN
Brigadier General, A.U.S.
Executive

10 March 1943

GENERAL ORDERS NO. 3
BLACKOUT

1. Hours of Blackout.
2. Use and Control of Lights During Hours of Blackout.
3. Motor Vehicle Blackout.
4. Traffic During Hours of Blackout.
5. Workers Going to Work in the Morning.
6. Personal Identification During Hours of Blackout.
7. Places of Amusement and Business.
8. Enforcement.

1. HOURS OF BLACKOUT.

1.01. City and County of Honolulu, District of Maui, District of Kauai, and District of Lanai-Molokai. The hours of blackout for the City and County of Honolulu, the District of Maui, the District of Kauai, and the District of Lanai-Molokai shall be as set forth in the following schedule for the periods of time indicated:

DATES				HOURS			
From		Through		From		To	
10 March	1943	14 March	1943	7:30 p.m.		7:00 a.m.	
15 March	1943	31 March	1943	7:45 p.m.		6:45 a.m.	
1 April	1943	14 April	1943	7:45 p.m.		6:30 a.m.	
15 April	1943	30 April	1943	7:45 p.m.		6:15 a.m.	
1 May	1943	31 May	1943	8:00 p.m.		6:00 a.m.	
1 June	1943	31 July	1943	8:15 p.m.		6:00 a.m.	
1 August	1943	31 August	1943	8:00 p.m.		6:15 a.m.	
1 September	1943	14 September	1943	7:45 p.m.		6:15 a.m.	
15 September	1943	30 September	1943	7:30 p.m.		6:30 a.m.	
1 October	1943	14 October	1943	7:15 p.m.		6:30 a.m.	
15 October	1943	31 October	1943	7:00 p.m.		6:30 a.m.	
1 November	1943	14 November	1943	7:00 p.m.		6:45 a.m.	
15 November	1943	14 December	1943	6:45 p.m.		7:00 a.m.	
15 December	1943	14 January	1944	7:00 p.m.		7:15 a.m.	

1.02. District of Hawaii. The hours of blackout for the District of Hawaii shall be as set forth in the following schedule for the periods of time indicated:

DATES				HOURS			
From		Through		From		To	
10 March	1943	14 March	1943	7:15 p.m.		6:45 a.m.	
15 March	1943	31 March	1943	7:30 p.m.		6:30 a.m.	
1 April	1943	14 April	1943	7:30 p.m.		6:15 a.m.	
15 April	1943	30 April	1943	7:30 p.m.		6:00 a.m.	
1 May	1943	31 May	1943	7:45 p.m.		5:45 a.m.	
1 June	1943	31 July	1943	8:00 p.m.		5:45 a.m.	
1 August	1943	31 August	1943	7:45 p.m.		6:00 a.m.	
1 September	1943	14 September	1943	7:30 p.m.		6:00 a.m.	
15 September	1943	30 September	1943	7:15 p.m.		6:15 a.m.	
1 October	1943	14 October	1943	7:00 p.m.		6:15 a.m.	
15 October	1943	31 October	1943	6:45 p.m.		6:15 a.m.	
1 November	1943	14 November	1943	6:45 p.m.		6:30 a.m.	
15 November	1943	14 December	1943	6:30 p.m.		6:45 a.m.	
15 December	1943	14 January	1944	6:45 p.m.		7:00 a.m.	

2. USE AND CONTROL OF LIGHTS DURING HOURS OF BLACKOUT.

2.01. General Restriction. During the hours of blackout, the use of exterior lights and interior lights which are visible on the outside of buildings, houses, or other structures is forbidden, except as is authorized by this General Orders.

2.02. Controlled Illumination. To provide a small amount of controlled illumination in homes and buildings sufficient to permit reasonable facility of movement without necessitating complete blackout of doors, windows and other openings, the use of limited lighting is authorized.

2.03. The following special requirements are prescribed for lamp bulbs used in the controlled lighting authorized in paragraph 2.02 above:

Watts—not more than 25 watts.

Volts—220 to 240 volts to operate on 110 to 120-volt current.

Base—medium screw.

Bulb—A19 Mazda or equal and internally frosted.

Bulb Coating—opaque except for circular aperture on bulb end.

Circular Aperture—maximum diameter 1 inch.

Opaque Coating Material—resistant to scratching or removal.

2.04. The following regulations are prescribed for the use of these lamp bulbs:

In small or medium-sized rooms (less than 200 square feet of floor area) only one lamp bulb shall be used per room.

In larger rooms and in corridors not more than one lamp bulb shall be used for each 200 square feet of floor area.

When more than one lamp bulb is used, the lamp bulbs shall be spaced at least 10 feet apart.

Lamp bulbs shall be placed at least 3 feet from any window, exterior door or opening and pointed towards the floor or ceiling.

Lamp bulbs shall not be pointed toward any window, exterior door, or other opening or mirror.

These lamp bulbs in no case shall be used on the outside of buildings except on the approval of the Provost Marshal. They will not be used on lanais except on the written approval of the local Air Raid Warden.

2.05. The use of the lamps authorized in this Title is not compulsory, but in the event they are not used, all blackout rules and regulations of the Military Governor shall be strictly observed.

2.06. Piers, Factories and Other Facilities. Any person, firm, or corporation who or which desires to operate and maintain any pier, factory or other facilities during the hours of blackout, shall make application to the Provost Marshal, Hawaiian Department, or the District Provost Marshal for special permission to do so.

2.07. Observation of Maximum Blackout in Piers, Factories, and Other Facilities. Any person, firm, or corporation who or which has been granted special permission by the Provost Marshal, Hawaiian Department, or the District Provost Marshal to operate and maintain any pier, factory, or other facilities during the hours of blackout, shall observe the maximum blackout consistent with the work to be done.

2.08. Special Blackout Regulations for Piers, Factories, and Other Facilities. In observing the maximum blackout consistent with the work to be done in any pier, factory, or other facilities authorized to be operated and maintained during hours of blackout pursuant to this General Orders, the following rules and regulations shall be complied with, in addition to any other provisions of the General Orders of the Military Governor relating to, or pertaining to, blackout restrictions:

Windows shall be painted or otherwise blacked-out, so as not to emit any light.

Entrances and exits of such structures will be opened only to the extent necessary for the ingress and egress of persons and the movement of materials.

The minimum amount of illumination consistent with the efficient operation of such pier, factory, or other facilities will be used.

Lights which are authorized to be burned in piers, factories, and other facilities during the hours of blackout shall be shaded, insofar as possible, to throw the illumination downward only, so as not to be directly visible from the air or outside.

2.09. Private Incineration. No person, firm, or corporation shall destroy, by burning, any refuse, waste, garbage, rubbish, paper, sticks, lumber, or any other matter out-of-doors, nor shall any private incineration be engaged in or allowed out-of-doors, during the hours of blackout or for one hour previous to blackout, except on written authority of the Provost Marshal.

2.10. Carrying Lighted Cigarettes, Cigars and Pipes in the Open During Hours of Blackout. The carrying of lighted cigarettes, cigars, and pipes in the open and the use of matches and lighters in the open for the purpose of lighting cigarettes, cigars, and pipes, during the hours of blackout, except during air raids, air raid alarms and attacks, hereby is permitted.

2.11. Flashlights. Flashlights may be used during the hours of blackout. Except as is otherwise authorized in this paragraph, all flashlights shall be painted or otherwise fixed so as to give off a blue light. Military Police and members of the Civilian Police Department on night duty are authorized to use orange or red cellophane, paint, or other material, so as to give off a red or orange light, on the lens of their flashlights. Air Raid and Fire Wardens on night duty are authorized to use green cellophane, paint, or other materials, so as to give off a green light, on the lens of their flashlights.

2.12. Excessive Illumination. No person, firm, or corporation shall use, or cause to be used, excessively, any means of illumination during the hours of blackout.

2.13. Extinguishment of Lights During Air Raid and Other Attacks. No person, firm, or corporation shall, in case of an air raid, air raid alarm, attack, or invasion, during the hours of blackout, burn, or cause to be burned, any lights which will be visible out-of-doors, nor shall any person, firm, or corporation rekindle or turn on again such lights until the "All Clear" signal is sounded.

2.14. Businesses and other activities operating at night in the Kauai District, in such a manner as to require the use of outside lighting, shall comply with the following special blackout regulations:

Plantations requesting permission to engage in night harvesting, must be equipped with operating lights so constructed that no beam of light will be projected upwards. The lights used will be of minimum intensity necessary for operations and safety to personnel involved.

One or more radio receiving sets sealed to Station KTOH, with an operator constantly in attendance, will be continuously tuned to the Station in the immediate vicinity of any night harvesting project in order that all lights may be extinguished without delay in the event an air raid or other warning should be broadcast.

Prior to the conducting of any authorized night harvesting operations by plantations, the Plans and Training Officer, District Headquarters, Kalaheo, Kauai, will be advised in order that the proper military and naval authorities may have knowledge of the locations in which lights will be exposed.

All other businesses or activities requesting permission to violate blackout regulations will comply with the above requirements with respect to the amount and type of out-

side lighting used, and a radio or other approved means of communication will be immediately available for the reception of notices to extinguish lights. Upon receipt of any application for permission to operate in violation of blackout restrictions subject to the above provisions, the District Provost Marshal will inspect the installations under actual night operating conditions and if they are approved, will so notify the Plans and Training Officer at District Headquarters. Following official approval, the applicant will receive from District Headquarters a certificate of authority to operate during blackout hours.

Applications will be considered only from businesses or industries engaged in production of essentials necessary for the war effort or otherwise connected with the National Defense Program.

3. MOTOR VEHICLE BLACKOUT.

3.01. All motor vehicles operating during the hours of blackout shall conform to the specifications as set forth in the following paragraphs.

3.02. Headlights. Two (2) approved blackout driving headlights shall be used on each motor vehicle, except on motorcycles and motor scooters, which shall have but one (1). Such lamps shall have the necessary color design as described below, with a slot which emits white light for driving. This slot shall be covered by a metal hood. Except as shown in paragraphs 3.07 and 3.11 below, the mounting height of the headlights shall be not less than twenty-four (24) inches nor more than fifty-five (55) inches measured from road level to the bottom of the slot, and in no case higher than the top of the rim of the steering wheel. With the vehicle on level surface and carrying a capacity load, the unit shall be so adjusted that the bottom of the slot is horizontal and so aimed that the visual cut-off up the top of the beam on a vertical screen 10 feet in front of the lamp is at least four (4) inches below the bottom of the horizontal slot in the headlight and in no instances higher than fifty-one (51) inches from the road level. When mounted on motorcycles or motor scooters, the lamp shall be placed on the front as near the center as possible to normal line of operator's vision and far enough forward to eliminate any objectionable reflection of light from any portion of the vehicle.

The upper sector of the headlight shall be painted a deep red color of brightness of 3 and not to exceed 3.5 foot-lamberts (this light will be visible at a distance of one thousand (1,000) and not over one thousand five hundred (1,500) feet). The thickness of the red band at the center of the vertical axis shall be at least 1½ inches and not to exceed 2½ inches. Paint shall be sprayed on the lens instead of brushing, thus producing an even surface. The other portion of the headlight, with the exception of the white light slot, shall be painted black or lusterless olive drab.

White Light Slot. Except as shown in paragraphs 3.06 to 3.13, below, the white light slot for all motor vehicles shall be one-eighth (⅛) inch wide by two (2) inches long and placed at right angles to the vertical axis of the light. The bottom of the slot shall be located at the focal point of the lens which is about three-fourths (¾) inch below the center of the headlight bulb, but in no case shall it be more than one (1) inch below the center of the bulb.

Metal Shield or Hood Over Slot. The metal shield or hood over the white light slot shall be of twenty (20) to twenty-eight (28) gauge sheet metal, extending from side to side of the headlamp and to be tightly clamped to the outer rim of the headlamp. At the center of the vertical axis of light, the shield shall have an angle of from forty-five (45) to seventy (70) degrees from the vertical axis at the face of the lens, and sloped downward so that the outer edge of the shield will be at least 1¾ inches and not more than 2½ inches from the lens at the narrowest part of the shield. The outer edge of the shields shall be designed so that a lip protrudes to cover the white light slot, this lip to be one-fourth (¼) inch long, and to be of sufficient width to extend a minimum of one-half (½) inch over each end of the white light slot. The outer edge of the shield shall be folded back approximately three-eighths (⅜) inch to provide stiffness for the shield. The ends of the shield shall be closed and extended sufficiently back into the lamp to provide a clip to hold the shield in position on the headlamp. The inner face of the shield, or face on the lens side, shall be made to fit snugly to the curvature of the lens. Due to various types of headlights now in use on vehicles, the curvature of the shield shall be cut to fit each individual type of lens. The lip of the shield, when in proper position, and when the vehicle is fully loaded, shall give the adjustment prescribed in paragraph 3.02 supra. The shield shall be painted black or lusterless olive drab on the exterior and interior surfaces. Suitable mastic will be applied around the circumference of the lens at the junction of the glass with the retaining rim, and between the inner face of the shield and headlight lens, to properly shield any light at these points.

3.03. Combination Tail and Stop Lamp, Reflectors, and Additional Equipment. One tail, or combination tail and stop, lamp shall be securely mounted on the extreme rear of the vehicle and as near the left side as is practicable with red color as described below and aimed straight to the rear, so that it will be clearly visible to traffic approaching from the rear. Except as specified in paragraph 3.11 below, such lamps shall be mounted not less than twenty (20) inches and not more than fifty (50) inches above the road level. When mounted on motorcycles or motor scooters, this lamp shall be mounted on the rear fender. The tail light shall have a round circle one-half (½) inch in diameter of red color as prescribed for headlights in paragraph 3.02 above. The remainder of the lens shall be painted black or lusterless olive drab.

An additional tail, or combination tail and stop, lamp as described hereinabove shall be securely mounted on the extreme rear of all motor vehicle combinations one hundred (100) inches and more in width as near the right side as is practicable, and at the same height and alignment as the left combination tail and stop lamp.

Two approved red reflectors may be mounted on all over-sized motor vehicles, as hereinabove described, on the extreme rear, and two approved amber reflectors may be mounted on the extreme front, on each side, as low on the vehicles as practicable and in no case higher than thirty (30) inches above the road level.

3.04. Instrument and Dashboard Lights, Interior, and Exterior Lights. Instrument and dashboard lights shall be extinguished unless illumination provided therefor is of low intensity and deep red in color. Except as shown in paragraph 3.08 below, all other interior lights in the vehicle shall be extinguished and rendered inoperative. All exterior lights not authorized by this General Orders shall be removed or rendered inoperative.

3.05. Testing of Lights. The intensity of brightness of red used on headlights and tail lights shall be tested by the brightness meter manufactured by the Weston Electric Company, by the gauge designed and tested by the Department Engineer, by the Official Headlight Testing Stations operated by the U. S. Army Ordnance Department, or by other methods when approved by the Office of the Military Governor. The size and location of the white light slot, relative to the lip on the metal shield, shall be tested by a suitable screen to insure that the headlights conform with specifications set forth herein (if vehicle is tested with less than capacity load, suitable allowances will be made to insure that the adjustment will meet these specifications when vehicle is loaded to capacity). This adjustment will be made by moving the entire headlamp. The shield will not be bent unless it is impossible to make this adjustment otherwise.

3.06. Lights for Special Vehicles. Such vehicles as are described in paragraphs 3.07 to 3.13 below hereby are authorized to have the lights provided for in said paragraphs of this General Orders.

3.07. Trucks of Over 3-Ton Rated Capacity. All lights for trucks of over 3-ton rated capacity will conform to specifications set forth herein, except that the white light slot of the headlights may be increased to three-eighths (⅜) inch wide by three (3) inches long.

Vehicles in this category may have lights mounted at a height in excess of fifty-five (55) inches measured from the bottom of the slot to road level provided that visual cut-off up the top of the beam on a vertical screen ten (10) feet in front of lamp is at least four (4) inches below the bottom of the horizontal slot and in no case higher than fifty-three (53) inches from road level when vehicle is carrying a capacity load.

3.08. Busses. All lights for busses will conform to specifications set forth herein except that the white light slot of the headlights may be increased to three-eighths (⅜) inch wide by three (3) inches long.

The route markers on all busses will be illuminated with a red light of low intensity.

A maximum of ten (10) interior dome lights, of low intensity may be used in each bus.

3.09. Fire Department Trucks. All lights on Fire Department trucks will conform to specifications set forth

herein, except that the white light slot of the headlights may be one-half (½) inch wide by three (3) inches long.

If needed, Fire Department trucks may use a hooded white spotlight when going to a fire during peaceful times, but when returning from a fire, the headlights prescribed above will be used. In case of a blitz or other emergency situation, no spotlights will be used. The hood for the white spotlight will encircle the circumference of the light and be at least two (2) inches longer than the diameter of the lens of the spotlight.

3.10. Ambulances, Doctors' Vehicles, and Utility Vehicles. All lights of ambulances and utility vehicles will conform to specifications set forth herein except that the white light slot of the headlights may be three-eighths (⅜) inch wide by three (3) inches long.

All lights on motor vehicles owned and operated by, or direction of, or under the supervision of, a physician or surgeon in the practice of his profession will conform to the specifications set forth herein, except that the white light slot of the headlights may be one-fourth (¼) inch wide by two (2) inches long.

When responding to emergency calls, ambulances and utility vehicles may use a hooded white spotlight during peaceful times, if needed, but when returning to their stations, only the headlights prescribed will be used. In case of a blitz or other similar emergency situation, no spotlight will be used. The hood will encircle the circumference of the spotlight and will be at least two (2) inches longer than the diameter of the lens of the spotlight.

·3.11. Lumber Carriers. Headlights on lumber carriers will conform to specifications set forth herein, with the following exceptions:

White light slot on the headlights may be three-fourths (¾) inch wide by three (3) inches long;

The outer edge of the metal shield will not have the lip prescribed for other vehicles;

With the vehicle on level surface the headlights shall be so adjusted that the bottom of the slot is horizontal and so aimed that the visual cut-off up the top of the beam of a vertical screen thirty (30) feet in front of lamp is not higher than fifty-three (53) inches from the road level; and

The tail light may be mounted at the same height as the headlights.

Lumber carriers will be allowed to have one hooded white spotlight on the front of the carrier, at the top and one hooded spotlight on the rear left side, near the seat of the operator. In peaceful times, these spotlights may be used when carrying loads of unusual length (over thirty-five (35) feet) when loading and unloading, and when maneuvering the vehicle in unusually difficult places. In case of a blitz or other similar emergency situation, no spotlight will be used. The hood will encircle the circumference of the spotlight and be at least two (2) inches longer than the diameter of the lens of the spotlight.

3.12. Police Cars. All lights of police cars will conform strictly with specifications set forth herein, except that the white light slot of the headlights may be one-fourth (¼) inch wide by two (2) inches long.

Police cars may be equipped with a hooded white spotlight, which may be used during peaceful times when responding to emergency calls or in other emergency situations. In case of a blitz or other emergency no spotlights will be used. The hood will encircle the circumference of the spotlight and be two (2) inches longer than the diameter of the lens of the spotlight.

3.13. Road Sweepers. All lights on road sweepers will conform strictly with specifications set forth herein, except that the white light slot of the headlights may be one-fourth (¼) inch wide by three (3) inches long.

Road sweepers may be equipped with a hooded spotlight of low power for the purpose of defining the curb line of the road. In case of a blitz or other emergency situation, no spotlight will be used. The hood will encircle the circumference of the spotlight and be two (2) inches longer than the diameter of the lens of the spotlight.

3.14. Any shop, paint shop, or garage which is equipped to paint and install shields and test headlights, so that they meet specifications set forth herein, are authorized to perform this work. These shops may be inspected regularly by the Department Ordnance Officer. Headquarters Hawaiian Department, or his duly authorized representative.

3.15. Upon installation, painting or testing of "motor vehicle blackout lights, the shop performing the work will affix a gum sticker to the inside lower right corner of the windshield. The sticker will be not more than one (1) inch wide by 2½ inches long. The face of this sticker will show that the lights have been tested and adjusted. The reverse of the sticker will be filled in to indicate the date, organization, and name of the individual performing the adjustment and test.

3.16. No shop, paint shop, or garage shall install shields or paint headlights without performing the proper test and adjustment to meet specifications set forth herein, nor shall any person tamper with the lens or shields of headlights after they have been inspected and approved.

4. TRAFFIC DURING HOURS OF BLACKOUT.

4.01. Enemy Aliens. No enemy alien shall be present on the streets and highways, in parks, and on beaches, either on foot or in vehicles, during the hours of blackout.

4.02. Persons Other Than Enemy Aliens. Except as is hereinafter authorized, no person shall be present on the streets and highways, in parks, and on beaches either on foot or in vehicles, during the hours of blackout after 10:00 P.M.

4.03. Certain Persons Permitted Out-of-Doors After 10:00 P.M. The following classes of persons are excepted from the restrictions of paragraph 4.02 above:

Personnel of the Armed Forces of the United States and allied nations on duty or proceeding to and from duty;

Law enforcement officers on duty or proceeding to and from duty;

Civilian personnel required to be on the streets and highways during such hours because of their employment on defense work, by public utilities, in civilian defense activities, or by the government, or while proceeding directly to and from work;

Doctors on call;

Persons holding Police passes issued since December 7, 1941;

Persons holding special passes issued and approved by the Provost Marshal, Military Police, or Civilian Police; and

Enemy aliens transported in motor vehicles during the hours of blackout by drivers of non-enemy ancestry upon written approval of the Provost Marshal.

4.04. Vehicular and Passenger Traffic During Blackout. Any person except an enemy alien may drive, or ride as a passenger in, a motor vehicle on the streets and highways during blackout hours from the commencement of the period thereof until ten o'clock P.M., but not thereafter during said blackout hours unless duly authorized pursuant to the General Orders of the Military Governor. Motor vehicles driven pursuant to this paragraph 4.04 during blackout hours shall conform with all other blackout regulations with respect to equipment and manner of operation of such motor vehicles.

4.05. Twenty Miles Speed Limit. Except as authorized by the civil or military police, no person shall operate any vehicle at a rate of speed in excess of twenty (20) miles per hour during hours of blackout.

4.06. No Parking. No person shall park any vehicle on any public thoroughfare, street, or highway, during the hours of blackout.

4.07. Removal of Keys From, and Locking Ignition of, Parked Cars. No person shall allow the keys of any motor vehicle, of which he is the owner or operator, to remain therein, during the hours of blackout, while such vehicle remains properly and lawfully unattended; nor shall any person leave any motor vehicle, of which he is the owner or operator, during the hours of blackout, without first having locked the ignition thereof if possible.

Nothing contained in paragraph 4.07 shall be construed to relieve any person of the restriction imposed by paragraph 4.06 hereof.

4.08. Taxicabs Allowed on Streets After 5:30 A.M. All taxicabs, except those owned or operated by enemy aliens, are authorized to be operated and to be on the streets and highways of the Territory of Hawaii after 5:30 A.M. daily.

4.09. No person shall, during the hours of blackout, violate any statute of the Territory of Hawaii or any ordinance, resolution, by-law, regulation, or rule of any city, city and county, county, or other municipal corporation or political subdivision of the Territory of Hawaii, regulating or relating to traffic, now in force or hereinafter in force; and all such traffic violations or offenses occurring during the hours of blackout hereby are made

violations or offenses of and punishable under the General Orders of the Military Governor.

5. WORKERS GOING TO WORK IN THE MORNING.

5.01. Men and women who must leave their homes before the termination of the hours of blackout in order to reach their places of employment between the hours of 7:00 and 8:00 A.M., respectively, are permitted to proceed on the streets and highways of the Territory of Hawaii in motor vehicles or on foot after 5:30 A.M. Such workers shall leave their homes as late as possible.

5.02. Between the hours of 5:30 A.M. and the termination of the hours of blackout, all blackout rules and regulations of the Military Governor shall be observed. Motor vehicles shall proceed with all caution necessary with safety, and shall comply with the maximum speed limit as prescribed by this General Orders.

5.03. No enemy alien shall be present on the streets or highways between the hours of 5:30 A.M. and the termination of the hours of blackout, unless special permission of the Provost Marshal or his duly authorized representative has first been secured.

5.04. Nothing contained in this Title 5 shall be construed to permit the use of light or other means of illumination during hours of blackout, except in compliance with all blackout rules and regulations of the Military Governor.

5.05. Children under the age of 16 years will not be permitted on the streets and highways between the hours of 5:30 A.M. and the termination of the hours of blackout, unless accompanied by one of their parents or some other adult person, and unless their travel is directly connected with their parents or guardians proceeding to work.

6. PERSONAL IDENTIFICATION DURING HOURS OF BLACKOUT.

6.01. All persons required to be on the streets and highways during the hours of blackout after 10:00 P.M. shall carry an identification badge, pass, or letter from their employer evidencing their right to be on the streets, and any such person who may be stopped by the civil or military police during said hours of blackout shall identify himself promptly.

7. PLACES OF AMUSEMENT AND BUSINESS.

7.01. All persons, firms, and corporations who operate and maintain places of business and amusement shall comply with all the blackout rules and regulations of the Military Governor during that period of the hours of blackout that the said places of business and amusement remain open and are operated.

8. ENFORCEMENT.

8.01. Enforcement by Provost Marshal. The Provost Marshal, Hawaiian Department, shall have the power to control the sufficiency and effectiveness of the blackout and shall enforce all rules, regulations, and General Orders of the Military Governor relating to, or pertaining to, blackout in the Territory of Hawaii.

8.02. Penalty for Violations. Any person, firm or corporation, who violates, refuses, fails, or neglects to comply with any of the provisions of this General Orders, or who evades or attempts to evade any of the provisions of this General Orders, upon conviction thereof, shall be punished by confinement, with or without hard labor, not to exceed one (1) year, or by a fine not to exceed one thousand dollars ($1,000.00), or by both such confinement and fine.

By order of the Military Governor of the Territory of Hawaii:

THOMAS H. GREEN
Brigadier General, A. U. S.
Executive

10 March 1943

GENERAL ORDERS NO. 10
LABOR

1. Policy.
2. Registration.
3. Employment.
4. Wages.
5. Hours of Work and Overtime.
6. Use of Labor.
7. Appeal Agency.
8. Child Labor.

1. POLICY.

1.01. The following policies are announced for the information and guidance of employers employing the services of (a) employees of the United States under the War Department or the Navy Department; (b) workers employed on construction and other projects under the War Department or the Navy Department; (c) stevedores and other workers employed on docks and dock facilities; and (d) employees of public utilities. The same policies shall be equally applicable to employees of the above-mentioned employing agencies.

2. REGISTRATION.

2.01. Any person, now or hereafter employed by any of the employers to whom reference is made in Paragraph 1.01, and who ceases to be so employed, shall, within two (2) days after ceasing to be so employed, register or re-register with the nearest office of the United States Employment Service.

2.02. Every employer described in Paragraph 1.01 shall notify the nearest office of the United States Employment Service on Form USES-(H)1, prescribed by the United States Employment Service, of any employee added to such employer's payroll and on Form USES-(H)2, prescribed by the United States Employment Service, of any employee dropped from such employer's payroll, within two (2) days thereafter.

2.03. Any person, firm, or corporation who violates, refuses, fails or neglects to comply with any of the provisions of Paragraphs 2.01 and 2.02 above, upon conviction thereof, shall be fined not more than One Thousand Dollars ($1,000.00), or be imprisoned for not more than one (1) year, or both.

3. EMPLOYMENT.

3.01. Employers described in Paragraph 1.01 may maintain their own labor recruiting facilities.

3.02. The United States Employment Service hereby is designated as the central employment agency for the distribution of civilian labor hereby required to register, and shall allocate labor in the fulfillment of employers' requisitions in accordance with priorities established by the Office of the Military Governor.

3.03. No employer described in Paragraph 1.01 shall employ or offer to employ an individual formerly, now, or hereafter in the employment of other such employers, unless and until such individual shall have presented to the employing agency a bona fide release without prejudice, on Form USES-(H)2, from his last previous employer or from the Director of Labor Control, and evidence of registration on Form USES-350, or Form USES-506.

3.04. Any individual, who is, has been, or hereafter shall be, employed by any employer described in Paragraph 1.01, who presents himself to any other such agency and secures or attempts to secure employment without having a bona fide release without prejudice from his last previous employer, or from the Director of Labor Control, or in any way misrepresents his employment status with regard to such release, shall, upon conviction, be fined not more than two hundred dollars ($200.00), or be imprisoned for not more than two (2) months, or both.

3.05. Any employer or employer's agent who shall cause any individual to be employed in contravention of Paragraph 3.03 hereof, shall, upon conviction, be fined not more than two hundred dollars ($200.00), or be imprisoned for not more than two (2) months, or both.

4. WAGES.

4.01. Revised Wage Schedule No. 9, dated 3 May 1942 and effective at the beginning of the first payroll period after 3 May 1942, hereby is designated as the standard wage scale for workers engaged in work on construction and other projects under the War Department or the Navy Department. No person seeking work or employed on construction or other projects under the War Department or the Navy Department, shall be employed at a rate less

than, or in excess of the standard rate for the job as listed in Wage Schedule No. 9, and as same may be revised from time to time, as approved by the Military Governor.

4.02. Federal agencies under the War Department or the Navy Department shall continue their regularly established wage schedules.

5. HOURS OF WORK AND OVERTIME.

5.01. Normal work week for employees on construction and other projects under the War Department or the Navy Department shall be six (6) days of eight (8) hours each. The maximum number of hours worked in any seven (7) consecutive days shall not exceed fifty-six (56), except in cases of emergency and with the approval of the Chief of Military or Naval Service concerned.

5.02. Normal work week for employees of the United States under the War Department or Navy Department shall conform to applicable Federal regulations.

5.03. Employees on construction and other projects under the War Department or the Navy Department shall be paid overtime at the rate of one and one-half the regular rate for overtime in excess of forty-four (44) hours per week, or in excess of eight (8) hours in any one day. Double the regular rate will be paid for work performed on the seventh consecutive work day. One and one-half the regular rate will be paid for work performed on any of the following days only: New Year's Day, Fourth of July, Labor Day, Thanksgiving Day, Christmas Day and Memorial Day.

5.04. Paragraph 5.03 above shall not apply to employees who are in a supervisory capacity on a monthly salary basis.

5.05. Employees of the United States under the War Department and the Navy Department shall be paid overtime in accordance with applicable Federal regulations.

5.06. For employees engaged on construction and other projects under the War Department and the Navy Department, work shall be so scheduled that all employees shall receive one (1) day off in seven (7). Sunday work per se shall not be considered overtime, and no overtime shall be paid for Sunday except when it is worked consecutively in excess of six (6) days.

5.07. The provisions of any contract between individual employees, labor unions, and employers engaged on construction and other projects under the War Department or the Navy Department, in conflict with the provisions of this General Orders hereby are suspended.

6. USE OF LABOR.

6.01. Terms of labor contracts between individuals and employers engaged on construction and other projects under the War Department or the Navy Department which restrict or specify the nature of work to be performed, hereby are suspended.

6.02. Any person now or hereafter employed by any employer described in Paragraph 1.01 hereof shall report regularly to the job to which he is ordered by said employer.

6.03. Employers and employers' agents described in Paragraph 1.01 are directed to refrain from discriminatory practices toward employees with regard to releases or other matters relating to termination of employment.

6.04. No employer or employer's agent shall fail or refuse to abide by the decisions of the Director of Labor Control on any matters within the meaning of Paragraph 6.03.

6.05. Any person, firm, or corporation who or which violates, refuses, fails, or neglects to comply with any of the provisions of Paragraphs 6.01 to 6.04 inclusive, or who or which evades or attempts to evade any of the provisions of said Paragraphs 6.01 to 6.04, inclusive, upon conviction thereof, if a natural person, shall be punished by confinement, with or without hard labor, not to exceed two (2) months, or by a fine not to exceed two hundred dollars ($200.00), or by both such confinement and fine, or, if a corporation or other than a natural person, by a fine not to exceed two hundred dollars ($200.00).

7. APPEAL AGENCY.

7.01. Persons discharged with prejudice from employment with employers mentioned in Paragraph 1.01 hereof, may appeal their cases to the Appeal Agency, Office of the Director of Labor Control, for decision as to whether or not they may be allowed to continue work with another employer.

7.02. The Director of Labor Control, Office of the Military Governor, hereby is designated as the Appeal Agency for persons discharged with prejudice by employers described in Paragraph 1.01. Any individual not satisfied with the decision of the Appeal Agency may appeal his case to the Labor Control Board of the Military Governor.

8. CHILD LABOR.

8.01. Employers described in Paragraph 1.01 shall comply with the provisions of Section 18 of Chapter 259-B of the Revised Laws of Hawaii 1935, as enacted by Act 237 of the Session Laws of Hawaii 1939, as amended by Act 319, Session Laws of Hawaii, Regular Session 1941.

By order of the Military Governor of the Territory of Hawaii:

THOMAS H. GREEN
Brigadier General, A.U.S.
Executive

10 March 1943

GENERAL ORDERS NO. 14
ORGANIZATION OF THE OFFICE OF THE MILITARY GOVERNOR

1. Executive Section.
2. District Representatives of the Military Governor.
3. Plans and Operations.
4. Central Identification Bureau.
5. Appointments.
6. Location of the Office of the Military Governor.

1. EXECUTIVE SECTION.

1.01. Executive. The Executive and Assistant Executive of the Military Governor and others designated by them shall function on behalf of the Military Governor in carrying out the administration of all policies and operations of martial law and in coordinating and controlling all functions connected with such administration.

1.02. Law Enforcement. The military commissions, provost courts, and the Provost Court Commissioner will carry out the functions assigned to them in General Orders No. 2, this office, 10 March 1943, and amendments and additions thereto.

1.03. Legal Section. This section shall handle all matters with reference to military commissions and provost courts including review and appeal therefrom and recommendations to the Military Governor thereon, and shall render legal advice to the Military Governor and handle such other related matters as the Executive of the Military Governor may direct.

1.04. Public Information. Press releases and other information will be made available to the public by this section as ordered by the Military Governor.

1.05. Personnel. This section shall procure and administer the necessary personnel for the office operation of the Military Governor and perform such other related functions as directed.

1.06. Finance. This section shall handle all matters of finance connected with the office of the Military Governor and procure and administer supplies and equipment therefor.

1.07. Statistics and Engineering. This section shall handle all matters related to statistics and engineering referred to it by the Military Governor.

1.08. Trans-Pacific Travel. This section shall handle all matters concerning priorities of trans-Pacific travel and make recommendations to the Military Governor with reference thereto.

1.09. Military Property Comptroller. The Military Property Comptroller will carry out the functions set forth in Title 2, of General Orders No. 11., this office, 10 March 1943, and any amendments or additions thereto.

1.10. Internee and Evacuee Property Coordinator. The Internee and Evacuee Property Coordinator will carry out the functions set forth in Title 3. of General Orders No. 11., this office, 10 March 1943, and any amendments or additions thereto.

1.11. Hawaiian Department Alien Processing Center. The Hawaiian Department Alien Processing Center will handle all matters with reference to the internment or evacuation of persons in the Territory of Hawaii which are referred to it by the Military Governor.

2. DISTRICT REPRESENTATIVES OF THE MILITARY GOVERNOR.

2.01. The Commanding Generals of the Hawaii, Maui, Kauai, and Molokai-Lanai districts hereby are appointed Representatives of the Military Governor and hereby are charged with assisting in the administration and enforcement of the policies and orders of the Military Governor in their respective districts.

2.02. Representatives of the various sections and bureaus of the Office of the Military Governor will be appointed within the Districts of Hawaii, Maui, Kauai, and Molokai-Lanai as the situation may require. Such representatives shall be appointed by the Military Governor upon recommendation of the Commanding Generals of the respective districts acting as District Representatives of the Military Governor.

3. PLANS AND OPERATIONS.

3.01. Director of Plans and Operations. Under the direction of the Military Governor, the Director of Plans and Operations will make plans for, and control, coordinate, and supervise the activities of, such functional sections of the Office of the Military Governor as the Military Governor may direct and designate from time to time.

3.02. Director of Cargo and Passenger Control. In order to expedite the handling of all shipments at all Territorial ports, the Director of Cargo and Passenger Control is hereby directed to coordinate all port facilities.

3.03. Authority of Director of Cargo and Passenger Control. The Director of Cargo and Passenger Control will, to the extent directed by the Military Governor:

Supervise, coordinate and regulate dockage and stevedoring; barges, tugs, and floating equipment; the loading and discharging of fuel, including the use of fuel lines; transportation and other facilities necessary to expedite the handling of cargo and passengers; and the disposition of all cargo until removed from the dock area at all docks and wharves in the Port of Honolulu and in other Territorial ports;

Supervise, coordinate, and regulate, in accordance with priorities set by civilian agencies and transmitted to the Director of Cargo and Passenger Control by the Director of Plans and Operations, the allocation to vessels of all commercial cargo; and, in accordance with advice of the Army Transportation Corps, all Army cargo and vessels offered for shipment out of the Territory or between the islands;

Organize and set up an Assistant Director of Cargo and Passenger Control, together with such added personnel as the Military Governor may authorize, at each of the outlying ports of the Territory, to carry out the operations prescribed above.

3.04. Section of Labor Control. Under the direction of the Director of Labor Control, this section shall administer all matters pertaining to labor as promulgated by the Military Governor in General Orders No. 10, this office 10 March 1943, and any amendments or additions thereto.

3.05. Labor Control Board. A Labor Control Board hereby is created to investigate and arbitrate such labor disputes as may arise under the provisions of General Orders No. 10, this office, 10 March 1943, and any amendments or additions thereto, as well as such other labor disputes as may be referred to it by the Military Governor, and shall recommend to the Military Governor such labor policies as it shall deem advisable for the successful prosecution of the war effort.

This Labor Control Board shall consist of seven members as follows:

Director of Labor Control, Chairman
One (1) representative of the U. S. Army
One (1) representative of the U. S. Navy
Two (2) representatives of the American Federation of Labor
One (1) representative of the Congress for Industrial Organization
One (1) representative of industry, appointed on recommendation of the Honolulu Chamber of Commerce.

The decisions of this Labor Control Board shall not be final until approved by the Military Governor.

4. CENTRAL IDENTIFICATION BUREAU.

4.01. The Central Identification Bureau will operate under a director appointed by the Military Governor and is charged with the registration of persons and the issuance of means of identification as required by the provisions of General Orders No. 8, this office, 10 March 1943, and any amendments or additions thereto.

5. APPOINTMENTS.

5.01. The following appointments to the offices indicated hereby are made:

Major General James A. Woodruff, U.S.A., Director of the Central Identification Bureau;

Colonel B. F. Hayford, F.A., Director of Plans and Operations;

Commander Ernest Gray, U.S.N.R., Director of Cargo and Passenger Control;

Mr. John R. Mead, Director of Labor Control;

Mr. Alfred E. Tree, Military Property Comptroller;

Lieutenant Dwight H. Lowrey, Inf., Internee and Evacuee Property Coordinator.

5.02. The following officers are hereby designated District Military Property Comptrollers and also District Internee and Evacuee Property Coordinators in their respective districts:

Major William P. Crum, F.A., District of Kauai;

Major John D. Hagon, F.A., District of Maui;

Major Thomas E. G. Paradine, Inf., District of Hawaii.

6. LOCATION OF THE OFFICE OF THE MILITARY GOVERNOR.

6.01. The Office of the Military Governor of the Territory of Hawaii shall be located at Iolani Palace, Honolulu, T. H.

6.02. An Office of the Military Governor shall also be maintained in each district, including the Hawaii District, the Kauai District, the Maui District, and the Molokai-Lanai District, at such location as may be designated within the district by the Commanding General of each district acting as District Representative of the Military Governor.

By order of the Military Governor of the Territory of Hawaii:

THOMAS H. GREEN
Brigadier General, A.U.S.
Executive

TERRITORY OF HAWAII
OFFICE OF THE MILITARY GOVERNOR
IOLANI PALACE
HONOLULU, T.H.

26 April 1943

GENERAL ORDERS)
NO. 20   )

AMENDMENTS TO GENERAL ORDERS

1. AMENDMENT TO GENERAL ORDERS NO. 10, THIS OFFICE,
10 MARCH 1943.

1.01. Paragraph numbered 5.03, Title 5, General
Orders No. 10, this office, 10 March 1943, hereby is
amended to read as follows:

"5.03. Employees on construction and other projects under the War Department or the Navy Department
shall be paid overtime at the rate of one and one-half
the regular rate for overtime in excess of forty-four
(44) hours per week, or in excess of eight (8) hours in
any one day. Where, because of emergency conditions,
an employee is required to work for seven consecutive
days in any regularly scheduled work-week a premium
wage of double time compensation shall be paid for work
on the seventh day. One and one-half regular rate will
be paid for work performed on any of the following days
only: New Year's Day, Fourth of July, Labor Day,
Thanksgiving Day, Christmas Day and Memorial Day."

By order of the Military Governor of the Territory
of Hawaii:

/S/ Wm. R. C. Morrison
WM. R. C. MORRISON
Colonel, J.A.G.D.
Executive

A TRUE COPY:

ROBERT B. GRIFFITH
Captain, Infantry

TERRITORY OF HAWAII
OFFICE OF THE MILITARY GOVERNOR
IOLANI PALACE
HONOLULU, T.H.

18 June 1943

GENERAL ORDERS)
NO. 24   )

AMENDMENTS TO GENERAL ORDERS

1. AMENDMENT TO GENERAL ORDERS NO. 10, THIS
OFFICE, 10 MARCH 1943.

1.01. Paragraph numbered 4.01, Title 4, General
Orders No. 10, this office, 10 March 1943, hereby is
amended to read as follows:

"4.01. Revised Wage Schedule No. 9 (Third Re-
issue), dated 16 June 1943 and effective at the beginning of the first pay roll period after 16 June
1943, hereby is designated as the standard wage scale
for workers engaged in work on construction and other
projects under the War Department or the Navy Department, and employees of such other employers as may be
designated from time to time by the Military Governor.
No persons seeking work or employed on construction or
other projects under the War Department or the Navy
Department, or with other employers designated by the
Military Governor, shall be employed at a rate less
than, or in excess of, the standard rate for the job
as listed in said Revised Wage Schedule No. 9 (Third
Reissue) as now established or as the same may be revised from time to time as approved by the Military
Governor."

By order of the Military Governor of the Territory of Hawaii:

/S/ Wm. R. C. Morrison
WM. R. C. MORRISON
Colonel, J.A.G.D.
Executive

A TRUE COPY:

ROBERT B. GRIFFITH
Major, Infantry

TERRITORY OF HAWAII
OFFICE OF THE MILITARY GOVERNOR
IOLANI PALACE
HONOLULU, T. H.

25 August 1943

GENERAL ORDERS)
NO. 31   )

HABEAS CORPUS PROCEEDINGS AND INTERFERENCE
WITH MILITARY PERSONNEL IN PERFORMANCE OF
MILITARY FUNCTIONS PROHIBITED.

1. PURPOSE.

1.01. This General Orders is issued to eliminate, prevent, and prohibit interference with military personnel in
the performance of their military functions or duties within
the Territory of Hawaii, and to eliminate, prevent, and prohibit interference with military operations within the Territory of Hawaii, and thereby to further the defense and
internal security of the Territory of Hawaii.

2. HABEAS CORPUS PROCEEDINGS PROHIBITED.

2.01. No clerk, deputy clerk, other officer, or
employee of the District Court of the United States for the
Territory of Hawaii, or of any court of the Territory of
Hawaii, shall accept or receive for filing in such clerk's
office, deposit for filing, or file, or allow, authorize, or
permit to be deposited for filing, or to be filed in such
clerk's office, or with such clerk, any application or petition for a writ of habeas corpus, or make, issue, or execute
any summons, citation, decree, order, or other process in any
habeas corpus proceedings.

2.02. No judge of the District Court of the United
States for the Territory of Hawaii or of any court of of
or within the Territory of Hawaii, shall accept or receive for
filing with, in, or before such judge or court, or in the
office of the clerk of such court, or with such clerk, deposit
for filing or file or allow, authorize, order, or permit to be
filed with, in or before such judge or court, or in the office
of such clerk or with such clerk, any application or petition
for a writ of habeas corpus.

- 1 -

G. O. NO. 31, O.M.G., 25 August 1943

2.03. No judge of the District Court of the United
States for the Territory of Hawaii or of any other court
of or within the Territory of Hawaii, shall authorize,
allow, decree, order, direct, or permit any habeas corpus
proceedings to be commenced, maintained, or prosecuted before or by such judge or in or before the court in or over
which such judge sits or presides; nor shall any such judge
maintain, prosecute, hear, try, or determine in whole or
in part, any habeas corpus proceedings or any phase of, or
matter related to or in any way connected with, any habeas
corpus proceedings.

2.04. No judge of the District Court of the United
States for the Territory of Hawaii or any other court
of or within the Territory of Hawaii, shall issue any
writ of habeas corpus, order that any writ of habeas corpus
issue or be issued, or authorize, direct, permit, or allow
any writ of habeas corpus to issue, or be issued, from the
court over which or in which such judge presides or sits,
or from the office of the clerk of said court, or by the
clerk of said court.

2.05. No person, either in his own behalf or as
attorney, agent, or in any way for or on behalf of another
person, shall present to, file or attempt to file, or
deposit for filing, any application or petition for a writ
of habeas corpus, to or with the clerk, deputy clerk, a
judge, other officer, or employee of the District Court
of the United States for the Territory of Hawaii, or of
any court of or within the Territory of Hawaii; nor shall
any person, either in his own behalf or as attorney, agent,
or in any way for or on behalf of another person, commence,
maintain, or prosecute any habeas corpus proceedings in or
before the District Court of the United States for the
Territory of Hawaii or in or before any other court of or
within the Territory of Hawaii.

2.06. Neither the United States Marshal for the
Territory of Hawaii, any deputy or employee of such marshal,
or any other officer or employee of the District Court of
the United States for the Territory of Hawaii, or of any
other court of or within the Territory of Hawaii shall accept

- 2 -

G. O. NO. 31, O.M.G., 25 August 1943

or receive for service an application or petition for a writ of habeas corpus or copy thereof, or any writ of habeas corpus, any summons, citation, order, decree, warrant, or process of any kind in a habeas corpus proceedings; nor shall the United States Marshal for the Territory of Hawaii, any deputy of such marshal, or any other officer or employee of the District Court of the United States for the Territory of Hawaii, or any officer or employee of any court of or within the Territory of Hawaii, serve or attempt to serve any application or petition for a writ of habeas corpus or copy thereof, or any writ of habeas corpus, or any summons, citation, mandate, decree, order, warrant, or process of any kind in a habeas corpus proceedings or issued or arising out of any matter or proceeding related to or in any way connected with a habeas corpus proceedings.

2.07. Any judge of the District Court of the United States for the Territory of Hawaii, or of any other court of or within the Territory of Hawaii, before whom a habeas corpus proceedings is pending, shall forthwith discontinue such habeas corpus proceedings, and shall not maintain or prosecute, or allow, permit, or authorize to be maintained or prosecuted before such judge or the court in which such judge sits or presides, such habeas corpus proceedings any further, and hereafter shall not hear, try, or determine said habeas corpus proceedings or any phase of or matter related to or in any way connected with or arising out of such habeas corpus proceedings; nor, except as authorized in paragraphs 2.08 and 2.09 herein, shall any such judge hereafter issue any order, decree, mandate, summons, citation, warrant, or process of any kind in any such pending habeas corpus proceedings, or in any matter, action, or proceedings arising out of, related to, or in any way connected with any pending habeas corpus proceedings; and such judge forthwith shall withdraw, revoke, and rescind any order, decree, mandate, summons, citation, warrant, or process of any kind, remaining unexecuted in any pending habeas corpus proceedings or in any matter, action, or proceedings arising out of, related to, or in any way connected with any pending habeas corpus proceedings.

2.08. Neither the Honorable Delbert E. Metzger, Judge, District Court of the United States in and for the

- 3 -

G. O. NO. 31, O.M.G., 25 August 1943

Territory of Hawaii, nor any other judge of the said District Court of the United States in and for the Territory of Hawaii, shall make or issue, or order, direct, or cause to be made or issued, any process, mandate, summons, citation, order, decree, decision, determination, direction, or action in or relative to, or arising out of, by reason or because of, that certain habeas corpus proceedings now pending in the District Court of the United States in and for the Territory of Hawaii substantially styled or entitled as follows: "In the Matter of the Application of Walter Glockner," and bearing file or identification number or mark "H. C. 295," in the office of the Clerk of the District Court of the United States in and for the Territory of Hawaii. The said Delbert E. Metzger, Judge, District Court of the United States in and for the Territory of Hawaii, forthwith and immediately shall stay, refrain from, cause to be stayed, and desist from, all pending or further action or proceedings in said habeas corpus proceedings, or in any matter, action, or proceedings arising out of, related to, or in any way connected with, such pending habeas corpus proceedings.

2.09. Neither the Honorable Delbert E. Metzger, Judge, District Court of the United States in and for the Territory of Hawaii, nor any other judge of the said District Court of the United States in and for the Territory of Hawaii, shall make or issue, or order, direct, or cause to be made or issued, any process, citation, order, decree, decision, determination, direction, or action in or relative to, or arising out of, by reason or because of, that certain habeas corpus proceedings now pending in the District Court of the United States in and for the Territory of Hawaii substantially styled or entitled as follows: "In the Matter of the Application of Erwin R. Seifert," and bearing file or identification number or mark "H. C. 296," in the office of the Clerk of the District Court of the United States in and for the Territory of Hawaii. The said Delbert E. Metzger, Judge, District Court of the United States in and for the Territory of Hawaii, forthwith and immediately shall stay, refrain from, cause to be stayed, and desist from, all pending or further action or proceedings in said habeas corpus proceedings, or in any matter, action, or proceedings arising out of, related to, or in any way connected with, such pending habeas corpus proceedings.

- 4 -

G. O. NO. 31, O.M.G., 25 August 1943

3. INTERFERENCE WITH MILITARY PERSONNEL PROHIBITED.

3.01. No judge of the District Court of the United States for the Territory of Hawaii, or any court of the Territory of Hawaii, no United States Marshal for the Territory of Hawaii or his deputy, nor other public officer, deputy of such public officer, public employee, or any other person, shall, for any cause, whether or not such cause is deemed lawful cause by such judge, or other public officer, public employee, or any other person, in any manner, way, or form impede, oppose, or interfere with the Commanding General, United States Army Forces, Central Pacific Area, or with any other member of the armed forces of the United States, in his performance of his military functions, military duties, or military orders, or in his performance of any orders heretofore or hereafter issued by the Military Governor of the Territory of Hawaii regardless of whether or not such order or orders are published in the newspapers of the Territory of Hawaii; provided, however, that nothing contained in this paragraph shall be construed or deemed to prohibit municipal police officers from arresting members of the armed forces for traffic offenses triable by the Provost Courts.

4. PROVISIONS OF THIS GENERAL ORDERS TO BE LIBERALLY CONSTRUED.

4.01. Except where otherwise clearly indicated, in addition to being applicable to habeas corpus proceedings hereafter commenced, the provisions of this General Orders shall be applicable to habeas corpus proceedings heretofore commenced and now pending in the District Court of the United States for the Territory of Hawaii or in any other court of the Territory of Hawaii. The provisions of this General Orders shall be liberally construed so that the purposes for which this General Orders is issued, set forth in Paragraph 1.01, may be fully effected and accomplished.

- 5 -

G. O. NO. 31, O.M.G., 25 August 1943

5. PENALTIES.

5.01. Any judge of the District Court of the United States in and for the Territory of Hawaii, any United States Marshal or Deputy United States Marshal in and for the Territory of Hawaii, or any other public officer, deputy of such other public officer, public employee, or any other person, who directly or indirectly, expressly or impliedly, in any manner, shape, or form, shall violate, attempt to violate, evade, or attempt to evade, or aid, assist, or abet, in any violation of, any provision of this General Orders, upon conviction thereof by a Provost Court heretofore or hereafter appointed by the Military Governor of the Territory of Hawaii, shall be punished by confinement, with or without hard labor, for a period not to exceed five (5) years, or by a fine not to exceed five thousand dollars ($5,000.00), or by both such confinement and fine, or if convicted thereof by a Military Commission heretofore or hereafter appointed by the Military Governor of the Territory of Hawaii shall be punished as such Military Commission shall determine.

6. ISSUANCE OF THIS GENERAL ORDERS IS NECESSARY EXERCISE OF MARTIAL LAW POWERS OF MILITARY COMMANDER IN THIS THEATER OF WAR.

6.01. This General Orders is issued by the undersigned as the Military Governor of the Territory of Hawaii and as the Military Commander of the military forces of the United States in this theater of war in which martial law has been established and exists. This General Orders is a necessary exercise of the martial law powers of the undersigned as Military Commander of the military forces of the United States in this theater of war.

(S) Robert C. Richardson, Jr
ROBERT C. RICHARDSON, JR.
Lieutenant General, United States Army
Commanding General, United States Army
Forces, Central Pacific Area
Military Governor of the Territory of Hawaii

A TRUE COPY:

Wm. R C Morrison
WM. R. C. MORRISON
Colonel, J.A.G.D.
Executive

- 6 -

TERRITORY OF HAWAII
OFFICE OF THE MILITARY GOVERNOR
IOLANI PALACE
HONOLULU, T.H.

14 October 1943

GENERAL ORDERS)
   NO. 38   )

RESCISSION OF GENERAL ORDERS

1. RESCISSION OF GENERAL ORDERS NO. 31, THIS
OFFICE, 25 AUGUST 1943.

   1.01. General Orders No. 31, this office,
25 August 1943, hereby is rescinded.

   By order of the Military Governor of the Territory
of Hawaii:

/s/ Wm. R. C. Morrison
WM. R. C. MORRISON
Colonel, J.A.G.D.
Executive

A TRUE COPY:

ROBERT B. GRIFFITH
Major, Infantry

G.O. NO. 40, O.M.G., 1 November 1943

   1.03. Paragraph numbered 2.02, Title 2, General
Orders No. 10, this office, 10 March 1943, hereby is
amended to read as follows:

"2.02. Every employer described in Paragraph 1.01
shall notify the nearest office of the United States
Employment Service on Form 14-E, Section of Labor Control,
Office of the Military Governor, of any employee dropped
from such employer's pay roll, within two (2) days
thereafter."

   1.04. Paragraph numbered 3.03, Title 3, General
Orders No. 10, this office, 10 March 1943, hereby is
amended to read as follows:

"3.03. No employer described in Paragraph 1.01
shall employ or offer to employ an individual formerly,
now, or hereafter in the employment of other such
employers, unless and until, such individual shall have
presented to the employing agency a bona fide release,
without prejudice, on Form 14-E, Section of Labor Control,
Office of the Military Governor, from his last previous
employer, or from the Director of Labor Control and
evidence of referral on Form USES-508."

   1.05. Paragraph numbered 4.01, Title 4, General
Orders No. 10, this office, 10 March 1943, as amended by
Paragraph numbered 1.01, General Orders No. 24, this
office, 18 June 1943, hereby is amended to read as follows:

"4.01. Revised Wage Schedule No. 9, (Fourth Re-Issue),
dated 1 November 1943, and effective at the beginning of
the first pay roll period after 1 November 1943, hereby
is designated as the standard wage scale, except as noted
in Paragraph 4.03, for workers engaged in work on construction and other projects under the War Department or the
Navy Department and employers of such other employees as
may be designated from time to time by the Military
Governor. No persons seeking work or employed on construction or other projects under the War Department or
the Navy Department, or with other employers designated
by the Military Governor, shall be employed at a rate
less than, or in excess of, the standard rate for the job
as listed in said Revised Wage Schedule No. 9, (Fourth Re-
Issue), as now established or as the same may be revised
from time to time as approved by the Military Governor."

- 2 -

TERRITORY OF HAWAII
OFFICE OF THE MILITARY GOVERNOR
IOLANI PALACE
HONOLULU, T.H.

1 November 1943

GENERAL ORDERS)
   NO. 40   )

AMENDMENTS TO GENERAL ORDERS

1. AMENDMENTS TO GENERAL ORDERS NO. 10, THIS
OFFICE, 10 MARCH 1943.

   1.01. Paragraph 1.01, Title 1, General Orders
No. 10, this office, 10 March 1943, hereby is amended
to read as follows:

"1.01. The following policies are announced for
the information and guidance of employers employing
the services of (a) employees of the United States under
the War Department or the Navy Department; (b) workers
employed on construction and other projects under the
War Department or the Navy Department; (c) stevedores
and other workers employed on docks and dock facilities;
and (d) employees of public utilities. The same
policies shall be equally applicable to employees of
the above-mentioned employing agencies. Nothing herein
shall be construed as superseding or in conflict with
the provisions of the Fair Labor Standards Act of 1938
or the Walsh Healey Public Contracts Act."

   1.02. Paragraph numbered 2.01, Title 2, General
Orders No. 10, this office, 10 March 1943, hereby is
amended to read as follows:

"2.01. Any person now or hereafter employed by any
of the employers to whom reference is made in Paragraph
1.01 and who ceases to be so employed, shall, within two
(2) days after ceasing to be so employed, register or re-
register at the nearest office of the U. S. Employment
Service and shall not accept employment with any other
employer in the Territory of Hawaii, regardless of whether
such employer is or is not an employer described in Paragraph 1.01, until so directed by the U. S. Employment
Service."

- 1 -

G.O. NO. 40, O.M.G., 1 November 1943

   1.06. General Orders No. 10, this office, 10 March
1943, hereby is amended by adding to Title 4 of said
General Orders No. 10 a new paragraph to be numbered and
known as Paragraph 4.03, Title 4, General Orders No. 10,
Office of the Military Governor, 10 March 1943, and to
read as follows:

"4.03. The provisions of contracts, or extensions
thereof, between individuals and employers engaged on
construction or other projects under the War Department
or the Navy Department, relative to wages shall not be
abrogated without the written consent of the individual."

   1.07. Paragraph numbered 5.03, Title 5, General
Orders No. 10, this office, 10 March 1943, as amended by
Paragraph numbered 1.01, Title 1, General Orders No. 20,
this office, 26 April 1943, hereby is amended to read
as follows:

"5.03. Employees on construction and other projects
under the War Department or the Navy Department shall be
paid overtime at the rate of one and one-half the regular
rate, for overtime in excess of forty (40) hours per week,
or in excess of eight (8) hours in any one day, except as
noted in Paragraphs 5.08 and 5.09. Where, because of
emergency conditions, an employee is required to work for
seven consecutive days in any regularly scheduled work-
week, a premium wage of double time compensation shall be
paid for work on the seventh day. One and one-half
regular rate will be paid for work performed on any of
the following days only: New Year's Day, Fourth of July,
Labor Day, Thanksgiving Day, Christmas Day and Memorial
Day."

   1.08. Paragraph numbered 5.06, Title 5, General
Orders No. 10, this office, 10 March 1943, hereby is
amended to read as follows:

"5.06. For employees engaged on construction and
other projects under the War Department or the Navy
Department, work shall be so scheduled that all employees
shall receive one (1) day off in seven (7). Sunday work
per se shall not be considered overtime, and no overtime
shall be paid for Sunday except when it is worked
consecutively in excess of five (5) days."

- 3 -

G.O. NO. 40, O.M.G., 1 November 1943

1.09. General Orders No. 10, this office, 10 March 1943, hereby is amended by adding to Title 5 of said General Orders No. 10, two new paragraphs to be respectively numbered and known as Paragraphs 5.08 and 5.09, Title 5, General Orders No. 10, Office of the Military Governor, 10 March 1943, and to read as follows:

"5.08. Persons employed on construction or other projects under the War Department or the Navy Department in connection with derricks, dredges, drill rigs and tugs shall be paid overtime on the basis of one and one-half times the regular rate of pay for hours worked in excess of eight (8) hours in any one day or hours in excess of forty-eight (48) hours per week.

"5.09. The provisions of contracts, or extensions thereof, between individuals and employers engaged on construction or other projects under the War Department or the Navy Department relative to hours of work and overtime shall not be abrogated without the written consent of the individual.

1.10. General Orders No. 10, this office, 10 March 1943, hereby is amended by adding thereto a new title and two new paragraphs to be respectively numbered and known as Title 9, General Orders No. 10, Office of the Military Governor, 10 March 1943, and Paragraphs 9.01 and 9.02, Title 9, General Orders No. 10, Office of the Military Governor, 10 March 1943, and to read as follows:

"9. SUBSISTENCE AND QUARTERS.

"9.01. The provisions of contracts, or extensions thereof, between individuals and employers engaged on construction and other projects under the War Department or the Navy Department relative to subsistence and quarters shall not be abrogated without the written consent of the individual.

"9.02. The practice of furnishing free board and lodging, or cash payment in lieu thereof, to persons

4 --

G.O. NO. 40, O.M.G., 1 November 1943

employed locally or on new contracts shall be discontinued effective 1 November 1943."

By order of the Military Governor of the Territory of Hawaii:

/s/ Wm. R. C. Morrison
WM. R. C. MORRISON
Colonel, J.A.G.D.
Executive

A TRUE COPY:

ROBERT B. GRIFFITH
Major, Infantry

- 5 -

4 May 1944

GENERAL ORDERS)
NO. 57)

AMENDMENTS TO GENERAL ORDERS

1. AMENDMENTS TO GENERAL ORDERS NO. 3, THIS OFFICE, 10 MARCH 1943.

1.01. General Orders No. 3, this office, 10 March 1943, as amended, hereby is amended to read as follows:

"GENERAL ORDERS)   10 March 1943
NO. 3)

CURFEW

1. Definition.
2. Traffic During Hours of Curfew.
3. Personal Identification During Hours of Curfew.
4. Flashlights.
5. Motor Vehicle Blackout.
6. Enforcement.

"1. DEFINITION.

"1.01. The term "hours of curfew," "during the hours of curfew," "curfew," or similar language, as used in this General Orders or in any other General Orders of the Military Governor, unless the use thereof in such General Orders clearly indicates otherwise, shall include and hereby is defined to mean that period of time between ten o'clock P. M. of one day and five-thirty o'clock A. M. of the following day.

"1.02. The term "hours of darkness" as used in this General Orders, or in any other General Orders of the Military Governor, unless the use thereof in such General Orders clearly indicates otherwise, shall include and hereby is defined to mean that period of time between one-half (1/2) hour after sunset and one-half (1/2) hour before sunrise.

- 1 -

G.O. NO. 57, O.M.G., 4 May 1944

"2. TRAFFIC DURING HOURS OF CURFEW.

"2.01. Except as is hereinafter authorized by Subparagraph 7, Paragraph 2.03, no enemy alien shall be present on the streets and highways, in parks, and on beaches, either on foot or in vehicles, during the hours of curfew.

"2.02. Except as is hereinafter authorized, no person shall be present on the streets and highways, in parks, and on beaches, either on foot or in vehicles, during the hours of curfew.

"2.03. The following classes of persons are excepted from the restrictions of Paragraph 2.02 above:

Personnel of the Armed Forces of the United States and allied nations on duty or proceeding to and from duty;

Law enforcement officers on duty or proceeding to and from duty;

Civilian personnel required to be on the streets and highways during such hours because of their employment on defense work, by public utilities, in civilian defense activities, or by the government, or while proceeding directly to and from work;

Doctors on call;

Persons holding Police passes issued since December 7, 1941;

Persons holding special passes issued and approved by the Provost Marshal, United States Army Forces, Central Pacific Area, Military Police, or Civilian Police; and

Enemy aliens transported in motor vehicles during the hours of curfew by drivers of non-enemy ancestry upon written approval of the Provost Marshal, United States Army Forces, Central Pacific Area.

"2.04. No person may drive, operate, or ride as a passenger in, a motor vehicle on the streets and highways within the Territory of Hawaii, during the hours of curfew unless duly authorized to do so by or pursuant to the General Orders of the Military Governor or otherwise first authorized by the said Military Governor. No person authorized pursuant to this Paragraph numbered 2.04 shall drive a motor vehicle during the hours of curfew unless said motor vehicle shall conform with all blackout regulations of the Military Governor relating to equipment for and manner of operation of such motor vehicle.

- 2 -

G.O. NO. 57, O.M.G., 4 May 1944

"3. PERSONAL IDENTIFICATION DURING HOURS OF CURFEW.

"3.01. All persons required to be on the streets and highways during the hours of curfew shall carry an identification badge, pass, or letter from their employer evidencing their right to be on the streets, and any such person who may be stopped by the civil or military police during said hours of curfew shall identify himself promptly.

"4. FLASHLIGHTS.

"4.01. Flashlights may be used, either indoors or outdoors, at any time or times, during the hours of curfew, subject, however, to the provisions of this paragraph. Military police, members of the United States Navy Shore Patrol, and civilian police officers are authorized to use flashlights with red or orange light, during said hours, either indoors or outdoors, while engaged in the performance of their official duties. Air Raid Wardens and Fire Wardens are authorized to use flashlights with a green light during said hours, either indoors or outdoors, while engaged in the performance of their official duties as such wardens. No person other than a member of the military police, or a member of said shore patrol, or such a civilian police officer engaged in the performance of official duties as aforesaid, shall use a flashlight with a red or orange light at any time during said hours of curfew, nor shall any person other than an Air Raid Warden or Fire Warden engaged in the performance of official duties as aforesaid, use a flashlight with a green light at any time during said hours of curfew. Any person may use a flashlight with a white light, either indoors or outdoors, during said hours of curfew.

"5. MOTOR VEHICLE BLACKOUT.

"5.01. No person shall drive or operate any motor vehicle at any time during the hours of darkness unless headlights shall be installed, maintained, and used on said motor vehicle in conformity with the specifications and provisions set forth in the following paragraphs of this Title.

"5.02. Headlights. When motor vehicles are driven at any time during the hours of darkness, two (2) approved blackout driving headlights constructed, installed, and maintained as herein required, shall be used on each motor vehicle, except on motorcycles and motor scooters, which shall have but one (1)

- 3 -

G.O. NO. 57, O.M.G., 4 May 1944

headlight. Such headlights shall have the necessary color design as described below. Each headlight shall be covered by a metal shield or hood as described below. The mounting height of said headlight shall be not less than twenty-four (24) inches nor more than fifty-five (55) inches measured from road level to the extended forward edge of the said shield or hood of the headlight, and in no case higher than the top of the rim of the steering wheel. With the vehicle on level surface and carrying a capacity load, the headlight unit shall be so adjusted that the extended forward edge of the shield or hood of the headlight of such vehicle shall be parallel to and fixed at at least eleven-sixteenths (11/16) inch below the horizontal center line of the headlight lens and so aimed that the visual cut-off at the top of the beam on a vertical screen ten (10) feet in front of the headlight is at least four (4) inches below the extended forward edge of the shield or hood of the headlight of such vehicle and in no instance higher than fifty-one (51) inches from the road level. When mounted on motorcycles or motor scooters the headlight shall be placed on the front as near the center as possible to normal line of operator's vision and far enough forward to eliminate any objectionable reflection of light from any portion of the vehicle.

"All that portion of the headlight lens above the junction of the headlight lens with the shield or hood shall be painted black, or lustorless olive drab, except that where such upper portion of such headlight is now painted a deep red color, said color shall be of brightness of three (3) and not exceeding 3.5 foot lamberts, and said red colored paint may be retained until such time as repainting is necessary. Paint shall be sprayed on such upper portion of such headlight instead of brushing thus producing an even surface. The portion of the headlight lens of such vehicle below the junction of the headlight lens with the shield or hood described in this General Orders need not be painted.

"Metal Shield or Hood. The metal shield or hood over the headlight lens shall be twenty (20) to twenty-eight (28) gauge sheet metal, extending from side to side of the headlight. The extended forward edge of the shield or hood of such headlight shall be parallel to and fixed at at least eleven-sixteenths (11/16) inch below the horizontal center line of the headlight lens, and shall be tightly clamped to the outer rim of the headlight. At the center of the vertical axis of light, the shield or hood shall have an angle of from forty-five (45) to seventy

- 4 -

G.O. NO. 57, O.M.G., 4 May 1944

(70) degrees from the vertical axis at the face of the headlight lens and sloped downward so that the outer edge of the shield or hood shall be at least one and three-quarters (1-3/4) inches and not more than two and one-half (2-1/2) inches from the headlight lens at the narrowest part of the shield or hood. The outer edge of the shield or hood shall be folded back approximately three-eighths (3/8) inch to provide stiffness for the shield or hood. The ends of the shield or hood shall be closed and extended sufficiently back into the headlight to provide a clip to hold the shield or hood in position on the headlight. The inner face of the shield or hood, or face on the lens side, shall be made to fit snugly to the curvature of the lens. Due to the various types of headlights now in use on vehicles, the curvature of the shield or hood shall be cut to fit each individual type of headlight lens. The shield or hood edge, when in proper position, shall give the adjustment prescribed in Paragraph 5.02, supra. The shield or hood shall be painted black or lusterless olive drab on the exterior and interior surfaces. Suitable mastic shall be applied around the circumference of the headlight lens at the junction of the headlight lens with the retaining rim and between the outer face of the shield or hood and headlight lens, to properly shield any light at these points.

"5.03. No person, at any time or times during the hours of darkness, shall use or operate a taillight or lamp, or combination tail and stop light or lamp, or any other light on the rear of a vehicle, which allows a white light, a red light, or a light of any color to shine upward. Otherwise than as provided in the preceding sentence, and subject to territorial laws, city and county ordinances, and county ordinances, a person may use, at any time or times during the hours of darkness, the taillight or lamp or taillights or lamps, or a combination tail and stop light or lamp and the other lights and lamps on the rear of a vehicle, regardless of the color, brightness, or quantity of light emanating therefrom.

"5.04. Instrument and Dashboard Lights, Interior and Exterior Lights. Instrument and dashboard lights may be used, during the hours of darkness, providing they are of low intensity and do not permit light to be reflected from the interior to the exterior of the vehicle. Interior lights to permit facilitation of passenger ingress and egress may be used, during the hours of darkness, only at the time the vehicle is not in motion.

- 5 -

G.O. NO. 57, O.M.G., 4 May 1944

Except as authorized by this title of this General Orders, all other lights shall be removed or rendered inoperative.

"5.05. Testing of Lights. The intensity of brightness of red used on headlights and tail lights shall conform to the specifications set forth in Paragraph 5.02, supra, and shall be tested by the brightness meter manufactured by the Weston Electric Company, by the gauge designed and tested by the Department Engineer, or by other methods approved by the Office of the Military Governor. The direction of the beam of the headlight relative to the metal shield or hood, shall be tested by a suitable screen to insure that the headlight conforms to specifications set forth herein. This adjustment shall be made by moving the entire headlight or with the adjusting screws provided for headlight beam adjustment, but the shield or hood portion shall not be altered.

"5.06. Trucks of Over 3-Ton Rated Capacity. All lights for trucks of over 3-Ton rated capacity shall conform to the specifications set forth herein, except that vehicles in this category may have lights mounted at a height in excess of fifty-five (55) inches measured from the road level to the extended forward edge of the shield or hood of the headlight, provided that visual cut-off at the top of the beam on a vertical screen ten (10) feet in front of headlight is at least four (4) inches below the extended forward edge of the shield or hood of the headlight of such vehicle, and in no instance higher than fifty-three (53) inches from the road level when the vehicle is carrying a capacity load.

"5.07. Busses. All lights for busses shall conform to the specifications set forth herein.

"The route markers on all busses shall be illuminated with a red light of low intensity.

"Separate red stop light indicators mounted on the rear of all passenger carrying busses may be used.

"5.08. Fire Department Trucks. All lights on Fire Department trucks shall conform to specifications set forth herein. If needed, Fire Department trucks may use a hooded white spotlight when going to a fire, but when returning from a fire, only the headlights prescribed above will be used, provided, however, that in case of a blitz or other similar situation, no spotlight

G.O. NO. 57, O.M.G., 4 May 194

shall be used. The hood for the white spotlight shall encircle the circumference of the light and shall protrude from the face of the lens horizontally a distance of at least two (2) inches greater than the diameter of the lens of the spotlight.

"5.09. Ambulances. All lights on ambulances shall confor to specifications set forth herein. When responding to emergen calls, ambulances may use a hooded white spotlight, if needed, but when returning to their stations, only the headlights prescribed above shall be used, provided, however, that in case of a blitz or other similar situation, no spotlight shall be used. The hood shall encircle the circumference of the spotlight and shall protrude from the face of the lens horizontally a distance of at least two (2) inches greater than the diameter of the lens of the spotlight.

"5.10. Lumber Carriers. Headlights on lumber carriers shall conform to specifications set forth herein. With the vehicle on level surface the headlights shall be so adjusted that the extended forward edge of the headlight is horizontal and is so aimed that the visual cut-off at the top of the beam on a vertical screen thirty (30) feet in front of the headlight is not higher than fifty-three (53) inches from the road level when the vehicle is carrying a capacity load.

"Lumber carriers may have one (1) hooded white spotlight on the front of the carrier, at the top and one (1) hooded spotlight on the rear left side, near the seat of the operator. These spotlights may be used when carrying loads of unusual length (over thirty-five (35) feet), when loading and unloading, and when maneuvering the vehicle in unusually difficult places, provided, however, that in case of a blitz or other similar situation, no spotlight shall be used. The hood shall encircle the circumference of the spotlight and shall protrude from the face of the lens horizontally a distance of at least two (2) inches greater than the diameter of the lens of the spotlight.

"5.11. Road Sweepers. All lights on road sweepers shall conform to specifications set forth herein. Road sweepers may be equipped with a hooded spotlight of low power for the purpose of defining the curb line of the road, provided, however, that in case of a blitz or other emergency situation, no spotlight

- 7 -

G.O. NO. 57, O.M.G., 4 May 1944

shall be used. The hood shall encircle the circumference of the spotlight and shall protrude from the face of the lens horizontally a distance of at least two (2) inches greater than the diameter of the lens of the spotlight.

"5.12. Police Cars. All lights on police cars shall conform to specifications set forth herein. Police cars may be equipped with a hooded white spotlight, which may be used when responding to emergency calls or in other emergency situations, provided, however, that in case of a blitz or other similar situation, no spotlight shall be used. The hood shall encircle the circumference of the spotlight and shall protrude from the face of the lens horizontally a distance of at least two (2) inches greater than the diameter of the lens of the spotlight

"5.13. Oversized trucks and trailers now equipped with running marker lights may use such lights providing they are of low intensity and shed only sufficient illumination to outline the vehicles on which they are used.

"5.14. The owner of any motor vehicle, or any paint shop or garage which is equipped to paint and install shields and test headlights, so that they meet specifications set forth herein, is authorized to perform this work.

"5.15. No person, firm, or corporation shall install shields or paint headlights without performing, or causing to be performed, the proper test and adjustment to meet specifications set forth herein, nor shall any person tamper with the lens or shield of headlights after they have been adjusted, tested, inspected, and approved.

"5.16. Traffic signal lights and street lights shielded as the Military Governor may direct may be used at full strength at all times during the hours of darkness. Maximum lighting in the interior of busses and trains, during the hours of darkness, is authorized.

"6. ENFORCEMENT.

"6.01. Enforcement by Provost Marshal. The Provost Marshal, United States Army Forces, Central Pacific Area, shall have the power to control the effectiveness of the motor vehicle blackout and curfew and shall enforce all rules, regulations, and General

- 8 -

G.O. NO. 57, O.M.G., 4 May 1944

Orders of the Military Governor relating to, or pertaining to, motor vehicle blackout and curfew in the Territory of Hawaii.

"6.02. Penalty for Violations. Any person, firm or corporation, who violates, refuses, fails, or neglects to comply with any of the provisions of this General Orders, or who evades or attempts to evade any of the provisions of this General Orders, upon conviction thereof, shall be punished by confinement, with or without hard labor, not to exceed one (1) year, or by a fine not to exceed one thousand dollars ($1,000.00), or by both such confinement and fine."

/s/ Robert C. Richardson, Jr.
ROBERT C. RICHARDSON, JR.
Lieutenant General, United States Army
Commanding General, United States Army
Forces, Central Pacific Area
Military Governor of the Territory of Hawaii

A TRUE COPY:

[signature]

ROBERT B. GRIFFITH
Major, Infantry

- 9 -

TERRITORY OF HAWAII
OFFICE OF INTERNAL SECURITY
IOLANI PALACE GROUNDS
HONOLULU 2, T. H.

21 July 1944

GENERAL ORDERS }
NO. 63   }

Announcement is made that the name of the Office of the Military Governor hereby is changed to "Office of Internal Security".

/s/ Robert C. Richardson, Jr.
ROBERT C. RICHARDSON, JR.
Lieutenant General, United States Army
Commanding General, United States Army
Forces, Central Pacific Area

A TRUE COPY:

[signature]

ROBERT B. GRIFFITH
Major, Infantry

TERRITORY OF HAWAII
OFFICE OF INTERNAL SECURITY
IOLANI PALACE GROUNDS
HONOLULU 2, T. H.

1 August 1944

GENERAL ORDERS)
NO. 64)

AMENDMENTS TO GENERAL ORDERS

1. AMENDMENTS TO GENERAL ORDERS NO. 1, OFFICE OF THE MILITARY GOVERNOR, 10 March 1943.

1.01. Paragraph numbered 1.01, Title 1, General Orders No. 1, Office of the Military Governor, 10 March 1943, hereby is amended to read as follows:

"1.01. William R. C. Morrison, Colonel, J.A.G.D., hereby is appointed Executive of the Commanding General, Pacific Ocean Areas, Office of Internal Security."

/s/ Robert C. Richardson, Jr.
ROBERT C. RICHARDSON, JR.
Lieutenant General, United States Army
Commanding General, United States Army
Forces, Pacific Ocean Areas

A TRUE COPY:

ROBERT B. GRIFFITH
Major, Infantry

G. O. NO. 68, O.I.S., 21 August 1944

"2. EMPLOYMENT STABILIZATION PROGRAM.

"2.01. The Employment Stabilization Program for the Labor Shortage Area, City and County of Honolulu, Territory of Hawaii, is hereby designated as the governing set of rules and regulations applicable to all employers and employees described in Paragraph 1.01.

"3. REGISTRATION AND EMPLOYMENT.

"3.01. Every employer described in Paragraph 1.01 shall notify the nearest office of the United States Employment Service, on such forms as may be prescribed by the United States Employment Service, of any employee added to or dropped from such employer's pay roll, within two (2) days thereafter. Any person, now or hereafter employed by any of the employers to whom reference is made in Paragraph 1.01 and who ceases to be so employed, shall, within two (2) days after ceasing to be so employed, register or re-register with the nearest office of the United States Employment Service. Any person now or hereafter employed by any employer described in Paragraph 1.01 hereof shall report regularly to the job to which he is assigned and shall observe the conditions of the Employment Stabilization Program."

2. AMENDMENTS TO GENERAL ORDERS NO. 14, OFFICE OF THE MILITARY GOVERNOR, 10 MARCH 1943.

2.01. Paragraph numbered 3.04, Title 3, General Orders No. 14, Office of the Military Governor, 10 March 1943, hereby is amended to read as follows:

"3.04. Labor Section. Under the direction of the Labor Director, this section shall administer all matters pertaining to labor, Office of Internal Security."

- 2 -

TERRITORY OF HAWAII
OFFICE OF INTERNAL SECURITY
IOLANI PALACE GROUNDS
HONOLULU 2, T. H.

21 August 1944

GENERAL ORDERS)
NO. 68)

AMENDMENTS TO GENERAL ORDERS

1. AMENDMENTS TO GENERAL ORDERS NO. 10, OFFICE OF THE MILITARY GOVERNOR, 10 MARCH 1943.

1.01. General Orders No. 10, Office of the Military Governor, 10 March 1943, as amended, hereby is amended to read as follows:

"GENERAL ORDERS)
NO. 10)   10 March 1943

LABOR

1. Policy.
2. Employment Stabilization Program.
3. Registration and Employment.

"1. POLICY.

"1.01. The following policies are announced for the information and guidance of the following employers and their employees in the Labor Shortage Area, City and County of Honolulu, Territory of Hawaii; (a) agencies of the United States under the War Department or the Navy Department; (b) employers engaged on construction or other projects under the War Department or the Navy Department; (c) employers engaged in stevedoring and other work on docks and dock facilities; and (d) public utilities.

- 1 -

G. O. NO. 68, O.I.S., 21 August 1944

2.02 Paragraph numbered 3.08, Title 3, General Orders No. 14, Office of the Military Governor, 10 March 1943, hereby is rescinded.

/s/ Robert C. Richardson, Jr.
ROBERT C. RICHARDSON, JR.
Lieutenant General, United States Army
Commanding General, United States Army
Forces, Pacific Ocean Areas

A TRUE COPY:

ROBERT B. GRIFFITH
Major, Infantry

- 3 -

OFFICE OF INTERNAL SECURITY
IOLANI PALACE GROUNDS
HONOLULU, T. H.

24 October 1944

SECURITY ORDER NO. 1
ENEMY ALIENS

The Commanding General, United States Army Forces, Pacific Ocean Areas, finds that this Security Order No. 1 is required in order to protect national-defense material, national-defense premises, and national-defense utilities, as defined by Section 4, Act of April 20, 1918, Chapter 59, 40 Stat. 533, as amended by the Act of November 30, 1940, Chapter 926, 54 Stat. 1220, and by the Act of August 21, 1941, Chapter 388, 55 Stat. 655 (USC, Title 50, Section 104), from espionage and sabotage, and for the maintenance of military and internal security and the efficient utilization of available facilities in the Territory of Hawaii and that military necessity exists for said Security Order.

1. DEFINITION OF "ENEMY ALIEN" AND "ALIEN ENEMY."

1.01. The term "Enemy Alien" or "Alien Enemy" as used in the foregoing Proclamation and this Security Order No. 1, or in any other Proclamation, restriction, order, rule, regulation or instruction of the undersigned Military Commander, unless the use thereof in such Proclamation, restriction, order, rule, regulation or instruction clearly indicates otherwise, shall include and hereby is defined to mean all natives, citizens, denizens, or subjects of Japan, Germany, or of any other nation or government hostile to the United States, who are within the Territory of Hawaii Military Area, and not actually naturalized within the United States, provided, however, that the term "Enemy Alien," or "Alien Enemy," as used in Paragraphs 2.01, and 2.03, Title 2, Security Order No. 3, and as used in Paragraph 2.02, Title 2, of this Security Order No. 1, shall not include nor mean any Korean or any person of Korean ancestry or of Korean racial extraction.

2. POLICY TOWARDS ENEMY ALIENS.

2.01. All enemy aliens hereby are enjoined to preserve the peace towards the United States and to refrain from crime against the public safety, and from violating the laws of the United States and laws of the Territory of Hawaii and to refrain from actual hostility or giving information, aid, or comfort to the enemies of the United States, and to comply strictly with the regulations which hereby are, or may be, from time to time promulgated by the President of the United States or the undersigned Military Commander, and so long as they shall conduct themselves in accordance with law, they shall be undistrubed in the peaceful pursuit of their lives and occupations and be accorded the consideration due to all peaceful and law-abiding persons, except so far as restrictions may be necessary for their own protection and for the safety of the United States. All citizens of the United States are enjoined to preserve the peace and to treat them with all such friendliness as may be compatible with loyalty and allegiance to the United States.

2.02. Enemy aliens hereby are permitted to go about their business and visit friends and relatives throughout the day without special permits or passes except during the hours of curfew and as may be otherwise limited by Public Proclamation No. 1 and the restrictions, orders, rules, regulations, and instructions herein contained, or hereafter promulgated.

2.03. All enemy aliens who fail to conduct themselves as so enjoined, in addition to being liable to restraint, shall be subject to all other penalties prescribed by law and by the Proclamations, restrictions, orders, rules, regulations and instructions of the undersigned Military Commander.

3. REGULATION OF CONDUCT OF ENEMY ALIENS.

3.01. All enemy aliens within the Territory of Hawaii Military Area shall comply strictly with the regulations and restrictions as set forth in the following paragraphs.

3.02. No enemy alien shall commit, aid, or abet any hostile act against the United States, or give information, aid, or comfort to its enemies.

3.03. No enemy alien within the Territory of Hawaii Military Area shall write, print, publish, utter, or otherwise make any attack or threats against the Government or Congress of the United States, or any branch thereof, or against the measures or policy of the United States, or against the person or property of any person in the military, naval or civil service of the United States or of the Territory of Hawaii.

3.04. All enemy aliens shall carry on their person the alien registration card or certificate issued to them at the time of their registration under Section III of the Act of June 28, 1940.

3.05. No enemy alien shall change his place of residence or occupation within the Territory of Hawaii Military Area without first having obtained the approval of the Provost Marshal, United States Army Forces, Central Pacific Base Command. This requirement does not eliminate the necessity of complying with the provisions of Section 35 of the Act of June 28, 1940 (54 Stat. 675).

3.06. No enemy alien shall undertake an air flight or ascent into the air in any aircraft, balloon, or flying machine of any sort, whether owned governmentally, commercially, or privately, except upon written authority of the Office of the Assistant Chief of Staff, G-2, Headquarters Central Pacific Base Command, acting for the undersigned Military Commander.

3.07. Except as may be otherwise authorized by the undersigned Military Commander, no enemy alien shall have in his actual or constructive possession at any time or place, or use or operate, any of the following listed articles:
Firearms;

Weapons or implements of war or component parts thereof;
Ammunition;
Bombs;
Explosives or material used in the manufacture of explosives;
Short-wave radio receiving sets;
Transmitting sets;
Signal devices;
Codes or ciphers;
Cameras;
Materials and supplies used for the developing and printing of photographs;
Paper, documents or books in which there may be invisible writing, photographs, sketches, pictures, drawings, maps or graphical representations of any military or naval installations or equipment, of any arms, ammunition, implements of war, or devices or things used or intended to be used in the combat equipment of the land or naval forces of the United States, or of any military or naval post, camp or station;
Binoculars, field glasses, telescopes, or any other device used or designed for use for making observations at distances.
Any enemy alien having in his possession or under his control any article

listed above will forthwith report the possession of such article to the Office of Internal Security where he will receive instructions for the disposition thereof. Dealers, handlers, and brokers having quantities of such articles will submit a complete inventory thereof to the Office of Internal Security where they will receive instructions for the disposition thereof.

3.08. Any article of the classes of property listed above found in the possession of any enemy alien shall be subject to seizure and the possessor shall be subject to trial and punishment.

ROBERT C. RICHARDSON, JR.
Lieutenant General, United States Army
Commanding General, United States Army
Forces, Pacific Ocean Areas
Military Commander, Territory of Hawaii
Military Area

OFFICIAL COPY:
WM. R. C. MORRISON
Brigadier General, U.S.A.
Executive

OFFICE OF INTERNAL SECURITY
IOLANI PALACE GROUNDS
HONOLULU, T. H.

24 October 1944

SECURITY ORDER NO. 3
CURFEW

The Commanding General, United States Army Forces, Pacific Areas, finds that this Security Order No. 3 is required in order to protect national-defense material, national-defense premises, and national-defense utilities, as defined by Section 4, Act of April 20, 1918, Chapter 59, 40 Stat. 533, as amended by the Act of November 30, 1940, Chapter 926, 54 Stat. 1220, and the Act of August 21, 1941, Chapter 388, 55 Stat. 655 (USC, Title 50, Section 104), from espionage and sabotage, and for the maintenance of military and internal security and the efficient utilization of available facilities in the Territory of Hawaii and that military necessity exists for said Security Order.

1. DEFINITION.

1.01. The term "hours of curfew," "during the hours of curfew," "curfew," or similar language, as used in this Security Order or in any other Proclamation restriction, order, rule, regulation or instruction of the undersigned Military Commander, unless the use thereof in such Proclamation, restriction, order, rule, regulation or instruction clearly indicates otherwise, shall include and hereby is defined to mean that period of time between ten o'clock P.M. of one day and five-thirty o'clock A.M. of the following day.

1.02. The term "hours of darkness" as used in any Proclamation, restriction, order, rule, regulation or instruction of the undersigned Military Commander, unless the use thereof in such Proclamation, restriction, order, rule, regulation or instruction clearly indicates otherwise, shall include and hereby is defined to mean that period of time between one-half ($\frac{1}{2}$) hour after sunset and one-half ($\frac{1}{2}$) hour before sunrise.

2. TRAFFIC DURING HOURS OF CURFEW.

2.01. Except as is hereinafter authorized by subparagraph 7, Paragraph 2.03, no enemy alien shall be present on the streets and highways, in parks, and on beaches, either on foot or in vehicles, during the hours of curfew.

2.02. Except as is hereinafter authorized, no person shall be present on the streets and highways, in parks, and on beaches. either on foot or in vehicles. during the hours of curfew.

2.03. The following classes of persons are excepted from the restrictions of Paragraph 2.02 above:

Personnel of the Armed Forces of the United States and allied nations on duty or proceeding to and from duty;

Law enforcement officers on duty or proceeding to and from duty;

Civilian personnel required to be on the streets and highways during such hours because of their employment on defense work, by public utilities, in civilian defense activities, or by the government, or while proceeding directly to and from work;

Doctors on call;

Persons holding Police passes issued since December 7, 1941;

Persons holding special passes issued and approved by the Provost Marshal, United States Army Forces, Pacific Ocean Areas, Provost Marshal, United States Army Forces, Central Pacific Base Command, Military Police, or Civilian Police; and

Enemy aliens transported in motor vehicles during the hours of curfew by drivers of non-enemy ancestry upon written approval of the Provost Marshal, United States Army Forces, Central Pacific Base Command.

2.04. No person may drive, operate, or ride as a passenger in, a motor vehicle on the streets and highways within the Territory of Hawaii Military Area, during the hours of curfew unless duly authorized to do so by or pursuant to any Proclamation, restriction, order, rule, regulation or instruction of the undersigned Military Commander or otherwise first authorized by the said Military Commander.

3. PERSONAL IDENTIFICATION DURING HOURS OF CURFEW

3.01. All persons required to be on the streets and highways during the hours

of curfew shall carry an identification badge, pass, or letter from their employer evidencing their right to be on the streets, and any such person who may be stopped by the civil or military police during said hours of curfew shall identify himself promptly.

4. FLASHLIGHTS.

4.01. Flashlights may be used, either indoors or outdoors, at any time or times, during the hours of curfew, subject, however, to the provisions of this paragraph. Military police, members of the United States Navy Shore Patrol, and civilian police officers are authorized to use flashlights with red or orange light, during said hours, either indoors or outdoors, while engaged in the performance of their official duties. Air Raid Wardens and Fire Wardens are authorized to use flashlights with green light during said hours, either indoors or outdoors, while engaged in the performance of their official duties as such wardens. No person other than a member of the military police, or a member of said shore patrol, or such a civilian police officer engaged in the performance of official duties as aforesaid, shall use a flashlight with a red or orange light at any time during said hours of curfew, nor shall any person other than an Air Raid Warden or Fire Warden engaged in the performance of official duties as aforesaid, use a flashlight with a green light at any time during said hours of curfew. Any person may use a flashlight with a white light, either indoors or outdoors, during said hours of curfew.

5. ENFORCEMENT.

5.01. Enforcement by Provost Marshal. The Provost Marshal, United States Army Forces, Central Pacific Base Command, shall have the power to control the effectiveness of curfew and shall enforce all Proclamations, restrictions, orders, rules, regulations and instructions of the undersigned Military Commander relating to, or pertaining to, curfew in the Territory of Hawaii Military Area.

ROBERT C. RICHARDSON, JR.
Lieutenant General, United States Army
Commanding General, United States Army
Forces, Pacific Ocean Areas
Military Commander, Territory of Hawaii
Military Area

OFFICIAL COPY:
WM. R. C. MORRISON
Brigadier General, U.S.A.
Executive

OFFICE OF INTERNAL SECURITY
Iolani Palace Grounds
Honolulu 2, T. H.

July 1945

SECURITY ORDER NO. 10
RESCISSION OF SECURITY ORDER
1. RESCISSION OF SECURITY ORDER NO. 3, THIS OFFICE, 24 OCTOBER 1944.
    1.01. Security Order No. 3, this office, 24 October 1944, hereby is rescinded.

(S)   ROBERT C. RICHARDSON, JR.
Lieutenant General, United States Army
Commanding General, United States Army
Forces, Pacific Ocean Areas
Military Commander, Territory of Hawaii
Military Area

(Adv.—July 11, 1945)

OFFICE OF INTERNAL SECURITY
Iolani Palace Grounds
Honolulu 2, T. H.

7 July 1945

SECURITY ORDER NO. 11
AMENDMENTS TO SECURITY ORDERS

The Commanding General, United States Army Forces, Pacific Ocean Areas, finds that this Security Order No. 11 is required in order to protect national-defense material, national-defense premises, and national-defense utilities, as defined by Section 4, Act of April 20, 1918, Chapter 59, 40 Stat. 533, as amended by the Act of November 30, 1940, Chapter 926, 54 Stat. 1220, and the Act of August 21, 1941 Chapter 388, 55 Stat. 655 (USC, Title 50, Section 104), from espionage and sabotage, and for the maintenance of military and internal security and the efficient utilization of available facilities in the Territory of Hawaii and that military necessity exists for said Security Order.

1. AMENDMENTS TO SECURITY ORDER NO. 1, THIS OFFICE, 24 OCTOBER 1944.

1.01 Paragraph numbered 1.01, Title 1, Security Order No. 1, this office, 24 October 1944, hereby is amended to read as follows:

"1.01. The term "Enemy Alien" or "Alien Enemy" as used in Public Proclamation Number One of the Military Commander, Territory of Hawaii Military Area, dated 24 October 1944, and this Security Order No. 1, or in any other Proclamation, restriction, order, rule, regulation or instruction of the undersigned Military Commander, unless the use thereof in such Proclamation, restriction, order, rule, regulation or instruction clearly indicates otherwise, shall include and hereby is defined to mean all natives, citizens, denizens, or subjects of Japan, Germany, or of any other nation or government hostile to the United States, who are within the Territory of Hawaii Military Area, and not actually naturalized within the United States."

1.02. Paragraph numbered 2.02, Title 2, Security Order No. 1, this office, 24 October 1944, hereby is amended to read as follows:

"2.02. Enemy aliens hereby are permitted to go about their business and visit friends and relatives throughout the day or night without special permits or passes except as may be otherwise limited by the Proclamations, restrictions, orders, rules, regulations, and instructions of the undersigned Military Commander."

2. AMENDMENT TO SECURITY ORDER NO. 2, THIS OFFICE, 24 OCTOBER 1944.

2.01 Security Order No. 2, this office, 24 October 1944, hereby is amended by adding to Title 7 of said Security Order No. 2, a new paragraph to be numbered and known as Paragraph 7.04, Title 7, Security Order No. 2, Office of Internal Security, 24 October 1944, and to read as follows:

"7.04. The term "hours of darkness" as used in any Proclamation, restriction, order, rule, regulation or instruction of the undersigned Military Commander, unless the use thereof in such Proclamation, restriction, order, rule, regulation or instruction clearly indicates otherwise, shall include and hereby is defined to mean that period of time between one-half (½) hour after sunset and one-half (½) hour before sunrise."

(S)   ROBERT C. RICHARDSON, JR.
Lieutenant General, United States Army
Commanding General, United States Army
Forces, Pacific Ocean Areas
Military Commander, Territory of Hawaii
Military Area

(Adv.—July 11, 1945)

TERRITORY OF HAWAII
Department of the Attorney General
Honolulu

December 1, 1942

Honorable Ingram M. Stainback
Governor of Hawaii
Honolulu, Hawaii

My dear Governor:

At your request I make the following report on the government of Hawaii. On December 7, 1941 your predecessor, Governor Poindexter, virtually abdicated his office, turned over all functions of government to the Commanding General, including the functions of the judicial officers of the Territory. This he purported to do under the Organic Act[1] which gave him no such power.

General Short assumed the title of "military governor" and from then on he and his successor, General Emmons, continued to exercise increasing stringent controls over the civil population of these islands regardless of whether or not they have any basis in military necessity.

These controls are exercised in the form of general orders issued from the "Office of the Military Governor." They proceed upon the theory that the Constitution itself and all federal and territorial laws may be freely ignored or suspended at the will of the commanding general; that he is at liberty to rule the civil population by military order and substitute his will for that of the Congress, or the Legislature of Hawaii.

It would seem clear that since Hawaii is not a conquered nation or in rebellion against the authority of the United States, the federal and territorial laws are still in force, subject only to such modifications as may be imposed by the commanding general based upon military necessity. The basic error that the will of the commander is law regardless of whether his commands are justifiable on the ground of military necessity results in nothing but confusion in every activity of civil life, whether it be the government of Hawaii or the private activities of the inhabitants.

THE OFFICE OF "THE MILITARY GOVERNOR"

There is no basis either in federal or territorial law for the use of the term "military governor." This phrase is unknown to our law even

---

[1] This section authorizes the governor to ". . . call upon the commanders of the military and naval forces of the United States . . . to prevent or suppress lawless violence, invasion, insurrection or rebellion in said Territory, and he may, in case of rebellion or invasion, or imminent danger thereof, when the public safety requires it, suspend the privilege of the writ of habeas corpus, or place the Territory or any part thereof, under martial law until communication can be had with the President and his decision thereon made known." 31 Stat. (1900) 153, 48 U.S.C. (1940) Sec. 532.

in times of the direst emergency; it is a term properly applied only to areas in rebellion or conquered nations. It is, I regret to say, an apt expression for the rule which exists here.

The office of the "military governor" was organized by G.O. No. 56, copies of which are enclosed. I am also enclosing copies of a functional chart prepared by the military authorities. From an examination of this chart, you will observe that for all practical purposes there is nothing to be done by the Governor of Hawaii, designated on the chart as "civil governor"; nor for the territorial and county governments. All of the affairs of the government are placed under the direction of the executive of the so-called "military governor."

I also enclose a more recent modification of this chart, which, you will note, places the subject of price control in the hands of the Office of Price Administration, directly under the executive of the "military governor." In fact, price regulations, which originate and are prepared by the OPA, at the present time are issued as orders of the "military governor." In fact, Mr. Karl Borders, the director of the OPA in Hawaii, a federal employee, is appointed as director of price control by the Military Governor under G.O. No. 159. The enforcement of such orders is, of course, in the provost courts.

On the staff of the military governor are a large number of civilian employees who are engaged in purely civilian activities, such as food control, labor control, materials and supplies control, land transportation control, and cold storage. The November budget for this office is $40,608.41, exclusive of the $25,000 for new buildings. This monthly charge is paid out of the $15,000,000 allocated by the President for the relief of the civil population of Hawaii.

G.O. No. 56 purports to place the director of civilian defense under the control of the "military governor." Section III, 2, *b*, provides: "The Director of Civilian Defense shall to the extent directed by the Military Governor," perform his duties as director of civilian defense. This, of course, is directly contrary to the existing legal situation. The Office of Civilian Defense was created pursuant to the Hawaii Defense Act (Act 24, Sp. S.L. 1941). The funds originally expended in the administration of this office were funds provided by the territorial legislature. These were soon exhausted and federal funds were made available under the Independent Offices Appropriation Act of 1942, Public Law 28, 77th Congress, First Session, which appropriated $25,000,000 "to enable the President, through appropriate agencies of government, to provide for emergencies affecting national security and for each and every purpose connected therewith."

By letter of January 12, 1942, addressed to the Secretary of the Interior the President appropriated and allotted $15,000,000.00

> "for any and all emergencies due to the existing war conditions for the protection, care and relief of the civilian population in the Territory of Hawaii . . . while this allocation is being made to you, I assume that the money will be transferred as and when needed to the Governor of Hawaii for expenditure in connection with emergency situations which may arise."

Pursuant to the foregoing authorization, the Secretary of the Interior radioed Governor Poindexter "you are hereby designated to authorize obligation for the $15,000,000 allotment from emergency fund for protection and relief of civilian population of Hawaii." From the foregoing, it is abundantly clear that the funds appropriated by Congress are to be expended by the Governor of Hawaii acting under direction of the Secretary of the Interior for the purposes designated in the letter of allocation.

Since the original allocation of this fund was made, the military authorities here have attempted to dictate its use. It is with these funds (allocated for the relief of the civilian population) the "military governor" has been able to create a rule which for all practical purposes completely supersedes civilian authority.

The "military governor" took over food production and distribution including the stimulation of locally grown products. This section formerly was in charge of Colonel White, who has since been made a general. Although a large amount of money has been expended in this activity, it has proved a complete failure, just as complete a failure as the attempt by the "military governor" to exercise price control. Several weeks ago the "military governor" apparently decided to turn this activity back into civilian hands. Curiously enough, instead of relinquishing the assumed power and returning it to the territorial government, the "military governor" selected a civilian of his own choosing and appointed him director of food production (G.O. No. 153).

In other words, a civilian affair which the military authorities desire to abandon, is not relinquished to the lawfully constituted authorities but turned over to civilians selected by the "military governor," who are not responsible to either the territorial or federal authorities. Whether this was an intentional affront to civilian authority or was simply accidental is immaterial, the fact remains that to accomplish this task (which had already been under investigation by this department at your request) a territorial agency with duly constituted powers emanating from the civilian government including such powers as control over certain public lands would have to be created. You would not be warranted in turning these lands over to any private individual even though he had been appointed by the "military governor," since such an individual would not be responsible by law to the territorial authorities.

The "military governor" has a public relations section (a staff of four) who feed the press with news designed to place military rule in a favorable light and suppress news reflecting any dissatisfaction with it. In addition to this set-up, Mr. Lorrin P. Thurston, the manager of the *Honolulu Advertiser*, one of the two daily papers printed in this city, has been appointed as "Public Relations Advisor to the Military Governor" (G.O. No. 155). It is unfortunate that this newspaper has thus foreclosed itself from being of any public service in criticizing the existing military rule.

At the present time, the "military governor" exercises control over almost every civilian activity whether governmental or private, the principal exception is the realm of taxation. These fields may be summarized as follows:

    (1)   The courts, civil and criminal

(2) Municipal affairs, operation of taxi cabs, rent control, rubbish and garbage disposal, house numbering, traffic regulations, one-way streets, no parking zones, and control over the police
(3) Labor
(4) The press
(5) The Office of Civilian Defense
(6) Public health, civilian hospitals, and water works
(7) Prisons, jails and insane asylum
(8) Price control
(9) Liquor
(10) Food control and production
(11) Land transportation
(12) Gasoline rationing
(13) Materials and supplies, including all WPB functions
(14) Fiscal matters, including the collection and disposition of fines and receipts from liquor commissions
(15) Use of territorial and county properties and institutions
(16) Incarceration of military prisoners in territorial prisons and county jails

The above fields do not, of course, include those matters which are of military nature such as regulations of movement about the water front, army posts and military installations, censorship of wireless messages, firearms, radios, evacuation areas, air raids, poison, curfew and blackout, all of which are subject to stringent military orders.

The enclosed chart was prepared by the "Office of the Military Governor," which clearly illustrates the Army's conception of the plan of civil government in Hawaii. You will note that the "civil governor" as well as the mayor, territorial government and county governments, appear as appendages on the left, evidently having no governmental functions to perform. The remainder of the chart places all activities therein designated under the direction of the "executive section," which means under the direction of General Green, who is known as the "executive to the military governor."

Since your appointment of Mr. E. E. Black as director of the Office of Civilian Defense, I believe the military authorities are beginning to realize that funds disbursed by the Office of Civilian Defense are funds appropriated by Congress allocated by the President for the "relief of the civil population of Hawaii" and expendable by the Governor of Hawaii acting under the direction of the Department of the Interior. These funds cannot be expended without your approval.

Since the "Office of the Military Governor" cannot operate without very substantial funds, it is at this point you can exercise your most effective control since you, acting under direction of the Secretary of the Interior, have the only lawful authority over the disbursement of the $15,000,000 allocated for the relief of the civilian population of Hawaii. I recommend that in consultation with the Secretary of the Interior you eliminate, at the earliest possible moment, the budget for the Office of the Military Governor in its entirety, and whatever functions performed by that office that are of any value be placed directly under the control of the Director of the Office of Civilian Defense.

THE COURTS

On December 7, 1941 all courts (civil and criminal) were ordered closed by the Commanding General. On December 16 there was some relaxation of this order which permit them to try certain classes of civil cases. A further reopening of the civil courts was permitted on January 27, 1942.

In place of the criminal courts of this Territory there have been erected on all the islands provost courts and military commissions for the trial of all manner of offenses from the smallest misdemeanor to crimes carrying the death penalty. Trials have been conducted without regard to whether or not the subject matter is in any manner related to the prosecution of the war. These military tribunals are manned largely by army officers without legal training. Those who may have had any training in the law seem to have forgotten all they ever knew about the subject.

Lawyers who appear before these tribunals are frequently treated with contempt and suspicion. Many citizens appear without counsel, they know, generally speaking, that no matter what evidence is produced the "trial" will result in a conviction. An acquittal before these tribunals is a rare animal. Accordingly, in most cases a plea of guilty is entered in order to avoid the imposition of a more severe penalty. Those who have the temerity to enter a plea of not guilty are dealt with more severely for having chosen that course.

Heavy fines and long prison sentences are meted out in many cases for comparatively trivial violations of military orders. The former practice of making people donate blood or buy bonds in expiation of their sins has been abandoned. In some instances persons have been found guilty of violating "the spirit of martial law" or "the spirit" of general orders, notwithstanding the act for which they are charged is not prohibited either by statute or military order.

The accused is not furnished with a copy of the charge against him but is permitted to examine the prosecutor's copy. Trials take place in crowded courtrooms in which the officers in charge are fully armed. The witnesses are brought before the provost judges en masse and stand in a circle about the bench together with the accused. The assemblage tells the judge their views of the matter. Cross-examination of witnesses is tolerated with none too much patience by the court.

There have been instances in which arrests have been made and the accused kept in jail three or four days awaiting trial, even in the case of comparatively minor offenses. With the writ of habeas corpus suspended the unfortunate accused in such cases is without remedy.

Shortly after you took office, General Orders No. 133 was promulgated, which purported to be a relaxation of the prohibition imposed upon the courts by the military authorities. That order, together with General Orders No. 135, preserves to the military tribunals a very large share of criminal jurisdiction. Moreover, it has the effect of circumscribing and limiting the jurisdiction of the courts of the land to such an extent that they are but little better off than they were prior to its promulgation. General Orders No. 135 purports to define the jurisdiction of the federal and territorial courts. The prohibition against the territorial courts includes all crimes against the government, espionage, violation of the Selective Service and Training Act, vagrancy, prostitution, public health, traffic ordinances, driving while drunk, and all violations of military orders. Not only are a large number of purely non-military offenses denied to the ordinary courts but a large class of persons are not triable only before military courts. This class includes not only members of the armed forces but any person engaged in any defense activity under the direction of the Army, or the Navy, or the "military governor" (G.O. Nos. 133, 135).

There are possibly fifty thousand persons employed on defense contracts on this island. In addition to this, there are many civilian employees of the Army, the Navy and the "military governor." Employees of public utilities are tried before military courts, for example, if a utility bus driver has a traffic accident he goes before the provost, whereas if the driver is working for a bakery he is tried in civil courts.

General Orders No. 135, 4, *b*, provides in part:

> "The determination of the status of such persons, and whether an offense is committed within the scope of employment shall rest with the Military Governor whose decision shall be final."

This order also specifically provides that the determination of the jurisdiction of federal courts, territorial courts and military tribunals "shall be determined by the Military Governor whose decision shall be final." The order reserves to the military authorities the right to take any particular case from the civil courts and turn it over to the military for trial.

> "Notwithstanding any provision of this or any other order of the Military Governor to the contrary, the Military Governor may, whenever in his opinion such action be necessary in the public interest, exercise jurisdiction at any time over any crime or offense or person, and direct that the same be tried before a Military Commission or Provost court." (G.O. No. 135, Sec. 7.)

The "military governor" has appointed what he styles a coordinator of courts. At the present time this is Captain Edward N. Sylva, who was formerly one of the deputies in this office. I am informed that as cases come in Mr. Sylva makes a determination whether or not they should be tried by the courts of the land or tried before the military tribunals. His determination is final.

The proceedings in these military tribunals are not only shocking to a lawyer but to anyone with a sense of fair play. Severe and bizarre sentences are meted out by persons untrained in the law. The feeling of the public is that they are guilty before they step inside the courtroom and their main problem is to escape with as light a sentence as possible.

CENSORSHIP OF THE PRESS

There exists no free press in Hawaii today. The press operates under a strict military censorship, not only the censorship that the mainland press presently complains of (i.e., insufficient information about the war), but in addition, censorship which prohibits publication of certain news of general interest not related to the conduct of the war. The "military governor" controls the press through a licensing system permitting it to publish "under such conditions and regulations as shall be prescribed from time to time by the Military Governor" (G.O. No. 14). When the editor of the *Star-Bulletin* wrote an editorial which mildly criticized the administration of civil affairs he was promptly given to understand that the offense would not be tolerated by the "military governor."

Murders and rapes have occurred in Honolulu, yet the press is forbidden to publish these incidents. The press is denied access to police files.

The prostitution problem is a good illustration of how censorship operates. For many years the evil of prostitution has been efficiently handled by the local police by segregating these unfortunates in certain areas and placing them under police supervision. After the outbreak of war the Army decided to take over. As a result prostitutes were scattered throughout the residential districts of this city, and people who did not care to have their houses devoted to this purpose experienced difficulty in regaining possession of their premises. When this subject got a little "hot" the Army decided to return jurisdiction to the Police Commission, which was done in part. The police proceeded to enforce their prior regulations and a three week strike ensued. Nothing appeared in the public press in regard to this strike nor was the press permitted to say that prostitution was being controlled by the Army.

There is always the possibility that censorship may be made effective by the "military governor's" control of the importation of news print. His office regulates the allocation of shipping space and the importation of all commodities.

In addition to the censorship of the press we have complete censorship of the mails. This, until lately, has been under the supervision of the Army and is now under the censorship bureau. The Act of Congress (Second War Powers Act, 1942, 55 Stat. 840) permits the censorship of mails from the United States to foreign countries. It does not authorize the censorship of mails between territories and other parts of the United States. There is pending in Congress legislation which will legalize the present censorship.

LABOR

Perhaps the greatest inroad on the liberty of the individual, next to abrogation of the Bill of Rights, is G.O. No. 91, which has the effect of freezing labor.

This order prohibits army and navy agencies, contractors, federal, territorial and county agencies, hospitals, public utilities and stevedoring companies from employing any individual formerly in the employment of any such agency unless the individual presents a release without prejudice from his private employer. Moreover, any individual who refuses to report to his job after ordered to report by his employer is subject to a $200 fine or imprisonment for two months.

It is essential, of course, that labor should not be constantly changing jobs. However, insofar as this order applies to private employers, it strikes at the very heart of the fundamental liberties of the individual. Employees of the electric company, the gas company and the bus company, for instance, under this order are frozen to their jobs and prohibited from seeking employment elsewhere. This results in great dissatisfaction in these employees, particularly when they see others engaged in similar work receiving substantially higher wages.

Instances have come to my attention in which bus drivers have purposely had accidents hoping that they would obtain a discharge on the ground of negligence so that they will be free to seek other employment. Industrial mobilization, when carried out by the government under a general law, is one thing, but freezing men to their jobs for the benefit of private employers who thereby profit by the services of the employees, in my opinion, is a very different matter. Those in command here seem to lose sight of the fact that the Civil War and the Thirteenth Amendment are generally considered to have put at rest involuntary servitude in the United States "or any place subject to their jurisdiction."

CONCLUSION

It is easy enough to understand the cause that brought about our present situation—the combination of a military and naval disaster on December 7 coupled with the fact that our affairs were in the hands of an aged and weak governor who readily surrendered all powers to the Commanding General. Whatever might be said for his course on December 7 and the days that immediately followed, it cannot be said that present conditions warrant the continuance of the present military rule.

It might be wondered how the public of this Territory have acquiesced so long in a reign that is so contrary to every tradition of America. I believe that there are several reasons. The first is fear. To the average citizen the present regime is an anathema. However, he is never sure of his ground and is fearful of punishment and hence remains inarticulate. He is also afraid lest his criticism of existing conditions will stamp him as unpatriotic.

The second reason is censorship. I feel safe in saying that no place in America, and probably few elsewhere, have been subjected to the rigid censorship which exists here. By the censorship of the press and all means of communication, there is a virtual blackout on information available to the public concerning civil affairs in Hawaii. Some information trickles back via visitors returning to the mainland.

The third reason is the fact of the large number of Army and Navy personnel and the employees of these services including the civilians working for the "military governor." The latter class have a financial interest in maintaining the status quo.

The last, but not the least important, reason is the existence of a small number of fascist-minded business men. They are influential with the "Office of the Military Governor." This group, I regret to say, favor the military regime with all its stringent controls of labor, severe and arbitrary penalties for infractions of orders. To be sure, they want to win the war, but they are also interested in profits and find it extremely convenient to obtain whatsoever they desire in the form of an order from the military authorities. They are not hampered either by democratic processes, such as legislation, or by territorial civil servants who, as a rule, are far more able to deal with the shrewd man of business than the average army officer.

This report, already too long, is by no means exhaustive of the problems that exist under the present military rule. The solution of our present difficulties cannot be reached here but can only be settled in Washington.

I understand that in no single instance has any general order been submitted to you before it is promulgated. This is consistent with the view that the governorship is a mere figurehead and that the real governor of Hawaii is the "military governor." The situation can be clarified by reaching an agreement on the following points:

(1) The restoration of the courts to their normal functions, reserving to the military tribunals only those cases directly affecting the prosecution of war, such as sabotage, espionage, violation of the Articles of War, or crimes in and about military establishments. The jurisdiction to be determined by the United States District Court for Hawaii.

(2) A restoration to the territorial government of all civilian functions. This would involve the relinquishment by the military of all the civil functions presently usurped under military rule, such as food, price and liquor controls.

(3) The abolition of the assumption of military governorship by the Commanding General.

(4) A rescission of all general orders heretofore issued which are not based upon military necessity and an agreement that in the future the military orders dealing with the civilian population and civil government be predicated upon the ground of military necessity and, except in case of a real emergency which will not admit of delay, that such orders be submitted to you for approval before issuance.

In the event such a program cannot be agreed upon, the only alternative would seem to be the issuance of a proclamation terminating martial law. This, of course, should not be done without first having obtained the approval of the President. It could be done without restoring the privilege of the writ of habeas corpus. This would have the effect of placing us in approximately the same situation as exists in the West Coast where there is, in fact, a form of martial law, except that the writ of habeas corpus has not been suspended there. This would afford the military all necessary power, restore to civil authorities all civilian functions, and preserve to the citizen the substance of the Bill of Rights.

Respectfully yours,

/sgd/ GARNER ANTHONY
Attorney General

INDEX

(Material in Appendixes not included)

STANFORD BOOKS IN WORLD POLITICS

————————GRAHAM H. STUART, *Editor*————————

Date Due